INTRODUCING RELIGION

INTRODUCING RELIGION

Readings from the Classic Theorists

~

Daniel L. Pals

New York   Oxford
OXFORD UNIVERSITY PRESS
2009

OXFORD

UNIVERSITY PRESS

Oxford University Press, Inc., publishes works that further
Oxford University's objective of excellence
in research, scholarship, and education.

Oxford   New York
Auckland   Cape Town   Dar es Salaam   Hong Kong   Karachi
Kuala Lumpur   Madrid   Melbourne   Mexico City   Nairobi
New Delhi   Shanghai   Taipei   Toronto

With offices in
Argentina   Austria   Brazil   Chile   Czech Republic   France   Greece
Guatemala   Hungary   Italy   Japan   Poland   Portugal   Singapore
South Korea   Switzerland   Thailand   Turkey   Ukraine   Vietnam

Library of Congress Cataloging-in-Publication Data

Introducing religion : readings from the classic theorists / [edited] by
Daniel L. Pals.
      p.   cm.
   Includes bibliographical references.
      ISBN   978-0-19-518149-4 (pbk. : alk. paper)   ISBN   978-0-19-518148-7
(hardcover : alk. paper)
   1. Religion—Philosophy.   I. Pals, Daniel L.
      BL51.I6565 2009
      200—dc22   2008028657

For Carmela and Eve,
lifelong assiduous readers

Contents

〜

Preface

$\sim$

The idea for this book was not originally mine. It arose, indirectly, out of casual conversations with colleagues in the discipline of Religious Studies who had adopted *Eight* (and the earlier *Seven*) *Theories of Religion* for use in their college and university classrooms. They and others raised the familiar question of how best to engage students in greater depth with the classic debates over religion once their first meeting with theorists such as these—and the general outline of their theories—has occurred. It was not hard to articulate the ideal: The sooner students engage with theories unmediated, in the original form and idiom of argument, the better. The sooner they encounter a theory in a primary source and wrestle with its ideas in their original formulation, the greater the intellectual gain from the exercise.

None of this rather idle professorial thought turned to action, however, until Oxford's Executive Editor Robert Miller proposed to me a book that would actually do what was envisioned: move students from an initial second-order acquaintance with the classic theorists into sustained first-hand engagement with the axioms, evidence, and arguments of their works. At the very least, such a project could be seen as a modest complement to an expository account like *Eight Theories*, adding the benefit of example to exposition. But it could also offer considerably more. By presenting (where possible) readings of more than minimal length, carefully selected to follow the key turns and evidential claims of an argument, a work of this kind could draw students into the process of "thinking along with" the theorist at hand. It could encourage them not only to grasp the broad architecture of a theory, but to trace its blueprint and judge for themselves the quality of its design and engineering. And it could thereby push them to the crucial "next step" in learning—nudging them page by page to construe and critically engage a theory, to track its assembly, appraise it both analytically and comparatively, and work through the logic of its arguments as they develop. The prospect of promoting that kind of active intellectual engagement is what led me willingly to sign on to Robert's proposal. The result is the collection of readings that appear in these pages. Whether the book succeeds in achieving its goal will be for others to judge. The goal itself, I venture to say, can hardly be open to dispute.

Readers familiar with either *Seven* or *Eight Theories* will notice already in this book's table of contents certain choices more suited to an anthology than an introductory exposition. In those earlier works, the Victorian anthropologists E. B. Tylor and James Frazer were treated in combination because of the close affinity in their aims and methods. But Tylor's *Primitive Culture* and Frazer's *Golden Bough* were independently important works of wide cultural influence, separated by nearly a generation in time and by certain noticeable differences of emphasis and argument. Hence in this volume the selections from these books are introduced and reprinted separately, in chapters that allow for some comparison of their subtler explanatory differences and similarities. Similarly, in *Eight Theories* an effort was made to place Max Weber's celebrated *Protestant Ethic and the Spirit of Capitalism* in the context of his broader sociological inquiries and his ambitious global project centered on the "economic ethic" of the world's religions. Here, however, the argument of *The Protestant Ethic* is highlighted and presented at considerable length, chiefly because it offers the most sustained and subtle exhibit we have of a major theorist who, in contrast to Marx, Freud, and Durkheim, finds religious belief not to be a mere effect of other causes, but itself a cause of other effects—in fact the historically decisive agent in generating the most profound transformation of economic and social life in human history. To enlist one's energies in following that argument is to capitalize on a singular opportunity for historical analysis and theoretical comparison. What better way, after all, to appreciate the powerful appeal of Durkheim's or Marx's reductionism than to track by comparison Weber's sustained exercise in *Verstehen* that runs counter to it? To do so, however, a student must engage with more than a brief excerpt; the text at hand must be of a scale sufficient to trace the key features of the argument as they emerge. Thus the choice—and scale—of the selection from *The Protestant Ethic* as compared to the selections from other of Weber's works that, quite arguably, are of equal interest and importance.

This collection also offers selections from William James and Rudolf Otto. Though they did not appear in *Seven* or *Eight Theories*, no one doubts that they were theorists of real importance, whose *Varieties of Religious Experience* in the former case and *Idea of the Holy* in the latter hold a rightful place alongside the other classic studies from theory of religion's "axial age" at the turn of the twentieth century. Accordingly, substantial readings from those works appear in this collection, offering further occasion for comparative analysis and criticism.

The reference to most of these readings as "substantial" requires one note of clarification, or (better said) caution, pertaining to the chapter on Freud. In my view Freud's short essay *The Future of an Illusion* presents the most compelling form of his reductionist psychological account of the origin of religious belief. It is the least dependent on unprovable prehistoric or early historical speculation and most closely tied to his professional and empirical inquiries into the nature of neurosis. The selection provided here, however, is unusually brief—insufficient, actually, to convey in full measure the design and character of Freud's discussion. This reason for this is that by policy W. W. Norton Inc., which holds the American rights to the translation of this work, would not allow more than ten percent of the text to be reprinted in this volume. Given that *The Future of an Illusion* is a brief work—less a book than extended essay—this constraint meant that the amount of material reprinted here could come to barely more this than five pages of the original text. The result is a less than satisfying representation of Freud's argument; moreover, its brevity leaves the misleading impression that *The Future of an Illusion* is a study of less significance theoretically than either *Totem and Taboo* or *Moses* and *Moses and Monotheism*, which stand here on either side of it represented in passages of greater, more suitable length. Readers and instructors should be aware of this imbalance.

Two further notes about the presentation of the texts are in order. First, as these passages are provided mainly for students, not scholars, footnotes have been almost entirely deleted. In most all of these works, the main purpose of the notes is to provide documentation from sources, so their absence need not detract discernibly from engagement with the core elements of the discussions. The one obvious exception, of course, is Max Weber, whose notes—Teutonic in both number and scale—pursue intriguing complementary lines of inquiry well beyond the text above them. But, again, those paths can here be left to specialists instead of students, whom they are more likely to distract than enlighten in this instructional context. The main line of Weber's expositions in the passages reprinted here can be followed quite profitably without them. Second, any enterprise of this kind requires abbreviation, which means elision. Conventional triple-dot ellipses are used to mark all deletions, both within and beyond a paragraph, that comprise less than two pages of the original text. Any deletion of greater length is denoted by the following ornament: ∼. On those occasions where, after an elision, the text is taken up again from within a paragraph, rather than at its start, I have chosen not to use ellipsis dots at re-entry, so as not to clutter the texts more than is minimally required. As things stand, there are more than few ellipses in these readings, but all are necessary to be faithful to the original sources.

In addition to being the principal audience for this book, I am pleased to note that students have played an integral role in producing it. I am grateful especially to a diligent group of student assistants here at the University of Miami: Jessica Cornett, Jessica Misener, Adrienne Faris, Christine Mantis, Kait Ginder, and Soledad Galindo. At various points over several semesters, they assumed the tedious labor of input-typing, scanning, and proofreading of texts—a markedly greater measure of text, as things transpired, than readers who see this final version will ever quite know. Thanks are certainly due also to the quietly efficient and talented staff here in the Office of the Dean in our College of Arts and Sciences. In scores of ways, Rose Glemaud, Angie Callesis, and Lee Ingram (who also assisted with scanning and input) have always been ready to offer virtually instant assistance with whatever was needed—a last-minute query, a tutorial on international faxes, a phone call, a photocopy, or a publisher's address, all of which were offered beyond the call of their normal administrative duties. They should know that I noticed, even if not often enough. Also among professional debts, I owe much to the patience and flexibility of Michael Halleran, Dean of the College at Miami, to whom I report as Associate Dean. Over the 2007–2008 academic year especially, and although he had first claim on my time and efforts, he made allowances not easy for him to make, given the scale of the responsibilities he carries.

Appreciations go also to the editorial and production staff at Oxford University Press: Emily Voigt, Sarah Calabi, Yelena Bromberg, Lisa Grzan, and doubtless other names unknown. Sarah Calabi has been especially skillful (and sympathetic) in guiding me through often fog-shrouded terrain of copyrights and publisher permissions. Robert Miller I have already mentioned. Though this book owes much to his editorial intuition, it owes perhaps even more to his personal understanding. When unexpected family adversity delayed my work in its earlier stages, he stood by considerately and was prepared to wait. For that I am most grateful.

Finally, and yet again, I need to thank my both my wife Phyllis and daughter Katharine for their love, their time, and their tolerance of a personal penchant for working in hours not meant for work. Phyllis did more than tolerate. She was an integral part of this project from the beginning, a virtual ghost editor (if that is the term), commenting on the selections, editing the texts, proofreading the typescripts, correcting drafts of the chapter introductions, assisting in the hunt for rights-holders, and advising on strategies to secure the needed permissions. All of us need anchors; she and Katie are mine.

DANIEL PALS

Introduction

~

"Religion is the soul of civilization." The aim of historian Will Durant in making this remark was not to confess his personal piety, but to recognize a simple reality. In one form or another, religious beliefs and behaviors stand at the core of every civilization that humanity has created; similarly so for every tribe or village anthropologists have visited. Almost invariably, the effort to understand a clan, a community, or a culture draws us at some point into its religion—the network of its ultimate beliefs and values. But if religion is a key to explaining society, how is the phenomenon of religion itself to be explained? If we trace the character of a culture to its underlying ideas and ideals, then to what, in turn, do we trace those ideas and ideals themselves? How do *they* originate and operate? Questions of this kind hold particular interest for theorists of religion.

This book assembles a number of "classic" texts authored by theorists who played a formative role in the modern enterprise of explaining religion. Most worked in the decades before and after the turn of the twentieth century, a period of great intellectual ferment in both Europe and North America. The birth of capitalist economies, the growth of science and industry, the rise of democratic ideals, revolutionary ideologies, and mass communication—these distinctively modern developments occasioned almost everywhere searching reassessments of accepted ideas and established institutions. Religious ideas and institutions were no exception. The lead in the enterprise of reconsidering religion was taken not by theologians, but by scholars outside of the churches and synagogues, who relied on new methods of scientific scholarship rather than the authority of the Bible or articles of dogma. Their efforts yielded inquiries of a kind unknown to earlier epochs, as a quick glance backward in religious history makes clear.

If in the heart of the Middle Ages one were to have asked the random "person on the pathway" why she believed as she did, there was a ready theological answer at hand. The Christian faith is eternal truth, delivered by the prophets and apostles, preserved in the scriptures, and transmitted by the authority of the church. Those who embrace this truth know how to explain their belief: it comes from God. The standing of those who reject it can be equally explained. They have been ensnared by Satan, the Great Deceiver. Jews and Muslims, for example, have come near the truth, but not near enough. The former accept only its Old Testament preface; the latter have overlaid it with the errors of the Quran. The plight of still other peoples beyond the reach of these scriptural faiths is much the same. Their minds have been darkened by error.

For centuries, this conception both of religion and of the explanation for religion had been a fixed feature of the Christian sensibility in the Western world. Religion, it was everywhere held, is God's revealed truth, to be either recognized by faith or rejected in perverse unbelief.

At the beginning of the modern era, however, this frame of mind began to change—significantly. Shortly after 1500, the Church of Rome, the anchor of religious authority in Christendom, found itself under assault by Protestant reformers and princes in the North of Europe. Led by the German monk Martin Luther and the lawyer John Calvin in France and Switzerland, the theologians of the Protestant Reformation repudiated the Catholic claim to sole ownership of Christian doctrine and Biblical truth. Fierce theological debate erupted; new religious sects multiplied; repression, persecution, and religious wars followed. Amid protracted battles that were fought over the very foundations of faith, thoughtful believers on all sides grew hesitant about things once beyond question. Divine truth might be one and eternal. But with the Christian consensus in tatters, no single institution could insist, as the Roman Church once did, on sole and undisputed possession of it. Luther and the Pope claimed equally to speak for God, but they disagreed vehemently on what the divine message was. Inevitably in such a circumstance, it became difficult for thoughtful people to believe in a singular system of religious truth—or that the simple embrace of divine revelation was the only explanation for it. Meanwhile, as conflict raged in Christianity's homeland, explorers, traders, and missionaries were deeply engaged in travel abroad—to Asia and Africa, as well as the New World. Their aims were conquest, commerce, and conversion. Missionaries took charge of the last endeavor, under sacred pledge to bring alien peoples into the Church. They converted many, but not without some consequences that were quite unintended. In China, Jesuit fathers were surprised to discover a civilization with a level of order and decency superior to their own, wracked as it was with religious hatred and strife. Though not drawn from the Bible, the moral wisdom of Confucius seemed to the Jesuit teacher Matteo Ricci comparable in dignity to the commandments of Moses or Christ's Sermon on the Mount. Living in the court of China's emperor, the missionary came near to becoming himself the convert. In India also, Jesuit missionaries found a form of spirituality so appealing that some, like the great Roberto di Nobili, freely adopted the manner and habits of the Hindu Brahmins. In America, still others developed a respect for its native peoples who, also without divine revelation, had come to worship a single Great Spirit not unlike the Christian Creator of heaven and earth.

As accounts of these non-Western, but still admirable, beliefs and practices flowed back into Europe, the notion that all of religion could be explained theologically came under additional challenge. In due course, spokesmen in the succeeding century, the celebrated "Age of Enlightenment," introduced an idea that spoke to both the cry for tolerance and the new global awareness: the concept of a pure and ancient "natural religion," universal in scope and free of divisive theological dogmas. The enticing thought that there might have been a simple and quite rational religion of nature, a creed embraced by the entire human race in its earliest ages, captured the imagination of the most influential thinkers of the day. Voltaire and Denis Diderot in France, Jefferson and Franklin in the American colonies, and notable others in England, Germany, and elsewhere subscribed to this "Deism": the nondogmatic, nonmiraculous belief in a single Creator God, a system of natural laws (both physical and moral), and the prospect of an afterlife of rewards and punishments. In this elegantly simple creed Deists found the common religion of all races—unvisited by special revelations and uncorrupted by priests. This original religion of humanity fostered brotherhood among all peoples. And because it was natural rather than supernatural, it could be explained as arising from human reason rather than divine revelation, just as physicists like the great Isaac Newton (1643–1727) could apply reason to account for the motions of both circling planets and falling apples under a single explanatory principle.

Deists prized rationality, but were tone-deaf to the deep emotions that give form and vitality to the religious life. Devout souls, both Catholic and Protestant, repudiated this aspect of the Deist program. They insisted that true religion was found not in the "God of the philosophers," as mathematician Blaise Pascal put it, but in "the reasons of the heart," which only the heart can know. This commitment to heart-felt faith over the Deists' rationalistic religion of the head was shared by a variety of Pietists, Revivalists, and Romantics, the last of these comprising an assortment of writers, scholars, and poets who celebrated just what most Deists despised—the beauty and emotional appeal of churches, temples, and rituals, of ceremonies and prayers, of saints, the supernatural, and all that pertains to the life of devotion. For Romantics, the institutions and history of religion do not corrupt its spirit. They keep it safe, and bear its torch.

In the later 1700s and early years of the century following, it was the curious convergence of these two opposing perspectives—rationalist Deism and religious Romanticism—that inspired several of the first attempts to account theoretically for the origin and growth of religion. French scholar Charles De Brosses (1709–1777) examined ancient polytheism and the worship of fetishes, while the German Romantics Johann Herder (1744–1803) and Friedrich Schelling (1775–1854) made early efforts of a similar kind, developing new appreciations of mythology and spirituality (including Indian philosophy).

The contrasting temperaments of the Deist and the Romantic combined most intriguingly some decades later in the person of Friedrich Max Müller (1823–1900), a learned German linguist who had traveled to England to prepare an edition of India's oldest sacred books, the *Vedas*, written in the ancient Sanskrit language. Religiously, Müller was in part an Enlightenment rationalist; he embraced the view of German philosopher Immanuel Kant (1724–1804), who anchored religion in the two cardinal doctrines of Deism: belief in a Creator God and the claims of the human conscience, nature's "moral law within." But he was also a Romantic—deeply sentimental, attuned to mysticism, and attentive to whatever signs of divinity he could discern in either the beauty of the natural world or the historic strivings of the human spirit. To these attributes he added another: a commitment to the methods of modern historical and empirical science. Müller believed that it was possible to assemble facts, frame generalizations, and work toward a comprehensive theory of the origin of religion among all peoples. By sustained historical and scientific labor, he felt, we can place ourselves far back in time, recover the earliest religious notions of the human race, and follow their historical changes, whether of degeneration or development (he in fact believed the former), until we come to the present day. Recent advances in the study of history, language, mythology, archaeology, and anthropology had paved the way for this new "science of religion," as he described it in a noteworthy series of lectures delivered at London's Royal Institution in the Winter of 1870. Instead of just speculating aimlessly about the nature of religion, he argued, scholars can at last proceed scientifically to formulate the general principles—the scientific "laws of development"—that underlie religious behavior, just as we might trace the growth of language, technology, agriculture, or any other human institution.

Not only in Müller's lectures, but in other writings of his day, we can notice a remarkable enthusiasm about the inquiries that were being undertaken. Science, it was agreed, could provide reliable knowledge. Fact alone, and not private attachments to revelation or inspiration, furnished the sure footing on which theories could be made to stand. Such was the confidence of Müller and his peers in both the facts at hand and the science employed to confirm them, that they fully expected to explain by their methods the entire phenomenon of religion—its origin, historical growth, and worldwide variations. For the most part, that same expansive and ambitious set of goals may be said also to guide most of the theorists who appear in the chapters that follow.

Looking back on it from the present, of course, this buoyant hope of isolating some general theory, some set of scientifically derived principles that might explain all of the varied circumstances and endeavors that figure in human religious behavior, seems to us unrealistic in the extreme. We are humbler today. The most notable efforts of current theorists are considerably more limited in character. Even so, the prospect of framing a general theory of religion has not been given up easily. And in a sense, why should it be? Cosmologists and physicists have not given up the goal of a "unified field theory" even though finding it has proved far more difficult than they once imagined. Religionists can hardly be thought unreasonable to seek something similar.

"Religion" and "Theory": Some Preliminaries

Before going further, it may be helpful at this point to take an initial reading on what is meant by both "religion" and "theory"—the two terms central to all of the selections presented here. Most people have an intuitive idea of what religion is. They are likely to think of belief in a God or of one of the major world religions—Hinduism, for example, or Christianity, or Buddhism. Or they may expect discussions of sacred scriptures and rituals, of prophets and priests, prayer or meditation, ceremonies, sainthood, or sacrifice and systems of salvation. Those first impressions are sufficient enough for the moment; we can say more later on.

Most people also have some general idea of what a theory is. When Newton explained planetary motion by formulating the impressive physical law of gravitational attraction, he produced a theory of the first order. How? By bringing an enormously wide range of different occurrences and processes into a connection that could be stated in a single mathematical formula. Similarly, if not quite so impressively, our theorists seek to explain, by appeal to a general principle, or set of principles, why people from a wide variety of cultures believe and behave as they do religiously. Interpreters try to go beyond specific instances to find their common thread. What they seek is a general understanding of the nature of religion through theory.

As with "religion," so with "theory," we should notice also that few of the discussions presented in the chapters ahead will rest content with the notions of common sense once the issues have been seriously engaged. They develop further classifications and distinctions. In the matter of definition, for example, some theorists strongly prefer a *substantive* formulation, which builds on everyday understandings. They define religion in terms of the *content*, or *ideas*, that religious people affirm and find valuable. Other definitions are better described as *functional* in character. They put ideas and beliefs aside and center instead on what religion does for people psychologically or sociologically: how it provides, say, a sense of individual well-being or of group solidarity. This substantive-functional distinction extends beyond definitions to entire theories as well. Theorists who advocate substantive approaches tend to seek explanations that are intellectual and rational, or consciously psychological and emotional. People are religious, they say, because certain ideas strike them as true and valuable, or satisfy certain deeply felt needs, to a point where they are impelled to live by them. This kind of theory is sometimes described as "interpretive" rather than "explanatory." It presumes that since religions are practiced by human persons, only theories that appeal to conscious human motives can explain how and why people behave as they do. Interpretive theorists avoid the word "explanation" because they find it more appropriate to impersonal processes than to activities guided by human intentions. Functional theorists, by contrast, think rather differently. They find more impersonal explanatory methods to be as applicable to human actions as they are to natural processes—and with clear reason. For them human actions ultimately are shaped by underlying social structures, psychological forces, or even biological drives, and not (or not just) by the conscious thoughts and aims that religious people themselves imagine to be governing their actions. In the chapters to come, we shall see this kind of functionalist thinking on distinctive display in the works of theorists like Freud and Durkheim, as well as Marx and Engels. For the moment, however, it is enough to take note of the difference. The theorists will demonstrate it further in due course.

Comparing and Appraising Theories: Questions to Consider

In the chapters that follow, the classic theorists present their views in their own words. The limits of space require that the texts be edited, but each contributor claims space enough to offer his analysis or argument in its own distinctive strategy and style. Given that circumstance, it may be helpful also to address beforehand a few broad issues, applicable to all theories, which can assist in the process of comparing and appraising them. Here are five such questions to consider:

1) *How does the theorist define his subject?* What concept of religion does he develop as he proceeds? 2) *What type of theory is being offered?* Since, as we have seen, theories can be of quite different kinds, what specific form of explanation is offered in each case, and why? 3) *What is the range of the theory?* That is, how much of human religious behavior does it claim to explain? All of it? Most of it? Are there any exceptions, and why? And in that light, does the theory actually succeed in achieving what it claims? 4) *What evidence does the theorist appeal to?* Does the theory try to probe deeply into a few facts, ideas, or conditions, or does it spread itself widely to embrace as much of the seemingly relevant evidence as possible? And is the range of the evidence great enough to support the range of the theory? 5) *What relationship is there, if any, between the theorist's personal beliefs (or disbeliefs) and the explanation he chooses to advance?* Is the

author's personal religious faith or rejection of faith separable, or inseparable, from the theory he develops? Are certain types of theory to be associated with certain kinds of religious belief, or nonbelief? A brief comment on each of these issues is in order.

1. Defining Religion: A Point of Common Ground

People are occasionally inclined to say that religion is something so vague, so varied and diverse, or so personal and individual that it defies definition. It can mean almost anything to just about anyone; hence defining it is hopeless from the start. Interestingly, that is not the view of the theorists represented in this book. Although they disagree, often sharply, on explaining religion, they in fact differ less than one might suppose on the matter of defining it. By and large, they all presume that religion consists of belief or behavior associated with a supernatural realm of divine or spiritual beings. This is a point worth illustrating briefly.

Chapters 1 and 2 present two spokesmen for what some have called early, or "Victorian," anthropology: E. B. Tylor and James Frazer. Both of these theorists choose to define religion in quite straightforwardly supernaturalist terms. Tylor puts it perhaps most succinctly with his oft-cited minimum definition that describes religion simply as "belief in spiritual beings." Frazer, his disciple, takes over this minimal definition almost without change, though he prefers the term "supernatural beings." The French sociologist Emile Durkheim, who appears a bit later on, seems at first glance to take a quite different view; he defines religion instead as that which concerns "the sacred," as opposed to "the profane." But his view is not as different from the others as it seems. For Durkheim also presumes that, in the eyes of those who practice it, religion does after all consist of behaviors and beliefs (in his language, "representations") associated with a realm of reality inhabited by beings conceived to be spiritual or supernatural. It is true that he later moves away from this starting point to show the link between the religious and the social, but as he begins, he too finds that he must start where Tylor and Frazer do. This is even more emphatically the case with theologian Rudolf Otto, the Romanian comparativist Mircea Eliade, and American philosopher-psychologist William James, all of whom appear farther along in this collection. Eliade begins his analysis, like Durkheim, with a definition that relies on the paired concepts of the sacred and the profane. But he is also quite specific in stating what he means by "the sacred." It is, again, a realm of spiritual beings, as is also the case in Otto's *The Idea of the Holy* and James' *Varieties of Religious Belief*. Both of these latter works appeal to religious experience, which is defined by profound encounters with the realm of spirit or the supernatural. Sigmund Freud and Karl Marx make largely the same presumption. Critical as they may be of religion, they share with the other theorists the premise that it is by nature concerned with belief in gods, especially the monotheistic

Creator-Father God of the Judeo-Christian tradition. To be sure, they proceed later, like Durkheim, to argue that religion is not what believers imagine it to be, but in order to make that case, they must at the start understand it, with Tylor and Frazer and the others, as a form of "belief in spiritual beings."

E. E. Evans-Pritchard, whom we meet in a later chapter, prefers the term "mystical" in his studies because, unlike the cultures of the modern West, the tribal societies he explores have no clear concept of an opposition between a "natural" world and a "supernatural" one. Still, he makes it clear that the mystical realm is populated almost exclusively by extraordinary forces or divine spirits. Max Weber and Clifford Geertz can hardly be said to disagree. Weber's definition is quite expansive, embracing both the magical beliefs of simple villagers and what he calls the salvation religions of the prophets. In both the great traditions of Asia and the monotheistic faiths of the West, he finds religion to be centered on goals that transcend ordinary life in the present world; this realm of the transcendent is by definition the realm of the supernatural. Finally, in the theoretical essay "Religion as Cultural System," Geertz, a disciple of Weber, proceeds abstractly, appealing to the "conceptions of a general order of existence" that religion provides. What he means by those conceptions can be found in the field studies he undertook as a professional anthropologist, where it is clear that they refer in some cases to the God, angels, and demons of Islam, and in others to the spirits, magicians, and demons of native Indonesian animism.

In brief, then, we can see that although some say it less directly than others, all of our theorists are content, initially at least, to locate religion in those beliefs and practices associated with spiritual, or supernatural, beings. On the matter of defining religion, they work, broadly speaking, from common ground.

2. Types of Theory

Needless to say, the moment our theorists turn from definition to explanation, this consensus disappears. Because the same fact, or event, or behavior can often be explained in multiple ways, disagreement, and sometimes confusion, is not uncommon. In one of the selections to come, drawn from anthropologist E. E. Evans-Pritchard's *Theories of Primitive Religion,* he comments on how earlier theorists took a keen interest in finding the "origin" of religion, but were less than clear on the meaning of that term. The *historical* or *prehistorical* origin of religion is one thing; its *psychological* or *social* origin is another. The first would be found in certain specific events belonging to early ages of human society; the second refers to a condition, or characteristic, of human life presumably at work in all times and places. The one is a past occurrence; the other, a timeless condition, or feature, of all human existence.

The search for religious origins in the first sense of the word was a particular interest of theorists working in the later decades of the nineteenth century. Like others of their age, they thought in evolutionary terms. Influenced by notions of historical progress and especially by Charles Darwin's startling new theory of biological evolution, they were disposed to see religion as the product of a long process of growth, rooted in the earliest ages of the human past. Their inquiries led naturally enough to primitive peoples, because they were thought to display religion, as well as civilization, in its earliest and simplest form. In the well-worn evolutionist analogy, they formed the acorn out of which the oak of religion has grown. This evolutionary model is especially apparent in the works of Tylor and Frazer, but is discernible, under a somewhat different form, in the theories of Freud and Durkheim as well.

The chief problem with such evolutionary theories, of course, is that they seek knowledge of things exceedingly difficult to know, at least with any certainty. After all, the "earliest forms" of human religion and social life are subjects we must mostly guess about—and not with much skill. In the twentieth century, accordingly, theorists turned away from discussions of origins and toward more distinctively functional explanations. Their interest shifted to theories that stress those underlying psychological factors or social circumstances that always figure in the human condition. The most celebrated of these accounts, still very much alive in current debates, are the aggressively functionalist theories put forward by Freud and Durkheim, and by the followers of Karl Marx. As the texts to follow will make clear, all three of these theorists are dismissive of the claims of religion on its own terms; in a modern world ruled by science, they contend, religious statements should be dismissed on their face as absurd. And if so, then we can only turn to something subconscious, nonrational, or impersonal to explain why it persists. As will become apparent, Freud finds that "something" to be obsessional neurosis; for Marx it is the frustrated desire for economic justice; for Durkheim it is "society" with its compelling demands on the individual. In each case, these theorists pursue their functional explanations so aggressively that their accounts have come to be called "reductionist." They seek to reduce religion to something more basic than—something underneath and other than—what it claims to be on the surface. They seek not just to explain religion, but effectively to explain it away.

In differing ways, other theorists emphatically dissent from reductionism. Both William James and Rudolf Otto recognize the psychological roots of religious belief no less than Freud does, but they do not therefore dismiss it as obsessional neurosis. They find it grounded in normal, or even uniquely valuable, emotions. Simlarly Weber, Eliade, and Evans-Pritchard understand the social importance of religion, but they find significant misunderstandings in the reductionist analyses offered by Durkheim and Marx. They contend that there is nothing at all irrational or abnormal about religion; so there is no point in the reductionist effort to "explain it away." Weber, for example, finds it in the very nature of human beings to create systems of meaning to guide their actions; and so does Clifford Geertz. In that connection, we should also note, their views recall a feature of the approach taken by Tylor and Frazer that has on occasion gone unnoticed. The evolutionism of these Victorian pioneers in anthropology has been often and rightly criticized, but what some have called the "intellectualist" element of their program is another, and separate, thing. They believed that the first impulse to religion lay in the human desire to explain the world. Belief in the gods helped early peoples account for things that were otherwise mysterious or absurd. That claim certainly has its merits, and in an intriguing way, opponents of reductionism like Weber and Geertz partially reaffirm it. Evans-Pritchard does as well. In the selection presented here from his work among the Azande people of Africa, he observes that even when they seem absurd to outsiders, the religious beliefs of tribal peoples form coherent, orderly systems; they are neither chaotic nor irrational, just systems of thought that are different from those we employ in our culture, but equally designed to explain how the world works.

In the end, it should be apparent that this ongoing conceptual contest between reductionist functionalism, on the one hand, and various versions of anti-reductionist intellectualism or emotionalism, on the other, continues to weave itself subtly through theoretical debates to the present day.

3. The Range of Theories

As has been noted, most of these classic theorists draw a measure of their inspiration from Max Müller in believing that they can interpret or explain religion not just in one place or time, but across the ages and around the globe; they wish to account for religion taken, as it were, "in the round." But they do so in quite different ways. Tylor and Frazer feel they can explain, through the evolution of ideas, the entire history of religion as it first appeared and then developed throughout history. From their very different angles of vision, the three major reductionists show the same sweeping ambition, each resting his theory chiefly on some compelling general formula applied to a pivotal instance or paradigmatic case. Analogously, both James and Otto, as well as Weber and Eliade, take the entire spectrum of world religions into view, though their emphases clearly differ. In the selections presented here, James and Otto rely on emotional experiences which they take to be universal—an element of all the world's religions, while Eliade points to the universal reach of archaic religions and Weber to the great world systems, which encompass the vast majority of the world's population. Interestingly, however, the dissenters on this score are the only two (and more recent) theorists with actual experience of cultures other than their own as field-working anthropologists: Evans-Pritchard and Geertz. Since their concerns center on problems with evidence, we can describe them best in that light.

4. Evidence and Theory

An explanation is one thing; the method of proving it is another. If we look closely at the theorists represented here, most recognize that a truly global theory of religion requires an equally global approach to evidence. Tylor and Frazer, as we have already noted, set out to assemble a wide array of evidence from almost every corner of the far-flung British Empire. Mircea Eliade applies his vast learning to a similar purpose. At the same time, nearly all of their evidence is gathered from "primitive" or tribal societies—"archaic peoples," as Eliade calls them. Only Max Weber can be said to transcend this difficulty. The sweep of his learning is remarkably wide; he draws on an extraordinarily broad and yet precise knowledge of both simple and highly advanced cultures, including the great Eastern civilizations centered in India and China. Neither James nor Otto searches quite as widely as Weber or Eliade for materials and sources (though in works not presented here Otto displays an impressive grasp of Hinduism, as well as Western religions); still, they in principle make the same commitment to acquiring evidence from all traditions and cultures. The strength of this approach, certainly, lies in its honest attempt to make a complete "fit" between the scale of the theory and scope of the evidence. But its limits are no less obvious. It is a program exceptionally difficult to achieve in full measure, even by a team of collaborators, let alone by any single individual. Gaps in history, barriers of language, and the finite limits on the level of knowledge any individual, or group of individuals, can acquire—all of these are formidable obstacles to success.

Of course, these difficulties with evidence are rather neatly escaped by Freud and Marx. They see no need to search the world for data, for they feel that in obsessional neurosis or economic injustice they have found something better—the fundamental mechanism in all persons and societies that everywhere generates religion. With such formulas in hand there really is no need to explore the world seeking redundant examples to illustrate a process that yields the same effects everywhere. Both Marx and Freud are content to apply their theories chiefly to Judeo-Christian monotheism and let the verdict in that case stand for all other religions as well.

The remaining three theorists—Durkheim, Evans-Pritchard, and Geertz— think the problem of theory and evidence requires other measures. They find the "globalist" approach too unworkably broad, and the Western monotheistic focus of Marx and Freud too narrow. The solution, they say, must be found on another path. Durkheim's strategy is to rely on the case of Australia's aborigine peoples as a kind of singular paradigm, the "one well-made experiment," as he calls it, that is "valid universally." In his view, the aborigine clan, as the oldest and simplest form of human society, displays the "elementary forms" out of which the religions of all subsequent cultures have been constructed. Here too, however, we are left with a question not unlike the one that Marx and Freud leave for us: Is the very specific nature of this Australian evidence fully sufficient to support the universal claims that are made to rest upon it?

Durkheim's example enables us to see more clearly the reasoning behind the positions of E. E. Evans-Pritchard and Clifford Geertz. As these selections from their works will show, both theorists choose in the end to stop short of making any truly general explanatory claims about the nature of religion as a whole. The problem, they say, is in the evidence, which is just too limited, at least in its present state, to make comprehensive claims. Evans-Pritchard does express a kind of deferred hope that at some later time, well into the future, generalizations can be attempted again. But at present and in Africa alone, he observes, substantially more work in the form of specific case studies still needs to be completed. Geertz is even more hesitant. He comes near to announcing the end of all general theories in both anthropology and religion on the ground that truth lies always (and perhaps only) in the specifics of individual societies. As he indicates in the title of his most well-known book, what theorists today can offer is the interpretation of "cultures" in the plural, rather than any general theory of "culture" in the singular. And what is true of culture is equally true of religion. For the present, he feels, and probably also the future, the range of available evidence will almost certainly remain insufficient to support the range of general theories. He finds himself wondering whether "science" is any longer the best term to describe the study of religion, or of any other human cultural enterprise, as those inquires are carried on today.

5. Theory and Belief

None of the theorists who appear in the following pages should be considered a purely detached scholar, writing on a subject of no immediate personal interest. Each is also a human being, with personal convictions about religion that accompany his theoretical work. The relationship between those convictions and the explanation proposed is a quite individual matter, and sometimes very difficult to decipher.

There is, first, a sense in which all the theories on offer here present at least a possible problem for religious belief, for they all assume that confessional or theological statements are insufficient explanations. As we noted earlier, for some devout Christians and Jews their faith is exclusively the work of God; and some committed Muslims may see their submission to Allah in the same way. Nothing more need, or should, be said to explain why they believe as they do. When the issue is put in this form, the position of the theorist of religion almost unavoidably collides with that of the believer; for confessional statements of this kind cannot be counted in a science committed to the use only of evidence that both religious and nonreligious persons will acknowledge. On the opposite side of the matter, a number of theorists, especially those appearing here in the earlier chapters, take an equally uncompromising position against religious belief. As their discussions will show, both Tylor and Frazer were men of skeptical mind, who ultimately dismissed religion—in both its "savage" and civilized forms—as so much superstition and ignorance. In certain respects, their theories, which propose science as the modern replacement for religion, follow naturally from their personal atheism or agnosticism. The same can be said for the reductionist theories of Freud and Marx (though not entirely so for Durkheim). They find the claims of religion to be not only false, but pernicious and corruptive as well. Since for them religion cannot possibly be a normal and rational thing, the functional and reductive accounts of it they offer are really the only ones they regard as available. Reductionism in this respect would appear to be a natural theoretical child of atheism.

In light of the above, it is not hard to see why Rudolf Otto, a committed Protestant theologian, and Mircea Eliade, who displayed a lifelong sympathy for the religious temperament in both its Eastern and Western forms, would take stands opposed to reductionism. The same can be said, though in somewhat more moderated form, of William James, and even E. E. Evans-Pritchard. The former, a liberal American Protestant, was convinced that religious experience plays a constructive role in the individual human personality. The latter became a convert to Catholicism later in life; and in his encounters with the Azande and Nuer peoples, he developed (unlike Tylor and Frazer) a real appreciation for their religions. He found the reductionism of Freud, Marx, and Durkheim alien to the process of real understanding, and suggested later on in his career that religion is perhaps best understood only by those who have themselves had personal experience of it.

Yet if religious believers will tend to dissent from reductionist theories, at least of the aggressive type proposed by theorists like Marx and Freud, it does not follow that *only* believers will oppose such theories, or that opposition will arise only for religious reasons. Explanations such as these can be affirmed or opposed, conceivably, by theorists of any persuasion—on the quite purely scientific ground that they either are or are not adequate to explain religion, just as a theory of any other kind might be endorsed or opposed. On this point both Max Weber and his American disciple Clifford Geertz provide a pair of instructive examples. Both explicitly disavow religious commitments; they are personally atheist, or at best agnostic. In their explanatory work, however, both make clear their opposition to reductionist theories. They do not do so because reductionism presents any challenge to their personal beliefs, but simply because in their view it does not adequately explain the phenomenon of religion. As they see things, religion is too complex, too subtly multidimensional to be reduced to some principle such as Marx's class struggle or Freud's obsessional neurosis.

Such formulas, they contend, may explain some aspects of certain religions; they do not explain all of what occurs in any religion.

Behind the scenes, then, it is apparent that personal commitments play at the very least a discernibly motivating role in the development of all theories of religion. To those who have written out of antipathy toward religion, certain theories, most especially those of a reductionist character, seem only natural and right. To other theorists, more attuned to the religious temperament and sensibility, those formulas will appear unpersuasive and rival approaches more clearly compelling. That being said, the issues of personal belief that bear on the explanation and interpretation of religion are admittedly subtle and complex; inevitably, they allow for theories of quite different kinds to appear in combination with multiple variants of both belief and unbelief. Of that point, certainly, the theorists we meet here will provide quite ample proof in the chapters and pages to come.

1

E. B. Tylor: Animism and the Origin of Religion

Edward Burnett Tylor (1832–1917) was a pioneering figure in the systematic study of human society—an endeavor that later won him recognition, in some circles at least, as the "father of anthropology." Born into a prosperous London family and largely self-educated, he traveled as a young man to Mexico and Central America, where he observed the premodern customs of Native American peoples. He soon expanded these ethnological studies (as he called them) to other cultures, embracing texts from ancient civilizations, the folklore of old Europe, and reports of travelers to "primitive," or tribal, cultures across the globe. These efforts led to several books, one of which—the two-volume masterwork of his career—appeared in 1871 under the title *Primitive Culture: Researches into the Development of Mythology, Philosophy, Religion, Language, Art, and Custom* (1871). This ambitious project proved to be one of the most original and important books of the Victorian age—less significant in the long term than Darwin's famous *Origin of Species* (1859), but (in part because of Darwin) influential enough in its day. *Primitive Culture* passed through many editions, becoming in time both handbook and guidebook for others keen to pursue what came to be known as "Mr. Tylor's science."

Though raised in a religious family, Tylor early on renounced the Quaker beliefs of his parents. He held on principle that the truth about religion is best discovered not by listening to theologians, but by pursuing science—*social* science. Only by accumulating and closely comparing a wide range of facts from all ages and places, he contended, can we begin to understand the origin and character of religion—or for that matter any other human social endeavor. He took interest in Judaism and Christianity not as unique or revealed religions, but as particular cases of religion in general as it has developed in all human societies. It is worth noticing in the selections that follow just how many different examples Tylor brings to his discussions and how confident he is in framing comparisons among them. Those habits are typical of his approach, which came to be known as "the comparative method."

Two axioms that underpin Tylor's approach are also on display in these readings. The one can be called "intellectualist" individualism, the other "social evolutionism." Tylor assumes, first, that there is a certain uniformity—he calls it a "psychic unity"—to the human mind of all places and times. All have the capacity to think according to certain universal principles of logic and rationality; and all people, even the most primitive, or simple, use that capacity in similar fashion. Intellectually, he says, "all the world is a single country." But if all have the same intellect, that does not mean that all use it equally well. Primitive peoples are child-like; they reason by simple "association of ideas" which appear similar or connected—a method that may occasionally be correct but is often mistaken. Over time, however, societies do make progress in understanding. Through trial, error, and accumulated experience, they evolve. The patterns, or laws, that can be discerned in the development of human culture are "as definite as those which govern the motion of waves" and "the growth of plants and animals." Accordingly, we can actually chart certain broad stages of human progress. In what Tylor calls the "savage" stage of humanity, people hunted, gathered, and lived in simple villages. The later "barbaric" age, marked by the civilizations of Egypt, Babylonia, Greece, and Rome, saw the rise of agriculture, literacy, and life in cities. These stages have now of course been surpassed by the modern era, with its remarkable revolutions in commerce, industry, and technology.

Tylor recognizes that while cultures develop or change over time, not all do so in the same way or at the same pace. Industrial Britain of 1860 is different from rural Central America of the same year. That is because thinkers in England and Europe have been fortunate enough to make, and share, more intellectual progress in understanding the world than most tribal cultures have made. Similarly, within a single society, some people may be more intellectually advanced than others. There are always some people who hold beliefs that others have discarded. These things fall under the "doctrine of survivals"; they are beliefs and practices which linger on well after the day of their truth, or value, has passed. Archery, for example, was once a crucial skill, vital to the hunt. Today it is a recreation, a sport that entertains, rather than a skill needed to kill game. Tylor places the beliefs of the devout Christian majority of his day in this same category. Belief in God, the revealed Bible, the miraculous—in an age of science and technology, all of these must be seen as "survivals": ideas, no longer credible, that linger from an earlier, more primitive stage of human society.

Tylor contends that of all the associations of ideas made by primitive peoples, arguably none has been more influential than that which figured in the origin of religion. "The savage philosopher," he writes, was intrigued by two common occurrences: death and dreams. In the one case, the life within a person appears to separate from the physical body; in the other, a kind of phantom, or image, appears able to do the same. These two things can be accounted for if we make a next and natural step in logic and combine them into one—into the idea of a personal soul that mirrors the body and animates (from the Latin *anima*: spirit) it from within. With this step, the extremely useful principle of animism was born.

Once formulated, the doctrine of animism held for the primitive mind such strong appeal that it came to be applied to the widest imaginable range of phenomena. For if the human body is animated by a soul, why should the principle of an animating spirit not equally explain other elements of the natural world? Why should not plants and animals, the oceans and streams, storms and stars also be moved by souls? Further, if souls are separable from physical objects and organisms they animate, why should there not lie behind the physical world an entire realm of angelic and demonic spirits—like the gods of classical Greece and Rome—with no necessary attachment to physical objects at all? And why should the great monotheistic religions of our own civilization not be seen as belonging to the same line of development?

In the end Tylor contends that the origin of religion—the worship of multiple spirits and deities that is found in almost every primitive society on the globe, the system of belief that over time also produced the great monotheistic religions of the modern West—can be traced along a continuous line of social evolution back to the animist thinking of earliest humanity, to what he calls the first "general philosophy of man and nature" ever devised by the human race.

Stages in the Development of Human Civilization

The following sequence of passages from Primitive Culture *outlines Tylor's theory of social development, the doctrine of survivals, his account of the primitive logic*

FROM: *Primitive Culture: Researches into the Development of Mythology, Philosophy, Religion, Language, Art, and Custom*. Two volumes. Fourth Edition, Revised. London, John Murray, [1871] 1903.

that led to the idea of the soul, and the evolution of that idea into those of spirits and gods.

[O]n the definite basis of compared facts, ethnographers are able to set up at least a rough scale of civilization. Few would dispute that the following races are arranged rightly in order of culture: Australian, Tahitian, Aztec, Chinese, Italian. By treating the development of civilization on this plain ethnographic basis, many difficulties may be avoided which have embarrassed its discussion. This may be seen by a glance at the relation which theoretical principles of civilization bear to the transitions to be observed as matter of fact between the extremes of savage and cultured life.

From an ideal point of view, civilization may be looked upon as the general improvement of mankind by higher organization of the individual and of society, to the end of promoting at once man's goodness, power, and happiness. This theoretical civilization does in no small measure correspond with actual civilization, as traced by comparing savagery with barbarism, and barbarism with modern educated life. So far as we take into account only material and intellectual culture, this is especially true. Acquaintance with the physical laws of the world, and the accompanying power of adapting nature to man's own ends, are, on the whole, lowest among savages, mean among barbarians, and highest among modern educated nations. Thus a transition from the savage state to our own would be, practically, that very progress of art and knowledge which is one main element in the development of culture.

~

[W]hen we read descriptions of the hospitality, the gentleness, the bravery, the deep religious feeling of the North American Indians, we admit their claims to our sincere admiration; but we must not forget that they were hospitable literally to a fault, that their gentleness would pass with a flash of anger into frenzy, that their bravery was stained with cruel and treacherous malignity, that their religion expressed itself in absurd belief and useless ceremony. The ideal savage of the 18th century might be held up as a living reproof to vicious and frivolous London; but in sober fact, a Londoner who should attempt to lead the atrocious life which the real savage may lead with impunity and even respect, would be a criminal only allowed to follow his savage models during his short intervals out of gaol. Savage moral standards are real enough, but they are far looser and weaker than ours. We may, I think, apply the often-repeated comparison of savages to children as fairly to their moral as to their intellectual condition. The better savage social life seems in but unstable equilibrium, liable to be easily upset by a touch of distress, temptation, or violence, and then it becomes the worse savage life, which we know by so many dismal and hideous examples. Altogether, it may be admitted that some rude tribes lead a life to be envied by some barbarous races, and even by the outcasts of higher nations. But that any known savage tribe would not be improved by judicious civilization, is a proposition which no moralist would dare to make; while the general tenour of the evidence goes far to justify the view that on the whole the civilized man is not only wiser and more capable than the savage, but also better and happier, and that the barbarian stands between....

[T]he few remarks here made will have shown how loose must be the working-out of...rough-and-ready estimates of culture. In fact, much of the labour spent in investigating the progress and decline of civilization has been mis-spent, in premature attempts to treat that as a whole which is as yet only susceptible of divided study. The present comparatively narrow argument on the development of culture...takes cognizance principally of knowledge, art, and custom, and indeed only very partial cognizance within this field, the vast range of physical, political, social, and ethical considerations being left all but untouched. Its standard of reckoning progress and decline is not that of ideal good and evil, but of movement along a measured line from grade to grade of actual savagery, barbarism, and civilization. The thesis which I venture to sustain, within limits, is simply this, that the savage state in some measure represents an early condition of mankind, out of which the higher culture has gradually been developed or evolved, by processes still in regular operation as of old, the result showing that, on the whole, progress has far prevailed over relapse.

On this proposition, the main tendency of human society during its long term of existence has been to pass from a savage to a civilized state. Now all must admit a great part of this assertion to be not only truth, but truism.... It is mere matter of chronicle that modern civilization is a development of mediaeval civilization, which again is a development from civilization of the order represented in Greece, Assyria, or Egypt. Thus the higher culture being clearly traced back to what may be called the middle culture, the question which remains is, whether this middle culture may be traced back to the lower culture, that is, to savagery. To affirm this, is merely to assert that the same kind of development in culture which has gone on inside our range of knowledge has also gone on outside it, its course of proceeding being unaffected by our having or not having reporters present. If any one holds that human thought and action were worked out in primaeval times according to laws essentially other than those of the modern world, it is for him to prove by valid evidence this anomalous state of things, otherwise the doctrine of permanent principle will hold good, as in astronomy or geology. That the tendency of culture has been similar throughout the existence of human society, and that we may fairly judge from its known historic course what its prehistoric course may have been, is a theory clearly entitled to precedence as a fundamental principle of ethnographic research.

Gibbon, in his "Roman Empire," expresses in a few vigorous sentences his theory of the course of culture, as from savagery upward. Judged by the knowledge of nearly a century later, his remarks cannot, indeed, pass unquestioned....But, on the whole, the great historian's judgment seems so substantially that of the unprejudiced modern student of the progressionist school, that I gladly quote the passage here at length, and take it as a text to represent the development-theory of culture:—"The discoveries of ancient and modern navigators, and the domestic history, or tradition, of the most enlightened nations, represent the *human savage* naked both in mind and body, and destitute of laws, of arts, of ideas, and almost of language. From this abject condition, perhaps the primitive and universal state of man, he has gradually arisen to command the animals, to fertilise the earth, to traverse the ocean, and to measure the heavens. His progress in the improvement and exercise of his mental and corporeal faculties has been irregular and various; infinitely slow in the beginning and increasing by degrees with redoubled velocity: ages of laborious ascent have been followed by a moment of rapid downfall; and the several climates of the globe have felt the vicissitudes of light and darkness. Yet the experience of four thousand years should enlarge our hopes, and diminish our apprehensions: we cannot determine to what height the human species may aspire in their advances towards perfection; but it may safely be presumed that no people, unless the face of nature is changed, will relapse into their original barbarism."

~

The Theory of "Survivals"

When a custom, an art, or an opinion is fairly started in the world, disturbing influences may long affect it so slightly that it may keep its course from generation to generation, as a stream once settled in its bed will flow on for ages. This is mere permanence of culture; and the special wonder about it is that the change and revolution of human affairs should have left so many of its feeblest rivulets to run so long. On the Tatar steppes, six hundred years ago, it was an offence to tread on the threshold or touch the ropes in entering a tent, and so it appears to be still. Eighteen centuries ago Ovid mentions the vulgar Roman objection to marriages in May, which he not unreasonably explains by the occurrence in that month of the funeral rites of the Lemuralia....

The saying that marriages in May are unlucky survives to this day in England, a striking example of how an idea, the meaning of which has perished for ages, may continue to exist simply because it has existed.

Now there are thousands of cases of this kind which have become, so to speak, landmarks in the course of culture. When in the process of time there has come general change in the condition of a people, it is usual, notwithstanding, to find much that manifestly had not its origin in the new state of things, but has simply lasted on into it. On the strength of these survivals, it becomes possible to declare that the civilization of the people they are observed among must have been derived from an earlier state, in which the proper home and meaning of these things are to be found; and thus collections of such facts are to be worked as mines of historic knowledge. In dealing with such materials, experience of what actually happens is the main guide, and direct history has to teach us, first and foremost, how old habits hold their ground in the midst of a new culture which certainly would never have brought them in, but on the contrary presses hard to thrust them out. What this direct information is like, a single example may show. The Dayaks of Borneo were not accustomed to chop wood, as we do, by notching out V-shaped cuts. Accordingly, when the white man intruded among them with this among other novelties, they marked their disgust at the innovation by levying a fine on any of their own people who should be caught chopping in the European fashion; yet so well aware were the native woodcutters that the white man's plan was an improvement on their own, that they would use it surreptitiously when they could trust one another not to tell. The account is twenty years old, and very likely the foreign chop may have ceased to be an offence against Dayak conservatism, but its prohibition was a striking instance of survival by ancestral authority in the very teeth of common sense.

∼

Let us now put the theory of survival to a somewhat severe test, by seeking from it some explanation of the existence, in practice or memory, within the limits of modern civilized society, of…customs which civilized ideas totally fail to account for. Though we may not succeed in giving clear and absolute explanations of their motives, at any rate it is a step in advance to be able to refer their origins to savage or barbaric antiquity. Looking at these customs from the modern practical point of view, one is ridiculous, the others are atrocious, and all are senseless.…

In interpreting…customs connected with sneezing, it is needful to recognize a prevalent doctrine of the lower races, of which a full account will be given in another chapter. As a man's soul is considered to go in and out of his body, so it is with other spirits, particularly such as enter into patients and possess them or afflict them with disease. Among the less cultured races, the connexion of this idea with sneezing is best shown among the Zulus, a people firmly persuaded that kindly or angry spirits of the dead hover about them, do them good or harm, stand visibly before them in dreams, enter into them, and cause diseases in them.... The Zulu diviners or sorcerers are very apt to sneeze, which they regard as an indication of the presence of the spirits, whom they adore by saying "Makosi" (*i.e.* lords or masters). It is a suggestive example of the transition of such customs as these from one religion to another, that the Amakosa, who used to call on their divine ancestor Utixo when they sneezed, since their conversion to Christianity say, "Preserver, look upon me!" or "Creator of heaven and earth!"...Polynesia is another region where the sneezing salutation is well marked. In New Zealand, a charm was said to prevent evil when a child sneezed; if a Samoan sneezed, the bystanders said, "Life to you!" while in the Tongan group a sneeze on the starting of an expedition was a most evil presage.

∿

It is not strange that the existence of these absurd customs should have been for ages a puzzle to curious inquirers. Especially the legend-mongers took the matter in hand, and their attempts to devise historical explanations are on record in a group of philosophic myths, Greek, Jewish, Christian. Prometheus prays for the preservation of his artificial man, when it gives the first sign of life by a sneeze; Jacob prays that man's soul may not, as heretofore, depart from his body when he sneezes; Pope Gregory prays to avert the pestilence, in those days when the air was so deadly that he who sneezed died of it; and from these imaginary events legend declares that the use of the sneezing formulas was handed down.... [T]his idea shows itself clearly in Josephus' story of his having seen a certain Jew, named Eleazar, cure demoniacs in Vespasian's time, by drawing the demons out through their nostrils.... On the whole, though the sneezing superstition makes no approach to universality among mankind, its wide distribution is highly remarkable, and it would be an interesting problem to decide how far this wide distribution is due to independent growth in several regions, how far to conveyance from race to race, and how far to ancestral inheritance. Here it has only to be maintained that it was not originally an arbitrary and meaningless custom, but the working out of a principle. The...hints to be gained from the superstition and folklore of other races...connect the notions and practices as to sneezing with the ancient and savage doctrine of pervading and invading spirits, considered as good or evil, and treated accordingly. The lingering survivals of the quaint old formulas in modern Europe seem an unconscious record of the time when the explanation of sneezing had not yet been given over to physiology, but was still in the "theological stage."

∿

The principal key to the understanding of Occult Science is to consider it as based on the Association of Ideas, a faculty which lies at the very foundation of human reason, but in no small degree of human unreason also. Man, as yet in a low intellectual condition, having come to associate in thought those things which he found by experience to be connected in fact, proceeded erroneously to invert this action, and to conclude that association in thought must involve similar connexion to reality. He thus attempted to discover, to foretell, and to cause events by means of processes which we can now see to have only an ideal significance. By a vast mass of evidence from savage, barbaric, and civilized life, magic arts which have resulted from thus mistaking an ideal for a real connexion, may be clearly traced from the lower culture which they are of, to the higher culture which they are in. Such are the practices whereby a distant person is to be affected by acting on something closely associated with him—his property, clothes he has worn, and above all cuttings of his hair and nails. Not only do savages high and low like the Australians and Polynesians, and barbarians like the nations of Guinea, live in deadly terror of this spiteful craft—not only have the Parsis their sacred ritual prescribed for burying their cut hair and nails, lest demons and sorcerers do mischief with them, but the fear of leaving such clippings and parings about lest their former owner should be harmed through them, has by no means died out of European folklore, and the German peasant, during the days between his child's birth and baptism, objects to lend anything out of the house, lest witchcraft should be worked through it on the yet unconsecrated baby....

Magical arts in which the connexion is that of mere analogy or symbolism are endlessly numerous throughout the course of civilization. Their common theory may be readily made out from a few typical cases, and thence applied confidently to the general mass. The Australian will observe the track of an insect near a grave, to ascertain the direction where the sorcerer is to be found, by whose craft the man died. The Zulu may be seen chewing a bit of wood, in order, by this symbolic act, to soften the heart of the man he wants to buy oxen from, or of the woman he wants for a wife.... With quaint simplicity, the German cottager declares that if a dog howls looking downward, it portends a death; but if upward, then a recovery from sickness. Locks must be opened and bolts drawn in a dying man's house, that his soul may not be held fast.... Modern Servians, dancing and singing, lead about a little girl dressed in leaves and flowers, and pour bowls of water over her to make the rain come.... Fanciful as these notions are, it should be borne in mind that they come fairly under definite mental law, depending as they do on a principle of ideal association, of which we can quite understand the mental action, though we deny its practical results. The clever Lord Chesterfield, too clever to understand folly, may again be cited to prove this. He relates in one of his letters that the king had been ill, and that people generally expected the illness to be fatal, because the oldest lion in the Tower, about the king's age, had just died. "So wild and capricious is the human mind," he exclaims, by way of comment. But indeed the thought was neither wild nor capricious, it was simply such an argument from analogy as the educated world has at length painfully learnt to be worthless; but which, it is not too much to declare, would to this day carry considerable weight to the minds of four-fifths of the human race.

A glance at those magical arts which have been systematized into pseudo-sciences, shows the same underlying principle. The art of taking omens from seeing and meeting animals, which includes augury, is familiar to such savages as the Tupis of Brazil and the Dayaks of Borneo, and extends upward through classic civilization. The Maoris may give a sample of the character of its rules: they hold it unlucky if an owl hoots during a consultation, but a council of war is encouraged by prospect of victory when a hawk flies overhead; a flight of birds to the right of the war-sacrifice is propitious if the villages of the tribe are in that quarter, but if the omen is in the enemy's direction the war will be given up. Compare these with the Tatar rules, and it is obvious that similar thoughts lie at the source of both. Here a certain little owl's cry is a sound of terror, although there is a white owl which is lucky; but of all birds the white falcon is most prophetic, and the Kalmuk bows his thanks for the good omen when one flies by on the right, but seeing one on the left turns away his face and expects calamity.... Any one who takes the trouble to go into this subject in detail, and to study the classic, mediaeval, and oriental codes of rules, will find that the principle of direct symbolism still accounts for a fair proportion of them, though the rest may have lost their early significance, or may have been originally due to some other reason, or may have been arbitrarily invented (as a considerable proportion of such devices must necessarily be) to fill up the gaps in the system.

~

Animism: The Source of Religious Ideas

The first requisite in a systematic study of the religions of the lower races, is to lay down a rudimentary definition of religion. By requiring in this definition belief in a supreme deity or judgment after death, the adoration of idols or the practice of sacrifice, or other partially-diffused doctrines or rites, no doubt many tribes may be excluded from the category of religious. But such narrow definition has the fault of identifying religion rather with particular developments than with the deeper motive which underlies them. It seems best to fall back at once on this essential source, and simply to claim, as a minimum definition of Religion, the belief in Spiritual Beings.... It cannot be positively asserted that every existing tribe recognizes the belief in spiritual beings, for the native condition of a considerable number is obscure in this respect, and from the rapid change or extinction they are undergoing, may ever remain so.... Here, so far as I can judge from the immense mass of accessible evidence, we have to admit that the belief in spiritual beings appears among all low races with whom we have attained to thoroughly intimate acquaintance....

I purpose here, under the name of Animism, to investigate the deep-lying doctrine of Spiritual Beings, which embodies the very essence of Spiritualistic as opposed to Materialistic philosophy. Animism is not a new technical term, though now seldom used. From its special relation to the doctrine of the soul, it will be seen to have a peculiar appropriateness to the view here taken of the mode in which theological ideas have been developed among mankind....

Animism characterizes tribes very low in the scale of humanity, and thence ascends, deeply modified in its transmission, but from first to last preserving an unbroken continuity, into the midst of high modern culture. Doctrines adverse to it, so largely held by individuals or schools, are usually due not to early lowness of civilization, but to later changes in the intellectual course, to divergence from, or rejection of, ancestral faiths; and such newer developments do not affect the present enquiry as to the fundamental religious condition of mankind. Animism is, in fact, the groundwork of the Philosophy of Religion, from that of savages up to that of civilized men. And although it may at first seem to afford but a bare and meager definition of a minimum of religion, it will be found practically sufficient; for where the root is, the branches will generally be produced. It is habitually found that the theory of Animism divides into two great dogmas, forming parts of one consistent doctrine; first, concerning souls of individual creatures, capable of continued existence after the death or destruction of the body; second, concerning other spirits, upward to the rank of powerful deities. Spiritual beings are held to affect or control the events of the material world, and man's life here and hereafter; and it being considered that they hold intercourse with men, and receive pleasure or displeasure from human actions, the belief in their existence leads naturally, and it might almost be said inevitably, sooner or later to active reverence and propitiation. Thus Animism, in its full development, includes the belief in souls and in a future state, in controlling deities and subordinate spirits, these doctrines practically resulting in some kind of active worship. One great element of religion, that moral element which among the higher nations forms its most vital part, is indeed little represented in the religion of the lower races. It is not that these races have no moral sense or no moral standard, for both are strongly marked among them, if not in formal precept, at least in that traditional consensus of society which we call public opinion, according to which certain actions are held to be good or bad, right or wrong. It is that the conjunction of ethics and Animistic philosophy, so intimate and powerful in the higher culture, seems scarcely yet to have begun in the lower. I propose here hardly to touch upon the purely moral aspects of religion, but rather to study the animism of the world so far as it constitutes, as unquestionably it does constitute, an ancient and world-wide philosophy, of which belief is the theory and worship is the practice. Endeavouring to shape the materials for an enquiry hitherto strangely undervalued and neglected, it will now be my task to bring as clearly as may be into view the fundamental animism of the lower races, and in some slight and broken outline to trace its course into higher regions of civilization. Here let me state once for all two principal conditions under which the present research is carried on. First, as to the religious doctrines and practices examined, these are treated as belonging to theological systems devised by human reason, without supernatural aid or revelation; in other words, as being developments of Natural Religion. Second, as to the connexion between similar ideas and rites in the religions of the savage and the civilized world. While dwelling at some length on doctrines and ceremonies of the lower races, and sometimes particularizing for special reasons the related doctrines and ceremonies of the higher nations, it has not seemed my proper task to work out in detail the problems thus suggested among the philosophies and creeds of Christendom. Such applications, extending farthest from the direct scope of a work on primitive culture, are briefly stated in general terms, or touched in slight allusion, or taken for granted without remark. Educated readers possess the information required to work out their general bearing on theology, while more technical discussion is left to philosophers and theologians specially occupied with such arguments.

The first branch of the subject to be considered is the doctrine of human and other Souls.... What the doctrine of the soul is among the lower races may be explained in stating the present theory of its development. It seems as though thinking men, as yet at a low level of culture, were deeply impressed by two groups of biological problems. In the first place, what is it that makes the difference between a living body and a dead one; what causes waking, sleep, trance, disease, death? In the second place, what are those human shapes which appear in dreams and visions? Looking at these two groups of phenomena, the ancient savage philosophers probably made their first step by the obvious inference that every man has two things belonging to him, namely, a life and a phantom. These two are evidently in close connexion with the body, the life as enabling it to feel and think and act, the phantom as being its image or second self; both also, are perceived to be things separable form the body, the life as able to go away and leave it insensible or dead, the phantom as appearing to people at a distance from it. The second step would seem also easy for savages to make, seeing how extremely difficult civilized men have found it to unmake. It is merely to combine the life and the phantom. As both belong to the body, why should they not also belong to one another, and be manifestations of one and the same soul? Let them then be considered as united, and the result is that well-known conception which may be described as an apparitional-soul, a ghost-soul. This, at any rate, corresponds with the actual conception of the personal soul or spirit among the lower races; which may be defined as follows: It is a thin unsubstantial human image, in its nature a sort of vapour, film, or shadow; the cause of life and thought in the individual it animates; independently possessing the personal consciousness and volition of its corporal owner, past or present; capable of leaving the body far behind, to flash swiftly from place to place; mostly impalpable and invisible, yet also manifesting physical power, and especially appearing to men waking or asleep as a phantasm separate from the body of which it bears the likeness; continuing to exist and appear to men after the death of that body; able to enter into, possess, and act in the bodies of other men, of animals, and even of things. Though this definition is by no means of universal application, it has sufficient generality to be taken as a standard, modified by more or less divergence among any particular people. Far from these world-wide opinions being arbitrary or conventional products, it is seldom even justifiable to consider their uniformity among distant races as proving communication of any sort. They are doctrines answering in the most forcible way to the plain evidence of men's senses, as interpreted by a fairly consistent and rational primitive philosophy. So well, indeed, does primitive animism account for the facts of nature, that it has held its place into the higher levels of education. Though classic and mediaeval philosophy modified it much, and modern philosophy has handled it yet more unsparingly, it has so far retained the trace of its original character, that heirlooms of primitive ages may be claimed in the existing psychology of the civilized world. Out of the vast mass of evidence, collected among the most various and distant races of mankind, typical details may now be selected to display the earlier theory of the soul, the relation of the parts of this theory, and the manner in which these parts have been abandoned, modified, or kept up, along the course of culture.

To understand the popular conceptions of the human soul or spirit, it is instructive to notice the words which have been found suitable to express it. The ghost or phantasm seen by the dreamer or the visionary is an unsubstantial form, like a shadow, and thus the familiar term of the *shade* comes in to express the soul. Thus the Tasmanian word for the shadow is also that for the spirit; the Algonquin Indians describe a man's soul as *otahchuk,* "his shadow"; the Quiché language uses *natub* for "shadow, soul"; the Arawac *ujea* means "shadow, soul image"; the Abipones made the one word *loúkal* serve for "shadow, soul, echo, image." The Zulus not only use the word *tunzi* for "shadow, spirit, ghost," but they consider that at death the shadow of a man will in some way depart from the corpse, to become an ancestral spirit. The Basutos not only call the spirit remaining after death the *seriti* or "shadow," but they think that if a man walks on the river bank, a crocodile may seize his shadow in the water and draw him in; while in Old Calabar there is found the same identification of the spirit with the *ukpon* or "shadow," for a man to lose which is fatal. There are thus found among the lower races not only the types of those familiar classic terms, the *skia* and the *umbra*, but also what seems the fundamental thought of the stories of shadowless men still current in the folklore of Europe.... Thus the dead in Purgatory knew that Dante was alive when they saw that, unlike theirs, his figure cast a shadow on the ground. Other attributes are taken into the notion of soul or spirit, with especial regard to its being the cause of life. Thus the Caribs, connecting the pulses with spiritual beings, and especially considering that in the heart dwells man's chief soul, destined to a future heavenly life, could reasonably use the one word *iouanni* for "soul, life, heart." The Tongans supposed the soul to exist throughout the whole extension of the body, but particularly in the heart.... [T]he Basutos say of a dead man that his heart is gone out; and of one recovering from sickness that his heart is coming back. This corresponds to the familiar Old World view of the heart as the prime mover in life, thought, and passion....

The act of breathing, so characteristic of the higher animals during life, and coinciding so closely with life in its departure, has been repeatedly and naturally identified with the life or soul itself.... It is thus that West Australians used one word *waug* for "breath, spirit, soul;" that in the Netela language of California, *piuts* means "life, breath, soul;" that certain Greenlanders reckoned two souls to man, namely his shadow and his breath; that the Malays say the soul of the dying man escapes through his nostrils, and in Java use the same word *ñawa* for "breath, life, soul." How the notions of life, heart, breath, and phantom unite in the one conception of a soul or spirit, and at the same time how loose and vague such ideas are among barbaric races, is well brought into view in the answers to a religious inquest held in 1528 among the natives of Nicaragua. "When they die, there comes out of their mouth something that resembles a person, and is called *Julio* [Aztec *yuli* = to live]. This is like a person, but does not die, and the body remains here." ... The conception of the soul as breath may be followed up through Semitic and Aryan etymology, and thus into the main streams of the philosophy of the world. Hebrew shows *nephesh*, "breath," passing into all the meanings of "life, soul, mind, animal," while *ruach* and *neshamah* make the like transition from "breath" to "spirit;" and to these the Arabic *nefs* and *ruh* correspond. The same is the history of Sanskrit *atman* and *prâna*, of Greek *psychē* and *pneuma*, of Latin *animus, anima, spiritus.* So Slavonic *duch* has developed the meaning of "breath" into that of soul or spirit; and the dialects of the Gypsies have this word *dūk* with the meanings of "breath, spirit, ghost," whether these pariahs brought the word from India as part of their inheritance of Aryan speech, or whether they adopted it in their migration across Slavonic lands.

German *geist* and English *ghost*, too, may possibly have the same original sense of breath. And if any should think such expressions due to mere metaphor, they may judge the strength of the implied connexion between breath and spirit by cases of most unequivocal significance. Among the Seminoles of Florida, when a woman died in childbirth, the infant was held over her face to receive her parting spirit, and thus acquire strength and knowledge for its future use. These Indians could have well understood why at the death-bed of an ancient Roman, the nearest kinsman leant over to inhale the last breath of the departing.... Their state of mind is kept up to this day among Tyrolese peasants, who can still fancy a good man's soul to issue from his mouth at death like a little white cloud.

It will be shown that men, in their composite and confused notions of the soul, have brought into connexion a list of manifestations of life and thought even more multifarious than this. But also, seeking to avoid such perplexity of combination, they have sometimes endeavoured to define and classify more closely, especially by the theory that man has a combination of several kinds of spirit, soul, or image, to which different functions belong. Already among savage races such classification appears in full vigour. Thus the Fijians distinguish between man's "dark spirit" or shadow, which goes to Hades, and his "light spirit" or reflexion in water or a mirror, which stays near where he dies. The Malagasy say that the *saina* or mind vanishes at death, the *aina* or life becomes mere air, but the *matoatoa* or ghost hovers round the tomb. In North America, the duality of the soul is a strongly marked Algonquin belief; one soul goes out and sees dreams while the other remains behind; at death one of the two abides with the body, and for this the survivors leave offerings of food, while the other departs to the land of the dead. A division into three souls is also known, and the Dakotas say that man has four souls, one remaining with the corpse, one staying in the village, one going in the air, and one to the land of spirits....

The early animistic theory of vitality, regarding the function of life as caused by the soul, offers to the savage mind an explanation of several bodily and mental conditions, as being effects of a departure of the soul or some of its constituent spirits. This theory holds a wide and strong position in savage biology.

∼

[The] temporary exit of the soul has a world-wide application to the proceedings of the sorcerer, priest, or seer himself. He professes to send forth his spirit on distant journeys, and probably often believes his soul released for a time from its bodily prison.... Thus the Australian Native doctor is alleged to obtain his initiation by visiting the world of spirits in a trance of two or three days' duration; the Khond priest authenticates his claim to office by remaining from one to fourteen days in a languid and dreamy state, caused by one of his souls being away in the divine presence; the Greenland angekok's soul goes forth from his body to fetch his familiar demon; the Turanian shaman lies in lethargy while his soul departs to bring hidden wisdom from the land of spirits. The literature of more progressive races supplies similar accounts.... The typical classic case is the story of Hermotimos, whose prophetic soul went out from time to time to visit distant regions, till at last his wife burnt the lifeless body on the funeral pile, and when the poor soul came back, there was no longer a dwelling for it to animate....

This same doctrine forms one side of the theory of dreams prevalent among the lower races. Certain of the Greenlanders... consider that the soul quits the body in the night and goes out hunting, dancing, and visiting; their dreams, which are frequent and lively, having brought them to this opinion. Among the Indians of North America, we hear of the dreamer's soul leaving his body and wandering in quest of things attractive to it. These things the waking man must endeavor to obtain, lest his soul be troubled, and quit the body altogether. The New Zealanders considered the dreaming soul to leave the body and return, even traveling to the region of the dead to hold converse with its friends....

Another part has also a place here, the view that human souls come from without to visit the sleeper, who sees them as dreams. These two views are by no means incompatible. The North American Indians allowed themselves the alternative of supposing a dream to be either a visit from the soul of the person or object dreamt of, or a sight seen by the rational soul, gone out for an excursion while the sensitive soul remains in the body. So the Zulu may be visited in a dream by the shade of an ancestor, the itongo, who comes to warn him of danger, or he may himself be taken by the itongo in a dream to visit his distant people.... In the lower range of culture, it is perhaps most frequently taken for granted that a man's apparition in a dream is a visit from his disembodied spirit, which the dreamer, to use an expressive Ojibwa idiom, "sees when asleep." Such a thought comes out clearly in the Fijian opinion that a living man's spirit may leave the body, to trouble other people in their sleep; or in a recent account of an old Indian woman of British Columbia sending for the medicine-man to drive away the dead people who came to her every night. A modern observer's description of the state of mind of the negroes of South Guinea in this respect is extremely characteristic and instructive. "All their dreams are construed into visits from the spirits of their deceased friends. The cautions, hints, and warnings which come to them through this source are received with the most serious and deferential attention, and are always acted upon in their waking hours. The habit of relating their dreams, which is universal, greatly promotes the habit of dreaming itself, and hence their sleeping hours are characterized by almost as much intercourse with the dead as their waking are with the living. This is, no doubt, one of the reasons of their excessive superstitiousness.

Their imaginations become so lively that they can scarcely distinguish between their dreams and their waking thoughts, between the real and the ideal, and they consequently utter falsehood without intending, and profess to see things which never existed."

To the Greek of old, the dream-soul was what to the modern savage it still is. Sleep, loosing cares of mind, fell on Achilles as he lay by the sounding sea, and there stood over him the soul of Patroklos, like to him altogether in stature, and the beauteous eyes, and the voice, and the garments that wrapped his skin; he spake, and Achilles stretched out to grasp him with loving hands, but caught him not, and like a smoke the soul sped twittering below the earth. Along the ages that separate us from Homeric times, the apparition in dreams of men living or dead has been subject of philosophic speculation and of superstitious fear. . . .

The evidence of visions corresponds with the evidence of dreams in their bearing on primitive theories of the soul, and the two classes of phenomena substantiate and supplement one another. Even in healthy waking life, the savage or barbarian has never learnt to make the rigid distinction between subjective and objective, between imagination and reality, to enforce which is one of the main results of scientific education. Still less, when disordered in body and mind he sees around him phantom human forms, can he distrust the evidence of his very senses. Thus it comes to pass that throughout the lower civilization men believe, with the most vivid and intense belief, in the objective reality of the human specters which they see in sickness, exhaustion, or excitement. As will be hereafter noticed, one main reason of the practices of fasting, penance, narcotizing by drugs, and other means of bringing on morbid exaltation, is that the patients may obtain the sight of spectral beings, from whom they hope to gain spiritual knowledge and even worldly power. Human ghosts are among the principal of these phantasmal figures. There is no doubt that honest visionaries describe ghosts as they really appear to their perception, while even the impostors who pretend to see them conform to the descriptions thus established.

~

That the apparitional human soul bears the likeness of its fleshy body, is the principle implicitly accepted by all who believe it really and objectively present in dreams and visions. My own view is that nothing but dreams and visions could have ever put into men's minds such an idea as that of souls being ethereal images of bodies. It is thus habitually taken for granted in animistic philosophy, savage or civilized, that souls set free from the earthly body are recognized by a likeness to it which they still retain, whether as ghostly wanderers on earth or inhabitants of the world beyond the grave. . . . This world-wide thought, coming into view here in a multitude of cases from all grades of culture, needs no collection of ordinary instances to illustrate it. But a quaint and special group of beliefs will serve to display the thoroughness with which the soul is thus conceived as an image of the body. As a consistent corollary to such an opinion, it is argued that the mutilation of the body will have a corresponding effect upon the soul, and very low savage races have philosophy enough to work out this idea. Thus it was recorded of the Indians of Brazil by one of the early European visitors, that they "believe that the dead arrive in the other world wounded or hacked to pieces, in fact just as they left this." Thus, too, the Australian who has slain his enemy will cut off the right thumb of the corpse, so that although the spirit will become a hostile ghost, it cannot throw with its mutilated hand the shadowy spear, and may be safely left to wander, malignant but harmless....

In studying the nature of the souls as conceived among the lower races, and in tracing such conceptions onward among the higher, circumstantial details are available. It is as widely recognized among mankind that souls or ghosts have voices, as that they have visible forms, and indeed the evidence for both is of the same nature. Men who perceive evidently that souls do talk when they are present themselves in dream or vision, naturally take for granted at once the objective reality of the ghostly voice, and of the ghostly form from which it proceeds. This is involved in the series of narratives of spiritual communication with living men, from savagery onward to civilization, while the more modern doctrine of subjectivity of such phenomena recognizes the phenomena themselves, but offers a different explanation of them....

The conception of dreams and visions as caused by present objective figures, and the identification of such phantom souls with the shadow and the breath, has led many a people to treat souls as substantial material beings. Thus it is a usual proceeding to make openings through solid materials to allow souls to pass. The Iroquois in old time used to leave an opening in the grave for the lingering soul to visit its body, and some of them still bore holes in the coffin for the same purpose. The Malagasy sorcerer, for the cure of a sick man who had lost his soul, would make a hole in the burial-house to let out a spirit, which he would catch in his cap and so convey to the patient's head. The Chinese make a hole in the roof to let out the soul at death. And lastly, the custom of opening a window or door for the departing soul when it quits the body is to this day a very familiar superstition in France, Germany, and England.

⁓

Among rude races, the original conception of the human soul seems to have been that of ethereality, or vaporous materiality, which has held so large a place in human thought ever since. In fact, the later metaphysical notion of immateriality could scarcely have conveyed any meaning to a savage. It is moreover to be noticed that, as to the whole nature and action of apparitional souls, the lower philosophy escapes various difficulties which down to modern times have perplexed metaphysicians and theologians of the civilized world. Considering the thin ethereal body of the soul to be itself sufficient and suitable for visibility, movement, and speech, the primitive animists had no need of additional hypotheses to account for these manifestations....

Departing from the body at the time of death, the soul or spirit is considered set free to linger near the tomb, to wander on earth or flit in the air, or to travel the proper region of the spirits—the world beyond grave. The principal conceptions of the lower psychology as to a Future Life will be considered in the following chapters, but for the present purpose of investigating the theory of souls in general, it will be well to enter here upon one department of the subject. Men do not stop short at the persuasion that death releases the souls to a free and active existence, but they quite logically proceed to assist nature, by slaying men in order to liberate their souls for ghostly uses. Thus there arises one of the most wide-spread, distinct, and intelligible rites of animistic religion—that of funeral human sacrifice for the service of the dead. When a man of rank dies and his soul departs to its own place, wherever and whatever that place may be, it is a rational inference of early philosophy that the souls of attendants, slaves, and wives, put to death at his funeral, will make the same journey and continue their service in the next life, and the argument is frequently stretched further, to include the souls of new victims sacrificed in order that they may enter upon the same ghostly servitude. It will appear from the ethnography of this rite that it is not strongly marked in the very lowest levels of culture, but that, arising in the higher savagery, it develops itself in the barbaric stage, and thenceforth continues or dwindles in survival.

Of the murderous practices to which this opinion leads, remarkably distinct accounts may be cited from among tribes of the Indian Archipelago. The following account is given of the funerals of great men among the savage Kayans of Borneo:—"Slaves are killed in order that they may follow the deceased and attend upon him. Before they are killed the relations who surround them enjoin them to take great care of their master when they join him, to watch and shampoo him when he is indisposed, to be always near him, and to obey all his behests. The female relatives of the deceased then take a spear and slightly wound the victims, after which the males spear them to death." Again, the opinion of the Idaan is "that all whom they kill in this world shall attend them as slaves after death.... From the same principle they will purchase a slave, guilty of any capital crime, at fourfold his value, that they may be his executioners." With the same idea is connected the ferocious custom of "head-hunting," so prevalent among the Dayaks before Rajah Brooke's time. They considered that the owner of every human head they could procure would serve them in the next world, where, indeed, a man's rank would be according to his number of heads in this. They would continue the mourning for a dead man till a head was brought in to provide him with a slave to accompany him to the "habitation of souls"; a father who lost his child would go out and kill the first man he met, as a funeral ceremony; a young man might not marry till he had procured a head, and some tribes would bury with a dead man the first head he had taken, together with spears, cloth, rice, and betel. Waylaying and murdering men for their heads became, in fact, the Dayaks' national sport, and they remarked "the white men read books, we hunt for heads instead." Of such rites in the Pacific islands, the most hideously purposeful accounts reach us from the Fiji group. Till lately, a main part of the ceremony of a great man's funeral was the strangling of wives, friends, and slaves, for the distinct purpose of attending him into the world of spirits. Ordinarily the first victim was the wife of the deceased, and more than one if he had several, and their corpses, oiled as for a feast, clothed with new fringed girdles, with heads dressed and ornamented, and vermilion and turmeric powder spread on their faces and bosoms, were laid by the side of the dead warrior. Associates and inferior attendants were likewise slain, and these bodies were spoken of as "grass for bedding the grave." When Ra Mbithi, the pride of Somosomo, was lost at sea, seventeen of his wives were killed; and after the news of the massacre of the Namena people, in 1839, eighty women were strangled to accompany the spirits of their murdered husbands. Such sacrifices took place under the same pressure of public opinion which kept up the widow-burning in modern India. The Fijian widow was worked upon by her relatives with all the pressure of persuasion and of menace; she understood well that life to her henceforth would mean a wretched existence of neglect, disgrace, and destitution; and tyrannous custom, as hard to struggle against in the savage as in the civilized world, drove her to the grave. Thus, far from resisting, she became importunate for death and the new life to come, and till public opinion reached a more enlightened state, the missionaries often used their influence in vain to save from the strangling-cord some wife whom they could have rescued, but who herself refused to live. So repugnant to the native mind was the idea of a chieftain going unattended into the other world, that the missionaries' prohibition of the cherished custom was one reason of their dislike to Christianity. Many of the nominal Christians, when once a chief of theirs was shot from an ambush, esteemed it most fortunate that a stray shot at the same time killed a young man at a distance from him, and thus provided a companion for the spirit of the slain chief.

～

Animals... [being] considered in the primitive psychology to have souls like human beings, it follows as the simplest matter of course that tribes who kill wives and slaves, to dispatch their souls on errands of duty with their departed lords, may also kill animals in order that their spirits may do such service as is proper to them. The Pawnee warrior's horse is slain on his grave to be ready for him to mount again, and the Comanche's best horses are buried with his favorite weapons and his pipe, all alike to be used in the distant happy hunting-grounds.

~

Plants, partaking with animals the phenomena of life and death, health and sickness, not unnaturally have some kind of soul ascribed to them. In fact, the notion of a vegetable soul, common to plants and to the higher organisms possessing an animal soul in addition, was familiar to medieval philosophy, and is not yet forgotten by naturalists. But in the lower ranges of culture, at least within one wide district of the world, the souls of plants are much more fully identified with the souls of animals. The Society Islanders seem to have attributed "varua," i.e., surviving soul or spirit, not to men only but to animals and plants. The Dayaks of Borneo not only consider men and animals to have a spirit or living principle, whose departure from the body causes sickness and eventually death, but they also give to the rice its "samangat padi," or "spirit of the paddy," and they hold feasts to retain this soul securely, lest the crop should decay. . . .

Thus far the details of the lower animistic philosophy are not very unfamiliar to modern students. The primitive view of the souls of men and beasts, as asserted or acted on in the lower and middle levels of culture, so far belongs to current civilized thought, that those who hold the doctrine to be false, and the practices based upon it futile, can nevertheless understand and sympathise with the lower nations to whom they are matters of the most sober and serious conviction. Nor is even the notion of separable spirit or soul as the cause of life in plants too incongruous with ordinary ideas to be readily appreciable. But the theory of souls in the lower culture stretches beyond this limit, to take in a conception much stranger to modern thought. Certain high savage races distinctly hold, and a large proportion of other savage and barbarian races make a more or less close approach to, a theory of separable and surviving souls or spirits belonging to stocks and stones, weapons, boats, food, clothes, ornaments, and other objects which to us are not merely soulless but lifeless.

Yet, strange as such a notion may seem to us at first sight, if we place ourselves by an effort in the intellectual position of an uncultured tribe, and examine the theory of object-souls from their point of view, we shall hardly pronounce it irrational. In discussing the origin of myth, some account has been already given of the primitive stage of thought in which personality and life are ascribed not to men and beasts only, but to things. It has been shown how what we call inanimate objects—rivers, stones, trees, weapons, and so forth—are treated as living intelligent beings, talked to, propitiated, punished for the harm they do. Hume, whose "Natural History of Religion" is perhaps more than any other work the source of modern opinions as to the development of religion, comments on the influence of this personifying stage of thought. "There is an universal tendency among mankind to conceive all beings like themselves, and to transfer to every object those qualities with which they are familiarly acquainted, and of which they are intimately conscious. ... The *unknown causes*, which continually employ their thought, appearing always in the same aspect, are all apprehended to be of the same kind or species. Nor is it long before we ascribe to them thought and reason, and passion, and sometimes even the limbs and figures of men, in order to bring them nearer to a resemblance with ourselves." ... Our comprehension of the lower stages of mental culture depends much on the thoroughness with which we can appreciate this primitive, childlike conception, and in this our best guide may be the memory of our own childish days. He who recollects when there was still personality to him in posts and sticks, chairs and toys, may well understand how the infant philosophy of mankind could extend the notion of vitality to what modern science only recognizes as lifeless things; thus one main part of the lower animistic doctrine as to souls of objects is accounted for. The doctrine requires for its full conception of a soul not only life, but also a phantom or apparitional spirit; this development, however, follows without difficulty, for the evidence of dreams and visions applies to the spirits of objects in much the same manner as to human ghosts. Everyone who has seen visions while light-headed in fever, everyone who has ever dreamt a dream, has seen the phantoms of objects as well as of persons. How then can we charge the savage with far-fetched absurdity for taking into philosophy and religion an opinion which rests on the very evidence of the senses? The notion is implicitly recognized in his accounts of ghosts, which do not come naked, but clothed, and even armed; of course there must be spirits of garments and weapons, seeing that the spirits of men come bearing them. It will indeed place savage philosophy in no unfavorable light, if we compare this extreme animistic development of it with the popular opinion still surviving in civilized countries, as to ghosts and the nature of the human soul as connected with them.

∿

It remains to sum up in few words the doctrine of souls, in the various phases it has assumed from first to last among mankind. In the attempt to trace its main course through the successive grades of man's intellectual history, the evidence seems to accord best with a theory of its development, somewhat to the following effect. At the lowest levels of culture of which we have clear knowledge, the notion of a ghost-soul animating man while in the body, and appearing in dream and vision out of the body, is found deeply ingrained. There is no reason to think that this belief was learnt by savage tribes from contact with higher races, nor that it is a relic of higher culture from which the savage tribes have degenerated; for what is here treated as the primitive animistic doctrine is thoroughly at home among savages, who appear to hold it on the very evidence of their senses, interpreted on the biological principle which seems to the most reasonable. We may now and then hear the savage doctrines and practices concerning souls claimed as relics of a high religious culture pervading the primeval race of man. They are said to be traces of remote ancestral religion, kept up in scanty and perverted memory by tribes degraded from a nobler state. It is easy to see that such an explanation of some few facts, sundered from their connexion with the general array, may seem plausible to certain minds. But a large view of the subject can hardly leave such argument in possession. The animism of savages stands for and by itself; it explains its own origin. The animism of civilized men, while more appropriate to advanced knowledge, is in great measure only explicable as a developed product of the older and ruder system. It is the doctrines and rites of the lower races which are, according to their philosophy, results of point-blank natural evidence and acts of straightforward practical purpose. It is the doctrines and rites of the higher races which show survival of the old in the midst of the new, modification of the old to bring it into conformity with the new, abandonment of the old because it is no longer compatible with the new. Let us see at a glance in what general relation the doctrine of souls among savage tribes stands to the doctrine of souls amongst barbaric and cultured nations. Among races within the limits of savagery, the general doctrine of souls is found worked out with remarkable breadth and consistency. The souls of animals are recognized by a natural extension from the theory of human souls; the souls of trees and plants follow in some vague and partial way; and the souls of inanimate objects expand the general category to its extremest boundaries. Thenceforth, as we explore human thought onward from savage into barbarian and civilized life, we find a state of theory more conformed to positive science, but in itself less complete and consistent. Far on into civilization, men still act as though in some half-meant way they believe in souls or ghosts of objects, while nevertheless their knowledge of physical science is beyond so crude a philosophy. As to the doctrine of souls of plants, fragmentary evidence of the history of its breaking down in Asia is reaching us. In our own day and country, the notion of souls of beasts is to be seen dying out. Animism, indeed, seems to be drawing in its outposts, and concentrating itself on its first and main position, the doctrine of the human soul. This doctrine has undergone extreme modification in the course of culture. It has outlived the almost total loss of one great argument attached to it,—the objective reality of apparitional souls or ghosts seen in dreams and visions. The soul has given up its ethereal substance, and become an immaterial entity, "the shadows of a shade." Its theory is becoming separated from the investigations of biology and mental science, which now discuss the phenomena of life and thought, the senses and the intellect, the emotions and the will, on a ground-work of pure experience. There has arisen an intellectual product whose very existence is of the deepest significance, a "psychology" which has no longer anything to do with the "soul." The soul's place in modern thought is in the metaphysics of religion, and its especial office there is that of furnishing an intellectual side to the religious doctrine of the future life. Such are the alterations which have differenced the fundamental animistic belief in its course through successive periods of the world's culture. Yet it is evident that, notwithstanding all this profound change, the conception of the human soul is, as to its most essential nature, continuous from the philosophy of the savage thinker to that of the modern professor of theology. Its definition has remained from the first that of an animating, separable, surviving entity, the vehicle of individual personal existence. The theory of the soul is one principal part of a system of religious philosophy, which unites, in an unbroken line of mental connexion, the savage fetish-worshipper and the civilized Christian. The divisions which have separated the great religions of the world into intolerant and hostile sects are for the most part superficial in comparison with the deepest of all religious schisms, that which divides Animism from Materialism.

∽

Belief in Spirits and Gods

We have now to enter on the final topic of the investigation of Animism, by completing the classified survey of spiritual beings in general, from the myriad souls, elves, fairies, genii, conceived as filling their multifarious offices in man's life and the world's, up to the deities who reign, few and mighty, over the spiritual hierarchy. In spite of endless diversity of detail, the general principles of this investigation seem comparatively easy of access to the enquirer, if he will use the two keys which the foregoing studies supply: first, that spiritual beings are modelled by man on his primary conception of his own human soul, and second, that their purpose is to explain nature on the primitive childlike theory that it is truly and throughout "Animated Nature." ... [R]ude tribes of ancient men had within them this source of happiness, that they could explain to their own content the causes of things. For to them spiritual beings, elves and gnomes, ghosts and manes, demons and deities, were the living personal causes of universal life. "The first men found everything easy, the mysteries of nature were not so hidden from them as from us," said Jacob Böhme the mystic. True, we may well answer, if these primitive men believed in that animistic philosophy of nature which even now survives in the savage mind. They could ascribe to kind or hostile spirits all good and evil of their own lives, and all striking operations of nature; they lived in familiar intercourse with the living and powerful souls of their dead ancestors, with the spirits of the stream and grove, plain and mountains, they knew well the living mighty Sun pouring his beams of light and heat upon them, the living mighty Sea dashing her fierce billows on the shore, the great personal Heaven and Earth protecting and producing all things. For as the human body was held to live and act by virtue of its own inhabiting spirit-soul, so the operations of the world seemed to be carried on by the influence of other spirits. And thus Animism, starting as a philosophy of human life, extended and expanded itself till it became a philosophy of nature at large.

To the minds of the lower races it seems that all nature is possessed, pervaded, crowded, with spiritual beings. In seeking by a few types to give an idea of this conception of pervading Spirits in its savage and barbaric stage, it is not indeed possible to draw an absolute line of separation between spirits occupied in affecting for good and ill the life of Man, and spirits specially concerned in carrying on the operations of Nature. In fact these two classes of spiritual beings blend into one another as inextricably as do the original animistic doctrines they are based on. As, however, the spirits considered directly to affect the life and fortune of Man lie closest to the centre of the animistic scheme, it is well to give them precedence. The description and function of these beings extend upwards from among the rudest human tribes. Milligan writes of the Tasmanians: "They were polytheists, that is, they believed in guardian angels or spirits, and in a plurality of powerful, but generally evil-disposed beings, inhabiting crevices and caverns of rocky mountains, and making temporary abode in hollow trees and solitary valleys; of these a few were supposed to be of great power, while to the majority were imputed much of the nature and attributes of the goblins and elves of our native land." Oldfield writes of the aborigines of Australia, "The number of supernatural beings, feared if not loved, that they acknowledge, is exceedingly great; for not only are the heavens peopled with such, but the whole face of the country swarms with them; every thicket, most watering-places, and all rocky places abound with evil spirits. In like manner, every natural phenomenon is believed to be the work of demons, none of which seem of a benign nature, one and all apparently striving to do all imaginable mischief to the poor black fellow." It must be indeed an unhappy race among whom such a demonology could shape itself, and it is a relief to find that other people of low culture, while recognizing the same spiritual world swarming about them, do not find its main attribute to be spite against themselves. Among the Algonquin Indians of North America, Schoolcraft finds the very ground-work of their religion in the belief "that the whole visible and invisible creation is animated with various orders of malignant or benign spirits, who preside over the daily affairs and over the final destinies of men." Among the Khonds of Orissa, Macpherson describes the greater gods and tribal manes, and below these the order of minor and local deities: "They are the tutelary gods of every spot on earth, having power over the functions of nature which operate there, and over everything relating to human life in it. Their number is unlimited. They fill all nature, in which no power or object, from the sea to the clods of the field, is without its deity. They are the guardians of hills, groves, streams, foun-tains, paths, and hamlets, and are cognizant of every human action, want, and interest in the locality, where they preside." Describing the animistic mythology of the Turanian tribes of Asia and Europe, Castrén has said that every land, mountain, rock, river, brook, spring, tree, or whatsoever it may be, has a spirit for an inhabitant; the spirits of the trees and stones, of the lakes and brooks, hear with pleasure the wild man's pious prayers and accept his offerings. Such are the conceptions of the Guinea negro, who finds the abodes of his good and evil spirits in great rocks, hollow trees, mountains, deep rivers, dense groves, echoing caverns, and who passing silently by these sacred places leaves some offering, if it be but a leaf or a shell picked up on the beach. Such are examples which not unfairly picture the belief of the lower races in a world of spirits on earth, and such descriptions apply to the state of men's minds along the course of civilization.

~

Surveying the religions of the world and studying the descriptions of deity among race after race, we may recur to old polemical terms in order to define a dominant idea of theology at large. Man so habitually ascribes to his dei-ties human shape, human passions, human nature, that we may declare him an Anthropomorphite, an Anthropopathite, and (to complete the series) an Anthropophysite. In this state of religious thought, prevailing as it does through so immense a range among mankind, one of the strongest confirmations may be found of the theory here advanced concerning the development of Ani-mism. This theory that the conception of the human soul is the very "fons et origo" [fount and origin: ed.] of the conceptions of spirit and deity in general, has been already vouched for by the fact of human souls being held to pass into the characters of good and evil demons, and to ascend to the rank of deities. But beyond this, as we consider the nature of the great gods of the nations, in whom the vastest functions of the universe are vested, it will still be apparent that these mighty deities are modelled on human souls, that in great measure their feeling and sympathy, their character and habit, their will and action, even their material and form, display throughout their adaptations, exaggerations and distortions, characteristics shaped upon those of the human spirit. The key to investigation of the Dii Majorum Gentium [gods of most peoples: ed.] of the world is the reflex of humanity, and as we behold their figures in their proper districts of theology, memory ever brings back the Psalmist's words, "Thou thoughtest I was altogether as thyself."

The higher deities of Polytheism have their places in the general animistic system of mankind. Among nation after nation it is still clear how, man being the type of deity, human society and government became the model on which divine society and government were shaped. As chiefs and kings are among men, so are the great gods among the lesser spirits. They differ from the souls and minor spiritual beings which we have as yet chiefly considered, but the difference is rather of rank than of nature. They are personal spirits, reigning over personal spirits. Above the disembodied souls and manes, the local genii of rocks and fountains and trees, the host of good and evil demons, and the rest of the spiritual commonalty, stand these mightier deities, whose influence is less confined to local or individual interests, and who, as it pleases them, can act directly within their vast domain, or control and operate through the lower beings of their kind, their servants, agents, or mediators. The great gods of Polytheism, numerous and elaborately defined in the theology of the cultured world, do not however make their earliest appearance there. In the religions of the lower races their principal types were already cast, and thenceforward, for many an age of progressing or relapsing culture, it became the work of poet and priest, legend-monger and historian, theologian and philosopher, to develop and renew, to degrade and abolish, the mighty lords of the Pantheon.

With little exception, wherever a savage or barbaric system of religion is thoroughly described, great gods make their appearance in the spiritual world as distinctly as chiefs in the human tribe. In the lists, it is true, there are set down great deities, good or evil, who probably came in from modern Christian missionary teaching, or otherwise by contact with foreign religions. It is often difficult to distinguish from these the true local gods, animistic figures of native meaning and origin. Among the following polytheistic systems, examples may be found of such combinations, with the complex theological problems they suggest. Among Australians, above the swarming souls, nature-spirits, demons, there stand out mythic figures of higher divinity; Nguk-wonga, the Spirit of the Waters; Biam, who gives ceremonial songs and causes disease, and is perhaps the same as Baiame the creator; Nambajandi and Warrugura, lords of heaven and the nether world. In South America, if we look into the theology of the Manaos (whose name is well known in the famous legend of El Dorado and the golden city of Manoa), we see Mauari and Saraua, who may be called the Good and Evil Spirit, and beside the latter the two Gamainhas, Spirits of the Waters

and the Forest. In North America the description of a solemn Algonquin sacrifice introduces us to twelve dominant manitus or gods; first the Great Manitu
in heaven, then the Sun, Moon, Earth, Fire, Water, the House-god, the Indian
corn, and the four Winds or Cardinal Points. The Polynesian's crowd of manes,
and the lower ranks of deities of earth, sea, and air, stand below the great gods
of Peace and War, Oro and Tane the national deities of Tahiti and Huahine,
Raitubu the Sky-producer, Hina who aided in the work of forming the world,
her father Taaroa, the uncreate Creator who dwells in Heaven. Among the
Land Dayaks of Borneo, the commonalty of spirits consists of the souls of the
departed, and of such beings as dwell in the noble old forests on the tops of
lofty hills, or such as hover about villages and devour the stores of rice; above
these are Tapa, creator and preserver of man, and Iang, who taught the Dayaks
their religion, Jirong, whose function is the birth and death of men, and Tenabi,
who made, and still causes to flourish, the earth and all things therein save the
human race.

~

Among barbaric races we…find two conceptions current, the personal
divine Sea and the anthropomorphic Sea-god. These represent two stages of
development of one idea—the view of the natural object as itself an animated
being, and the separation of its animating fetish-soul as a distinct spiritual deity.
To follow the enquiry into classic times shows the same distinction as strongly
marked. When Kleomenes marched down to Thyrea, having slaughtered a bull
to the sea…he embarked his army in ships for the Tirynthian land and Nauplia.
Cicero makes Cotta remark to Balbus that "our generals, embarking on the sea,
have been accustomed to immolate a victim to the waves," and he goes on to
argue, not unfairly, that if the Earth herself is a goddess, what is she other than
Tellus, and "if the Earth, the Sea too, whom thou saidst to be Neptune." Here
is direct nature-worship in its extremest sense of fetish-worship. But in the
anthropomorphic stage appear that dim prae-Olympian figure of Nereus the
Old Man of the Sea, father of the Nereids in their ocean caves, and the Homeric
Poseidon the Earth-shaker, who stables his coursers in his cave in the Aegean
deeps, who harnesses the gold-maned steeds to his chariot and drives through
the dividing waves, while the subject sea-beasts come up at the passing of their
lord, a king so little bound to the element he governs, that he can come from
the brine to sit in the midst of the gods in the assembly on Olympos, and ask
the will of Zeus.

Fire-worship brings into view again, though under different aspects and
with different results, the problems presented by water-worship. The real
and absolute worship of fire falls into two great divisions, the first belonging
rather to fetishism, the second to polytheism proper, and the two apparently

representing an earlier and later stage of theological ideas. The first is the rude barbarian's adoration of the actual flame which he watches writhing, roaring, devouring like a live animal; the second belongs to an advanced generalization, that any individual fire is a manifestation of one general elemental being, the Fire-god. Unfortunately, evidence of the exact meaning of fire-worship among the lower races is scanty, while the transition from fetishism to polytheism seems a gradual process of which the stages elude close definition.

~

Animism and Monotheism

We now turn to the last objects of our present survey, those theological beliefs of the lower tribes of mankind which point more or less distinctly toward a doctrine of Monotheism. Here it is by no means proposed to examine savage ideas from the point of view of doctrinal theology, an undertaking which would demand arguments quite beyond the present range. Their treatment is limited to classifying the actual beliefs of the lower races, with some ethnographic considerations as to their origin and their relation to higher religions. For this purpose it is desirable to distinguish the prevalent doctrines of the uncultured world from absolute monotheism. At the outset, care is needed to exclude an ambiguity of which the importance often goes unnoticed. How are the mighty but subordinate divinities, recognized in different religions, to be classed? Beings who in Christian or Moslem theology would be called angels, saints, demons, would under the same definitions be called deities in polytheistic systems. . . . If the monotheistic criterion be simply made to consist in the Supreme Deity being held as creator of the universe and chief of the spiritual hierarchy, then its application to savage and barbaric theology will lead to perplexing consequences. Races of North and South America, of Africa, of Polynesia, recognizing a number of great deities, are usually and reasonably considered polytheists, yet under this definition their acknowledgement of a Supreme Creator, of which various cases will here be shown, would entitle them at the same time to the name of monotheists. To mark off the doctrines of the lower races, closer definition is required, assigning the distinctive attributes of deity to none save the Almighty Creator. It may be declared that, in this strict sense, no savage tribe of monotheists has been ever known. Nor are any fair representatives of the lower culture in a strict sense pantheists. The doctrine which they do widely hold, and which opens to them a course tending in one or other of these directions, is polytheism culminating in the rule of one supreme divinity. High above the doctrine of souls, of divine manes, of local nature-spirits, of the great deities of class and element, there are to be discerned in savage theology shadowings, quaint or majestic, of the conception of a Supreme Deity, henceforth to be traced onward in expanding power and brightening glory along the history of religion. It is no unimportant task, partial as it is, to select and group the typical data which show the nature and position of the doctrine of supremacy, as it comes into view within the lower culture....

In surveying the peoples of the world, the ethnographer finds some who are not shown to have any definite conception of a supreme deity; and even where such a conception is placed on record, it is sometimes so vaguely asserted, or on such questionable authority, that he can but take note of it and pass on. In numerous cases, however, illustrated by the following collection from different religions, certain leading ideas, singly or blended, may be traced. There are many savage and barbaric religions which solve their highest problem by the simple process of raising to divine primacy one of the gods of polytheism itself. Even the system of the manes-worshipper has been stretched to reach the limit of supreme deity, in the person of the primaeval ancestor. More frequently, it is the nature-worshipper's principle which has prevailed, giving to one of the great nature-deities the precedence of the rest. Here, by no recondite speculation, but by the plain teaching of nature, the choice has for the most part lain between two mighty visible divinities, the all-animating Sun and the all-encompassing Heaven. In the study of such schemes, we are on intellectual terra firma. There is among the religions of the lower races another notable group of systems, seemingly in close connection with the first. These display to us a heavenly pantheon arranged on the model of an earthly political constitution, where the commonalty are crowds of human souls and other tribes of world-pervading spirits, the aristocracy are great polytheistic gods, and the King is a Supreme Deity. To this comparatively intelligible side of the subject, a more perplexed and obscure side stands contrasted. Among men whose theory of the soul animating the body has already led them to suppose a divine spirit animating the huge mass of earth or sky, this idea needs but a last expansion to become a doctrine of the universe as animated by one greatest, all-pervading divinity, the World-Spirit. Moreover, where speculative philosophy, savage or cultured, grapples with the vast fundamental world-problem, the solution is attained by ascending from the Many to the One, by striving to discern through and beyond the Universe a First Cause. Let the basis of such reasoning be laid in the theological ground, then the First Cause is realized as the Supreme Deity. In such ways, the result of carrying to their utmost limits the animistic conceptions which pervade the philosophy of religion, alike among low races and high, is to reach an idea of as it were a soul of the world, a shaper, animator, ruler of the universe, a Great Spirit. In no small measure, such definition answers to that of the highest deity adored by the lower races of mankind. As we enter these regions of transcendental theology, however, we are not to wonder that the comparative distinctness belonging to conceptions of lower spiritual beings here fades away. Human souls, subordinate nature-spirits, and huge polytheistic nature-gods, carry with the defined special functions they perform some defined character and figure, but beyond such limits form and function blend into the infinite and universal in the thought of supreme divinity. To realize this vast idea, two especial ways are open, and both are trodden even by uncultured men. The first way is to fuse the attributes of the great polytheistic powers into more or less of common personality, thus conceiving that, after all, it is the same Highest Being who holds up the heavens, shines in the sun, smites his foes in the thunder, stands first in the human pedigree as the divine ancestor. The second way is to remove the limit of theologic speculation into the region of the indefinite and the inane. An unshaped divine entity looming vast, benevolent or too exalted to need human worship, too huge, too remote, too indifferent, too supine, too merely existent, to concern himself with the petty race of men,—this is a mystic form or formlessness in which religion has not seldom pictured the Supreme.

Thus, then, it appears that the theology of the lower races already reaches its climax in conceptions of Supreme Deity, and that these conceptions in the savage and barbaric world are no copies stamped from one common type, but outlines widely varying among mankind. The degeneration-theory, in some instances no doubt with justice, may claim such beliefs as mutilated and per-verted remnants of higher religions. Yet for the most part, the development-theory is competent to account for them without seeking their origin in grades of culture higher than those in which they are found existing. Looked upon as products of natural religion, such doctrines of divine supremacy seem in no way to transcend the powers of the low-cultured mind to reason out, nor of the low-cultured imagination to deck with mythic fancy. There have existed in times past, and do still exist, many savage or barbaric people who hold such views of a highest god as they may have attained to of themselves, without the aid of more cultured nations. Among these races, Animism has its distinct and consistent outcome, and Polytheism its distinct and consistent completion, in the doctrine of a Supreme Deity.

~

Savage Religion, Civilized Religion, and Ethics

Before now bringing these researches to a close, it will be well to state com-pactly the reasons for treating the animism of the modern savage world as more or less representing the animism of remotely ancient races of mankind. Savage animism, founded on a doctrine of souls carried to an extent far beyond its limits in the cultivated world, and thence expanding to a yet wider doctrine of spiritual beings animating and controlling the universe in all its parts, becomes a theory of personal causes developed into a general philosophy of man and nature.... The main issue of the problem is this, whether savage animism is a primary formation belonging to the lower culture, or whether it consists, mostly or entirely, of beliefs originating in some higher culture, and conveyed by adoption or degradation into the lower. The evidence for the first alternative, though not amounting to complete demonstration, seems reasonably strong, and not met by contrary evidence approaching it in force. The animism of the lower tribes, self-contained and self-supporting, maintained in close contact with that direct evidence of the senses on which it appears to be originally based, is a system which might quite reasonably exist among mankind, had they never anywhere risen above the savage condition. Now it does not seem that the animism of the higher nations stands in a connexion so direct and complete with their mental state. It is by no means so closely limited to doctrines evidenced by simple contemplation of nature. The doctrines of the lower animism appear in the higher often more and more modified, to bring them into accordance with an advancing intellectual condition, to adapt them at once to the limits of stricter science and the needs of higher faith; and in the higher animism these doctrines are retained side by side with other and special beliefs, of which the religions of the lower world show scarce a germ. In tracing the course of animistic thought from stage to stage of history, instruction is to be gained alike from the immensity of change and from the intensity of permanence. Savage animism, both by what it has and what it wants, seems to represent the earlier system in which began the age-long course of the education of the world. Especially it is to be noticed that various beliefs and practices, which in the lower animism stand firm upon their grounds as if they grew there, in the higher animism belong rather to peasants than philosophers, exist rather as ancestral relics than as products belonging to their age, are falling from full life into survival. Thus it is that savage religion can frequently explain doctrines and rites of civilized religion. The converse is far less often the case. Now this is a state of things which seems to carry a historical as well as a practical meaning. The degradation-theory would expect savages to hold beliefs and customs intelligible as broken-down relics of former higher civilization. The development-theory would expect civilized men to keep up belief and customs which have their reasonable meaning in less cultured states of society. So far as the study of survival enables us to judge between the two theories, it is seen that what is intelligible religion in the lower culture is often meaningless superstition in the higher, and thus the development-theory has the upper hand. Moreover, this evidence fits with the teaching of prehistoric archaeology. Savage life, carrying on into our own day the life of the Stone Age, may be legitimately claimed as representing remotely ancient conditions of mankind, intellectual and moral as well as material. If so, a low but progressive state of animistic religion occupies a like ground in savage and in primitive culture.

Lastly, a few words of explanation may be offered as to the topics which this survey has included and excluded. To those who have been accustomed to find theological subjects dealt with on a dogmatic, emotional, and ethical, rather than an ethnographic scheme, the present investigation may seem misleading, because one-sided. This one-sided treatment, however, has been adopted with full consideration. Thus, though the doctrines here examined bear not only on the development but the actual truth of religious systems, I have felt neither able nor willing to enter into this great argument fully and satisfactorily, while experience has shown that to dispose of such questions by an occasional dictatorial phrase is one of the most serious of errors. The scientific value of descriptions of savage and barbarous religions, drawn up by travellers and especially by missionaries, is often lowered by their controversial tone, and by the affectation of infallibility with which their relation to the absolutely true is settled. There is something pathetic in the simplicity with which a narrow student will judge the doctrines of a foreign religion by their antagonism or conformity to his own orthodoxy, on points where utter difference of opinion exists among the most learned and enlightened scholars. The systematizations of the lower religions, the reduction of their multifarious details to the few and simple ideas of primitive philosophy which form the common groundwork of them all, appeared to me an urgently needed contribution to the science of religion. This work I have carried out to the utmost of my power, and can now only leave the result in the hands of other students, whose province it is to deal with such evidence in wider schemes of argument. Again, the intellectual rather than the emotional side of religion has here been kept in view. Even in the life of the rudest savage, religious belief is associated with intense emotion, with awful reverence, with agonizing terror, with rapt ecstasy when sense and thought utterly transcend the common level of daily life. How much the more in faiths where not only does the believer experience such enthusiasm, but where his utmost feelings of love and hope, of justice and mercy, of fortitude and tenderness and self-sacrificing devotion, of unutterable misery and dazzling happiness, twine and clasp round the fabric of religion. Language, dropping at times from such words as soul and spirit their mere philosophic meaning, can use them in full conformity with this tendency of the religious mind, as phrases to convey a mystic sense of transcendent emotion. Yet of all this religion, the religion of vision and of passion, little indeed has been said in these pages, and even that little rather in incidental touches than with purpose. Those to whom religion means above all things religious feeling, may say of my argument that I have written soullessly of the soul, and unspiritually of spiritual things. Be it so: I accept the phrase not as needing an apology, but as expressing a plan. Scientific progress is at times most furthered by working along a distinct intellectual line, without being tempted to diverge from the main object to what lies beyond, in however intimate connexion. The anatomist does well to discuss bodily structure independently of the world of happiness and misery which depends upon it. It would be thought a mere impertinence for a strategist to preface a dissertation on the science of war, by an enquiry how far it is lawful for a Christian man to bear weapons and serve in the wars. My task has been here not to discuss Religion in all its bearings, but to portray in outline the great doctrine of Animism, as found in what I conceive to be its earliest stages among the lower races of mankind, and to show its transmission along the lines of religious thought.

The almost entire exclusion of ethical questions from this investigation has more than a mere reason of arrangement. It is due to the very nature of the subject. To some the statement may seem startling, yet the evidence seems to justify it, that the relation of morality to religion is one that only belongs in its rudiments, or not at all, to rudimentary civilization. The comparison of savage and civilized religions brings into view, by the side of deep-lying resemblance in their philosophy, a deep-lying contrast in their practical action on human life. So far as savage religion can stand as representing natural religion, the popular idea that the moral government of the universe is an essential tenet of natural religion simply falls to the ground. Savage animism is almost devoid of that ethical element which to the educated modern mind is the very mainspring of practical religion. Not, as I have said, that morality is absent from the life of the lower races. Without a code of morals, the very existence of the rudest tribe would be impossible; and indeed the moral standards of even savage races are to no small extent well-defined and praiseworthy. But these ethical laws stand on their own ground of tradition and public opinion, comparatively independent of the animistic beliefs and rites which exist beside them. The lower animism is not immoral, it is unmoral. For this plain reason, it has seemed desirable to keep the discussion of animism, as far as might be, separate from that of ethics. The general problem of the relation of morality to religion is difficult, intricate, and requiring immense array of evidence, and may be perhaps more profitably discussed in connexion with the ethnography of morals. To justify their present separation, it will be enough to refer in general terms to the accounts of savage tribes whose ideas have been little affected by civilized intercourse; proper caution being used not to trust vague statements about good and evil, but to ascertain whether these are what philosophic moralists would call virtue and vice, righteousness and wickedness, or whether they are mere personal advantage and disadvantage. The essential connexion of theology and morality is a fixed idea in many minds. But it is one of the lessons of history that subjects may maintain themselves independently for ages, till the event of coalescence takes place. In the course of history religion has in various ways attached to itself matters small and great outside its central scheme, such as prohibition of special meats, observance of special days, regulation of marriage as to kinship, division of society into castes, ordinance of social law and civil government. Looking at religion from a political point of view, as a practical influence on human society, it is clear that among its greatest powers has been its divine sanction of ethical laws, its theological enforcement of morality, its teaching of moral government of the universe, its supplanting the "continuance-doctrine" of a future life by the "retribution-doctrine" supplying moral motive in the present. But such alliance belongs almost wholly to religions above the savage level, not to the earlier and lower creeds. It will aid us to see how much more the fruit of religion belongs to ethical influence than to philosophical dogma, if we consider how the introduction of the moral element separates the religions of the world, united as they are throughout by one animistic principle, into two great classes, those lower systems whose best result is to supply a crude child-like natural philosophy and those higher faiths which implant on this the law of righteousness and of holiness, the inspiration of duty and of love.

2

James Frazer: Magic and the Rise of Religion

James George Frazer (1854–1941) was a gifted student of Greek literature and civilization who in later Victorian years became Tylor's most celebrated intellectual disciple. He embraced enthusiastically the comparative method of anthropological research. Like Tylor, he was raised in a religious household—Presbyterian rather than Quaker—but soon discarded the orthodox faith of his parents. Unlike Tylor, who was largely self-educated, Frazer from boyhood was to the academy born. In preparatory school he took multiple prizes in Latin and Greek. He won a fellowship to Trinity College, Cambridge University, where he continued to excel, afterward becoming a don and residing there for the rest of his life. It was during his student years at Cambridge that Frazer encountered *Primitive Culture* and found his perspective on classical civilization transformed. Anthropological inquiry, he concluded, could shed new light on ancient Greece and Rome, and by extension all forms of early human thought and life.

Frazer pursued his new program of cultural comparison with great energy, publishing studies that drew on an ever-widening field of sources—from folklore and legend to literature, mythology, and especially the personal reports of encounters with native peoples that flowed into England from the farther reaches of the British Empire. In 1890 he published *The Golden Bough,* later subtitled *A Study of Magic and Religion.* This capacious study of primitive rituals, customs, and beliefs drawn from cultures across the globe succeeded in raising Victorian anthropology to the pinnacle of its intellectual influence in Europe and North America. Nor was it a transient success. For twenty-five years, from the first to final edition, Frazer worked to revise and augment his discussions, until what had begun as a book ended as a virtual encyclopedia—a landmark from which later theorists of religion would draw examples and take their bearings.

The subtitle of *The Golden Bough* offers an instructive clue to its argument. Frazer agrees with Tylor that the reason for religious behavior is intellectual—and practical. Primitive peoples try to understand the world, so they can better survive in it. Hunters must find game to kill; farmers need rain for crops to grow. Animists suppose that if the gods control the world, prayer and sacrifice can persuade them. But for Frazer, this is not the full story. He finds the primitive mind governed by two systems of ideas. Animism is not the only, or even the oldest, form of primitive thought. Magic is.

The primitive magician assumes that the natural world is controlled not by personal spirits, or gods, but by certain influences, or "sympathies," that operate, impersonally, in accord with two principles: imitation and contact. Imitative magic presumes that "like affects like," as when a tribal rainmaker mimics the sound of thunder to bring rain from the sky. Contagious magic assumes that "part affects part"—as when a voodoo magician seeks to inflict harm from a distance by placing a curse on the hair or a fingernail of the intended victim. The first of the selections below presents Frazer's main discussion of primitive magic and its mechanisms. To support his claims, he offers evidence in great abundance and from a wide variety of cultures and locales. He attends also to primitive social structures, illustrating how the magician, who claims the greatest knowledge of nature's processes, most often holds the position of greatest social prestige and power. None of this, however, can disguise the fact that magic, at bottom, is false. It resembles modern science in seeking the "laws" of nature, but the laws that it frames are erroneous. Over time, with their trust in magic repeatedly betrayed, primitive people themselves draw the conclusion that magic is mistaken. It is this failure of magic that gives rise to religion.

Frazer's account of the transition from magic to religion was ingenious. His approach was to draw on both the animism and intellectual evolutionism he shared with Tylor and propose a simple sequence. We must notice, he says, just how religion differs from magic, and how, in a curious way, it represents an intellectual improvement upon it. The principles of magic are universal and iron-clad. If we perform the ritual of the thunder, the storm *must* occur as predicted. If it does not occur, there is reason to doubt the principle. Religion, by contrast, claims no such certitude. It confesses that the world is in the hands of the gods, who manage the forces of nature in their own interests, not those of humanity. In addition, in primitive societies the gods are many, with competing plans and purposes. We can plead with them, or pray and sacrifice to them, but we cannot guarantee the results we want. From the perspective of intellectual progress, then, this very uncertainty of religion must be seen as its virtue. It is an advance over magic because it accords better than magic with the world as we actually experience it.

With the coming of religion, certain other changes in primitive society naturally occur as well. The old magician-chieftain gives way to the priestly ruler, whose power rests not in magic but in his special ability to communicate with the gods, or just as often, in being himself worshiped as divine. None of this happens suddenly, of course; for long intervals the two systems overlapped and intermingled.

Like Tylor, Frazer also sees some evidence of intellectual progress within the realm of religion. Simple animism comes gradually to be replaced by complex polytheism, and polytheism by the monotheism of Judaism and Christianity. But these changes are eclipsed by the much greater change ushered in by the modern world: the rise of science and its applications in the form of technology. However long the rule of religion has been, its reign has come to an end. As it once supplanted magic, religion is now itself being supplanted by the observations and experimental proofs of science. Where it persists, it does so only as a survival, a fossil from a mental epoch now ended. Thus for Frazer, as for Tylor, the story of religion ends in a verdict serenely convergent with his own personal atheism. As *The Golden Bough* closes, Frazer brings to mind the image of religious faith slipping off the horizon, much like the sun setting slowly over the English countryside, dying—but unlike the sun, not to rise again. In *The Golden Bough* Frazer secured the fame of Victorian anthropology; however, as the methods of "Mr. Tylor's science" were at the time already coming under severe criticism, Frazer's achievement may be said also to have signaled the beginning of its demise.

The Forms and Uses of Magic

The sequence of selections below traces the main line of Frazer's argument from the distinction between magic and religion forward through the discussions of primitive applications, the transition from magic to religion, and the rise (and dangers) of ancient kingship to the replacement of both magic and religion by modern science.

Along with the view of the world as pervaded by spiritual forces, savage man has a different, and probably still older, conception in which we may detect a germ of the modern notion of natural law or the view of nature as a series of events occurring in an invariable order without the intervention of personal

---

FROM: *The Golden Bough: A Study in Magic and Religion.* One Volume. Abridged Edition. New York: The Macmillian Company, [1922] 1947.

agency. The germ of which I speak is involved in that sympathetic magic, as it may be called, which plays a large part in most systems of superstition.... [I]t is essential to have some acquaintance with the principles of magic and to form some conception of the extraordinary hold which that ancient system of superstition has had on the human mind in all ages and all countries. Accordingly, I propose to consider the subject in some detail.

The Principles of Magic.—If we analyze the principles of thought on which magic is based, they will probably be found to resolve themselves into two: first, that like produces like, or that an effect resembles its cause; and, second, that things which have once been in contact with each other continue to act on each other at a distance after the physical contact has been severed. The former principle may be called the Law of Similarity, the latter the Law of Contact or Contagion. From the first of these principles, namely the Law of Similarity, the magician infers that he can produce any effect he desires merely by imitating it: from the second he infers that whatever he does to a material object will affect equally the person with whom the object was once in contact, whether it formed part of his body or not. Charms based on the Law of Similarity may be called Homoeopathic or Imitative Magic. Charms based on the Law of Contact or Contagion may be called Contagious Magic. To denote the first of these branches of magic the term Homoeopathic is perhaps preferable, for the alternative term Imitative or Mimetic suggests, if it does not imply, a conscious agent who imitates, thereby limiting the scope of magic too narrowly. For the same principles which the magician applies in the practice of his art are implicitly believed by him to regulate the operations of inanimate nature; in other words, he tacitly assumes that the Laws of Similarity and Contact are of universal application and are not limited to human actions. In short, magic is a spurious system of natural law as well as a fallacious guide of conduct; it is a false science as well as an abortive art. Regarded as a system of natural law, that is, as a statement of the rules which determine the sequence of events throughout the world, it may be called Theoretical Magic: regarded as a set of precepts which human beings observe in order to compass their ends, it may be called Practical Magic. At the same time it is to be borne in mind that the primitive magician knows magic only on its practical side; he never analyses the mental processes on which his practice is based, never reflects on the abstract principles involved in his actions. With him, as with the vast majority of men, logic is implicit, not explicit: he reasons just as he digests his food in complete ignorance of the intellectual and physiological processes which are essential to the one operation and to the other. In short, to him magic is always an art, never a science; the very idea of science is lacking in his undeveloped mind. It is for the philosophic student to trace the train of thought which underlies the magician's practice; to draw out the few simple threads of which the tangled skein is composed;

to disengage the abstract principles from their concrete applications; in short, to discern the spurious science behind the bastard art.

If my analysis of the magician's logic is correct, its two great principles turn out to be merely two different misapplications of the association of ideas. Homoeopathic magic is founded on the association of ideas by similarity: contagious magic is founded on the association of ideas by contiguity. Homoeopathic magic commits the mistake of assuming that things which resemble each other are the same: contagious magic commits the mistake of assuming that things which have once been in contact with each other are always in contact. But in practice the two branches are often combined; or, to be more exact, while homoeopathic or imitative magic may be practiced by itself, contagious magic will generally be found to involve an application of the homoeopathic or imitative principle. Thus generally stated the two things may be a little difficult to grasp, but they will readily become intelligible when they are illustrated by particular examples. Both trains of thought are in fact extremely simple and elementary. It could hardly be otherwise, since they are familiar in the concrete, though certainly not in the abstract, to the crude intelligence not only of the savage, but of ignorant and dull-witted people everywhere. Both branches of magic, the homoeopathic and the contagious, may conveniently be comprehended under the general name of Sympathetic Magic, since both assume that things act on each other at a distance through a secret sympathy, the impulse being transmitted from one to the other by means of what we may conceive as a kind of invisible ether, not unlike that which is postulated by modern science for a precisely similar purpose, namely, to explain how things can physically affect each other through a space which appears to be empty.

It may be convenient to tabulate as follows the branches of magic according to the laws of thought which underlie them:

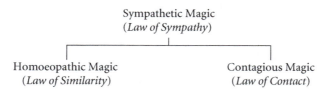

Sympathetic Magic
(*Law of Sympathy*)

Homoeopathic Magic   Contagious Magic
(*Law of Similarity*)   (*Law of Contact*)

I will now illustrate these two great branches of sympathetic magic by examples, beginning with homoeopathic magic.

Homoeopathic or Imitative Magic.—Perhaps the most familiar application of the principle that like produces like is the attempt which has been made by many peoples in many ages to injure or destroy an enemy by injuring or destroying an image of him, in the belief that, just as the image suffers, so does the man, and that when it perishes he must die. A few instances out of many may be given to prove at once the wide diffusion of the practice over the world and its remarkable persistence through the ages. For thousands of years ago it was known to the sorcerers of ancient India, Babylon, and Egypt, as well as of Greece and Rome, and at this day it is still resorted to by cunning and malignant savages in Australia, Africa, and Scotland. Thus the North American Indians, we are told, believe that by drawing the figure of a person in sand, ashes, or clay, or by considering any object as his body, and then pricking it with a sharp stick or doing it any other injury, they inflict a corresponding injury on the person represented. For example, when an Ojebway Indian desires to work evil on any one, he makes a little wooden image of his enemy and runs a needle into its head or heart, or he shoots an arrow into it, believing that wherever the needle pierces or the arrow strikes the image, his foe will the same instant be seized with a sharp pain in the corresponding part of his body; but if he intends to kill the person outright, he burns or buries the puppet, uttering certain magic words as he does so. The Peruvian Indians molded images of fat mixed with grain to imitate the persons whom they disliked or feared, and then burned the effigy on the road where the intended victim was to pass. This they called burning his soul.

A Malay charm of the same sort is as follows. Take parings of nails, hair, eyebrows, spittle, and so forth of your intended victim, enough to represent every part of his person, and then make them up into his likeness with wax.... Scorch the figure slowly by holding it over a lamp every night for seven nights, and say:

"*It is not the wax that I am scorching*
It is the liver, heart, and spleen of So-and-so that I scorch."

After the seventh time burn the figure, and your victim will die. This charm obviously combines the principles of homoeopathic and contagious magic; since the image which is made in the likeness of an enemy contains things which once were in contact with him, namely, his nails, hair, and spittle. Another form of the Malay charm, which resembles the Ojebway practice still more closely, is to make a corpse of wax... then pierce the eye of the image, and your enemy is blind; pierce the stomach, and he is sick; pierce the head, and his head aches.... If you would kill him outright, transfix the image from the head downwards; enshroud it as you would a corpse; pray over it as if you were praying over the dead; then bury it in the middle of a path where your victim will be sure to step over it....

If homoeopathic or imitative magic, working by means of images, has commonly been practiced for the spiteful purpose of putting obnoxious people out of the world, it has also, though far more rarely, been employed with the benevolent intention of helping others into it. In other words, it has been used to facilitate childbirth and to procure offspring for barren women. Thus among the Bataks of Sumatra a barren woman, who would become a mother, will make a wooden image of a child and hold it in her lap, believing that this will lead to the fulfillment of her wish. In the Babar Archipelago, when a woman desires to have a child, she invites a man who is himself the father of a large family to pray on her behalf to Upulero, the spirit of the sun....

Another beneficent use of homoeopathic magic is to heal or prevent sickness. The ancient Hindoos performed an elaborate ceremony, based on homoeopathic magic, for the cure of jaundice. Its main drift was to banish the yellow color to yellow creatures and yellow things, such as the sun, to which it properly belongs, and to procure for the patient a healthy red color from a living, vigorous source, namely, a red bull. With this intention, a priest recited the following spell: "Up to the sun shall go thy heart-ache and thy jaundice: in the color of the red bull do we envelop thee! We envelop thee in red tints, unto long life. May this person go unscathed and be free of yellow color!"...

Further, homoeopathic and in general sympathetic magic plays a great part in the measures taken by the rude hunter or fisherman to secure an abundant supply of food. On the principle that like produces like, many things are done by him and his friends in deliberate imitation of the result which he seeks to attain; and, on the other hand, many things are scrupulously avoided because they bear some more or less fanciful resemblance to others which would really be disastrous.

Nowhere is the theory of sympathetic magic more systematically carried into practice for the maintenance of the food supply than in the barren regions of Central Australia. Here the tribes are divided into a number of totem clans, each of which is charged with the duty of multiplying their totem for the good of the community by means of magical ceremonies. Most of the totems are edible animals and plants, and the general result supposed to be accomplished by these ceremonies is that of supplying the tribe with food and other necessaries. Often the rites consist of an imitation of the effect which the people desire to produce; in other words, their magic is homoeopathic or imitative. Thus among the Warramunga the headman of the white cockatoo totem seeks to multiply white cockatoos by holding an effigy of the bird and mimicking its cry. Among the Arunta the men of the witchety grub totem perform ceremonies for multiplying the grub which other members of the tribe use as food....

[I]t is to be observed that the system of sympathetic magic is not merely composed of positive precepts; it comprises a very large number of negative precepts, that is, prohibitions. It tells you not merely what to do, but also what to leave undone. The positive precepts are charms: the negative precepts are taboos. In fact the whole doctrine of taboo, or at all events a large part of it, would seem to be only a special application of sympathetic magic, with its two great laws of similarity and contact. Though these laws are certainly not formulated in so many words nor even conceived in the abstract by the savage, they are nevertheless implicitly believed by him to regulate the course of nature quite independently of human will. He thinks that if he acts in a certain way, certain consequences will inevitably follow in virtue of one or other of these laws; and if the consequences of a particular act appear to him likely to prove disagreeable or dangerous, he is naturally careful not to act in that way lest he should incur them. In other words, he abstains from doing that which, in accordance with his mistaken notions of cause and effect, he falsely believes would injure him; in short, he subjects himself to a taboo. Thus taboo is so far a negative application of practical magic. Positive magic or sorcery says, "Do this in order that so and so may happen." Negative magic or taboo says, "Do not do this, lest so and so should happen." The aim of positive magic or sorcery is to produce a desired event; the aim of negative magic or taboo is to avoid an undesirable one. But both consequences, the desirable and the undesirable, are supposed to be brought about in accordance with the laws of similarity and contact.... [T]hose negative precepts which we call taboo are just as vain and futile as those positive precepts which we call sorcery. The two things are merely opposite sides or poles of one great disastrous fallacy, a mistaken conception of the association of ideas. Of that fallacy, sorcery is the positive, and taboo the negative pole. If we give the general name of magic to the whole erroneous system, both theoretical and practical, then taboo may be defined as the negative side of practical magic. To put this in tabular form:

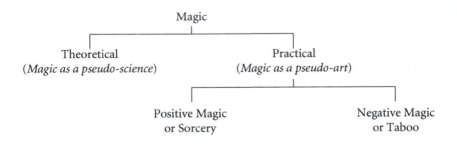

Among the taboos observed by savages none perhaps are more numerous or important than the prohibitions to eat certain foods, and of such prohibitions many are demonstrably derived from the law of similarity and are accordingly examples of negative magic. Just as the savage eats many animals or plants in order to acquire certain desirable qualities with which he believes them to be endowed, so he avoids eating many other animals and plants lest he should acquire certain undesirable qualities with which he believes them to be infected. In eating the former he practices positive magic; in abstaining from the latter he practices negative magic. Many examples of such positive magic will meet us later on; here I will give a few instances of such negative magic or taboo. For example, in Madagascar soldiers are forbidden to eat a number of foods lest on the principle of homoeopathic magic they should be tainted by certain dangerous or undesirable properties which are supposed to inhere in these particular viands. Thus they may not taste hedgehog, "as it is feared that this animal, from its propensity of coiling up into a ball when alarmed, will impart a timid shrinking disposition to those who partake of it." ... Further, the Malagasy soldier must eschew kidneys, because in the Malagasy language the word for kidney is the same as that for "shot"; so shot he would certainly be if he ate a kidney.

The reader may have observed that in some of the foregoing examples of taboos the magical influence is supposed to operate at considerable distances; thus among the Blackfeet Indians the wives and children of an eagle hunter are forbidden to use an awl during his absence, lest the eagles should scratch the distant husband and father; and again no male animal may be killed in the house of a Malagasy soldier while he is away at the wars, lest the killing of the animal should entail the killing of the man. This belief in the sympathetic influence exerted on each other by persons or things at a distance is of the essence of magic. Whatever doubts science may entertain as to the possibility of action at a distance, magic has none; faith in telepathy is one of its first principles. A modern advocate of the influence of mind upon mind at a distance would have no difficulty in convincing a savage; the savage believed in it long ago, and what is more, he acted on his belief with a logical consistency such as his civilized brother in the faith has not yet, so far as I am aware, exhibited in his conduct. For the savage is convinced not only that magical ceremonies affect persons and things afar off, but that the simplest acts of daily life may do so too. Hence on important occasions the behavior of friends and relations at a distance is often regulated by a more or less elaborate code of rules, the neglect of which by the one set of persons would, it is supposed, entail misfortune or even death on the absent ones. In particular when a party of men are out hunting or fighting, their kinsfolk at home are often expected to do certain things or to abstain from doing certain others, for the sake of ensuring the safety and success of the distant hunters or warriors. I will now give some instances of this magical telepathy both in its positive and in its negative aspect.

In Laos when an elephant hunter is starting for the chase, he warns his wife not to cut her hair or oil her body in his absence; for if she cut her hair the elephant would burst the toils, if she oiled herself it would slip through them. When a Dyak village has turned out to hunt wild pigs in the jungle, the people who stay at home may not touch oil or water with their hands during the absence of their friends; for if they did so, the hunters would all be "butter-fingered" and the prey would slip through their hands.

Elephant-hunters in East Africa believe that, if their wives prove unfaithful in their absence, this gives the elephant power over his pursuer, who will accordingly be killed or severely wounded. Hence if a hunter hears of his wife's misconduct, he abandons the chase and returns home. If a Wagogo hunter is unsuccessful, or is attacked by a lion, he attributes it to his wife's misbehavior at home, and returns to her in great wrath.... The Moxos Indians of Bolivia thought that if a hunter's wife was unfaithful to him in his absence he would be bitten by a serpent or a jaguar. Accordingly, if such an accident happened to him, it was sure to entail the punishment, and often the death, of the woman, whether she was innocent or guilty. An Aleutian hunter of sea-otters thinks that he cannot kill a single animal if during his absence from home his wife should be unfaithful or his sister unchaste....

Where beliefs like these prevail as to the sympathetic connection between friends at a distance, we need not wonder that above everything else war, with its stern yet stirring appeal to some of the deepest and tenderest of human emotions, should quicken in the anxious relations left behind a desire to turn the sympathetic bond to the utmost account for the benefit of the dear ones who may at any moment be fighting and dying far away....

In the island of Timor, while war is being waged, the high-priest never quits the temple; his food is brought to him or cooked inside; day and night he must keep the fire burning, for if he were to let it die out, disaster would befall the warriors and would continue so long as the hearth was cold....

Among the Tshi-speaking peoples of the Gold Coast the wives of men who are away with the army paint themselves white, and adorn their persons with beads and charms. On the day when a battle is expected to take place, they run about armed with guns, or sticks carved to look like guns, and taking green paw-paws (fruits shaped somewhat like a melon), they hack them with knives, as if they were chopping off the heads of the foe. The pantomime is no doubt merely an imitative charm, to enable the men to do to the enemy as the women do to the paw-paws.

～

Contagious Magic.—Thus far we have been considering chiefly that branch of sympathetic magic which may be called homoeopathic or imitative. Its leading principle, as we have seen, is that like produces like, or, in other words, that an effect resembles its cause. The other great branch of sympathetic magic, which I have called Contagious Magic, proceeds upon the notion that things which have once been conjoined must remain ever afterwards, even when quite dissevered from each other, in such a sympathetic relation that whatever is done to the one must similarly affect the other. Thus the logical basis of Contagious Magic, like that of Homoeopathic Magic, is a mistaken association of ideas; its physical basis, if we may speak of such a thing, like the physical basis of Homoeopathic Magic, is a material medium of some sort which, like the ether of modern physics, is assumed to unite distant objects and to convey impressions from one to the other. The most familiar example of Contagious Magic is the magical sympathy which is supposed to exist between a man and any severed portion of his person, as his hair or nails; so that whoever gets possession of human hair or nails may work his will, at any distance, upon the person for whom they were cut. This superstition is world wide.

~

The Baganda believe that every person is born with a double, and this double they identify with the afterbirth, which they regard as a second child. The mother buries the afterbirth at the root of a plantain tree, which then becomes sacred until the fruit has ripened, when it is plucked to furnish a sacred feast for the family....

Even in Europe many people still believe that a person's destiny is more or less bound up with that of his navel-string or afterbirth. Thus in Rhenish Bavaria the navel-string is kept for a while wrapped up in a piece of old linen, and then cut or pricked to pieces according as the child is a boy or girl, in order that he or she may grow up to be a skilful workman or a good seamstress....

A curious application of the doctrine of contagious magic is the relation commonly believed to exist between a wounded man and the agent of the wound, so that whatever is subsequently done by or to the agent must correspondingly affect the patient either for good or evil. Thus Pliny tells us that if you have wounded a man and are sorry for it, you have only to spit on the hand that gave the wound, and the pain of the sufferer will be instantly alleviated. In Melanesia, if a man's friends get possession of the arrow which wounded him, they keep it in a damp place or in cool leaves, for then the inflammation will be trifling and will soon subside. Meantime the enemy who shot the arrow is hard at work to aggravate the wound by all the means in his power. For this purpose he and his friends drink hot and burning juices and chew irritating leaves, for this will clearly inflame and irritate the wound. Further, they keep the bow near the fire to make the wound which it has inflicted hot; and for the same reason they put the arrow-head, if it has been recovered, into the fire.

~

The Magician's Progress.—We have now concluded our examination of the general principles of sympathetic magic. The examples by which I have illustrated them have been drawn for the most part from what may be called private magic, that is from magical rites and incantations practiced for the benefit or the injury of individuals. But in savage society there is commonly to be found in addition what we may call public magic, that is sorcery practiced for the benefit of the whole community. Wherever ceremonies of this sort are observed for the common good, it is obvious that the magician ceases to be merely a private practitioner and becomes to some extent a public functionary. The development of such a class of functionaries is of great importance for the political as well as the religious evolution of society. For when the welfare of the tribe is supposed to depend on the performance of these magical rites, the magician rises into a position of much influence and repute, and may readily acquire the rank and authority of a chief or king. The profession accordingly draws into its ranks some of the ablest and most ambitious men of the tribe, because it holds out to them a prospect of honour, wealth, and power such as hardly any other career could offer. The acuter minds perceive how easy it is to dupe their weaker brother and to play on his superstition for their own advantage. Not that the sorcerer is always a knave and impostor; he is often sincerely convinced that he really possesses those wonderful powers which the credulity of his fellows ascribes to him. But the more sagacious he is, the more likely he is to see through the fallacies which impose on duller wits. Thus the ablest members of the profession must tend to be more or less conscious deceivers; and it is just these men who in virtue of their superior ability will generally come to the top and win for themselves positions of the highest dignity and the most commanding authority. The pitfalls which beset the path of the professional sorcerer are many, and as a rule only the man of coolest head and sharpest wit will be able to steer his way through them safely. For it must always be remembered that every single profession and claim put forward by the magician as such is false; not one of them can be maintained without deception, conscious or unconscious. Accordingly the sorcerer who sincerely believes in his own extravagant pretensions is in far greater peril and is much more likely to be cut short in his career than the deliberate impostor. The honest wizard always expects that his charms and incantations will produce their supposed effect; and when they fail, not only really, as they always do, but conspicuously and disastrously, as they often do, he is taken aback: he is not, like his knavish colleague, ready with a plausible excuse to account for the failure.…

Thus, so far as the public profession of magic affected the constitution of savage society, it tended to place the control of affairs in the hands of the ablest man; it shifted the balance of power from the many to the one: it substituted a monarchy for a democracy, or rather for an oligarchy of old men; for in general the savage community is ruled, not by the whole body of adult males, but by a council of elders. The change, by whatever causes produced, and whatever the character of the early rulers, was on the whole very beneficial. For the rise of monarchy appears to be an essential condition of the emergence of mankind from savagery. No human being is so hide-bound by custom and tradition as your democratic savage; in no state of society consequently is progress so slow and difficult. The old notion that the savage is the freest of mankind is the reverse of the truth. He is a slave, not indeed to a visible master, but to the past, to the spirits of his dead forefathers, who haunt his steps from birth to death, and rule him with a rod of iron. What they did is the pattern of right, the unwritten law to which he yields a blind obedience. The least possible scope is thus afforded to superior talent to change old customs for the better. The ablest man is dragged down by the weakest and dullest, who necessarily sets the standard, since he cannot rise, while the other can fall. The surface of such a society presents a uniform dead level, so far as it is humanly possible to reduce the natural inequalities, the immeasurable real differences of inborn capacity and temper, to a false superficial appearance of equality. From this low and stagnant condition of affairs, which demagogues and dreamers in later times have lauded as the ideal state, the Golden Age, of humanity, everything that helps to raise society by opening a career to talent and proportioning the degrees of authority to men's natural abilities, deserves to be welcomed by all who have the real good of their fellows at heart. Once these elevating influences have begun to operate—and they cannot be for ever suppressed—the progress of civilization becomes comparatively rapid. The rise of one man to supreme power enables him to carry through changes in a single lifetime which previously many generations might not have sufficed to effect; and if, as will often happen, he is a man of intellect and energy above the common, he will readily avail himself of the opportunity. Even the whims and caprices of a tyrant may be of service in breaking the chain of custom which lies so heavy on the savage. As soon as the tribe ceases to be swayed by the timid and divided counsels of the elders, and yields to the direction of a single strong and resolute mind, it becomes formidable to its neighbours and enters on a career of aggrandizement, which at an early stage of history is often highly favourable to social, industrial, and intellectual progress. For extending its sway, partly by force of arms, partly by the voluntary submission of weaker tribes, the community soon acquires wealth and slaves, both of which, by relieving some classes from the perpetual struggle for a bare subsistence, afford them an opportunity of devoting themselves to the disinterested pursuit of knowledge which is the noblest and most powerful instrument to ameliorate the lot of man.

Intellectual progress, which reveals itself in the growth of art and science and the spread of more liberal views, cannot be dissociated from industrial or economic progress, and that in its turn receives an immense impulse from conquest and empire. It is no mere accident that the most vehement outbursts of activity of the human mind have followed close on the heels of victory, and that the great conquering races of the world have commonly done most to advance and spread civilization, thus healing in peace the wounds they inflicted in war. The Babylonians, the Greeks, the Romans, the Arabs are our witnesses in the past: we may yet live to see a similar outburst in Japan. Nor, to remount the stream of history to its sources, is it an accident that all the first great strides towards civilization have been made under despotic and theocratic governments, like those of Egypt, Babylon, and Peru, where the supreme ruler claimed and received the servile allegiance of his subjects in the double character of a king and a god. It is hardly too much to say that at this early epoch despotism is the best friend of humanity and, paradoxical as it may sound, of liberty. For after all there is more liberty in the best sense—liberty to think our own thoughts and to fashion our own destinies—under the most absolute despotism, the most grinding tyranny, than under the apparent freedom of savage life, where the individual's lot is cast from the cradle to the grave in the iron mould of hereditary custom.

So far, therefore, as the public profession of magic has been one of the roads by which the ablest men have passed to supreme power, it has contributed to emancipate mankind from the thralldom of tradition and to elevate them into a larger, freer life, with a broader outlook on the world. This is no small service rendered to humanity. And when we remember further that in another direction magic has paved the way for science, we are forced to admit that if the black art has done much evil, it has also been the source of much good; that if it is the child of error, it has yet been the mother of freedom and truth....

From Magic to Religion

Wherever sympathetic magic occurs in its pure unadulterated form, it assumes that in nature one event follows another necessarily and invariably without the intervention of any spiritual or personal agency. Thus its fundamental conception is identical with that of modern science; underlying the whole system is a faith, implicit but real and firm, in the order and uniformity of nature. The magician does not doubt that the same causes will always produce the same effects, that the performance of the proper ceremony, accompanied by the appropriate spell, will inevitably be attended by the desired result, unless, indeed, his incantations should chance to be thwarted and foiled by the more potent charms of another sorcerer. He supplicates no higher power: he sues the favor of no fickle and wayward being: he abases himself before no awful deity. Yet his power, great as he believes it to be, is by no means arbitrary and unlimited. He can wield it only so long as he strictly conforms to the rules of his art, or to what may be called the laws of nature as conceived by him. To neglect these rules, to break these laws in the smallest particular, is to incur failure, and may even expose the unskillful practitioner himself to the utmost peril. If he claims a sovereignty over nature, it is a constitutional sovereignty rigorously limited in its scope and exercised in exact conformity with ancient usage. Thus the analogy between the magical and the scientific conceptions of the world is close. In both of them the succession of events is assumed to be perfectly regular and certain, being determined by immutable laws, the operation of which can be foreseen and calculated precisely; the elements of caprice, of change, and of accident are banished from the course of nature. Both of them open up a seemingly boundless vista of possibilities to him who knows the vast and intricate mechanisms of the world. Hence the strong attraction which magic and science alike have exercised on the human mind; hence the powerful stimulus that both have given to the pursuit of knowledge....

The fatal flaw of magic lies not in its general assumption of a sequence of events determined by law, but in its total misconception of the nature of the particular laws which govern that sequence. If we analyze the various cases of sympathetic magic which have been passed in review in the preceding pages, and which may be taken as fair samples of the bulk, we shall find, as I have already indicated, that they are all mistaken applications of one or other of two great fundamental laws of thought, namely, the association of ideas by similarity and the association of ideas by contiguity in space or time. A mistaken association of similar ideas produces homoeopathic or imitative magic: a mistaken association of contiguous ideas produces contagious magic. The principles of association are excellent in themselves, and indeed absolutely essential to the working of the human mind. Legitimately applied they yield science; illegitimately applied they yield magic, the bastard sister of science. It is therefore a truism, almost a tautology, to say that all magic is necessarily false and barren; for were it ever to become true and fruitful, it would no longer be magic but science....

If magic is thus next of kin to science, we have still to enquire how it stands related to religion. But the view we take of that relation will necessarily be coloured by the idea which we have formed of the nature of religion itself; hence a writer may reasonably be expected to define his conception of religion before he proceeds to investigate its relation to magic.... By religion, then, I understand a propitiation or conciliation of powers superior to man which are believed to direct and control the course of nature and of human life. Thus defined, religion consists of two elements, a theoretical and a practical, namely, a belief in powers higher than man and an attempt to propitiate or please them.

Of the two, belief clearly comes first, since we must believe in the existence of a divine being before we can attempt to please him. But unless the belief leads to a corresponding practice, it is not a religion but merely a theology.... Hence belief and practice or, in theological language, faith and works are equally essential to religion, which cannot exist without both of them. But it is not necessary that religious practice should always take the form of a ritual; that is, it need not consist in the offering of sacrifice, the recitation of prayers, and other outward ceremonies. Its aim is to please the deity, and if the deity is one who delights in charity and mercy and purity more than in oblations of blood, the chanting of hymns, and the fumes of incense, his worshippers will best please him ... by being pure and merciful and charitable towards men, for in so doing they will imitate, so far as human infirmity allows, the perfections of the divine nature....

But if religion involves, first, a belief in superhuman beings who rule the world, and second, an attempt to win their favor, it clearly assumes that the course of nature is to some extent elastic or variable, and that we can persuade or induce the mighty beings who control it to deflect, for our benefit, the current of events from the channel in which they would otherwise flow. Now this implied elasticity or variability of nature is directly opposed to the principles of magic as well as of science, both of which assume that the processes of nature are rigid and invariable in their operation, and that they can as little be turned from their course by persuasion and entreaty as by threats and intimidation. The distinction between the two conflicting views of the universe turns on their answer to the crucial question, Are the forces which govern the world conscious and personal, or unconscious and impersonal? Religion, as a conciliation of the superhuman powers, assumes the former member of the alternative. For all conciliation implies that the being conciliated is a conscious or personal agent, that his conduct is in some measure uncertain, and that he can be prevailed upon to vary it in the desired direction by a judicious appeal to his interests, his appetites, or his emotions. Conciliation is never employed towards things which are regarded as inanimate, nor towards persons whose behavior in the particular circumstances is known to be determined with absolute certainty. Thus in so far as religion assumes the world to be directed by conscious agents who may be turned from their purpose by persuasion, it stands in fundamental antagonism to magic as well as to science, both of which take for granted that the course of nature is determined, not by the passions or caprice of personal beings, but by the operation of immutable laws acting mechanically. In magic, indeed, the assumption is only implicit, but in science it is explicit. It is true that magic often deals with spirits, which are personal agents of the kind assumed by religion; but whenever it does so in its proper form, it treats them exactly in the same fashion as it treats inanimate agents, that is, it constrains or coerces instead of conciliating or propitiating them as religion would do. Thus it assumes that all personal beings, whether human or divine, are in the last resort subject to those impersonal forces which control all things, but which neverthe-less can be turned to account by any one who knows how to manipulate them by the appropriate ceremonies and spells. In ancient Egypt, for example, the magicians claimed the power of compelling even the highest gods to do their bidding, and actually threatened them with destruction in case of disobedi-ence. Sometimes, without going quite so far as that, the wizard declared that he would scatter the bones of Osiris or reveal his sacred legend, if the god proved contumacious. Similarly in India at the present day the great Hindoo trinity itself of Brahma, Vishnu, and Siva is subject to the sorcerers, who, by means of their spells, exercise such an ascendancy over the mightiest deities, that these are bound submissively to execute on earth below, or in heaven above, whatever commands their masters the magicians may please to issue. There is a saying everywhere current in India: "The whole universe is subject to the gods; the gods are subject to the spells (*mantras*); the spells to the Brahmans; therefore the Brahmans are our gods."

This radical conflict of principle between magic and religion sufficiently explains the relentless hostility with which in history the priest has often pur-sued the magician. The haughty self-sufficiency of the magician, his arrogant demeanor towards the higher powers, and his unabashed claim to exercise a sway like theirs could not but revolt the priest, to whom, with his awful sense of the divine majesty, and his humble prostration in presence of it, such claims and such a demeanor must have appeared an impious and blasphemous usurpa-tion of prerogatives that belong to God alone. And sometimes, we may suspect, lower motives concurred to whet the edge of the priest's hostility. He professed to be the proper medium, the true intercessor between God and man, and no doubt his interests as well as his feelings were often injured by a rival practitio-ner, who preached a surer and smoother road to fortune than the rugged and slippery path of divine favour....

Yet though magic is thus found to fuse and amalgamate with religion in many ages and in many lands, there are some grounds for thinking that this fusion is not primitive, and that there was a time when man trusted to magic alone for the satisfaction of such wants as transcended his immediate animal cravings. In the first place a consideration of the fundamental notions of magic and religion may incline us to surmise that magic is older than religion in the history of humanity. We have seen that on the one hand magic is nothing but a mistaken application of the very simplest and most elementary processes of the mind, namely the association of ideas by virtue of resemblance or contiguity; and that on the other hand religion assumes the operation of conscious or per-sonal agents, superior to man, behind the visible screen of nature. Obviously the conception of personal agents is more complex than a simple recognition of the similarity or contiguity of ideas; and a theory which assumes that the course of nature is determined by conscious agents is more abstruse and recondite, and requires for its apprehension a far higher degree of intelligence and reflection, than the view that things succeed each other simply by reason of their contiguity or resemblance.... Thus, if magic be deduced immediately from elementary processes of reasoning, and be, in fact, an error into which the mind falls almost spontaneously, while religion rests on conceptions which the merely animal intelligence can hardly be supposed to have yet attained to, it becomes probable that magic arose before religion in the evolution of our race, and that man essayed to bend nature to his wishes by the sheer force of spells and enchantments before he strove to coax and mollify a coy, capricious, or irascible deity by the soft insinuation of prayer and sacrifice.

The conclusion which we have thus reached deductively from a consideration of the fundamental ideas of magic and religion is confirmed inductively by the observation that among the aborigines of Australia, the rudest savages as to whom we possess accurate information, magic is universally practiced, whereas religion in the sense of a propitiation or conciliation of the higher powers seems to be nearly unknown. Roughly speaking, all men in Australia are magicians, but not one is a priest; everybody fancies he can influence his fellows or the course of nature by sympathetic magic, but nobody dreams of propitiating gods by prayer and sacrifice.

But if in the most backward state of human society now known to us we find magic thus conspicuously present and religion conspicuously absent, may we not reasonably conjecture that the civilized races of the world have also at some period of their history passed through a similar intellectual phase, that they attempted to force the great powers of nature to do their pleasure before they thought of courting their favor by offerings and prayer—in short that, just as on the material side of human culture there has everywhere been an Age of Stone, so on the intellectual side there has everywhere been an Age of Magic? There are reasons for answering this question in the affirmative....

If an Age of Religion has thus everywhere, as I venture to surmise, been preceded by an Age of Magic, it is natural that we should enquire what causes have led mankind, or rather a portion of them, to abandon magic as a principle of faith and practice and to betake themselves to religion instead.... With all due diffidence... I would suggest that a tardy recognition of the inherent falsehood and barrenness of magic set the more thoughtful part of mankind to cast about for a truer theory of nature and more fruitful method of turning her resources to account. The shrewder intelligences must in time have come to perceive that magical ceremonies and incantations did not really effect the results which they were designed to produce, and which the majority of their simpler fellows still believed that they did actually produce. This great discovery of the inefficacy of magic must have wrought a radical though probably slow revolution in the minds of those who had the sagacity to make it. The discovery amounted to this, that men for the first time recognized their inability to manipulate at pleasure certain natural forces which hitherto they had believed to be completely within their control. It was a confession of human ignorance and weakness. Man saw that he had taken for causes what were no causes, and that all his efforts to work by means of these imaginary causes had been in vain. His painful toil had been wasted, his curious ingenuity had been squandered to no purpose....

Thus cut adrift from his ancient moorings and left to toss on a troubled sea of doubt and uncertainty, his old happy confidence in himself and his powers rudely shaken, our primitive philosopher must have been sadly perplexed and agitated till he came to rest, as in a quiet haven after a tempestuous voyage, in a new system of faith and practice, which seemed to offer a solution of his harassing doubts and a substitute, however precarious, for that sovereignty over nature which he had reluctantly abdicated. If the great world went on its way without the help of him or his fellows, it must surely be because there were other beings, like himself, but far stronger, who, unseen themselves, directed its course and brought about all the varied series of events which he had hitherto believed to be dependent on his own magic. It was they, as he now believed, and not he himself, who made the stormy wind to blow, the lightning to flash, and the thunder to roll; who had laid the foundations of the solid earth and set bounds to the restless sea that it might not pass; who caused all the glorious lights of heaven to shine;...who breathed into man's nostrils and made him live, or turned him to destruction by famine and pestilence and war. To these mighty beings, whose handiwork he traced in all the gorgeous and varied pageantry of nature, man now addressed himself, humbly confessing his dependence on their invisible power, and beseeching them of their mercy to furnish him with all good things, to defend him from the perils and dangers by which our mortal life is compassed about on every hand, and finally to bring his immortal spirit, freed from the burden of the body, to some happier world beyond the reach of pain and sorrow, where he might rest with them and with the spirits of good men in joy and felicity for ever.

In this, or some such way as this, the deeper minds may be conceived to have made the great transition from magic to religion. But even in them the change can hardly ever have been sudden; probably it proceeded very slowly, and required long ages for its more or less perfect accomplishment. For the recognition of man's powerlessness to influence the course of nature on a grand scale must have been gradual; he cannot have been shorn of the whole of his fancied dominion at a blow. Step by step he must have been driven back from his proud position; foot by foot he must have yielded, with a sigh, the ground which he had once viewed as his own. Now it would be the wind, now the rain, now the sunshine, now the thunder, that he confessed himself unable to wield at will; and as province after province of nature thus fell from his grasp, till what has once seemed a kingdom threatened to shrink into a prison, man must have been more and more profoundly impressed with a sense of his own helplessness and the might of the invisible beings by whom he believed himself to be surrounded. Thus religion, beginning as a slight and partial acknowledgement of powers superior to man, tends with the growth of knowledge to deepen into a confession of man's entire and absolute dependence on the divine; his old free bearing is exchanged for an attitude of lowliest prostration before the mysterious powers of the unseen, and his highest virtue is to submit his will to theirs; *In la sua voluntade é nostra pace* [In your will is our peace: ed.]....

The reader may well be tempted to ask, How was it that intelligent men did not sooner detect the fallacy of magic? How could they continue to cherish expectations that were invariably doomed to disappointment? With what heart persist in playing venerable antics that led to nothing, and mumbling solemn balderdash that remained without effect? Why cling to beliefs which were so flatly contradicted by experience? How dare to repeat experiments that had failed so often? The answer seems to be that the fallacy was far from easy to detect, the failure by no means obvious, since in many, perhaps in most cases, the desired event did actually follow, at a longer or shorter interval, the performance of the rite which was designed to bring it about; and a mind of more than common acuteness was needed to perceive that, even in these cases, the rite was not necessarily the cause of the event. A ceremony intended to make the wind blow or the rain fall, or to work the death of an enemy, will always be followed, sooner or later, by the occurrence it is meant to bring to pass; and primitive man may be excused for regarding the occurrence as a direct result of the ceremony, and the best possible proof of its efficacy. Similarly, rites observed in the morning to help the sun rise, and in spring to wake the dreaming earth from her winter sleep, will invariably appear to be crowned with success, at least within the temperate zones; for in these regions the sun lights his golden lamp in the east every morning, and year by year the vernal earth decks herself afresh with a rich mantle of green....

Magic, Magicians, and the Natural World

We have seen that in practice the magic art may be employed for the benefit either of individuals or of the whole community, and that according as it is directed to one or other of these two objects it may be called private or public magic. Further, I pointed out that the public magician occupies a position of great influence, from which, if he is a prudent and able man, he may advance step by step to the rank of a chief or king. Thus an examination of public magic conduces to an understanding of the early kingship, since in savage and barbarous society many chiefs and kings appear to owe their authority in great measure to their reputation as magicians.

Among the objects of public utility which magic may be employed to secure, the most essential is an adequate supply of food.... [P]urveyors of food—the hunter, the fisher, the farmer—all resort to magical practices in the pursuit of their various callings; but they do so as private individuals for the benefit of themselves and their families, rather than as public functionaries acting in the interest of the whole people. It is otherwise when the rites are performed not by the hunters, the fishers, the farmers themselves, but by professional magicians on their behalf. In primitive society, where uniformity of occupation is the rule,... every man is more or less his own magician; he practices charms and incantations for his own good and the injury of his enemies. But a great step in advance has been taken when a special class of magicians has been instituted; when, in other words, a number of men have been set apart for the express purpose of benefiting the whole community by their skill, whether that skill be directed to the healing of diseases, the forecasting of the future, the regulation of the weather, or any other object of general utility. The impotence of the means adopted by most of these practitioners to accomplish their ends ought not to blind us to the immense importance of the institution itself. Here is a body of men relieved, at least in the higher stages of savagery, from the need of earning their livelihood by hard manual toil, and allowed, nay, expected and encouraged, to prosecute researches into the secret ways of nature.

$\sim$

Magic and Religion

We have found that at an early stage of society men, ignorant of the secret processes of nature and of the narrow limits within which it is in our power to control and direct them, have commonly arrogated to themselves functions which in the present state of knowledge we should deem superhuman or divine. The illusion has been fostered and maintained by the same causes which begot it, namely the marvelous order and uniformity with which nature conducts her operations, the wheels of her great machine revolving with a smoothness and precision which enable the patient observer to anticipate in general the season, if not the very hour, when they will bring round the fulfillment of his hopes or the accomplishment of his fears.... [T]he springs which set the vast machine in motion...appear to ignorant man to lie within his reach: he fancies he can touch them and so work by magic art all manner of good to himself and evil to his foes. In time the fallacy of this belief becomes apparent to him: he discovers that there are things he cannot do, pleasures which he is unable of himself to procure, pains which even the most potent magician is powerless to avoid. The unattainable good, the inevitable ill, are now ascribed by him to the action of invisible powers, whose favor is joy and life, whose anger is misery and death. Thus magic tends to be displaced by religion, and the sorcerer by the priest. At this stage of thought the ultimate causes of things are conceived to be personal beings, many in number and often discordant in character, who partake of the nature and even of the frailty of man, though their might is greater than his, and their life far exceeds the span of his ephemeral existence.... Accordingly, so long as men look on their gods as beings akin to themselves and not raised to an unapproachable height above them, they believe it to be possible for those of their own number who surpass their fellows to attain to the divine rank after death or even in life. Incarnate human deities of this latter sort may be said to halt midway between the age of magic and the age of religion. If they bear the names and display the pomp of deities, the powers which they are supposed to wield are commonly those of their predecessor the magician. Like him, they are expected to guard their people against hostile enchantments, to heal them in sickness, to bless them with offspring, and to provide them with an abundant supply of food by regulating the weather and performing the other ceremonies which are deemed necessary to ensure the fertility of the earth and the multiplication of animals. Men who are credited with powers so lofty and far-reaching naturally hold the highest place in the land, and while the rift between the spiritual and the temporal spheres has not yet widened too far, they are supreme in civil as well as religious matters: in a word, they are kings as well as gods. Thus the divinity which hedges a king has its roots deep down in human history, and long ages pass before these are sapped by a profounder view of nature and man.

$\sim$

Magic and the Death of Kings

Kings killed when their Strength fails.... Now primitive peoples, as we have seen, sometimes believe that their safety and even that of the world is bound up with the life of one of these god-men or human incarnations of the divinity. Naturally, therefore, they take the utmost care of his life, out of a regard for their own. But no amount of care and precaution will prevent the man-god from growing old and feeble and at last dying. His worshippers have to lay their account with this sad necessity and to meet it as best they can. The danger is a formidable one; for if the course of nature is dependent on the man-god's life, what catastrophes may not be expected from the gradual enfeeblement of his powers and their final extinction in death? There is only one way of averting these dangers. The man-god must be killed as soon as he shows symptoms that his powers are beginning to fail, and his soul must be transferred to a vigorous successor before it has been seriously impaired by the threatened decay. The advantages of thus putting the man-god to death instead of allowing him to die of old age and disease are, to the savage, obvious enough. For if the man-god dies what we call a natural death, it means, according to the savage, that his soul has either voluntarily departed from his body and refuses to return, or more commonly that it has been extracted, or at least detained in its wanderings, by a demon or a sorcerer. In any of these cases the soul of the man-god is lost to his worshippers, and with it their prosperity is gone and their very existence endangered. Even if they could arrange to catch the soul of the dying god as it left his lips or his nostrils and so transfer it to a successor, this would not effect their purpose; for, dying of disease, his soul would necessarily leave his body in the last stage of weakness and exhaustion, and so enfeebled it would continue to drag out a languid, inert existence in any body to which it might be transferred. Whereas by slaying him his worshippers could, in the first place, make sure of catching his soul as it escaped and transferring it to a suitable successor; and, in the second place, by putting him to death before his natural force was abated, they would secure that the world should not fall into decay with the decay of the man-god. Every purpose, therefore, was answered, and all dangers averted by thus killing the man-god and transferring his soul, while yet at its prime, to a vigorous successor.

The mystic kings of Fire and Water in Cambodia are not allowed to die a natural death. Hence when one of them is seriously ill and the elders think that he cannot recover, they stab him to death. The people of Congo believed, as we have seen, that if their pontiff the Chitomé were to die a natural death, the world would perish, and the earth, which he alone sustained by his power and merit, would immediately be annihilated. Accordingly when he fell ill and seemed likely to die, the man who was destined to be his successor entered the pontiff's house with a rope or a club and strangled or clubbed him to death. The Ethiopian kings of Meroe were worshipped as gods; but whenever the priests chose, they sent a messenger to the king, ordering him to die, and alleging an oracle of the gods as their authority for the command....

Customs of the same sort appear to have prevailed in this part of Africa down to modern times. In some tribes of Fazoql the king had to administer justice daily under a certain tree. If from sickness or any other cause he was unable to discharge this duty for three whole days, he was hanged on the tree in a noose, which contained two razors so arranged that when the noose was drawn tight by the weight of the king's body they cut his throat.

A custom of putting their divine kings to death at the first symptoms of infirmity or old age prevailed until lately, if indeed it is even now extinct and not merely dormant, among the Shilluk of the White Nile, and in recent years it has been carefully investigated by Dr. C. G. Seligman. The reverence which the Shilluk pay to their king appears to arise chiefly from the conviction that he is a reincarnation of the spirit of Nyakang, the semi-divine hero who founded the dynasty and settled the tribe in their present territory. It is a fundamental article of the Shilluk creed that the spirit of the divine or semi-divine Nyakang is incarnate in the reigning king, who is accordingly himself invested to some extent with the character of a divinity. But while the Shilluk hold their kings in high, indeed religious reverence and take every precaution against their accidental death, nevertheless they cherish "the conviction that the king must not be allowed to become ill or senile, lest with his diminishing vigor the cattle should sicken and fail to bear their increase, the crops should rot in the fields, and man, stricken with disease, should die in ever-increasing numbers." To prevent these calamities it used to be the regular custom with the Shilluk to put the king to death whenever he showed signs of ill-health or failing strength. One of the fatal symptoms of decay was taken to be an incapacity to satisfy the sexual passions of his wives, of whom he has very many, distributed in a large number of houses at Fashoda. When this ominous weakness manifested itself, the wives reported it to the chiefs, who are popularly said to have intimated to the king his doom by spreading a white cloth over his face and knees as he lay slumbering in the heat of the sultry afternoon. Execution soon followed the sentence of death....

From Dr. Seligman's enquiries it appears that not only was the Shilluk king liable to be killed with due ceremony at the first symptoms of incipient decay, but even while he was yet in the prime of health and strength he might be attacked at any time by a rival and have to defend his crown in a combat to the death. According to the common Shilluk tradition any son of a king had the right thus to fight the king in possession and, if he succeeded in killing him, to reign in his stead. As every king had a large harem and many sons, the number of possible candidates for the throne at any time may well have been not inconsiderable, and the reigning monarch must have carried his life in his hand....

In general the principal element in the religion of the Shilluk would seem to be the worship which they pay to their sacred or divine kings, whether dead or alive. These are believed to be animated by a single divine spirit, which has been transmitted from the semi-mythical, but probably in substance historical, founder of the dynasty through all his successors to the present day. Hence, regarding their kings as incarnate divinities on whom the welfare of men, of cattle, and of the corn implicitly depends, the Shilluk naturally pay them the greatest respect and take every care of them; and however strange it may seem to us, their custom of putting the divine king to death as soon as he shows signs of ill-health or failing strength springs directly from their profound veneration for him and from their anxiety to preserve him, or rather the divine spirit by which he is animated, in the most perfect state of efficiency: nay, we may go further and say that their practice of regicide is the best proof they can give of the high regard in which they hold their kings. For they believe, as we have seen, that the king's life or spirit is so sympathetically bound up with the prosperity of the whole country, that if he fell ill or grew senile the cattle would sicken and cease to multiply, the crops would rot in the fields, and men would perish of widespread disease. Hence, in their opinion, the only way of averting these calamities is to put the king to death while he is still hale and hearty, in order that the divine spirit which he has inherited from his predecessors may be transmitted in turn by him to his successor while it is still in full vigor and has not yet been impaired by the weakness of disease and old age. In this connection the particular symptom which is commonly said to seal the king's death-warrant is highly significant; when he can no longer satisfy the passions of his numerous wives, in other words, when he has ceased, whether partially or wholly, to be able to reproduce his kind, it is time for him to die and to make room for a more vigorous successor. Taken along with the other reasons which are alleged for putting the king to death, this one suggests that the fertility of men, of cattle, and of the crops is believed to depend sympathetically on the generative power of the king, so that the complete failure of that power in him would involve a corresponding failure in men, animals, and plants, and would thereby entail at no distant date the entire extinction of all life, whether human, animal, or vegetable. No wonder, that with such a danger before their eyes the Shilluk should be most careful not to let the king die what we should call a natural death of sickness or old age.... The similar legends of the mysterious disappearance of early kings in other lands, for example at Rome and in Uganda, may well point to a similar custom of putting them to death for the purpose of preserving their life....

The Dinka are a congeries of independent tribes in the valley of the White Nile. They are essentially a pastoral people.... For their crops and above all for their pastures they depend on the regularity of the rains: in seasons of prolonged drought they are said to be reduced to great extremities. Hence the rainmaker is a very important personage among them to this day.... Yet in spite, or rather in virtue, of the high honor in which he is held, no Dinka rain-maker is allowed to die a natural death of sickness or old age; for the Dinka believe that if such an untoward event were to happen, the tribe would suffer from disease and famine, and the herds would not yield their increase. So when a rain-maker feels that he is growing old and infirm, he tells his children that he wishes to die. Among the Agar Dinka a large grave is dug and the rain-maker lies down in it, surrounded by his friends and relatives. From time to time he speaks to the people, recalling the past history of the tribe, reminding them how he has ruled and advised them, and instructing them how they are to act in the future. Then, when he has concluded his admonition, he bids them cover him up. So the earth is thrown down on him as he lies in the grave, and he soon dies of suffocation. Such, with minor variations, appears to be the regular end of the honorable career of a rain-maker in all the Dinka tribes. The Khor-Adar Dinka told Dr. Seligman that when they have dug the grave for their rain-maker they strangle him in his house. The father and paternal uncle of one of Dr. Seligman's informants had both been rain-makers and both had been killed in the most regular and orthodox fashion. Even if a rain-maker is quite young he will be put to death should he seem likely to perish of disease. Further, every precaution is taken to prevent a rain-maker from dying an accidental death, for such an end, though not nearly so serious a matter as death from illness or old age, would be sure to entail sickness on the tribe. As soon as a rain-maker is killed, his valuable spirit is supposed to pass to a suitable successor, whether a son or other near blood relation.

In the Central African kingdom of Bunyoro down to recent years custom required that as soon as the king fell seriously ill or began to break up from age, he should die by his own hand; for, according to an old prophecy, the throne would pass away from the dynasty if ever the king were to die a natural death. He killed himself by draining a poisoned cup. If he faltered or were too ill to ask for the cup, it was his wife's duty to administer the poison. When the king of Kibanga, on the Upper Congo, seems near his end, the sorcerers put a rope round his neck, which they draw gradually tighter till he dies. If the king of Gingiro happens to be wounded in war, he is put to death by his comrades, or, if they fail to kill him, by his kinsfolk, however hard he may beg for mercy.

~

Annual Death and Rebirth in Nature

The Magic of Spring.—The general explanation which we have been led to adopt of … many … ceremonies is that they are, or were in their origin, magical rites intended to ensure the revival of nature in spring. The means by which they were supposed to effect this end were imitation and sympathy. Led astray by his ignorance of the true causes of things, primitive man believed that in order to produce the great phenomena of nature on which his life depended he had only to imitate them, and that immediately by a secret sympathy or mystic influence the little drama which he acted in forest glade or mountain dell, on desert plain or wind-swept shore, would be taken up and repeated by mightier actors on a vaster stage.... To us, familiar as we are with the conception of the uniformity and regularity with which the great cosmic phenomena succeed each other, there seems little ground for apprehension that the causes which produce these effects will cease to operate, at least within the near future. But this confidence in the stability of nature is bred only by the experience which comes of wide observation and long tradition; and the savage, with his narrow sphere of observation and his short-lived tradition, lacks the very elements of that experience which alone could set his mind at rest in face of the ever-changing and often menacing aspects of nature. No wonder, therefore, that he is thrown into a panic by an eclipse, and thinks that the sun or the moon would surely perish, if he did not raise a clamour and shoot his puny shafts into the air to defend the luminaries from the monster who threatens to devour them. No wonder he is terrified when in the darkness of night a streak of sky is suddenly illumined by the flash of a meteor.... To the primitive savage, with his short memory and imperfect means of marking the flight of time, a year may well have been so long that he failed to recognize it as a cycle at all, and watched the changing aspects of earth and heaven with a perpetual wonder, alternately delighted and alarmed, elated and cast down, according as the vicissitudes of light and heat, of plant and animal life, ministered to his comfort or threatened his existence. In autumn when the withered leaves were whirled about the forest by the nipping blast, and he looked up at the bare boughs, could he feel sure that they would ever be green again? As day by day the sun sank lower and lower in the sky, could he be certain that the luminary would ever retrace his heavenly road? Even the waning moon, whose pale sickle rose thinner and thinner every night over the rim of the eastern horizon, may have excited in his mind a fear lest, when it had wholly vanished, there should be moons no more.

These and a thousand such misgivings may have thronged the fancy and troubled the peace of the man who first began to reflect on the mysteries of the world he lived in, and to take thought for a more distant future than the morrow. It was natural, therefore, that with such thoughts and fears he should have done all that in him lay to bring back the faded blossom to the bough, to swing the low sun of winter up to his old place in the summer sky, and to restore its orbed fullness to the silver lamp of the waning moon. We may smile at his vain endeavours if we please, but it was only by making a long series of experiments, of which some were almost inevitably doomed to failure, that man learned from experience the futility of some of his attempted methods and the fruitfulness of others. After all, magical ceremonies are nothing but experiments which have failed and which continue to be repeated merely because...the operator is unaware of their failure. With the advance of knowledge these ceremonies either cease to be performed altogether or are kept up from force of habit long after the intention with which they were instituted has been forgotten. Thus fallen from their high estate, no longer regarded as solemn rites on the punctual performance of which the welfare and even the life of the community depend, they sink gradually to the level of simple pageants, mummeries, and pastimes, till in the final stage of degeneration they are wholly abandoned by older people, and, from having once been the most serious occupation of the sage, become at last the idle sport of children. It is in this final stage of decay that most of the old magical rites of our European forefathers linger on at the present day, and even from this their last retreat they are fast being swept away by the rising tide of those multitudinous forces, moral, intellectual, and social, which are bearing mankind onward to a new and unknown goal. We may feel some natural regret at the disappearance of quaint customs and picturesque ceremonies, which have preserved...something of the flavour and freshness of the olden time, some breath of the springtime of the world; yet our regret will be lessened when we remember that these pretty pageants...had their origin in ignorance and superstition; that if they are a record of human endeavour, they are also a monument of fruitless ingenuity, of wasted labour, and of blighted hopes; and that for all their gay trappings—their flowers, their ribbons, and their music—they partake far more of tragedy than of farce....

In course of time the slow advance of knowledge, which has dispelled so many cherished illusions, convinced at least the more thoughtful portion of mankind that the alternations of summer and winter, of spring and autumn, were not merely the result of their own magical rites, but that some deeper cause, some mightier power, was at work behind the shifting scenes of nature. They now pictured to themselves the growth and decay of vegetation, the birth and death of living creatures, as effects of the waxing or waning strength of divine beings, of gods and goddesses, who were born and died, who married and begot children, on the pattern of human life.

Thus the old magical theory of the seasons was displaced, or rather supplemented by a religious theory. For although men now attributed the annual cycle of change primarily to corresponding changes in their deities, they still thought that by performing certain magical rites they could aid the god who was the principle of life, in his struggle with the opposing principle of death. They imagined that they could recruit his failing energies and even raise him from the dead. The ceremonies which they observed for this purpose were in substance a dramatic representation of the natural processes which they wished to facilitate; for it is a familiar tenet of magic that you can produce any desired effect by merely imitating it. And as they now explained the fluctuations of growth and decay, of reproduction and dissolution, by the marriage, the death, and the rebirth or revival of the gods, their religious or rather magical dramas turned in great measure on these themes. They set forth the fruitful union of the powers of fertility, the sad death of one at least of the divine partners, and his joyful resurrection. Thus a religious theory was blended with a magical practice. The combination is familiar in history. Indeed, few religions have ever succeeded in wholly extricating themselves from the old trammels of magic. The inconsistency of acting on two opposite principles, however it may vex the soul of the philosopher, rarely troubles the common man; indeed he is seldom even aware of it. His affair is to act, not to analyze the motives of his action. If mankind had always been logical and wise, history would not be a long chronicle of folly and crime.

Of the changes which the seasons bring with them, the most striking within the temperate zone are those which affect vegetation. Hence it is natural that in the magical dramas designed to dispel winter and bring back spring the emphasis should be laid on vegetation, and that trees and plants should figure in them.... To live and to cause to live, to eat food and to beget children, these were the primary wants of men in the past, and they will be the primary wants of men in the future so long as the world lasts. Other things may be added to enrich and beautify human life, but unless these wants are first satisfied, humanity itself must cease to exist. These two things, therefore, food and children, were what men chiefly sought to procure by the performance of magical rites for the regulation of the seasons.

Nowhere, apparently, have these rites been more widely and solemnly celebrated than in the lands which border the Eastern Mediterranean. Under the names of Osiris, Tammuz, Adonis, and Attis, the peoples of Egypt and Western Asia represented the yearly decay and revival of life, especially of vegetable life, which they personified as a god who annually died and rose again from the dead. In name and detail the rites varied from place to place: in substance they were the same.

~

Dying and Rising Gods

[I]f the explanation which I have adopted...is correct, the ceremony of the death and resurrection of Adonis must...have been a dramatic representation of the decay and revival of plant life. The inference thus based on the resemblance of the customs is confirmed by the following features in the legend and ritual of Adonis. His affinity with vegetation comes out at once in the common story of his birth. He was said to have been born from a myrrh-tree, the bark of which bursting, after a ten months' gestation, allowed the lovely infant to come forth.... Again, the story that Adonis spent half, or according to others a third, of the year in the lower world and the rest of it in the upper world, is explained most simply and naturally by supposing that he represented vegetation, especially the corn which lies buried in the earth half the year and reappears above the ground the other half.... [T]he annual death and revival of vegetation is a conception which readily presents itself to men in every stage of savagery and civilization; and the vastness of the scale on which this ever-recurring decay and regeneration takes place, together with man's intimate dependence on it for subsistence, combine to render it the most impressive annual occurrence in nature, at least within the temperate zones. It is no wonder that a phenomenon so important, so striking, and so universal should, by suggesting similar ideas, have given rise to similar rites in many lands. We may, therefore, accept as probable an explanation of the Adonis worship which accords so well with the facts of nature and with the analogy of similar rites in other lands....

This concentration, so to say, of the nature of Adonis upon the cereal crops is characteristic of the stage of culture reached by his worshippers in historical times. They had left the nomadic life of the wandering hunter and herdsman far behind them; for ages they had been settled on the land, and had depended for their subsistence mainly on the products of tillage. The berries and roots of the wilderness, the grass of the pastures, which had been matters of vital importance to their ruder forefathers, were now of little moment to them: more and more their thoughts and energies were engrossed by the staple of their life, the corn; more and more accordingly the propitiation of the deities of fertility in general and of the corn-spirit in particular tended to become the central feature of their religion. The aim they set before themselves in celebrating the rites was thoroughly practical. It was no vague poetical sentiment which prompted them to hail with joy the rebirth of vegetation and to mourn its decline. Hunger, felt or feared, was the mainspring of the worship of Adonis.

~

The Scapegoat and Atonement for Evil

[T]he employment of a divine man or animal as a scapegoat is especially to be noted; indeed, we are here directly concerned with the custom of banishing evils only in so far as these evils are believed to be transferred to a god who is afterwards slain.... [A]s has already been pointed out, the custom of killing a god dates from so early a period of human history that in later ages, even when the custom continues to be practiced, it is liable to be misinterpreted. The divine character of the animal or man is forgotten, and he comes to be regarded merely as an ordinary victim. This is especially likely to be the case when it is a divine man who is killed. For when a nation becomes civilized, if it does not drop human sacrifices altogether, it at least selects as victims only such wretches as would be put to death at any rate. Thus the killing of a god may sometimes come to be confounded with the execution of a criminal.

If we ask why a dying god should be chosen to take upon himself and carry away the sins and sorrows of the people, it may be suggested that in the practice of using the divinity as a scapegoat we have a combination of two customs which were at one time distinct and independent. On the one hand we have seen that it has been customary to kill the human or animal god in order to save his divine life from being weakened by the inroads of age. On the other hand we have seen that it has been customary to have a general expulsion of evils and sins once a year. Now, if it occurred to people to combine these two customs, the result would be the employment of the dying god as a scapegoat. He was killed, not originally to take away sin, but to save the divine life from the degeneracy of old age; but, since he had to be killed at any rate, people may have thought that they might as well seize the opportunity to lay upon him the burden of their sufferings and sins, in order that he might bear it away with him to the unknown world beyond the grave.

The use of the divinity as a scapegoat clears up the ambiguity which, as we saw, appears to hang about the European folk-custom of "carrying out Death." Grounds have been shown for believing that in this ceremony the so-called Death was originally the spirit of vegetation, who was annually slain in spring, in order that he might come to life again with all the vigour of youth. But, as I pointed out, there are certain features in the ceremony which are not explicable on this hypothesis alone. Such are the marks of joy with which the effigy of Death is carried out to be buried or burnt, and the fear and abhorrence of it manifested by the bearers. But these features become at once intelligible if we suppose that the Death was not merely the dying god of vegetation, but also a public scapegoat, upon whom were laid all the evils that had afflicted the people during the last year. Joy on such an occasion is natural and appropriate.... Again, the view that in these popular customs the Death is a scapegoat as well as a representative of the divine spirit of vegetation derives some support from the circumstance that its expulsion is always celebrated in spring and chiefly by Slavonic peoples. For the Slavonic year began in spring; and thus, in one of its aspects, the ceremony of "carrying out Death" would be an example of the widespread custom of expelling the accumulated evils of the old year before entering a new one.

～

The Golden Bough Concludes

We are at the end of our enquiry, but as often happens in the search after truth, if we have answered one question, we have raised many more. ...For the present we have journeyed far enough together, and it is time to part. Yet before we do so, we may well ask ourselves whether there is not some more general conclusion, some lesson, if possible, of hope and encouragement, to be drawn from the melancholy record of human error and folly which has engaged our attention in this book.

If then we consider, on the one hand, the essential similarity of man's chief wants everywhere and at all times, and on the other hand, the wide difference between the means he has adopted to satisfy them in different ages, we shall perhaps be disposed to conclude that the movement of the higher thought, so far as we can trace it, has on the whole been from magic through religion to science. In magic man depends on his own strength to meet the difficulties and dangers that beset him on every side. He believes in a certain established order of nature on which he can surely count, and which he can manipulate for his own ends. When he discovers his mistake, when he recognizes sadly that both the order of nature which he had assumed and the control which he had believed himself to exercise over it were purely imaginary, he ceases to rely on his own intelligence and his own unaided efforts, and throws himself humbly on the mercy of certain great invisible beings behind the veil of nature, to whom he now ascribes all those far-reaching powers which he once arrogated to himself. Thus in the acuter minds magic is gradually superseded by religion, which explains the succession of natural phenomena as regulated by the will, the passion, or the caprice of spiritual beings like man in kind, though vastly superior to him in power.

But as time goes on this explanation in its turn proves to be unsatisfactory. For it assumes that the succession of natural events is not determined by immutable laws, but is to some extent variable and irregular, and this assumption is not borne out by closer observation. On the contrary, the more we scrutinize that succession the more we are struck by the rigid uniformity, the punctual precision with which, wherever we can follow them, the operations of nature are carried on. Every great advance in knowledge has extended the sphere of order and correspondingly restricted the sphere of apparent disorder in the world, till now we are ready to anticipate that even in regions where chance and confusion appear still to reign, a fuller knowledge would everywhere reduce the seeming chaos to cosmos. Thus the keener minds, still pressing forward to a deeper solution of the mysteries of the universe, come to reject the religious theory of nature as inadequate, and to revert in a measure to the older standpoint of magic by postulating explicitly, what in magic had only been implicitly assumed, to wit, an inflexible regularity in the order of natural events, which, if carefully observed, enables us to foresee their course with certainty and to act accordingly. In short, religion, regarded as an explanation of nature, is displaced by science....

[W]hereas the order on which magic reckons is merely an extension, by false analogy, of the order in which ideas present themselves to our minds, the order laid down by science is derived from patient and exact observation of the phenomena themselves. The abundance, the solidity, and the splendor of the results already achieved by science are well fitted to inspire us with a cheerful confidence in the soundness of its method. Here at last, after groping about in the dark for countless ages, man has hit upon a clue to the labyrinth, a golden key that opens many locks in the treasury of nature. It is probably not too much to say that the hope of progress—moral and intellectual as well as material—in the future is bound up with the fortunes of science, and that every obstacle placed in the way of scientific discovery is a wrong to humanity....

In the last analysis magic, religion, and science are nothing but theories of thought; and as science has supplanted its predecessors, so it may hereafter be itself superseded by some more perfect hypothesis, perhaps by some totally different way of looking at the phenomena—of registering the shadows on the screen—of which we in this generation can form no idea. The advance of knowledge is an infinite progression towards a goal that for ever recedes.... Great things will come of that pursuit.... But a dark shadow lies athwart the far end of this fair prospect. For however vast the increase of knowledge and of power which the future may have in store for man, he can scarcely hope to stay the sweep of those great forces which seem to be making silently but relentlessly for the destruction of all this starry universe in which our earth swims as a speck or mote. In the ages to come man may be able to predict, perhaps even to control, the wayward courses of the winds and clouds, but hardly will his puny hands have strength to speed afresh our slackening planet in its orbit or rekindle the dying fire of the sun....

Without dipping so far into the future, we may illustrate the course which thought has hitherto run by likening it to a web woven of three different threads—the black thread of magic, the red thread of religion, and the white thread of science, if under science we may include those simple truths, drawn from observation of nature, of which men in all ages have possessed a store. Could we then survey the web of thought from the beginning, we should probably perceive it to be at first a checker of black and white, a patchwork of true and false notions, hardly tinged as yet by the red thread of religion. But carry your eye farther along the fabric and you will remark that, while the black and white checker still runs through it, there rests on the middle portion of the web, where religion has entered most deeply into its texture, a dark crimson stain, which shades off insensibly into a lighter tint as the white thread of science is woven more and more into the tissue. To a web thus checkered and stained, thus shot with threads of diverse hues, but gradually changing color the farther it is unrolled, the state of modern thought, with all its divergent aims and conflicting tendencies, may be compared. Will the great movement which for centuries has been slowly altering the complexion of thought be continued in the near future? or will a reaction set in which may arrest progress and even undo much that has been done? To keep up our parable, what will be the color of the web which the Fates are now weaving on the humming loom of time? will it be white or red? We cannot tell. A faint glimmering light illumines the backward portion of the web. Clouds and thick darkness hide the other end.

Our long voyage of discovery is over and our bark has drooped her weary sails in port at last. ... It is evening, and as we climb the long slope of the Appian way up to the Alban Hills, we look back and see the sky aflame with sunset, its golden glory resting like the aureole of a dying saint over Rome and touching with a crest of fire the dome of St. Peter's. The sight once seen can never be forgotten, but we turn from it and pursue our way darkling along the mountain side, till we come to Nemi and look down on the lake in its deep hollow, now fast disappearing in the evening shadows. The place has changed but little since Diana received the homage of her worshippers in the sacred grove. The temple of the sylvan goddess, indeed, has vanished and the King of the Wood no longer stands sentinel over the Golden Bough. But Nemi's woods are still green, and as the sunset fades above them in the west, there comes to us, borne on the swell of the wind, the sound of the church bells of Aricia ringing the Angelus. *Ave Maria!* Sweet and solemn they chime out from the distant town and die lingeringly away across the wide Campagnan marshes. *Le roi est mort, vive le roi! Ave Maria!* [The king is dead; long live the king. Hail Mary!: ed.]

3

Sigmund Freud: Religion as Neurosis

Sigmund Freud (1856–1939) was a towering presence in twentieth-century intellectual life. A thinker of fertile imagination and learned originality, he was a pioneering figure in the rise of psychology as a field of scientific inquiry. Perhaps more significantly, he has become, with Karl Marx, one of the two chief mentors of the modern mind. For some he is the icon of a revolution in sexual behavior and morality; for others, a fearless excavator of the depths of the human personality; for still others, the scourge of traditional religion and morality, and a somber prophet of the perils that shadow the future of civilization. Freud himself savored his position as outsider in a Victorian world, bent on disturbing the intellectual peace of the establishment. That posture of the brilliant dissenter, the modern Socrates in a complacent Athens, was the signature stance of his career.

In early years, Freud was an outstanding student, with a gift for languages, a capacious memory, and a keen interest in science. He pursued conventional medicine until he encountered Josef Breuer and Martin Charcot, two pioneers in the study of mental illness under whose influence he turned from physiological research on the brain to psychological study of the mind. In working with patients he developed a novel way of investigating—and treating—their disorders that he came to call "psychoanalysis." The technique centered on listening to patients, who were encouraged to report, by free association, whatever came into the mind: intimate secrets, distressing anxieties, and especially the contents of dreams. Freud's reflections on these clinical conversations led to *The Interpretation of Dreams,* published in the year 1900—fittingly enough, for this was the book that launched the "Freudian revolution" and would leave its mark on the entire century to come.

The *Interpretation of Dreams* introduced Freud's provocative idea of "the unconscious," a mysterious realm of the mind, beneath the conscious

71

self, that is the storehouse of suppressed memories, images, and urges too socially disruptive or personally painful to disclose. Dreams are mechanisms that release the repressed. Though they are natural features of the normal personality, they offer as well deep clues to the abnormal: to neurotic or even psychotic disorders.

Pscyhoanalysis was a theory as well as therapy. It was rooted in a new concept of the human personality that replaced the old categories of body and soul with Freud's now famous threefold partition of the self into the *superego* (carrying the moral demands of society), the *id* (reflecting the mindless urges of the body), and the *ego* (which strives to balance the conflict between the other two). In this scenario the self is not fixed; it is the site of an unceasing struggle of the *ego* to contain the conflicting pressures of the *superego* and the *id*. This portrait of the human self divided lies at the heart of the controversial theorem Freud introduced as the Oedipus complex: the desire of the young child sexually to possess one parent combined with hatred of the other as an unwanted rival. Oedipal issues apart, Freud found this idea of the personality in tension capable of illuminating every aspect of behavior, from the trivia of daily life to the great endeavors of art, literature, mythology, and, not least, religion.

Though references to religious ideas and practices appear throughout his writings, Freud's main engagements with religion occur in three works: *Totem and Taboo* (1913), *The Future of an Illusion* (1927), and *Moses and Monotheism* (1939). Selections from each of these works are provided in this chapter.

Totem and Taboo (1913)

Totem and Taboo is a work Freud regarded as one of his best, though it is less a book than a set of loosely linked essays influenced by evolutionary theory and the anthropological studies of Frazer, Tylor, and their associates. In it he proposed a historical circumstance that shocked middle class sensibilities. Among early humans, who lived in hordes, like apes and chimpanzees, the younger males grew jealous of their own father, murdered him, and took possession of his females. In fear afterward, they imposed a taboo against any new rebellion, and, assailed by guilt, they turned the father into a god, worshiping him in the form of an animal totem. Thus, out of the primal murder of the father have come both the oldest of humanity's moral commands—against murder (of the father) and incest (with his females)— as well as the beginnings of religion. It was a darkly fantastic story—calculated to outrage the guardians of conventionality; and it succeeded in its mission. Critics dismissed it as unverifiable—a purely speculative venture in prehistory. But Freud made no apologies, and the book won for itself a certain scandalous popularity.

The Future of an Illusion (1927)

The Future of an Illusion is a work quite different from *Totem and Taboo*. It does not speculate about prehistoric humanity, but centers on something that psychoanalysis is better equipped to address: the "manifest motives" of religious belief at all times and places. It also has at least the makings of a scientific argument—capable of at least some verification or disproof. We all know, says Freud, that the natural world is by no means friendly to our human aims and hopes. Disaster and disease ever threaten, and ultimately death conquers all. None of us easily accepts this harsh truth. We prefer the certitudes of childhood, when there was always a father present to give comfort in the dark of night and reassurance amid the dangers of the storm. As adults, we continue to crave that childhood security, though the world does not in fact offer it. Religion, however, pretends we can return to childhood; it invents a Father God who assures us of victory over every hardship, even death itself. It offers us an illusion—a form of belief arising merely from the immature wish that it be true. So, for humanity to persist in religious belief is to regress to its childhood, a condition that psychoanalysis can identify as neurotic. Religion, Freud thus concludes, is "the universal obsessional neurosis of humanity." Its appeal lies not in its rationality, but in the nonrational, purely emotional attachment to an illusion—a childish belief we hold simply because we wish it to be true.

Moses and Monotheism (1939)

Though *The Future of an Illusion* was potentially Freud's most persuasive statement on religion, it was not his last. His fascination with antiquity drew him late in life to his own Judaism and its foremost figure, the Prophet Moses, who, Freud guessed, had taken the idea of the one holy God from the Egyptian Pharoah Akenaton and given it to the Hebrews as they escaped from slavery. They grew tired of the hardships incurred, however, and in a desert rebellion, Moses was murdered. His monotheism was very nearly erased by a new and more violent religious creed, ugly by comparison with the original faith now lost, but suited to conquest of the land of promise. In the time of the great Hebrew prophets, however, the first faith was dramatically restored and reaffirmed. The original God of Moses returned to replace the God of vengeance and war and give shape to the true Judaism for the ages. For Freud, the parallel between the turbulent history of the Hebrews and what psychoanalysis finds in individual personalities is striking. In a case of neurosis, a traumatic event is forcibly repressed, only to return later on, often in a surprise eruption: a "return of the repressed." Similarly, in the fortunes of the Hebrews, no less than the murder in the primeval horde, a key psychic drama of the individual personality is played out in communal form on the stage of history. Society's dynamics mirror those of the individual.

Needless to say, this imaginative recreation of ancient Jewish history is as open to question as Freud's earlier speculations about a prehistoric tribal murder. But that has not displaced the fascination with his ideas that persists undiminished to the present day—among the current advocates of psychoanalytic theory, on the pages of journals in literary and social criticism, and in themes and ideas that continue to circulate in popular culture.

Totem and Taboo
The Origin of Religion and Morals: A Primeval Murder

In these selections Freud recounts the prehistoric "murder in the primeval horde" and finds in it the origins of morality, social constraint, and religion.

Let us call up the spectacle of a totem meal of the kind we have been discussing, amplified by a few probable features which we have not yet been able to consider. The clan is celebrating the ceremonial occasion by the cruel slaughter of its totem animal and is devouring it raw—blood, flesh and bones. The clansmen are there, dressed in the likeness of the totem and imitating it in sound and movement, as though they are seeking to stress their identity with it. Each man is conscious that he is performing an act forbidden to the individual and justifiable only through the participation of the whole clan; nor may

---

FROM: *Totem and Taboo: Some Points of Agreement between the Mental Lives of Savages and Neurotics.* In *Totem and Taboo and Other Works.* Volume 13 (1913–14) of *The Standard Edition of the Complete Psychological Works of Sigmund Freud.* Translated by James Strachey and edited in collaboration with Anna Freud. Copyright 1955. Hogarth Press. Reproduced by permission of Taylor & Francis Books, UK.

anyone absent himself from the killing and the meal. When the deed is done, the slaughtered animal is lamented and bewailed. The mourning is obligatory, imposed by dread of a threatened retribution. As [British biblical scholar: ed.] Robertson Smith... remarks of an analogous occasion, its chief purpose is to disclaim responsibility for the killing.

But the mourning is followed by demonstrations of festive rejoicing; every instinct is unfettered and there is license for every kind of gratification. Here we have easy access to an understanding of the nature of festivals in general. A festival is a permitted, or rather an obligatory, excess, a solemn breach of a prohibition. It is not that men commit the excesses because they are feeling happy as a result of some injunction they have received. It is rather that excess is of the essence of a festival; the festive feeling is produced by the liberty to do what is as a rule prohibited.

What are we to make, though, of the prelude to this festive joy—the mourning over the death of the animal? If the clansmen rejoice over the killing of the totem—a normally forbidden act—why do they mourn over it as well?

As we have seen, the clansmen acquire sanctity by consuming the totem: they reinforce their identification with it and with one another. Their festive feelings and all that follows from them might well be explained by the fact that they have taken into themselves the sacred life of which the substance of the totem is the vehicle.

Psycho-analysis has revealed that the totem animal is in reality a substitute for the father; and this tallies with the contradictory fact that, though the killing of the animal is as a rule forbidden, yet its killing is a festive occasion—with the fact that it is killed and yet mourned. The ambivalent emotional attitude, which to this day characterizes the father-complex in our children and which often persists into adult life, seems to extend to the totem animal in its capacity as substitute for the father.

If, now, we bring together the psycho-analytic translation of the totem with the fact of the totem meal and with Darwin's theories of the earliest state of human society, the possibility of a deeper understanding emerges—a glimpse of a hypothesis which may seem fantastic but which offers the advantage of establishing an unsuspected correlation between groups of phenomena that have hitherto been disconnected.

There is, of course, no place for the beginnings of totemism in Darwin's primal horde. All that we find there is a violent and jealous father who keeps all the females for himself and drives away his sons as they grow up. This earliest state of society has never been an object of observation. The most primitive kind of organization that we actually come across—and one that is in force to this day in certain tribes—consists of bands of males; these bands are composed of members with equal rights and are subject to the restrictions of the totemic system, including inheritance through the mother. Can this form of organization have developed out of the other one? And if so along what lines?

If we call the celebration of the totem meal to our help, we shall be able to find an answer. One day the brothers who had been driven out came together, killed and devoured their father and so made an end of the patriarchal horde. United, they had the courage to do and succeeded in doing what would have been impossible for them individually. (Some cultural advance, perhaps, command over some new weapon, had given them a sense of superior strength.) Cannibal savages as they were, it goes without saying that they devoured their victim as well as killing him. The violent primal father had doubtless been the feared and envied model of each one of the company of brothers: and in the act of devouring him they accomplished their identification with him, and each one of them acquired a portion of his strength. The totem meal, which is perhaps mankind's earliest festival, would thus be a repetition and a commemoration of this memorable and criminal deed, which was the beginning of so many things—of social organization, of moral restrictions and of religion.

In order that these later consequences may seem plausible, leaving their premises on one side, we need only suppose that the tumultuous mob of brothers were filled with the same contradictory feelings which we can see at work in the ambivalent father-complexes of our children and of our neurotic patients. They hated their father, who presented such a formidable obstacle to their craving for power and their sexual desires; but they loved and admired him too. After they had got rid of him, had satisfied their hatred and had put into effect their wish to identify themselves with him, the affection which had all this time been pushed under was bound to make itself felt. It did so in the form of remorse. A sense of guilt made its appearance, which in this instance coincided with the remorse felt by the whole group. The dead father became stronger than the living one had been—for events took the course we so often see them follow in human affairs to this day. What had up to then been prevented by his actual existence was thenceforward prohibited by the sons themselves, in accordance with the psychological procedure so familiar to us in psycho-analyses under the same name of "deferred obedience." They revoked their deed by forbidding the killing of the totem, the substitute for their father; and they renounced its fruits by resigning their claim to the women who had now been set free. They thus created out of their filial sense of guilt the two fundamental taboos of totemism, which for that very reason inevitably corresponded to the two repressed wishes of the Oedipus complex. Whoever contravened those taboos became guilty of the only two crimes with which primitive society concerned itself.

The two taboos of totemism with which human morality has its beginning are not on a par psychologically. The first of them, the law protecting the totem animal, is founded wholly on emotional motives: the father had actually been eliminated, and in no real sense could the deed be undone. But the second rule, the prohibition of incest, has a powerful practical basis as well. Sexual desires do not unite men but divide them. Though the brothers had banded together in order to overcome their father, they were all one another's rivals in regard to the women. Each of them would have wished, like his father, to have all the women to himself. The new organization would have collapsed in a struggle of all against all, for none of them was of such overmastering strength as to be able to take on his father's part with success. Thus the brothers had no alternative, if they were to live together, but—not, perhaps, until they had passed through many dangerous crises—to institute the law against incest, by which they all alike renounced the women whom they desired and who had been their chief motive for despatching their father. In this way they rescued the organization which had made them strong—and which may have been based on homosexual feelings and acts, originating perhaps during the period of their expulsion from the horde. Here, too, may perhaps have been the germ of the institution of matriarchy, described by [anthropologist Johann: ed.] Bachofen..., which was in turn replaced by the patriarchal organization of the family.

On the other hand, the claim of totemism to be regarded as a first attempt at a religion is based on the first of these two taboos—that upon taking the life of the totem animal. The animal struck the sons as a natural and obvious substitute for their father; but the treatment of it which they found imposed on themselves expressed more than the need to exhibit their remorse. They could attempt, in their relation to this surrogate father, to bring about a kind of reconciliation with their father. The totemic system was, as it were, a covenant with their father, in which he promised them everything that a childish imagination may expect from a father—protection, care and indulgence—while on their side they undertook to respect his life, that is to say, not to repeat the deed which had brought destruction on their real father. Totemism, moreover, contained an attempt at self-justification: "If our father had treated us in the way the totem does, we should never have felt tempted to kill him." In this fashion totemism helped to smooth things over and to make it possible to forget the event to which it owed its origin.

Features were thus brought into existence which continued thenceforward to have a determining influence on the nature of religion. Totemic religion arose from the filial sense of guilt, in an attempt to allay that feeling and to appease the father by deferred obedience to him. All later religions are seen to be attempts at solving the same problem. They vary according to the stage of civilization at which they arise and according to the methods which they adopt; but all have the same end in view and are reactions to the same great event, with which civilizations began and which, since it occurred, has not allowed mankind a moment's rest.

There is another feature which was already present in totemism and which has been preserved unaltered in religion. The tension of ambivalence was evidently too great for any contrivance to be able to counteract it; or it is possible that psychological conditions in general are unfavourable to getting rid of these antithetical conditions. However that may be, we find that the ambivalence implicit in the father-complex persists in totemism and in religions generally. Totemic religion not only comprised expressions of remorse and attempts at atonement, it also served as a remembrance of the triumph over the father. Satisfaction over that triumph led to the institution of the memorial festival of the totem meal, in which the restrictions of deferred obedience no longer held. Thus it became a duty to repeat the crime of parricide again and again in the sacrifice of the totem animal, whenever, as a result of the changing conditions of life, the cherished fruit of the crime—appropriation of the paternal attributes—threatened to disappear. We shall not be surprised to find that the element of filial rebelliousness also emerges, in the *later* products of religion, often in the strangest disguises and transformations.

Hitherto we have followed the developments of the *affectionate* current of feeling towards the father, transformed into remorse, as we find them in religion and in moral ordinances (which are not sharply distinguished in totemism). But we must not overlook the fact that it was in the main with the impulses that led to parricide that the victory lay. For a long time afterwards, the social fraternal feelings, which were the basis of the whole transformation, continued to exercise a profound influence on the development of society. They found expression in the sanctification of the blood tie, in the emphasis upon the solidarity of all life within the same clan. In thus guaranteeing one another's lives, the brothers were declaring that no one of them must be treated by another as their father was treated by them all jointly. They were precluding the possibility of a repetition of their father's fate. To the religiously-based prohibition against killing the totem was now added the socially-based prohibition against fratricide. It was not until long afterwards that the prohibition ceased to be limited to members of the clan and assumed the simple form: "Thou shalt do no more murder." The patriarchal horde was replaced in the first instance by the fraternal clan, whose existence was assured by the blood tie. Society was now based on complicity in the common crime; religion was based on the sense of guilt and the remorse attaching to it; while morality was based partly on the exigencies of this society and partly on the penance demanded by the sense of guilt.

Thus psycho-analysis, in contradiction to the more recent views of the totemic system but in agreement with the earlier ones, requires us to assume that totemism and exogamy were intimately connected and had a simultaneous origin.

A great number of powerful motives restrain me from any attempt at picturing the further development of religions from their origin in totemism to their condition to-day. I will only follow two threads whose course I can trace with especial clarity as they run through the pattern: the theme of the totemic sacrifice and the relation of son to father.

Robertson Smith has shown us that the ancient totem meal recurs in the original form of the sacrifice. The meaning of the act is the same: sanctification through participation in a common meal. The sense of guilt, which can only be allayed by the solidarity of all the participants, also persists. What is new is the clan deity, in whose supposed presence the sacrifice is performed, who participates in the meal as though he were a clansman, and with whom those who consume the meal become identified. How does the god come to be in a situation to which he was originally a stranger?

The answer might be that in the meantime the concept of God had emerged—from some unknown source—and had taken control of the whole of religious life; and that, like everything else that was to survive, the totem meal had been obliged to find a point of contact with the new system. The psycho-analysis of individual human beings, however, teaches us with quite special insistence that the god of each of them is formed in the likeness of his father, that his personal relation to God depends on his relation to his father in the flesh and oscillates and changes along with that relation, and that at bottom God is nothing other than an exalted father. As in the case of totemism, psychoanalysis recommends us to have faith in the believers who call God their father, just as the totem was called the tribal ancestor. If psycho-analysis deserves any attention, then—without prejudice to any other sources or meanings of the concept of God, upon which psycho-analysis can throw no light—the paternal element in that concept must be a most important one. But in that case the father is represented twice over in the situation of primitive sacrifice: once as God and once as the totemic animal victim. And, even granting the restricted number of explanations open to psycho-analysis, one must ask whether this is possible and what sense it can have.

We know that there are a multiplicity of relations between the god and the sacred animal (the totem or the sacrificial victim). (1) Each god usually has an animal (and quite often several animals) sacred to him. (2) In the case of certain specially sacred sacrifices—"mystic" sacrifices—the victim was precisely the animal sacred to the god.... (3) The god was often worshipped in the shape of an animal (or, to look at it in another way, animals were worshipped as gods) long after the age of totemism. (4) In myths the god often transforms himself into an animal, and frequently into the animal that is sacred to him.

It therefore seems plausible to suppose that the god himself was the totem animal, and that he developed out of it at a later stage of religious feeling. But we are relieved from the necessity for further discussion by the consideration that the totem is nothing other than a surrogate of the father. Thus, while the totem may be the *first* form of father-surrogate, the god will be a later one, in which the father has regained his human shape. A new creation such as this, derived from what constitutes the root of every form of religion—a longing for the father—might occur if in the process of time some fundamental change had taken place in man's relation to the father, and perhaps, too, in his relation to animals.

Signs of the occurrence of changes of this kind may easily be seen, even if we leave on one side the beginning of a mental estrangement from animals and the disrupting of totemism owing to domestication.... There was one factor in the state of affairs produced by the elimination of the father which was bound in the course of time to cause an enormous increase in the longing felt for him. Each single one of the brothers who had banded together for the purpose of killing their father was inspired by a wish to become like him and had given expression to it by incorporating parts of their father's surrogate in the totem meal. But, in consequence of the pressure exercised upon each participant by the fraternal clan as a whole, that wish could not be fulfilled. For the future no one could or might ever again attain the father's supreme power, even though that was what all of them had striven for. Thus after a long lapse of time their bitterness against their father, which had driven them to their deed, grew less, and their longing for him had increased; and it became possible for an ideal to emerge which embodied the unlimited power of the primal father against whom they had once fought as well as their readiness to submit to him. As a result of decisive cultural changes, the original democratic equality that had prevailed among all the individual clansmen became untenable; and there developed at the same time an inclination, based on veneration felt for particular human individuals, to revive the ancient paternal ideal by creating gods. The notion of a man becoming a god or of a god dying strikes us to-day as shockingly presumptuous; but even in classical antiquity there was nothing revolting in it. The elevation of the father who had once been murdered into a god from whom the clan claimed descent was a far more serious attempt at atonement than had been the ancient covenant with the totem....

It seems certain ... that the change in attitude to the father was not restricted to the sphere of religion but that it extended in a consistent manner to that other side of human life which had been affected by the father's removal—to social organization. With the introduction of father-deities a fatherless society gradually changed into one organized on a patriarchal basis. The family was a restoration of the former primal horde and it gave back to fathers a large portion of their former rights. There were once more fathers, but the social achievements of the fraternal clan had not been abandoned; and the gulf between the new fathers of a family and the unrestricted primal father of the horde was wide enough to guarantee the continuance of the religious craving, the persistence of an unappeased longing for the father.

We see, then, that in the scene of sacrifice before the god of the clan the father *is* in fact represented twice over—as the god and as the totemic animal victim.... The ambivalent attitude towards the father has found a plastic expression in it, and so, too, has the victory of the son's affectionate emotions over his hostile ones. The scene of the father's vanquishment, of his greatest defeat, has become the stuff for the representation of his supreme triumph. The importance which is everywhere, without exception, ascribed to sacrifice lies in the fact that it offers satisfaction to the father for the outrage inflicted on him in the same act in which that deed is commemorated.

As time went on, the animal lost its sacred character and the sacrifice lost its connection with the totem feast; it became a simple offering to the deity, an act of renunciation in favour of the god. God Himself had become so far exalted above mankind that He could only be approached through an intermediary—the priest....

Nevertheless it would be a mistake to suppose that the hostile impulses inherent in the father-complex were completely silenced during this period of revived paternal authority. On the contrary, the first phases of dominance of the two new father-surrogates—gods and kings—show the most energetic signs of the ambivalence that remains a characteristic of religion.

In his great work, *The Golden Bough,* Frazer...puts forward the view that the earliest kings of the Latin tribes were foreigners who played the part of a god and were solemnly executed at a particular festival. The annual sacrifice (or, as a variant, self-sacrifice) of a god seems to have been an essential element in the Semitic religions. The ceremonials of human sacrifice, performed in the most different parts of the inhabited globe, leave very little doubt that the victims met their end as representatives of the deity; and these sacrificial rites can be traced into late times, with an inanimate effigy or puppet taking the place of the living human being. The theanthropic [divine-human: ed.] sacrifice of the god, into which it is unfortunately impossible for me to enter here as fully as into animal sacrifice, throws a searching retrospective light upon the meaning of the older forms of sacrifice.... It confesses, with a frankness that could hardly be excelled, to the fact that the object of the act of sacrifice has always been the same—namely what is now worshipped as God, that is to say, the father. The problem of the relation between animal and human sacrifice thus admits of a simple solution. The original animal sacrifice was already a substitute for a human sacrifice—for the ceremonial killing of the father; so that, when the father-surrogate once more resumed its human shape, the animal sacrifice too could be changed back into a human sacrifice.

The memory of the first great act of sacrifice thus proved indestructible, in spite of every effort to forget it; and at the very point at which men sought to be at the farthest distance from the motives that led to it, its undistorted reproduction emerged in the form of the sacrifice of the god....

Let us assume it to be a fact, then, that in the course of the later development of religions the two driving factors, the son's sense of guilt and the son's rebelliousness, never became extinct. Whatever attempt was made at solving the religious problem, whatever kind of reconciliation was effected between these two opposing mental forces, sooner or later broke down, under the combined influence, no doubt, of historical events, cultural changes and internal psychical modifications.

∼

At the conclusion, then, of this exceedingly condensed inquiry, I should like to insist that its outcome shows that the beginnings of religion, morals, society and art converge in the Oedipus complex. This is in complete agreement with the psycho-analytic finding that the same complex constitutes the nucleus of all neuroses, so far as our present knowledge goes. It seems to me a most surprising discovery that the problems of social psychology, too, should prove soluble on the basis of one single concrete point—man's relation to his father. It is even possible that yet another psychological problem belongs in this same connection. I have often had occasion to point out that emotional ambivalence in the proper sense of the term—that is, the simultaneous existence of love and hate towards the same object—lies at the root of many cultural institutions. We know nothing of the origin of this ambivalence. One possible assumption is that it is a fundamental phenomenon of our emotional life. But it seems to me quite worth considering another possibility, namely that originally it formed no part of our emotional life but was acquired by the human race in connection with their father-complex, precisely where the psycho-analytic examination of modern individuals still finds it revealed at its strongest.

Before I bring my remarks to a close, however, I must find room to point out the uncertainties of my premises...[and] the difficulties involved in my conclusions...

No one can have failed to observe...that I have taken as the basis of my whole position the existence of a collective mind, in which mental processes occur just as they do in the mind of an individual....

Without the assumption of a collective mind, which makes it possible to neglect the interruptions of mental acts caused by the extinction of the individual, social psychology in general cannot exist....And what are the ways and means employed by one generation in order to hand on its mental states to the next one? I shall not pretend that...direct communication and tradition...are enough to account for the process. Social psychology shows very little interest, on the whole, in the manner in which the required continuity in the mental life of successive generations is established. A part of the problem seems to be met by the inheritance of psychical dispositions which, however, need to be given some sort of impetus in the life of the individual before they can be roused into actual operation.... The problem would seem even more difficult if we had to admit that mental impulses could be so completely suppressed as to leave no trace whatever behind them. But that is not the case.... For psycho-analysis has shown us that everyone possesses in his unconscious mental activity an apparatus which enables him to interpret other people's reactions, that is, to undo the distortions which other people have imposed on the expression of their feelings. An unconscious understanding such as this of all the customs, ceremonies and dogmas left behind by the original relation to the father may have made it possible for later generations to take over their heritage of emotion....

This creative sense of guilt still persists among us. We find it operating in an asocial manner in neurotics.... If, however, we inquire among these neurotics to discover what were the deeds which provoked these reactions, we shall be disappointed. We find no deeds, but only impulses and emotions...held back from their achievement. What lie behind the sense of guilt of neurotics are always *psychical* realities and never *factual* ones. What characterizes neurotics is that they prefer psychical to factual reality and react just as seriously to thoughts as normal people do to realities.

May not the same have been true of primitive men? We are justified in believing that, as one of the phenomena of their narcissistic organization, they overvalued their psychical acts to an extraordinary degree. Accordingly the mere hostile *impulse* against the father, the mere existence of a wishful *phantasy* of killing and devouring him, would have been enough to produce the moral reaction that created totemism and taboo. In this way we should avoid the necessity for deriving the origin of our cultural legacy, of which we justly feel so proud, from a hideous crime, revolting to all our feelings. No damage would thus be done to the causal chain stretching from the beginning to the present day, for psychical reality would be strong enough to bear the weight of these consequences.

The Future of an Illusion

In this essay—the clearest and most conversational of his discussions centered on religion—Freud draws an analogy between faith in God and obsessional neurosis; he finds religious belief rooted in a regression to the childhood need of a father to dispel life's terrors.

[I] n past times religious ideas, in spite of their incontrovertible lack of authentication, have exercised the strongest possible influence on mankind. This is a fresh psychological problem. We must ask where the inner force of those doctrines lies and to what it is that they owe their efficacy, independent as it is of recognition by reason.

VI

I think we have prepared the way sufficiently for an answer to both these questions. It will be found if we turn our attention to the psychical origin of religious ideas. These, which are given out as teachings, are not precipitates of experience or end results of thinking: they are illusions, fulfilments of the oldest, strongest and most urgent wishes of mankind. The secret of their strength lies in the strength of those wishes. As we already know, the terrifying impression of helplessness in childhood aroused the need for protection—for protection through love—which was provided by the father; and the recognition that this helplessness lasts throughout life made it necessary to cling to the existence of a father, but this time a more powerful one. Thus the benevolent rule of a divine Providence allays our fear of the dangers of life; the establishment of a moral world-order ensures the fulfilment of the demands of justice, which have so often remained unfulfilled in human civilization; and the prolongation of earthly existence in a future life provides the local and temporal framework in which these wish-fulfilments shall take place. Answers to the riddles that tempt the curiosity of man, such as how the universe began or what the relation is between body and mind, are developed in conformity with the underlying assumptions of this system. It is an enormous relief to the individual psyche if the conflicts of its childhood arising from the father-complex—conflicts which it has never wholly overcome—are removed from it and brought to a solution which is universally accepted.

When I say that these things are all illusions, I must define the meaning of the word. An illusion is not the same thing as an error; nor is it necessarily an error. Aristotle's belief that vermin are developed out of dung (a belief to which ignorant people still cling) was an error; so was the belief of a former generation of doctors that *tabes dorsalis* [atrophy of the spine: ed.] is the result of sexual excess. It would be incorrect to call these errors illusions. On the other hand, it was an illusion of Columbus's that he had discovered a new sea-route to the Indies. The part played by his wish in this error is very clear. One may describe as an illusion the assertion made by certain nationalists that the Indo-Germanic race is the only one capable of civilization; or the belief, which was only destroyed by psycho-analysis, that children are creatures without sexuality. What is characteristic of illusions is that they are derived from human wishes. In this respect they come near to psychiatric delusions. But they differ from them, too, apart from the more complicated structure of delusions. In the case of delusions, we emphasize as essential their being in contradiction with reality. Illusions need not necessarily be false—that is to say, unrealizable or in contradiction to reality. For instance, a middle-class girl may have the illusion that a prince will come and marry her. This is possible; and a few such cases have occurred. That the Messiah will come and found a golden age is much less likely. Whether one classifies this belief as an illusion or as something analogous to a delusion will depend on one's personal attitude. Examples of illusions which have proved true are not easy to find, but the illusion of the alchemists that all metals can be turned into gold might be one of them. The wish to have a great deal of gold, as much gold as possible, has, it is true, been a good deal damped by our present-day knowledge of the determinants of wealth, but chemistry no longer regards the transmutation of metals into gold as impossible. Thus we call a belief an illusion when a wish-fulfilment is a prominent factor in its motivation, and in doing so we disregard its relations to reality, just as the illusion itself sets no store by verification.

Having thus taken our bearings, let us return once more to the question of religious doctrines. We can now repeat that all of them are illusions and insusceptible of proof. No one can be compelled to think them true, to believe in them. Some of them are so improbable, so incompatible with everything we have laboriously discovered about the reality of the world, that we may compare them—if we pay proper regard to the psycho- logical differences—to delusions. Of the reality value of most of them we cannot judge; just as they cannot be proved, so they cannot be refuted. We still know too little to make a critical approach to them. The riddles of the universe reveal themselves only slowly to our investigation; there are many questions to which science to-day can give no answer. But scientific work is the only road which can lead us to a knowledge of reality outside ourselves. It is once again merely an illusion to expect anything from intuition and introspection; they can give us nothing but particulars about our own mental life, which are hard to interpret, never any information about the questions which religious doctrine finds it so easy to answer. It would be insolent to let one's own arbitrary will step into the breach and, according to one's personal estimate, declare this or that part of the religious system to be less or more acceptable. Such questions are too momentous for that; they might be called too sacred.

At this point one must expect to meet with an objection. "Well then, if even obdurate sceptics admit that the assertions of religion cannot be refuted by reason, why should I not believe in them, since they have so much on their side—tradition, the agreement of mankind, and all the consolations they offer?" Why not, indeed? Just as no one can be forced to believe, so no one can be forced to disbelieve. But do not let us be satisfied with deceiving ourselves that arguments like these take us along the road of correct thinking. If ever there was a case of a lame excuse we have it here. Ignorance is ignorance; no right to believe anything can be derived from it. In other matters no sensible person will behave so irresponsibly or rest content with such feeble grounds for his opinions and for the line he takes. It is only in the highest and most sacred things that he allows himself to do so. In reality these are only attempts at pretending to oneself or to other people that one is still firmly attached to religion, when one has long since cut oneself loose from it. Where questions of religion are concerned, people are guilty of every possible sort of dishonesty and intellectual misdemeanor. Philosophers stretch the meaning of words until they retain scarcely anything of their original sense. They give the name of "God" to some vague abstraction which they have created for themselves; having done so they can pose before all the world as deists, as believers in God, and they can even boast that they have recognized a higher, purer concept of God, notwithstanding that their God is now nothing more than an insubstantial shadow and no longer the mighty personality of religious doctrines. Critics persist in describing as "deeply religious" anyone who admits to a sense of man's insignificance or impotence in the face of the universe, although what constitutes the essence of the religious attitude is not this feeling but only the next step after it, the reaction to it which seeks a remedy for it. The man who goes no further, but humbly acquiesces in the small part which human beings play in the great world—such a man is, on the contrary, irreligious in the truest sense of the word.

To assess the truth-value of religious doctrines does not lie within the scope of the present enquiry. It is enough for us that we have recognized them as being, in their psychological nature, illusions. But we do not have to conceal the fact that this discovery also strongly influences our attitude to the question which must appear to many to be the most important of all. We know approximately at what periods and by what kind of men religious doctrines were created. If in addition we discover the motives which led to this, our attitude to the problem of religion will undergo a marked displacement. We shall tell ourselves that it would be very nice if there were a God who created the world and was a benevolent Providence, and if there were a moral order in the universe and an after-life; but it is a very striking fact that all this is exactly as we are bound to wish it to be. And it would be more remarkable still if our wretched, ignorant and downtrodden ancestors had succeeded in solving all these difficult riddles of the universe.

∼

We now observe that the store of religious ideas includes not only wish-fulfilments but important historical recollections. This concurrent influence of past and present must give religion a truly incomparable wealth of power. But perhaps with the help of an analogy yet another discovery may begin to dawn on us. Though it is not a good plan to transplant ideas far from the soil in which they grew up, yet here is a conformity which we cannot avoid pointing out. We know that a human child cannot successfully complete its development to the civilized stage without passing through a phase of neurosis sometimes of greater and sometimes of less distinctness. This is because so many instinctual demands which will later be unserviceable cannot be suppressed by the rational operation of the child's intellect but have to be tamed by acts of repression, behind which, as a rule, lies the motive of anxiety. Most of these infantile neuroses are overcome spontaneously in the course of growing up, and this is especially true of the obsessional neuroses of childhood. The remainder can be cleared up later still by psycho-analytic treatment. In just the same way, one might assume, humanity as a whole, in its development through the ages, fell into states analogous to the neuroses, and for the same reasons—namely because in the times of its ignorance and intellectual weakness the instinctual renunciations indispensable for man's communal existence had been achieved by it by means of purely affective forces. The precipitates of these processes resembling repression which took place in prehistoric times still remained attached to civilization for long periods. Religion would thus be the universal obsessional neurosis of humanity; like the obsessional neurosis of children, it arose out of the Oedipus complex, out of the relation to the father. If this view is right, it is to be supposed that a turning-away from religion is bound to occur with the fatal inevitability of a process of growth, and that we find ourselves at this very juncture in the middle of that phase of development. Our behaviour should therefore be modelled on that of a sensible teacher who does not oppose an impending new development but seeks to ease its path and mitigate the violence of its irruption. Our analogy does not, to be sure, exhaust the essential nature of religion. If, on the one hand, religion brings with it obsessional restrictions, exactly as an individual obsessional neurosis does, on the other hand it comprises a system of wishful illusions together with a disavowal of reality, such as we find in an isolated form nowhere else but in amentia, in a state of blissful hallucinatory confusion. But these are only analogies, by the help of which we endeavour to understand a social phenomenon; the pathology of the individual does not supply us with a fully valid counterpart.

It has been repeatedly pointed out (by myself and in particular by Theodor Reik) in how great detail the analogy between religion and obsessional neurosis can be followed out, and how many of the peculiarities and vicissitudes in the formation of religion can be understood in that light. And it tallies well with this that devout believers are safeguarded in a high degree against the risk of certain neurotic illnesses; their acceptance of the universal neurosis spares them the task of constructing a personal one.

Our knowledge of the historical worth of certain religious doctrines increases our respect for them, but does not invalidate our proposal that they should cease to be put forward as the reasons for the precepts of civilization. On the contrary! Those historical residues have helped us to view religious teachings, as it were, as neurotic relics, and we may now argue that the time has probably come, as it does in an analytic treatment, for replacing the effects of repression by the results of the rational operation of the intellect. We may foresee, but hardly regret, that such a process of remoulding will not stop at renouncing the solemn transfiguration of cultural precepts, but that a general revision of them will result in many of them being done away with. In this way our appointed task of reconciling men to civilization will to a great extent be achieved. We need not deplore the renunciation of historical truth when we put forward rational grounds for the precepts of civilization. The truths contained in religious doctrines are after all so distorted and systematically disguised that the mass of humanity cannot recognize them as truth.

～

I must contradict you when you go on to argue that men are completely unable to do without the consolation of the religious illusion, that without it they could not bear the troubles of life and the cruelties of reality. That is true, certainly, of the men into whom you have instilled the sweet—or bitter-sweet—poison from childhood onwards. But what of the other men, who have been sensibly brought up? Perhaps those who do not suffer from the neurosis will need no intoxicant to deaden it. They will, it is true, find themselves in a difficult situation. They will have to admit to themselves the full extent of their helplessness and their insignificance in the machinery of the universe; they can no longer be the centre of creation, no longer the object of tender care on the part of a beneficent Providence. They will be in the same position as a child who has left the parental house where he was so warm and comfortable. But surely infantilism is destined to be surmounted. Men cannot remain children for ever; they must in the end go out into "hostile life." We may call this "*education to reality.*" Need I confess to you that the sole purpose of my book is to point out the necessity for this forward step?

You are afraid, probably, that they will not stand up to the hard test? Well, let us at least hope they will. It is something, at any rate, to know that one is thrown upon one's own resources. One learns then to make a proper use of them. And men are not entirely without assistance. Their scientific knowledge has taught them much since the days of the Deluge, and it will increase their power still further. And, as for the great necessities of Fate, against which there is no help, they will learn to endure them with resignation. . . . By withdrawing their expectations from the other world and concentrating all their liberated energies into their life on earth, they will probably succeed in achieving a state of things in which life will become tolerable for everyone and civilization no longer oppressive to anyone.

Moses and Monotheism

Freud here argues that the prophet Moses was an Egyptian who acquired the doctrine of a strict, elevated monotheism from the Pharaoh Akenaten and passed it to the Hebrews when he led the Exodus from captivity. In the desert, however, he was murdered, and the doctrine was lost, or repressed, while a new faith in a darker deity of vengeance and warfare took its place. Later on, in a remarkable "return of the repressed," this Mosaic monotheism was recovered by the Hebrew prophets, thence to become the central article of Jewish faith and its legacy to the world.

Here, then, is the historical background of the events which have absorbed our interest. As a result of the conquests of the Eighteenth Dynasty, Egypt became a world-empire. The new imperialism was reflected in the development of the religious ideas, if not of the whole people, at least of its ruling and intellectually active upper stratum. Under the influence of the priests of the sun-god at On (Heliopolis), strengthened perhaps by impulses from Asia, the idea arose of a universal god Aten to whom restriction to a single country and a single people no longer applied. In the young Amenophis IV a Pharaoh came to the throne who had no higher interest than the development of this idea of a god.

[U. S. rights] FROM *Moses and Monotheism* by Sigmund Freud, translated by Katherine Jones, translation copyright 1939 by Alfred A. Knopf, Inc. and renewed 1967 by Ernst L. Freud and Anna Freud. Used by permission of Alfred A. Knopf, a division of Random House, Inc. [Canadian rights] Sigmund Freud © Copyrights. The Institute of Psycho-Analysis and The Hogarth Press for permission to quote from "Moses and Monotheism" (vol. 23) from *The Standard Edition of the Complete Psychological Works of Sigmund Freud* translated and edited by James Strachey. Reprinted by permission of The Random House Group Limited, United Kingdom.

He promoted the religion of Aten into the state religion, and through him the universal god became the *only* god: everything that was told of other gods was deceit and lies. With magnificent inflexibility he resisted every temptation to magical thought, and he rejected the illusion, so dear to Egyptians in particular, of a life after death. In an astonishing presentiment of later scientific discovery he recognized in the energy of solar radiation the source of all life on earth and worshipped it as the symbol of the power of his god. He boasted of his joy in the creation and of his life in Ma'at (truth and justice).

This is the first and perhaps the clearest case of a monotheist religion in human history; a deeper insight into the historical and psychological determinants of its origin would be of immeasurable value. Care has however been taken that none too much information about the Aten religion should reach us. Already under Akhenaten's feeble successors all that he had created collapsed. The vengeance of the priesthood which he had suppressed raged against his memory; the Aten religion was abolished, the capital city of the Pharaoh, who was branded as a criminal, was destroyed and plundered.... Akhenaten's reform seemed to be an episode doomed to be forgotten.

Thus far what is established historically; and now our hypothetical sequel begins. Among those in Akhenaten's *entourage* there was a man who was perhaps called Tuthmosis, like many other people at that time—the name is not of great importance except that its second component must have been "—mose." He was in a high position and a convinced adherent of the Aten religion, but, in contrast to the meditative king, he was energetic and passionate. For him the death of Akhenaten and the abolition of his religion meant the end of all his expectations. He could remain in Egypt only as an outlaw or as a renegade. Perhaps as governor of the frontier province he had come in contact with a Semitic tribe which had immigrated into it a few generations earlier. Under the necessity of his disappointment and loneliness he turned to these foreigners and with them sought compensation for his losses. He chose them as his people and tried to realize his ideals in them. After he had left Egypt with them, accompanied by his followers, he made them holy by the mark of circumcision, gave them laws and introduced them into the doctrines of the Aten religion, which the Egyptians had just thrown off....

We must take the period of the interregnum after 1350 B.C. as the date of the Exodus from Egypt. The interval of time which followed, up to the completion of the occupation of the land of Canaan, is particularly inscrutable. Modern historical research has been able to extract two facts from the obscurity which the biblical narrative has left, or rather created, at this point. The first of these facts, discovered by Ernst Sellin, is that the Jews, who, even by the account in the Bible, were headstrong and unruly towards their law-giver and leader, rose against him one day, killed him and threw off the religion of the Aten which had been imposed on them, just as the Egyptians had thrown it off earlier. The second fact, demonstrated by Eduard Meyer, is that those Jews who had returned from Egypt united later on with closely related tribes in the region between Palestine, the Sinai Peninsula and Arabia, and that there, in a well-watered locality named Kadesh, under the influence of the Arabian Midianites, they took on a new religion, the worship of the volcano god Yahweh. Soon after this they were ready to invade Canaan as conquerors....

Our interest follows the fortunes of Moses and of his doctrines, to which the rising of the Jews had only apparently put an end. From the account given by the Yahwist, which was written down in about 1000 B.C. but was certainly based on earlier records, we have discovered that the union and the founding of the religion at Kadesh were accompanied by a compromise in which the two sides are still easily distinguishable. The one partner was only concerned to disavow the novelty and foreign character of the god Yahweh and to increase his claim to the people's devotion; the other partner was anxious not to sacrifice to him precious memories of the liberation from Egypt and of the grand figure of the leader, Moses. The second side succeeded, too, in introducing both the fact and the man into the new account of prehistory, in retaining at least the external mark of the religion of Moses—circumcision—and possibly in establishing certain restrictions on the use of the name of the new god. As we have said, the representatives of these claims were the descendants of the followers of Moses, the Levites, who were separated from his contemporaries and compatriots by only a few generations and were still attached to his memory by a living recollection. The poetically embellished narrative which we attribute to the Yahwist, and to his later rival the Elohist, were like mausoleums beneath which, withdrawn from the knowledge of later generations, the true account of those early things—of the nature of the Mosaic religion and of the violent end of the great man—was, as it were, to find its eternal rest. And if we have guessed what happened correctly, there is nothing left about it that is puzzling; but it might very well have signified the final end of the Moses episode in the history of the Jewish people.

The remarkable thing, however, is that that was not the case—that the most powerful effects of the people's experiences were to come to light only later and to force their way into reality in the course of many centuries. It is unlikely that Yahweh differed much in character from the gods of the surrounding peoples and tribes. It is true that he struggled with them, just as the peoples themselves fought with one another, but we cannot suppose that it came into the head of a Yahweh-worshipper of those days to deny the existence of the gods of Canaan or Moab or Amalek, and so on, any more than to deny the existence of the peoples who believed in them.

The monotheist idea, which had flared up with Akhenaten, had grown dark once more and was to remain in darkness for a long time to come.... Going back to earlier times, we may say that the god Yahweh certainly bore no resemblance to the Mosaic god. Aten had been a pacifist like his representative on earth—or more properly, his prototype—the Pharaoh Akhenaten, who looked on passively while the world-empire conquered by his ancestors fell to pieces. No doubt Yahweh was better suited to a people who were starting out to occupy new homelands by force. And everything in the Mosaic god that deserved admiration was quite beyond the comprehension of the primitive masses.

~

The Latency Period and Tradition

We confess the belief... that the idea of a single god, as well as the rejection of magically effective ceremonial and the stress upon ethical demands made in his name, were in fact Mosaic doctrines, to which no attention was paid to begin with, but which, after a long interval had elapsed, came into operation and eventually became permanently established. How are we to explain a delayed effect of this kind and where do we meet with a similar phenomenon?...

It may happen that a man who has experienced some frightful accident—a railway collision, for instance—leaves the scene of the event apparently uninjured. In the course of the next few weeks, however, he develops a number of severe psychical and motor symptoms which can only be traced to his shock, the concussion or whatever else it was. He now has a "traumatic neurosis." It is a quite unintelligible—that is to say, new—fact. The time that has passed between the accident and the first appearance of the symptoms is described as the "incubation period," in a clear allusion to the pathology of infectious diseases. On reflection, it must strike us that, in spite of the fundamental difference between the two cases—the problem of traumatic neurosis and that of Jewish monotheism—there is nevertheless one point of agreement: namely, in the characteristic that might be described as "latency." According to our assured hypothesis, in the history of the Jewish religion there was a long period after the defection from the religion of Moses during which no sign was to be detected of the monotheist idea, of the contempt for ceremonial or of the great emphasis on ethics. We are thus prepared for the possibility that the solution of our problem is to be looked for in a particular psychological situation....

The Jewish people had abandoned the Aten religion brought to them by Moses and had turned to the worship of another god who differed little from the Baalim [fertility gods: ed.] of the neighbouring peoples. All the tendentious efforts of later times failed to disguise this shameful fact. But the Mosaic religion had not vanished without leaving a trace; some sort of memory of it had kept alive—a possibly obscured and distorted tradition. And it was this tradition of a great past which continued to operate (from the background, as it were), which gradually acquired more and more power over people's minds and which in the end succeeded in changing the god Yahweh into the Mosaic god and in re-awakening into life the religion of Moses that had been introduced and then abandoned long centuries before. That a tradition thus sunk in oblivion should exercise such a powerful effect on the mental life of a people is an unfamiliar idea to us. We find ourselves here in the field of group psychology, where we do not feel at home. We shall look about for analogies, for facts that are at least of a similar nature, even though in different fields. And facts of that sort are, I believe, to be found....

The Analogy

The only satisfying analogy to the remarkable course of events that we have found in the history of the Jewish religion lies in an apparently remote field; but it is very complete, and approaches identity. In it we once more come upon the phenomenon of latency, the emergence of unintelligible manifestations calling for an explanation and an early, and later forgotten, event as a necessary determinant....

This analogy is met with in psychopathology, in the genesis of human neuroses—in a field, that is to say, belonging to the psychology of individuals, while religious phenomena have of course to be reckoned as part of group psychology. We shall see that this analogy is not so surprising as might at first be thought—indeed that it is more like a postulate.

We give the name of *traumas* to those impressions, experienced early and later forgotten, to which we attach such great importance in the aetiology of the neuroses.... We must often resign ourselves to saying that all we have before us is an unusual, abnormal reaction to experiences and demands which affect everyone, but are worked over and dealt with by other people in another manner which may be called normal. When we have nothing else at our disposal for explaining a neurosis but hereditary and constitutional dispositions, we are naturally tempted to say that it was not acquired but developed.

~

And now let us enquire about latency.... A trauma in childhood may be followed immediately by a neurotic outbreak, an infantile neurosis, with an abundance of efforts at defence, and accompanied by the formation of symptoms. This neurosis may last a considerable time and cause marked disturbances, but it may also run a latent course and be overlooked.... Not until later does the change take place with which the definitive neurosis becomes manifest as a belated effect of the trauma. This occurs either at the irruption of puberty or some while later. In the former case it happens because the instincts, intensified by physical maturation, are able now to take up the struggle again in which they were at first defeated by the defence.... The phenomenon of a latency of the neurosis between the first reactions to the trauma and the later outbreak of the illness must be regarded as typical.

∼

Application

Early trauma—defence—latency—outbreak of neurotic illness—partial return of the repressed. Such is the formula which we have laid down for the development of a neurosis. The reader is now invited to take the step of supposing that something occurred in the life of the human species similar to what occurs in the life of individuals: of supposing, that is, that here too events occurred of a sexually aggressive nature, which left behind them permanent consequences but were for the most part fended off and forgotten, and which after a long latency came into effect and created phenomena similar to symptoms in their structure and purpose.

We believe that we can guess these events and we propose to show that their symptom-like consequences are the phenomena of religion. Since the emergence of the idea of evolution no longer leaves room for doubt that the human race has a prehistory, and since this is unknown—that is, forgotten—a conclusion of this kind almost carries the weight of a postulate. When we learn that in both cases the operative and forgotten traumas relate to life in the human family, we can greet this as a highly welcome, unforeseen bonus which has not been called for by our discussions up to this point.

∼

What is the place of religion in this connection? I think we are completely justified in regarding totemism, with its worship of a father-substitute, with its ambivalence as shown by the totem meal, with its institution of memorial festivals and of prohibitions whose infringement was punished by death—we are justified, I say, in regarding totemism as the first form in which religion was manifested in human history and in confirming the fact of its having been linked from the first with social regulations and moral obligations....

The first step away from totemism was the humanizing of the being who was worshipped. In place of the animals, human gods appear, whose derivation from the totem is not concealed....

If our account of primaeval history is accepted as on the whole worthy of belief, two sorts of elements will be recognized in religious doctrines and rituals: on the one hand fixations to the ancient history of the family and survivals of it, and on the other hand revivals of the past and returns, after long intervals, of what has been forgotten. It is this last portion which, hitherto overlooked and therefore not understood, is to be demonstrated here in at least one impressive instance.

It is worth specially stressing the fact that each portion which returns from oblivion asserts itself with peculiar force, exercises an incomparably powerful influence on people in the mass, and raises an irresistible claim to truth against which logical objections remain powerless: a kind of *"credo quia absurdum"* ["I believe because it is absurd.": ed.]. This remarkable feature can only be understood on the pattern of the delusions of psychotics.... We must grant an ingredient such as this of what may be called *historical* truth to the dogmas of religion as well, which, it is true, bear the character of psychotic symptoms but which, as group phenomena, escape the curse of isolation.

No other portion of the history of religion has become so clear to us as the introduction of monotheism into Judaism and its continuation in Christianity—if we leave on one side the development which we can trace no less uninterruptedly, from the animal totem to the human god with his regular companions. (Each of the four Christian evangelists still has his own favourite animal.) If we provisionally accept the world-empire of the Pharaohs as the determining cause of the emergence of the monotheist idea, we see that that idea, released from its native soil and transferred to another people was, after a long period of latency, taken hold of by them, preserved by them as a precious possession and, in turn, itself kept them alive by giving them pride in being a chosen people: it was the religion of their primal father to which were attached their hope of reward, of distinction and finally of world-dominion....

The re-establishment of the primal father in his historic rights was a great step forward but it could not be the end. The other portions of the prehistoric tragedy insisted on being recognized. It is not easy to discern what set this process in motion. It appears as though a growing sense of guilt had taken hold of the Jewish people, or perhaps of the whole civilized world of the time, as a precursor to the return of the repressed material. Till at last one of these Jewish people found, in justifying a politico-religious agitator, the occasion for detaching a new—the Christian—religion from Judaism.

～

On further reflection I must admit that I have behaved for a long time as though the inheritance of memory-traces of the experience of our ancestors, independently of direct communication and of the influence of education by the setting of an example, were established beyond question. When I spoke of the survival of a tradition among a people or of the formation of a people's character, I had mostly in mind an inherited tradition of this kind and not one transmitted by communication. Or at least I made no distinction between the two and was not clearly aware of my audacity in neglecting to do so. My position, no doubt, is made more difficult by the present attitude of biological science, which refuses to hear of the inheritance of acquired characters by succeeding generations. I must, however, in all modesty confess that nevertheless I cannot do without this factor in biological evolution....

If we assume the survival of these memory-traces in the archaic heritage, we have bridged the gulf between individual and group psychology: we can deal with peoples as we do with an individual neurotic. Granted that at the time we have no stronger evidence for the presence of memory-traces in the archaic heritage than the residual phenomena of the work of analysis..., yet this evidence seems to us strong enough to postulate that such is the fact. If it is not so, we shall not advance a step further along the path we entered on, either in analysis or in group psychology....

A tradition that was based only on communication could not lead to the compulsive character that attaches to religious phenomena....It must have undergone the fate of being repressed, the condition of lingering in the unconscious, before it is able to display such powerful effects on its return, to bring the masses under its spell, as we have seen with astonishment and hitherto without comprehension in the case of religious tradition. And this consideration weighs heavily in favour of our believing that things really happened in the way we have tried to picture them or at least in some similar way.

~

There is no doubt that it was a mighty prototype of a father which, in the person of Moses, stooped to the poor Jewish bondsmen to assure them that they were his dear children. And no less overwhelming must have been the effect upon them of the idea of an only, eternal, almighty God, to whom they were not too mean for him to make a covenant with them and who promised to care for them if they remained loyal to his worship. It was probably not easy for them to distinguish the image of the man Moses from that of his God; and their feeling was right in this, for Moses may have introduced traits of his own personality into the character of his God—such as his wrathful temper and his relentlessness. And if, this being so, they killed their great man one day, they were only repeating a misdeed which in ancient times has been committed, as prescribed by law, against the Divine King and which, as we know, went back to a still more ancient prototype....

We cannot follow the chain of events further, but if we have rightly recognized these first steps, the monotheist idea returned like a boomerang to the land of its origin. Thus it seems unfruitful to try to fix the credit due to an individual in connection with a new idea. It is clear that many have shared in its development and made contributions to it. And, again it would obviously be unjust to break off the chain of causes at Moses and to neglect what was effected by those who succeeded him and carried on his idea, the Jewish Prophets. The seed of monotheism failed to ripen in Egypt. The same thing might have happened in Israel after the people had thrown off the burdensome and exacting religion. But there constantly arose from the Jewish people men who revived the fading tradition, who renewed the admonitions and demands made by Moses, and who did not rest till what was lost had been established once again. In the course of constant efforts over centuries, and finally owing to two great reforms, one before and one after the Babylonian exile, the transformation was accomplished of the popular god Yahweh into the God whose worship had been forced upon the Jews by Moses. And evidence of the presence of a peculiar psychical aptitude in the masses who had become the Jewish people is revealed by the fact that they were able to produce so many individuals prepared to take on the burdens of the religion of Moses in return for the reward of being the chosen people and perhaps for some other prizes of a similar degree.

∼

The religion of Moses did not produce its effects immediately but in a remarkably indirect manner. This does not mean to say simply that it did not work at once, that it took long periods of time, hundreds of years, to deploy its full effect, for that is self-evident when it is a question of the imprinting of a people's character. But the restriction relates to a fact which we have derived from the history of the Jewish religion or, if you like, have introduced into it. We have said that after a certain time the Jewish people rejected the religion of Moses... —whether they did so completely or retained some of its precepts we cannot guess. If we suppose that in the long period of the seizure of Canaan and the struggle with the peoples inhabiting it the Yahweh religion did not differ essentially from the worship of the other Baalim..., we shall be on historical ground in spite of all the later tendentious efforts to throw a veil over this shaming state of things.

The religion of Moses, however, had not disappeared without leaving a trace. A kind of memory of it had survived, obscured and distorted, supported, perhaps, among individual members of the priestly caste by ancient records. And it was this tradition of a great past which continued to work in the background, as it were, which gradually gained more and more power over men's minds, and which finally succeeded in transforming the god Yahweh into the god of Moses and in calling back to life the religion of Moses which had been established and then abandoned long centuries earlier.

4

Emile Durkheim: The Social as Sacred

If Freud is the name that comes first to mind as the architect of psychoanalytic psychology, something similar can be said of his French contemporary, Emile Durkheim, a figure pivotal to the rise of scientific sociology. Durkheim (1858–1917) championed the key role of society in shaping every dimension of human thought and behavior. His unique achievement arises from a determination to examine all elements of human life—work and leisure, crime and punishment, language and logic, the self and others, education, politics, the arts, and most especially the rituals and beliefs of religion—as inescapably social endeavors.

The stress on society and its influence is familiar enough today, when terms like "social mobility" and "social reform" appear in everyone's conversation. But that familiarity itself is a tribute to Durkheim. In his day, accounts of human belief and behavior tended by default to be strongly individualistic. Durkheim disagreed. For him, humans do not just exist; they *belong*. From the beginning of life, they are bound to communities: to a family or clan, a town, a church, or a political party. He saw these social templates and ties as so important that they need nothing less than a professional discipline—sociology—specifically committed to understanding them.

Durkheim was born in 1858 at Epinal, near Strasbourg in northeastern France. The son of a rabbi, he was raised, like Freud, as a Jew in a predominantly Roman Catholic city and nation. He was a brilliant student, who won a place at the prestigious Ecole Normale Superieur in Paris and later took a professorial appointment at the University of Bordeaux, where a position was created for him. There he pursued an ambitious program of sociological research, writing articles and reviews, creating a new scholarly journal, *L'Anee Sociologique,* and publishing three books: *The Division of Labor* (1893), *The Rules of Sociological Method* (1895), and *Suicide* (1897), the last an intriguing exploration of the social pressures affecting this deeply personal act of despair.

Durkheim's scientific sociology was new, but not without roots. He had read Tylor and Frazer, and took inspiration from his own teacher, Numa Denys Fustel de Coulanges, whose acclaimed study, *The Ancient City* (1864), stressed the role of religion in Greek and Roman communities. He also drew on earlier French thinkers: Baron de Montesquieu from the age of Enlightenment, the socialist St. Simon, and the positivist Auguste Comte. From their writings and others, Durkheim concluded that the modern Western world is set apart from other, earlier societies by two momentous events—the political earthquake of the French Revolution and the economic tidal wave of the industrial revolution.

In 1902 Durkheim was appointed Professor at the University of Paris, achieving the pinnacle of academic prestige in France. While in that post, he devoted his inquiries more directly to the theme of religion. The result, after ten years of labor, was the masterwork of his career: *The Elementary Forms of the Religious Life,* published in 1912. The selections provided here are taken from this book—now a classic text in the theory of religion.

The title of *The Elementary Forms* discloses its theme. Durkheim seeks to uncover certain fundamental units, or building blocks, of religion—what he describes as its "ever present causes" in all places and times. He does not believe that these causes can be found through the comparative method practiced by Tylor and Frazer, who drew on too many examples from too many places and cultures. Far better, he felt, to fix attention on just one primitive culture and draw from the on-scene reports of people who have taken time actually to immerse themselves in its life. Such accounts were in fact available in the careful field studies that had been prepared by two English anthropologists, Baldwin Spencer and F. J. Gillen, and others who had lived among the remote Aborgine peoples of Australia. For Durkheim, one such "well made experiment" offered more value to sociological science than all the tomes of Tylor and Frazer combined.

Durkheim departed from the Victorians, and from Freud, in another way. For him the defining essential of religion was not belief in spiritual, or supernatural, beings, but the distinction that all societies make between things sacred and things profane. The sacred is the realm of important matters, the great concerns that affect the life of the entire community; the profane, in contrast, is the realm of things personal and private, the daily minor needs of the individual. Religion is the system of beliefs and practices related to sacred things, the vital issues of the community; it should be distinguished clearly from an enterprise like magic, whose main interest is the minor, petty interests and ailments of individuals.

Durkheim noticed that at the center of Aborigine religion stands the very thing that so fascinated Freud: worship of the totem. Each of the

Australian clans centers its rituals on a single sacred figure—usually an animal, occasionally a plant—to which it is exclusively attached. The totem image stands at the center of all its assemblies and governs all aspects of clan life. It is surrounded with taboos. While all other animals can be killed and eaten, the clan's totem may not—except on special, sacred occasions when it is ritually sacrificed, and all consume it in a celebratory feast. In simple terms we could say that an Aborigine clan worships its totem, but the truth is actually more subtle. For it is not really the totem itself—the cockatiel or frog or crow, seen as a divinity—that draws the worship of the clan. It is rather what Durkheim calls the "totemic principle"—an impersonal force within and behind the totem. What can this be? He answers: "The god of the clan, the totemic principle, can therefore be nothing else than the clan itself, personified and represented to the imagination under the visible form of the animal or vegetable which serves as totem." In worship of this totem divinity, the clan worships itself essentially, and claims the loyalty and lives of its members.

Once this fundamental fact—that worship of god is worship of the clan—has been recognized, says Durkheim, the remaining pieces in the puzzle of primitive society fit naturally into place. The totem symbol, carved in wood or stone, conveys the permanence of the social community; totemism provides systems of order and classification, connecting persons to clans and dividing clans from each other; totemism explains both the idea and immortality of the soul; the soul is "the clan within" each individual, calling for the denial of the body's selfish physical desires to promote the welfare of the group; the immortality of the soul is simply an affirmation that while individuals die, the clan lives on. Over time the ancestral souls become the clan's guardian spirits, and as they grow in both power and prestige, they become gods.

In the last part of his discussion Durkheim turns from beliefs to rituals. Rituals in his view are more central to religion than beliefs, which invariably change from one time or place to the next. Rituals are performed in two main types of cult—the positive and negative—plus a third called piacular. Taboos, or prohibitions, are the chief instances of negative ritual. They stress the importance of self-sacrifice over self-indulgence, placing the good of the clan first, the interests of self second. The positive cult is illustrated in the great *intichiuma* ceremony, where religious sentiment runs deep and emotions high, and individuals renew their commitment to the life and health of the clan. Similarly, on the solemn occasion of piacular rites, held at times of crisis or death, mourning is not just a private act. Its purpose is to grieve the loss, and repair the injury, to the community.

In the end, says Durkheim, all of the truly "elementary forms" of religion can be found on display in the totemism of Australian primitive culture: the separation of sacred from profane, the social aim and purpose of worship, the ideas of the soul, conscience, and immortality, belief in ancestral spirits and gods, and the basic forms of ritual. In and through all of these aspects, it is apparent that the entire tapestry of religion is in its essence social. Its real nature is not to make claims about the existence of gods, forgiveness of sins, or life after death. For all of these are simply symbolic representations of profoundly social needs and sentiments. Religion's true role is not to bring people to a god or offer them salvation in a realm beyond; it is rather to anchor them, here and now, in the clan, the community that shapes and sustains their lives.

The originality of this argument as Durkheim patiently develops it in *The Elementary Forms* lies not just in its inventive account of religion as both mirror and template of a primitive society, but in the unusually various and fertile applications it offers for discerning the role of religion in societies of other places and times, including our own.

Defining Religion: The Sacred and the Profane

The following series of selections traces the architecture of Durkheim's argument, beginning from his distinctive definition of religion in terms of the sacred and profane and continuing through his selection of Aborigine culture as his test case, his discussion of the soul, immortality, and asceticism, his account of the rise of the gods, and finally his address to the importance of rituals: positive, negative, and piacular.

Religious phenomena are naturally arranged in two fundamental categories: beliefs and rites. The first are states of opinion, and consist in representations; the second are determined modes of action. Between these two classes of facts there is all the difference which separates thought from action.

The rites can be defined and distinguished from other human practices, moral practices, for example, only by the special nature of their object. A moral rule prescribes certain manners of acting to us, just as a rite does, but which are addressed to a different class of objects. So it is the object of the rite which must be characterized, if we are to characterize the rite itself. Now it is in the beliefs that the special nature of this object is expressed. It is possible to define the rite only after we have defined the belief.

FROM: *The Elementary Forms of the Religious Life.* Translated by Joseph Ward Swain. London: George Allen & Unwinn Ltd., [1912] 1915.

All known religious beliefs, whether simple or complex, present one common characteristic: they presuppose a classification of all the things, real and ideal, of which men think, into two classes or opposed groups, generally designated by two distinct terms which are translated well enough by the words *profane* and *sacred (profane, sacré?)*. This division of the world into two domains, the one containing all that is sacred, the other all that is profane, is the distinctive trait of religious thought; the beliefs, myths, dogmas and legends are either representations or systems of representations which express the nature of sacred things, the virtues and powers which are attributed to them, or their relations with each other and with profane things. But by sacred things one must not understand simply those personal beings which are called gods or spirits; a rock, a tree, a spring, a pebble, a piece of wood, a house, in a word, anything can be sacred. A rite can have this character; in fact, the rite does not exist which does not have it to a certain degree.... The circle of sacred objects cannot be determined, then, once for all. Its extent varies infinitely, according to the different religions. That is how Buddhism is a religion: in default of gods, it admits the existence of sacred things, namely, the four noble truths and the practices derived from them.

Up to the present we have confined ourselves to enumerating a certain number of sacred things as examples: we must now show by what general characteristics they are to be distinguished from profane things.

One might be tempted, first of all, to define them by the place they are generally assigned in the hierarchy of things. They are naturally considered superior in dignity and power to profane things, and particularly to man, when he is only a man and has nothing sacred about him. One thinks of himself as occupying an inferior and dependent position in relation to them; and surely this conception is not without some truth. Only there is nothing in it which is really characteristic of the sacred.

On the other hand, it must not be lost to view that there are sacred things of every degree, and that there are some in relation to which a man feels himself relatively at his ease. An amulet has a sacred character, yet the respect which it inspires is nothing exceptional. Even before his gods, a man is not always in such a marked state of inferiority; for it very frequently happens that he exercises a veritable physical constraint upon them to obtain what he desires. He beats the fetich with which he is not contented, but only to reconcile himself with it again, if in the end it shows itself more docile to the wishes of its adorer. To have rain, he throws stones into the spring or sacred lake where the god of rain is thought to reside; he believes that by this means he forces him to come out and show himself. Moreover, if it is true that man depends upon his gods, this dependence is reciprocal. The gods also have need of man; without offerings and sacrifices they would die. We shall even have occasion to show that this dependence of the gods upon their worshippers is maintained even in the most idealistic religions.

But if a purely hierarchic distinction is a criterium at once too general and too imprecise, there is nothing left with which to characterize the sacred in its relation to the profane except their heterogeneity. However, this heterogeneity is sufficient to characterize this classification of things and to distinguish it from all others, because it is very particular: *it is absolute*. In all the history of human thought there exists no other example of two categories of things so profoundly differentiated or so radically opposed to one another. The traditional opposition of good and bad is nothing beside this; for the good and bad are only two opposed species of the same class, namely morals.…

The two worlds are not only conceived of as separate, but as even hostile and jealous rivals of each other. Since men cannot fully belong to one except on condition of leaving the other completely, they are exhorted to withdraw themselves completely from the profane world, in order to lead an exclusively religious life. Hence comes the monasticism which is artificially organized outside of and apart from the natural environment in which the ordinary man leads the life of this world, in a different one, closed to the first, and nearly its contrary. Hence comes the mystic asceticism whose object is to root out from man all the attachment for the profane world that remains in him. From that come all the forms of religious suicide, the logical working-out of this asceticism; for the only manner of fully escaping the profane life is, after all, to forsake all life.

The opposition of these two classes manifests itself outwardly with a visible sign by which we can easily recognize this very special classification, wherever it exists. Since the idea of the sacred is always and everywhere separated from the idea of the profane in the thought of men, and since we picture a sort of logical chasm between the two, the mind irresistibly refuses to allow the two corresponding things to be confounded, or even to be merely put in contact with each other; for such a promiscuity, or even too direct a contiguity, would contradict too violently the dissociation of these ideas in the mind. The sacred thing is *par excellence* that which the profane should not touch, and cannot touch with impunity. To be sure, this interdiction cannot go so far as to make all communication between the two worlds impossible; for if the profane could in no way enter into relations with the sacred, this latter could be good for nothing. But, in addition to the fact that this establishment of relations is always a delicate operation in itself, demanding great precautions and a more or less complicated initiation, it is quite impossible, unless the profane is to lose its specific characteristics and become sacred after a fashion and to a certain degree itself. The two classes cannot even approach each other and keep their own nature at the same time.

Thus we arrive at the first criterium of religious beliefs. Undoubtedly there are secondary species within these two fundamental classes which, in their turn, are more or less incompatible with each other. But the real characteristic of religious phenomena is that they always suppose a bipartite division of the whole universe, known and knowable, into two classes which embrace all that exists, but which radically exclude each other. Sacred things are those which the interdictions protect and isolate; profane things, those to which these interdictions are applied and which must remain at a distance from the first. Religious beliefs are the representations which express the nature of sacred things and the relations which they sustain, either with each other or with profane things. Finally, rites are the rules of conduct which prescribe how a man should comport himself in the presence of these sacred objects....

However, this definition is not yet complete, for it is equally applicable to two sorts of facts which, while being related to each other, must be distinguished nevertheless: these are magic and religion.

Magic, too, is made up of beliefs and rites. Like religion, it has its myths and its dogmas; only they are more elementary, undoubtedly because, seeking technical and utilitarian ends, it does not waste its time in pure speculation. It has its ceremonies, sacrifices, lustrations, prayers, chants and dances as well....

Here is how a line of demarcation can be traced between these two domains.

The really religious beliefs are always common to a determined group, which makes profession of adhering to them and of practising the rites connected with them. They are not merely received individually by all the members of this group; they are something belonging to the group, and they make its unity. The individuals which compose it feel themselves united to each other by the simple fact that they have a common faith. A society whose members are united by the fact that they think in the same way in regard to the sacred world and its relations with the profane world, and by the fact that they translate these common ideas into common practices, is what is called a Church. In all history, we do not find a single religion without a Church....

It is quite another matter with magic. To be sure, the belief in magic is always more or less general; it is very frequently diffused in large masses of the population, and there are even peoples where it has as many adherents as the real religion. But it does not result in binding together those who adhere to it, nor in uniting them into a group leading a common life. *There is no Church of magic.* Between the magician and the individuals who consult him, as between these individuals themselves, there are no lasting bonds which make them members of the same moral community, comparable to that formed by the believers in the same god or the observers of the same cult. The magician has a clientele and not a Church, and it is very possible that his clients have no other relations between each other, or even do not know each other; even the relations which they have with him are generally accidental and transient; they are just like those of a sick man with his physician....

There still remain those contemporary aspirations towards a religion which would consist entirely in internal and subjective states, and which would be constructed freely by each of us. But howsoever real these aspirations may be, they cannot affect our definition, for this is to be applied only to facts already realized, and not to uncertain possibilities. One can define religions such as they are, or such as they have been, but not such as they more or less vaguely tend to become. It is possible that this religious individualism is destined to be realized in facts; but before we can say just how far this may be the case, we must first know what religion is, of what elements it is made up, from what causes it results, and what function it fulfils—all questions whose solution cannot be foreseen before the threshold of our study has been passed. It is only at the close of this study that we can attempt to anticipate the future.

Thus we arrive at the following definition: *A religion is a unified system of beliefs and practices relative to sacred things, that is to say, things set apart and forbidden—beliefs and practices which unite into one single moral community called a Church, all those who adhere to them.* The second element which thus finds a place in our definition is no less essential than the first; for by showing that the idea of religion is inseparable from that of the Church, it makes it clear that religion should be an eminently collective thing.

∽

Since neither man nor nature have of themselves a sacred character, they must get it from another source. Aside from the human individual and the psychical world, there should be some other reality, in relation to which... all religion... has a significance and objective value. In other words, beyond those which we have called animistic and naturistic, there should be another sort of cult, more fundamental and more primitive, of which the first are only derived forms or particular aspects.

In fact, this cult does exist: it is the one to which ethnologists have given the name of totemism.

∽

[I]t is clear that Australia is the most favourable field for the study of totemism, and therefore we shall make it the principal area of our observations....

In his *Totemism* Frazer sought especially to collect all the traces of totemism which could be found in history or ethnography. He was thus led to include in his study societies the nature and degree of whose cultures differs most widely.... This manner of procedure is not at all surprising for a disciple of the anthropological school. For this school does not seek to locate religions in the social environments of which they are a part.... For researches of this sort, all peoples can be called upon equally well. It is true that they prefer the more primitive peoples...; but...equally well among the most civilized peoples, it is but natural they too should be called as witnesses. Consequently, all those who pass as being not too far removed from the origins, and who are confusedly lumped together under the rather imprecise rubric of *savages,* are put on the same plane and consulted indifferently. Since from this point of view facts have an interest only in proportion to their generality, they consider themselves obliged to collect as large a number as possible of them; the circle of comparisons could not become to large.

Our method will not be such a one....

[W]e propose to limit our research to Australian societies.... They are perfectly homogeneous, for though it is possible to distinguish varieties among them, they all belong to one common type.... Also, Australian totemism is the variety for which our documents are the most complete.... [T]hat which we propose to study in this work is the most primitive and simple religion which it is possible to find. It is therefore natural that to discover it, we address ourselves to societies as slightly evolved as possible, for it is evidently there that we have the greatest chance of finding it and studying it well. Now there are no societies which present this characteristic to a higher degree than Australian ones. Not only is their civilization the most rudimentary—the house and even the hut are still unknown—but also their organization is the most primitive and simple which is actually known.

~

The Totem as Name and as Emblem

Owing to its nature, our study will include two parts. Since every religion is made up of intellectual conceptions and ritual practices, we must deal successively with the beliefs and rites which compose the totemic religion. These two elements of the religious life are too closely connected with each other to allow of any radical separation. In principle, the cult is derived from the beliefs, yet it reacts upon them; the myth is frequently modeled after the rite in order to account for it, especially when its sense is no longer apparent. On the other hand, there are beliefs which are clearly manifested only through the rites which express them. So these two parts of our analysis cannot fail to overlap. However, these two orders of facts are so different that it is indispensable to study them separately. And since it is impossible to understand anything about a religion while unacquainted with the ideas upon which it rests, we must seek to become acquainted with these latter first of all.

But it is not our intention to retrace all the speculations into which the religious thought, even of the Australians alone, has run. The things we wish to reach are the elementary notions at the basis of the religion, but there is no need of following them through all the development, sometimes very confused, which the mythological imagination of these peoples has given them. We shall make use of myths when they enable us to understand these fundamental ideas better, but we shall not make mythology itself the subject of our studies. In so far as this is a work of art, it does not fall within the jurisdiction of the simple science of religions. Also, the intellectual evolution from which it results is of too great a complexity to be studied indirectly and from a foreign point of view. It constitutes a very difficult problem which must be treated by itself, for itself and with a method peculiar to itself.

Among the beliefs upon which totemism rests, the most important are naturally those concerning the totem; it is with these that we must begin.

At the basis of nearly all the Australian tribes we find a group which holds a preponderating place in the collective life: this is the clan. Two essential traits characterize it.

In the first place, the individuals who compose it consider themselves united by a bond of kinship, but one which is of a very special nature. This relationship does not come from the fact that they have definite blood connections with one another; they are relatives from the mere fact that they have the same name. They are not fathers and mothers, sons or daughters, uncles or nephews of one another in the sense which we now give these words; yet they think of themselves as forming a single family, which is large or small according to the dimensions of the clan, merely because they are collectively designated by the same word.... The species of things which serves to designate the clan collectively is called its totem. The totem of the clan is also that of each of its members.

Each clan has its totem, which belongs to it alone; two different clans of the same tribe cannot have the same. In fact, one is a member of a clan merely because he has a certain name. All who bear this name are members of it for that very reason; in whatever manner they may be spread over the tribal territory, they all have the same relations of kinship with one another....

In regard to the word totem, we may say that it is the one employed by the Ojibway, an Algonquin tribe, to designate the sort of thing whose name the clan bears. Although this expression is not at all Australian, and is found only in one single society in America, ethnographers have definitely adopted it, and use it to denote, in a general way, the system which we are describing....

[N]ormally the totem is not an individual, but a species or a variety: it is not such and such a kangaroo or crow, but the kangaroo or crow in general. Sometimes, however, it is a particular object.

∽

[T]he totem is not merely a name; it is an emblem, a veritable coat-of-arms whose analogies with the arms of heraldry have often been remarked.... Thus when the Indians entered into relations with the Europeans and contracts were formed between them, it was with its totem that each clan sealed the treaties thus concluded.

The nobles of the feudal period carved, engraved and designed in every way their coats-of-arms upon the walls of their castles, their arms, and every sort of object that belonged to them; the blacks of Australia and the Indians of North America do the same thing with their totems....

But totemic images are not placed only upon the walls of their houses, the sides of their canoes, their arms, their utensils and their tombs; they are also found on the bodies of the men. They do not put their coat-of-arms merely upon the things which they possess, but they put it upon their persons; they imprint it upon their flesh, it becomes a part of them, and this world of representations is even by far the more important one.

~

These totemic decorations enable us to see that the totem is not merely a name and an emblem. It is in the course of the religious ceremonies that they are employed; they are a part of the liturgy; so while the totem is a collective label, it also has a religious character. In fact, it is in connection with it, that things are classified as sacred or profane. It is the very type of sacred thing.

The tribes of Central Australia, especially the Arunta, the Loritja, the Kaitish, the Unmatjera, and the Ilpirra, make constant use of certain instruments in their rites which are called the churinga.... They are pieces of wood or bits of polished stone.... Upon each of these is engraved a design representing the totem of this same group. A certain number of the churinga have a hole at one end, through which goes a thread.... By means of the thread by which they are suspended, they are whirled rapidly in the air in such a way as to produce a sort of humming.... These sorts of churinga are ... bull roarers [sacred sound-making devices: ed.]....

In fact, every churinga, for whatever purpose it may be employed, is counted among the eminently sacred things; there are none which surpass it in religious dignity. This is indicated even by the word which is used to designate them. It is not only a substantive but also an adjective meaning sacred.... Churinga, when used substantively, therefore designates the thing whose essential characteristic is sacredness. Profane persons, that is to say, women and young men not yet initiated into the religious life, may not touch or even see the churinga; they are only allowed to look at it from a distance, and even this is only on rare occasions.

~

Society Frames Our Categories of Thought

We are beginning to see that totemism is a much more complex religion than it first appeared to be. We have already distinguished three classes of things which it recognizes as sacred, in varying degrees: the totemic emblem, the animal or plant whose appearance this emblem reproduces, and the members of the clan. However, this list is not yet complete. In fact, a religion is not merely a collection of fragmentary beliefs in regard to special objects like those we have just been discussing. To a greater or less extent, all known religions have been systems of ideas which tend to embrace the universality of things, and to give us a complete representation of the world. If totemism is to be considered as a religion comparable to the others, it too should offer us a conception of the universe. As a matter of fact, it does satisfy this condition.

~

[W]e have shown what light these facts throw upon the way in which the idea of a kind or class was formed in humanity. In fact, these systematic [totem: ed.] classifications are the first we meet with in history, and we have just seen that they are modeled upon the social organization, or rather that they have taken the forms of society as their framework. . . . It is because men were organized that they have been able to organize things, for in classifying these latter, they limited themselves to giving them places in the groups they formed themselves. And if these different classes of things are not merely put next to each other, but are arranged according to a unified plan, it is because the social groups with which they commingle themselves are unified and, through their union, form an organic whole, the tribe. The unity of these first logical systems merely reproduces the unity of the society. Thus we have an occasion for verifying the proposition which we laid down at the commencement of this work, and for assuring ourselves that the fundamental notions of the intellect, the essential categories of thought, may be the product of social factors. The above-mentioned facts show clearly that this is the case with the very notion of category itself.

However, it is not our intention to deny that the individual intellect has of itself the power of perceiving resemblances between the different objects of which it is conscious. Quite on the contrary, it is clear that even the most primitive and simple classifications presuppose this faculty. The Australian does not place things in the same clan or in different clans at random. For him as for us, similar images attract one another, while opposed ones repel one another, and it is on the basis of these feelings of affinity or of repulsion that he classifies the corresponding things in one place or another. . . .

The idea of class is an instrument of thought which has obviously been constructed by men. But in constructing it, we have at least had need of a model; for how could this idea ever have been born, if there had been nothing either in us or around us which was capable of suggesting it to us? To reply that it was given to us *a priori* is not to reply at all; this lazy man's solution is, as has been said, the death of analysis. But it is hard to see where we could have found this indispensable model except in the spectacle of the collective life. In fact, a class is not an ideal, but a clearly defined group of things between which internal relationships exist, similar to those of kindred. Now the only groups of this sort known from experience are those formed by men in associating themselves.... In all probability, we would never have thought of uniting the beings of the universe into homogeneous groups, called classes, if we had not the example of human societies before our eyes....

But these primitive classifications have a no less direct interest for the origins of religious thought....

[T]he men of the clan and the things which are classified in it form by their union a solid system, all of whose parts are united and vibrate sympathetically. This organization, which at first may have appeared to us as purely logical, is at the same time moral. A single principle animates it and makes its unity: this is the totem. Just as a man who belongs to the Crow clan has within him something of this animal, so the rain, since it is of the same clan and belongs to the same totem, is also necessarily considered as being "the same thing as a crow"; for the same reason, the moon is a black cockatoo, the sun a white cockatoo, every black-nut tree a pelican, etc. All the beings arranged in a single clan, whether men, animals, plants or inanimate objects, are merely forms of the totemic being....

But we also know that the totemic animal is a sacred being. All the things that are classified in the clan of which it is the emblem have this same character, because in one sense, they are animals of the same species, just as the man is. They, too, are sacred, and the classifications which locate them in relation to the other things of the universe, by that very act give them a place in the religious world. For this reason, the animals or plants among these may not be eaten freely by the human members of the clan.

~

The Totem as Symbol of the Clan and Its God

Since totemism is everywhere dominated by the idea of a quasi-divine principle, imminent in certain categories of men and things and thought of under the form of an animal or vegetable, the explanation of this religion is essentially the explanation of this belief; to arrive at this, we must seek to learn how men have been led to construct this idea and out of what materials they have constructed it.…

It is the figurative representation of this plant or animal and the totemic emblems and symbols of every sort, which have the greatest sanctity; so it is in them that is found the source of that religious nature, of which the real objects represented by these emblems receive only a reflection.

Thus the totem is before all a symbol, a material expression of something else. But of what?

From the analysis to which we have been giving our attention, it is evident that it expresses and symbolizes two different sorts of things. In the first place, it is the outward and visible form of what we have called the totemic principle or god. But it is also the symbol of the determined society called the clan. It is its flag; it is the sign by which each clan distinguishes itself from the others, the visible mark of its personality, a mark borne by everything which is a part of the clan under any title whatsoever, men, beasts or things. So if it is at once the symbol of the god and of the society, is that not because the god and the society are only one? How could the emblem of the group have been able to become the figure of this quasi-divinity, if the group and the divinity were two distinct realities? The god of the clan, the totemic principle, can therefore be nothing else than the clan itself, personified and represented to the imagination under the visible form of the animal or vegetable which serves as totem.

But how has this apotheosis been possible, and how did it happen to take place in this fashion?

In a general way, it is unquestionable that a society has all that is necessary to arouse the sensation of the divine in minds, merely by the power that it has over them; for to its members it is what a god is to his worshippers. In fact, a god is, first of all, a being whom men think of as superior to themselves, and upon whom they feel that they depend. Whether it be a conscious personality, such as Zeus or Jahveh, or merely abstract forces such as those in play in totemism, the worshipper, in the one case as in the other, believes himself held to certain manners of acting which are imposed upon him by the nature of the sacred principle with which he feels that he is in communion. Now society also gives us the sensation of a perpetual dependence. Since it has a nature which is peculiar to itself and different from our individual nature, it pursues ends which are likewise special to it; but, as it cannot attain them except through our intermediacy; it imperiously demands our aid. It requires that, forgetful of our own interests, we make ourselves its servitors, and it submits us to every sort of inconvenience, privation and sacrifice, without which social life would be impossible. It is because of this that at every instant we are obliged to submit ourselves to rules of conduct and of thought which we have neither made nor desired, and which are sometimes even contrary to our most fundamental inclinations and instincts....

Now the ways of action to which society is strongly enough attached to impose them upon its members, are, by that very fact, marked with a distinctive sign provocative of respect. Since they are elaborated in common, the vigour with which they have been thought of by each particular mind is retained in all the other minds, and reciprocally. The representations which express them within each of us have an intensity which no purely private states of consciousness could ever attain; for they have the strength of the innumerable individual representations which have served to form each of them. It is society who speaks through the mouths of those who affirm them in our presence; it is society whom we hear in hearing them; and the voice of all has an accent which that of one alone could never have. The very violence with which society reacts, by way of blame or material suppression, against every attempted dissidence, contributes to strengthening its empire by manifesting the common conviction through this burst of ardor. In a word, when something is the object of such a state of opinion, the representation which each individual has of it gains a power of action from its origins and the conditions in which it was born, which even those feel who do not submit themselves to it. It tends to repel the representations which contradict it, and it keeps them at a distance; on the other hand, it commands those acts which will realize it, and it does so, not by a material coercion or by the perspective of something of this sort, but by the simple radiation of the mental energy which it contains. It has an efficacy coming solely from its psychical properties, and it is by just this sign that moral authority is recognized. So opinion, primarily a social thing, is a source of authority, and it might even be asked whether all authority is not the daughter of opinion. It may be objected that science is often the antagonist of opinion, whose errors it combats and rectifies. But it cannot succeed in this task if it does not have sufficient authority, and I can obtain this authority only from opinion itself. If a people did not have faith in science, all the scientific demonstrations in the world would be without any influence whatsoever over their minds. Even today, if science happened to resist a very strong current of public opinion, it would risk losing its credit there.

Since it is in spiritual ways that social pressure exercises itself, it could not fail to give men the idea that outside themselves there exist one or several powers, both moral and, at the same time, efficacious, upon which they depend. They must think of these powers, at least in part, as outside themselves, for these address them in a tone of command and sometimes even order them to do violence to their most natural inclinations. It is undoubtedly true that if they were able to see that these influences which they feel emanate from society, then the mythological system of interpretations would never be born. But social action follows ways that are too circuitous and obscure, and employs psychical mechanisms that are too complex to allow the ordinary observer to see whence it comes. As long as scientific analysis does not come to teach it to them, men know well that they must invent by themselves the idea of these powers with which they feel themselves in connection, and from that, we are able to catch a glimpse of the way by which they were led to represent them under forms that are really foreign to their nature and to transfigure them by thought.

But a god is not merely an authority upon whom we depend; it is a force upon which our strength relies. The man who has obeyed his god and who, for this reason, believes the god is with him, approaches the world with confidence and with the feeling of an increased energy. Likewise, social action does not confine itself to demanding sacrifices, privations and efforts from us. For the collective force is not entirely outside of us; it does not act upon us wholly from without; but rather, since society cannot exist except in and through individual consciousnesses, this force must also penetrate us and organize itself within us; it thus becomes an integral part of our being and by that very fact this is elevated and magnified.

There are occasions when this strengthening and vivifying action of society is especially apparent. In the midst of an assembly animated by common passion, we become susceptible of acts and sentiments of which we are incapable when reduced to our own forces; and when the assembly is dissolved and when, finding ourselves alone again, we fall back to our ordinary level, we are then able to measure the height to which we have been raised above ourselves. History abounds in examples of this sort. It is enough to think of the night of the Fourth of August, 1789, when an assembly was suddenly led to an act of sacrifice and abnegation which each of its members had refused the day before, and at which they were all surprised the day after. This is why all parties, political, economic, or confessional, are careful to have periodical reunions where their members may revivify their common faith by manifesting it in common. To strengthen those sentiments which, if left to themselves, would soon weaken, it is sufficient to bring those who hold them together and to put them into closer and more active relations with one another. This is the explanation of the particular attitude of a man speaking to a crowd, at least if he has succeeded in entering into communion with it. His language has a grandiloquence that would be ridiculous in ordinary circumstances; his gestures show a certain domination; his very thought is impatient of all rules, and easily falls into all sorts of excesses. It is because he feels within him an abnormal over-supply of force which overflows and tries to burst out from him. . . .

But it is not only in exceptional circumstances that this stimulating action of society makes itself felt; there is not, so to speak, a moment in our lives when some current of energy does not come to us from without. The man who has done his duty finds, in the manifestations of every sort expressing the sympathy, esteem or affection which his fellows have for him, a feeling of comfort, of which he does not ordinarily take account, but which sustains him, none the less. The sentiments which society has for him raise the sentiments which he has for himself. Because he is in moral harmony with his comrades, he has more confidence, courage and boldness in action, just like the believer who thinks that he feels the regard of his god turned graciously towards him. It thus produces, as it were, a perpetual sustenance for our moral nature. Since this varies with a multitude of external circumstances, as our relations with the groups about us are more or less active and as these groups themselves vary, we cannot fail to feel that this moral support depends upon an external cause; but we do not perceive where this cause is nor what it is. So we ordinarily think of it under the form of a moral power which, though immanent in us, represents within us something not ourselves: this is the moral conscience, of which, by the way, men have never made even a slightly distinct representation except by the aid of religious symbols.

In addition to these free forces which are constantly coming to renew our own, there are others which are fixed in the methods and traditions which we employ. We speak a language that we did not make; we use instruments that we did not invent; we invoke rights that we did not found; a treasury of knowledge is transmitted to each generation that it did not gather itself, etc. It is to society that we owe these varied benefits of civilization, and if we do not ordinarily see the source from which we get them, we at least know that they are not our own work. Now it is these things that give man his own place among things; a man is a man only because he is civilized. So he could not escape the feeling that outside of him there are active causes from which he gets the characteristic attributes of his nature and which, as benevolent powers, assist him, protect him and assure him of a privileged fate. And of course he must attribute to these powers a dignity corresponding to the great value of the good things he attributes to them.

Thus the environment in which we live seems to us to be peopled with forces that are at once imperious and helpful, august and gracious, and with which we have relations. Since they exercise over us a pressure of which we are conscious, we are forced to localize them outside ourselves, just as we do for the objective causes of our sensations. . . .

If . . . [a society] happens to fall in love with a man and if it thinks it has found in him the principal aspirations that move it, as well as the means of satisfying them, this man will be raised above the others and, as it were, deified.

Opinion will invest him with a majesty exactly analogous to that protecting the gods. This is what has happened to so many sovereigns in whom their age had faith: if they were not made gods, they were at least regarded as direct representatives of the deity. And the fact that it is society alone which is the author of these varieties of apotheosis, is evident since it frequently chances to consecrate men thus who have no right to it from their own merit. The simple deference inspired by men invested with high social functions is not different in nature from religious respect.... In Melanesia and Polynesia, for example, it is said that an influential man has *mana,* and that his influence is due to this *mana.* However, it is evident that his situation is due solely to the importance attributed to him by public opinion....

This aptitude of society for setting itself up as a god or for creating gods was never more apparent than during the first years of the French Revolution. At this time, in fact, under the influence of the general enthusiasm, things purely laical by nature were transformed by public opinion into sacred things: these were the Fatherland, Liberty, Reason. A religion tended to become established which had its dogmas, symbols, altars and feasts. It was to these spontaneous aspirations that the cult of Reason and the Supreme Being attempted to give a sort of official satisfaction. It is true that this religious renovation had only an ephemeral duration. But that was because the patriotic enthusiasm which at first transported the masses soon relaxed. The cause being gone, the effect could not remain. But this experiment, though short-lived, keeps all its sociological interest. It remains true that in one determined case we have seen society and its essential ideas become, directly and with no transfiguration of any sort, the object of a veritable cult.

All these facts allow us to catch glimpses of how the clan was able to awaken within its members the idea that outside of them there exist forces which dominate them and at the same time sustain them, that is to say in fine, religious forces: it is because there is no society with which the primitive is more directly and closely connected. The bonds uniting him to the tribe are much more lax and more feebly felt. Although this is not at all strange or foreign to him, it is with the people of his own clan that he has the greatest number of things in common; it is the action of this group that he feels the most directly; so it is this also which, in preference to all others, should express itself in religious symbols.

But this first explanation has been too general, for it is applicable to every sort of society indifferently, and consequently to every sort of religion. Let us attempt to determine exactly what form this collective action takes in the clan and how it arouses the sensation of sacredness there. For there is no place where it is more easily observable or more apparent in its results.

~

The Power of Sacred Ceremonies

[I]t is in the midst of... effervescent social environments and out of this efferves-cence itself that the religious idea seems to be born. The theory that this is really its origin is confirmed by the fact that in Australia the really religious activity is almost entirely confined to the moments when these assemblies are held.... The religious life of the Australian passes through successive phases of complete lull and of super-excitation, and social life oscillates in the same rhythm. This puts clearly into evidence the bond uniting them to one another.... By concen-trating itself almost entirely in certain determined moments, the collective life has been able to attain its greatest intensity and efficacy, and consequently to give men a more active sentiment of the double existence they lead and of the double nature in which they participate.

But this explanation is still incomplete. We have shown how the clan, by the manner in which it acts upon its members, awakens within them the idea of external forces which dominate them and exalt them; but we must still demand how it happens that these forces are thought of under the form of totems, that is to say, in the shape of an animal or plant.

It is because this animal or plant has given its name to the clan and serves it as emblem. In fact, it is a well-known law that the sentiments aroused in us by something spontaneously attach themselves to the symbol which represents them. For us, black is a sign of mourning; it also suggests sad impressions and ideas. This transference of sentiments comes simply from the fact that the idea of a thing and the idea of its symbol are closely united in our minds; the result is that the emotions provoked by the one extend contagiously to the other. But this contagion, which takes place in every case to a certain degree, is much more complete and more marked when the symbol is something simple, definite and easily representable.... For we are unable to consider an abstract entity, which we can represent only laboriously and confusedly, the source of the strong sen-timents which we feel. We cannot explain them to ourselves except by connect-ing them to some concrete object of whose reality we are vividly aware.... It is this which is loved, feared, respected; it is to this that we are grateful; it is for this that we sacrifice ourselves. The soldier who dies for his flag, dies for his country; but as a matter of fact, in his own consciousness, it is the flag that has the first place....

Now the totem is the flag of the clan. It is therefore natural that the impres-sions aroused by the clan in individual minds—impressions of dependence and of increased vitality—should fix themselves to the idea of the totem rather than that of the clan: for the clan is too complex a reality to be represented clearly in all its complex unity by such rudimentary intelligences. More than that, the primitive does not even see that these impressions come to him from the group. He does not know that the coming together of a number of men associated in the same life results in disengaging new energies, which transform each of them. All that he knows is that he is raised above himself and that he sees a different life from the one he ordinarily leads. However, he must connect these sensations to some external object as their cause. Now what does he see about him? On every side those things which appeal to his senses and strike his imagination are the numerous images of the totem. They are the waninga and the nurtunja, which are symbols of the sacred being. They are churinga and bull-roarers, upon which are generally carved combinations of lines having the same significance. They are...totemic marks. How could this image, repeated everywhere and in all sorts of forms, fail to stand out with exceptional relief in his mind? Placed thus in the centre of the scene, it becomes representative. The sentiments experienced fix themselves upon it, for it is the only concrete object upon which they can fix themselves. It continues to bring them to mind and to evoke them even after the assembly has dissolved, for it survives the assembly, being carved upon the instruments of the cult, upon the sides of rocks, upon bucklers etc. By it, the emotions experienced are perpetually sustained and revived. Everything happens just as if they inspired them directly....

When this point is once established, we are in a position to understand all that is essential in the totemic beliefs.

Since religious force is nothing other than the collective and anonymous force of the clan, and since this can be represented in the mind only in the form of the totem, the totemic emblem is like the visible body of the god. Therefore, it is from it that those kindly or dreadful actions seem to emanate, which the cult seeks to provoke or prevent; consequently, it is to it that the cult is addressed. This is the explanation of why it holds the first place in the series of sacred things.

But the clan, like every other sort of society, can live only in and through the individual consciousnesses that compose it. So if religious force, in so far as it is conceived as incorporated in the totemic emblem, appears to be outside of the individuals and to be endowed with a sort of transcendence over them, it, like the clan of which it is the symbol, can be realized only in and through them; in this sense, it is imminent in them and they necessarily represent it as such. They feel it present and active within them, for it is this which raises them to a superior life. This is why men have believed that they contain within them a principle comparable to the one residing in the totem, and consequently, why they have attributed a sacred character to themselves, but one less marked than that of the emblem. It is because the emblem is the pre-eminent source of the religious life; the man participates in it only indirectly, as he is well aware; he takes into account the fact that the force that transports him into the world of sacred things is not inherent in him, but comes to him from the outside.

But for still another reason, the animals or vegetables of the totemic species should have the same character, and even to a higher degree. If the totemic principle is nothing else than the clan, it is the clan thought of under the material form of the totemic emblem; now this form is also that of the concrete beings whose name the clan bears. Owing to this resemblance, they could not fail to evoke sentiments analogous to those aroused by the emblem itself. Since the latter is the object of a religious respect, they too should inspire respect of the same sort and appear to be sacred. Having external forms so nearly identical, it would be impossible for the native not to attribute to them forces of the same nature. It is therefore forbidden to kill or eat the totemic animal, since its flesh is believed to have the positive virtues resulting from the rites; it is because it resembles the emblem of the clan, that is to say, it is in its own image.…

But even if the totemic principle has its preferred seat in a determined species of animal or vegetable, it cannot remain localized there. A sacred character is to a high degree contagious; it therefore spreads out from the totemic being to everything that is closely or remotely connected with it. The religious sentiments inspired by the animal are communicated to the substances upon which it is nourished and which serve to make or remake its flesh and blood, to the things that resemble it, and to the different beings with which it has constant relations. Thus, little by little, sub-totems are attached to the totems and from the cosmological systems expressed by the primitive classifications. At last, the whole world is divided up among the totemic principles of each tribe.

We are now able to explain the origin of the ambiguity of religious forces as they appear in history, and how they are physical as well as human, moral as well as material. They are moral powers because they are made up entirely of the impressions this moral being, the group, arouses in those other moral beings, its individual members; they do not translate the manner in which physical things affect our senses, but the way in which the collective consciousness acts upon individual consciousnesses. Their authority is only one form of the moral ascendancy of society over its members. But, on the other hand, since they are conceived of under material forms, they could not fail to be regarded as closely related to material things. Therefore they dominate the two worlds. Their residence is in men, but at the same time they are the vital principles of things. They animate minds and discipline them, but it is also they who make plants grow and animals reproduce. It is this double nature which has enabled religion to be like the womb from which come all the leading germs of human civilization. Since it has been made to embrace all of reality, the physical world as well as the moral one, the forces that move bodies as well as those that move minds have been conceived in a religious form. That is how the most diverse methods and practices, both those that make possible the continuation of the moral life (law, morals, beaux-arts) and those serving the material life (the natural, technical and practical sciences), are either directly or indirectly derived from religion.

~

The Idea of the Soul

In the preceding chapters we have been studying the fundamental principles of the totemic religion. We have seen that no idea of soul or spirit or mythical personality is to be found among these. Yet, even if the idea of spiritual beings is not at the foundation of totemism or, consequently, of religious thought in general, still, there is no religion where this notion is not met with. So it is important to see how it is formed. To make sure that it is the product of a secondary formation, we must discover the way in which it is derived from the more essential conceptions which we have just described and explained.

Among the various spiritual beings, there is one which should receive our attention first of all because it is the prototype after which the others have been constructed: this is the soul.

Just as there is no known society without a religion, so there exist none, howsoever crudely organized they may be, where we do not find a whole system of collective representations concerning the soul, its origin and its destiny.... [A]ll the Australian societies admit that every human body shelters an interior being, the principle of the life which animates it: this is the soul....

[The soul] is distinct and independent of the body, for during this life it can leave it at any moment. It does leave it during sleep, fainting spells, etc. It may even remain absent for some time without entailing death; however, during these absences life is weakened and even stops if the soul does not return home. But it is especially at death that this distinction and independence manifest themselves with the greatest clarity. While the body no longer exists and no visible traces of it remain, the soul continues to live: it leads an autonomous existence in another world.

But howsoever real this duality may be, it is in no way absolute. It would show a grave misunderstanding to represent the body as a sort of habitat in which the soul resides, but with which it has only external relations. Quite on the contrary, it is united to it by the closest bonds; it is separable from it only imperfectly and with difficulty....

But a moment does arrive when the final separation is accomplished; the liberated soul takes flight. But by nature it is so intimately associated with the body that this removal cannot take place without a profound change in its condition. So it takes a new name also. Although keeping all the distinctive traits of the individual whom it animated, his humours and his good and bad qualities, still it has become a new being. From that moment a new existence commences for it.

It goes to the land of souls....

Such are the beliefs relative to the soul and its destiny, in their most primitive form, and reduced to their most essential traits. We must now attempt to explain them. What is it that has been able to lead men into thinking that there are two beings in them, one of which possesses these very special characteristics which we have just enumerated?

~

[W]e reach the conclusion that, in a general way, the soul is nothing other than the totemic principle incarnate in each individual. And there is nothing to surprise us in this derivation. We already know that this principle is immanent in each of the members of the clan. But in penetrating into these individuals, it must inevitably individualize itself. Because the consciousnesses, of which it becomes thus an integral part, differ from each other, it differentiates itself according to their image.... Of course it remains something outside of and foreign to the man, but the portion of it which each is believed to possess cannot fail to contract close affinities with the particular subject in which it resides; it becomes his to certain extent. Thus it has two contradictory characteristics, but whose coexistence is one of the distinctive features of the notion of the soul. To-day, as formerly, the soul is what is best and most profound in ourselves, and the pre-eminent part of our being; yet it is also a passing guest which comes from the outside, which leads in us an existence distinct from that of the body, and which should one day regain its entire independence. In a word, just as society exists only in and through individuals, the totemic principle exists only in and through the individual consciousnesses whose association forms the clan. If they did not feel it in them it would not exist; it is they who put it into things. So it must of necessity be divided and distributed among them. Each of these fragments is a soul.

~

The universality of these conceptions extends, of course, to the conclusion which we have deduced from them, that is, to the explanation of the idea of the soul which we have proposed. Its general acceptability is also proved by the following facts. We know that each individual contains within him something of that anonymous force which is diffused in the sacred species; he is a member of this species himself. But as an empirical and visible being, he is not, for, in spite of the symbolic designs and marks with which he decorates his body, there is nothing in him to suggest the form of an animal or plant. So it must be that there is another being in him, in whom he recognizes himself, but whom he represents in the form of an animal or vegetable species. Now is it not evident that this double can only be the soul, since the soul is, of itself, already a double of the subject whom it animates?...

~

The Immortality of the Soul

[T]he belief in the immortality of the soul is the only way in which men were able to explain a fact which could not fail to attract their attention; this fact is the perpetuity of the life of the group. Individuals must die, but the clan survives. So the forces which give it life must have the same perpetuity. Now these forces are the souls which animate individual bodies; for it is in them and through them that the group is realized. For this reason, it is necessary that they endure. It is even necessary that in enduring, they remain always the same; for, as the clan always keeps its characteristic appearance, the spiritual substance out of which is made must be thought of as qualitatively invariable. Since it is always the same clan with the same totemic principle it is necessary that the souls be the same, for souls are only the totemic principle broken up and particularized.... And this belief, in spite of its symbolic character, is not without a certain objective truth. For though the group may not be immortal in the absolute sense of the word, still it is true that it endures longer than the individuals and that it is born and incarnated afresh in each new generation....

Thus the causes leading to the first beliefs in a future life had no connections with the functions to be filled at a later period by the institutions beyond the tomb. But when that had once appeared, they were soon utilized for other purposes besides those which had been their original reasons for existence. Even in the Australian societies, we see them beginning to organize themselves for this other purpose. Moreover, there was no need of any fundamental transformation for this. How true it is that the same social institution can successively fulfil different functions without changing its nature!

~

The totem, as the ancestor, is the soul of the individual, but externalized and invested with powers superior to those it is believed to possess while within the organism. Now this duplication is the result of a psychological necessity; for it only expresses the nature of the soul which, as we have seen, is double. In one sense, it is ours: it expresses our personality. But at the same time, it is outside of us, for it is only the reaching into us of a religious force which is outside of us. We cannot confound ourselves with it completely, for we attribute to it an excellence and a dignity by which it rises far above us and our empirical individuality. So there is a whole part of ourselves which we tend to project into the outside. This way of thinking of ourselves is so well established in our nature that we cannot escape it, even when we attempt to regard ourselves without having recourse to any religious symbols. Our moral consciousness is like a nucleus about which the idea of the soul forms itself; yet when it speaks to us, it gives the effect of an outside power, superior to us, which gives us our law and judges us, but which also aids and sustains us. When we have it on our side we feel ourselves to be stronger against the trials of life, and better assured of triumphing over them, just as the Australian who, when trusting in his ancestor or his personal totem, feels himself more valiant against his enemies. So there is something objective at the basis of these conceptions, whether we have in mind the Roman *genius,* the individual totem, or the Alcheringa ancestor; and this is why they have survived, in various forms, up to the present day. Everything goes just as if we really had two souls; one which is within us, or rather, which is us; the other which is above us, and whose function it is to control and assist the first one. Frazer thought that the individual totem was an external soul; but he believed that this exteriority was the result of an artifice and a magic ruse. In reality, it is implied in the very constitution of the idea of the soul.

~

The Gods

We have already seen how the notion of mythical ancestors is implied in the very principles upon which totemism rests, for each of them is a totemic being. Now, though the great gods are certainly superior to these, still, there are only differences of degree between them; we pass from the first to the second with no break of continuity. In fact, a great god is himself an ancestor of especial importance. They frequently speak to us about him as though he were a man, endowed, to be sure, with more than human powers, but one who lived a human life upon the earth. He is pictured as a great hunter, a powerful magician, or the founder of the tribe. He was the first man....

The notion of a supreme god even depends so closely upon the entire system of the totemic beliefs that it still bears their mark. Tundun is a divine hero, as we have just seen, who is very close to the tribal divinity; now among the Kurnai, the same word means totem. Similarly among the Arunta, Altjira is the name of a great god; it is also the name of the maternal totem....

In order to account for the bonds uniting them to one another, no matter what clan they belonged to, men imagined that they were all descended from the same stock and that they were all descended from a single father, to whom they owe their existence, though he owed his to no one....

We thus reach the highest conception to which totemism has arrived. This is the point where it touches and prepares the religions which are to follow, and aids us in understanding them. But at the same time, we are able to see that this culminating idea is united without any interruption to the crudest beliefs which we analysed to start with.

In fact, the great tribal god is only an ancestral spirit who finally won a pre-eminent place. The ancestral spirits are only entities forged in the image of the individual souls whose origin they are destined to explain. The souls, in their turn, are only the form taken by the impersonal forces which we found at the basis of totemism, as they individualize themselves in the human body. The unity of the system is as great as its complexity.

In this work of elaboration, the idea of the soul has undoubtedly played an important part: it is through it that the idea of personality has been introduced into the domain of religion. But it is not true that, as the theorists of animism maintain, it contains the germ of the whole religion. First of all, it presupposes the notion of *mana* or the totemic principle of which it is only a special form. Then, if the spirits and gods could not be conceived before the soul, they are, nevertheless, more than mere human souls, liberated by death; else whence would come their supernatural powers? The idea of the soul has merely served to direct the mythological imagination in a new way and to suggest to it constructions of a new sort. But the matter for these conceptions has been taken, not from the representation of the soul, but from this reservoir of the anonymous and diffused forces which constitute the original foundation of religions. The creation of mythical personalities has only been another way of thinking of these essential forces. As for the notion of the great god, it is due entirely to the sentiment whose action we have already observed in the genesis of the most specifically totemic beliefs: this is the tribal sentiment. In fact, we have seen that totemism was not the work of isolated clans, but that it was always elaborated in the body of a tribe which was to some degree conscious of its unity. It is for this reason that the different cults peculiar to each clan mutually touch and complete each other in such a way as to form a unified whole. Now it is this same sentiment of a tribal unity which is expressed in the conception of a supreme god, common to the tribe as a whole. So they are quite the same causes which are active at the bottom and at the top of this religious system.

However, up to the present, we have considered the religious representations as if they were self-sufficient and could be explained by themselves. But in reality, they are inseparable from the rites, not only because they manifest themselves there, but also because they, in their turn, feel the influence of these.

Of course the cult depends upon the beliefs, but it also reacts upon them. So in order to understand them better, it is important to understand it better. The moment has come for undertaking its study.

~

Rituals of Denial

The Negative Cult and Its Functions
The Ascetic Rites

We do not have the intention of attempting a complete description of the primitive cult in what is to follow. Being preoccupied especially with reaching that which is most elementary and most fundamental in the religious life, we shall not attempt to reconstruct in detail the frequently confused multiplicity of all the ritual forms. But out of the midst of this extreme diversity of practices we should like to touch upon the most characteristic attitudes which the primitive observes in the celebration of his cult, to classify the most general forms of his rites, and to determine their origins and significance, in order that we may control and, if there is occasion, make more definite the results to which the analysis of the beliefs has led us.

Every cult presents a double aspect, one negative, the other positive. In reality, of course, the two sorts of rites which we denominate thus are closely associated; we shall see that they suppose one another. But still, they are different and, if it is only to understand their connection, it is necessary to distinguish them.

By definition, sacred beings are separated beings. That which characterizes them is that there is a break of continuity between them and the profane beings. Normally, the first are outside the others. A whole group of rites has the object of realizing this state of separation which is essential. Since their function is to prevent undue mixings and to keep one of these two domains from encroaching upon the other, they are only able to impose abstentions or negative acts. Therefore, we propose to give the name negative cult to the system formed by these special rites. They do not prescribe certain acts to the faithful, but confine themselves to forbidding certain ways of acting; so they all take the form of interdictions, or as is commonly said by ethnographers, of *taboos*. This latter word is the one used in the Polynesian languages to designate the institution in virtue of which certain things are withdrawn from common use; it is also an adjective expressing the distinctive characteristic of these kinds of things. We have already had occasion to show how hard it is to translate a strictly local and dialectical expression like this into a generic term.

There is no religion where there are no interdictions and where they do not play a considerable part; so it is regrettable that the consecrated terminology should seem to make so universal an institution into a peculiarity of Polynesia. The expression *interdicts* or *interdictions* seems to us to be much more preferable. However, the word taboo, like the word totem, is so customary that it would show an excess of purism to prohibit it systematically; also, the inconveniences it may have are attenuated when its real meaning and importance have once been definitely stated....

There is [a]...system of religious interdictions...which separates, not different species of sacred things, but all that is sacred from all that is profane. So it is derived immediately from the notion of sacredness itself, and it limits itself to expressing and realizing this. Thus it furnishes the material for a veritable cult, and even of a cult which is at the basis of all the others; for the attitude which it prescribes is one from which the worshipper must never depart in all his relations with the sacred. It is what we call the negative cult. We may say that its interdicts are the religious interdicts *par excellence*.

Before all are the interdictions of contact; these are the original taboos, of which the others are scarcely more than particular varieties. They rest upon the principle that the profane should never touch the sacred. We have seen already that the uninitiated may not touch the churinga or the bull-roarers under any circumstances. If adults are allowed the free use of them, it is because initiation has conferred a sacred character upon them. Blood, and especially that which flows during the initiation, has a religious virtue; it is under the same interdict. It is the same with the hair....

An exceptionally intimate contact is the one resulting from the absorption of food. Hence comes the interdiction against eating the sacred animals or vegetables, and especially those serving as totems. Such an act appears so very sacrilegious that the prohibition covers even adults, or at least, the majority of them....

Besides the sacred things, there are words and sounds which have the same character; they should not pass the lips of the profane or enter their ears. There are ritual songs which women must not hear under pain of death. They may hear the noise of the bull-roarers, but only from a distance....

In general, all acts characteristic of the ordinary life are forbidden while those of the religious life are taking place. The act of eating is, of itself, profane; for it takes place every day, it satisfies essentially utilitarian and material needs and it is a part of our ordinary existence. This is why it is prohibited in religious times....

For this same reason, all temporal occupations are suspended while the great religious solemnities are taking place.... The distinctive character of the feast-days in all known religions is the cessation of work and the suspension of public and private life, in so far as it does not have a religious objective. This repose is not merely a sort of temporary relaxation which men have given themselves in order to give themselves up more freely to the sentiments of joy ordinarily awakened by the feast-days; for there are sad feasts, consecrated to mourning and repentance, and during which this cessation is no less obligatory. This is because work is an eminent form of profane activity: it has no other apparent end than to provide for the temporal necessities of life; it puts us in relations with ordinary things only. On feast days, on the contrary, the religious life attains an exceptional degree of intensity. So the contrast between the two forms of existence is especially marked at this moment; consequently, they cannot remain near to each other. A man cannot approach his god intimately while he still bears on him marks of his profane life; inversely, he cannot return to his usual occupations when a rite has just sanctified him. So the ritual day of rest is only one particular case of the general incompatibility separating the sacred from the profane; it is the result of an interdiction....

[T]he religious life and the profane life cannot coexist in the same place. If the former is to develop, a special spot must be placed at its disposition, from which the second is excluded. Hence comes the founding of temples and sanctuaries; these are the spots awarded to sacred beings and things and serve them as residences, for they cannot establish themselves in any place except on the condition of entirely appropriating to themselves all within a certain distance. Such arrangements are so indispensable to all religious life that even the most inferior religions cannot do without them.... Likewise, the religious life and the profane life cannot coexist in the same unit of time. It is necessary to assign determined days or periods to the first, from which all profane occupations are excluded. Thus feast days are born. There is no religion, and, consequently, no society which has not known and practiced this division of time into two distinct parts, alternating with one another according to a law varying with the peoples and the civilizations; as we have already pointed out, it was probably the necessity of this alternation which led men to introduce into the continuity and homogeneity of duration, certain distinctions and differentiations which it does not naturally have. Of course, it is almost impossible that the religious life should ever succeed in concentrating itself hermetically in the places and times which are thus attributed to it; it is inevitable that a little of it should filter out. There are always some sacred things outside the sanctuaries; there are some rites that can be celebrated on work-days. But these are sacred things of the second rank and rites of a lesser importance. Concentration remains the dominating characteristic of this organization. Generally this concentration is complete for all that concerns the public cult, which cannot be celebrated except in common. The individual, private cult is the only one which comes very near to the temporal life. Thus the contrast between these two successive phases of human life attains its maximum of intensity in the inferior societies; for it is there that the individual cult is the most rudimentary....

In fact, owing to the barrier which separates the sacred from the profane, a man cannot enter into intimate relations with sacred things except after ridding himself of all that is profane in him. He cannot lead a religious life of even a slight intensity unless he commences by withdrawing more or less completely from the temporal life. So the negative cult is in one sense a means in view of an end: it is a condition of access to the positive cult. It does not confine itself to protecting sacred beings from vulgar contact; it acts upon the worshipper himself and modifies his condition positively. The man who has submitted himself to its prescribed interdictions is not the same afterwards as he was before....

[T]here are circumstances when a whole system of interdictions is concentrated on one man; in these cases, their effects accumulate, and thus become more manifest. This takes place in Australia at the time of the initiation. The neophyte is submitted to a great variety of negative rites. He must withdraw from the society in which his existence has been passed up till then, and from almost all human society. Not only is it forbidden for him to see women and uninitiated persons, but he also goes to live in the brush, far from his fellows, under the direction of some old men who serve him as godfathers....

In the light of these facts, we are able to understand what asceticism is, what place it occupies in the religious life and whence come the virtues which have generally been attributed to it. In fact, there is no interdict, the observance of which does not have an ascetic character to a certain degree. Abstaining from something which may be useful or from a form of activity which, since it is usual, should answer to some human need, is, of necessity, imposing constraints and renunciations. So in order to have real asceticism, it is sufficient for these practices to develop in such a way as to become the basis of a veritable scheme of life....

It follows that asceticism is not a rare, exceptional and nearly abnormal fruit of the religious life, as some have supposed it to be; on the contrary, it is one of its essential elements. Every religion contains it, at least in germ, for there are none in which a system of interdicts is not found. Their only difference in this regard which there may be between cults is that this germ is more or less developed in different ones. It should also be added that there probably is not a single one in which this development does not take, at least temporarily, the characteristic traits of real asceticism. This is what generally takes place at certain critical periods when, for a relatively short time, it is necessary to bring about a grave change of condition in a subject. Then, in order to introduce him more rapidly into the circle of sacred things with which he must be put in contact, he is separated violently from the profane world; but this does not come without many abstinences and an exceptional recrudescence of the system of interdicts. Now this is just what happens in Australia at the moment of initiation....

But abstinences and privations do not come without suffering. We hold to the profane world by all the fibers of our flesh; our senses attach us to it; our life depends upon it. It is not merely the natural theatre of our activity; it penetrates us from every side; it is a part of ourselves. So we cannot detach ourselves from it without doing violence to our nature and without painfully wounding our instincts. In other words, the negative cult cannot develop without causing suffering. Pain is one of its necessary conditions.

~

Self-Denial as an Essential Element of Religion

At the beginning of this work, we said that all the essential elements of religious thought and life ought to be found, at least in germ, in the most primitive religions: the preceding facts confirm this assertion. If there is any one belief which is believed to be peculiar to the most recent and idealistic religions, it is the one attributing a sanctifying power to sorrow.... In fact, it is by the way in which he braves suffering that the greatness of a man is best manifested. He never rises above himself with more brilliancy than when he subdues his own nature to the point of making it follow a way contrary to the one it would spontaneously take. By this, he distinguishes himself from all the other creatures who follow blindly wherever pleasure calls them; by this, he makes a place apart for himself in the world. Suffering is the sign that certain of the bonds attaching him to his profane environment are broken; so it testifies that he is partially freed from this environment, and, consequently, it is justly considered the instrument of deliverance....

Sacrifices and privations do not come without privations which cost the worshipper dear. Even if the rites do not demand material gifts from him, they require his time and his strength. In order to serve his gods, he must forget himself; to make for them a fitting place in his own life, he must sacrifice his profane interests. The positive cult is possible only when a man is trained to renouncement, to abnegation, to detachment from self, and consequently to suffering. It is necessary that he have no dread of them: he cannot even fulfil his duties joyfully unless he loves them to some extent. But for that, it is necessary that he train himself, and it is to this that the ascetic practices tend. So the suffering which they impose is not arbitrary and sterile cruelty; it is a necessary school, where men form and temper themselves, and acquire the qualities of disinterestedness and endurance without which there would be no religion. If this result is to be obtained, it is even a good thing that the ascetic ideal be incarnated eminently in certain persons, whose speciality, so to speak, it is to represent, almost with excess, this aspect of the ritual life; for they are like so many living models, inciting to effort. Such is the historic role of the great ascetics. When their deeds and acts are analyzed in detail, one asks himself what useful end they can have. He is struck by the fact that there is something excessive in the disdain they profess for all that ordinarily impassions men. But these exaggerations are necessary to sustain among the believers a sufficient disgust for an easy life and common pleasures. It is necessary that an elite put the end too high, if the crowd is not to put it too low. It is necessary that some exaggerate, if the average is to remain at a fitting level.

But asceticism does not serve religious ends only. Here, as elsewhere, religious interests are only the symbolic form of social and moral interests. The ideal beings to whom the cults are addressed are not the only ones who demand of their followers a certain disdain for suffering: society itself is possible only at this price. Though exalting the strength of man, it is frequently rude to individuals; it necessarily demands perpetual sacrifices from them; it is constantly doing violence to our natural appetites, just because it raises us above ourselves. If we are going to fulfil our duties towards it, then we must be prepared to do violence to our instincts sometimes and to ascend the decline of nature when it is necessary. So there is an asceticism which, being inherent in all social life, is destined to survive all the mythologies and all the dogmas; it is an integral part of all human culture. At bottom, this is the asceticism which is the reason for the existence of and the justification of that which has been taught by the religions of all times.

~

Rituals of Affirmation and Celebration

The Positive Cult

Whatever the importance of the negative cult may be, and though it may indirectly have positive effects, it does not contain its reason for existence in itself; it introduces one to the religious life, but it supposes this more than it constitutes it. If it orders the worshipper to flee from the profane world, it is to bring him nearer to the sacred world. Men have never thought that their duties towards religious forces might be reduced to a simple abstinence from all commerce; they have always believed that they upheld positive and bilateral relations with them, whose regulation and organization is the function of a group of ritual practices. To this special system of rites we give the name of *positive cult*.

For some time we almost completely ignored the positive cult of the totemic religion and what it consists in. We knew almost nothing more than the initiation rites, and we do not know those sufficiently well even now. But the observations... on the tribes of central Australia, have partially filled this gap in our information. There is one ceremony especially which these explorers have taken particular pains to describe to us and which, moreover, seems to dominate the whole totemic cult: this is the one that the Arunta, according to Spencer and Gillen, call the *Intichiuma*....

~

These rites are certainly among the most primitive that have ever been observed. No determined mythical personality appears in them; there is no question of gods or spirits that are properly so called; it is only vaguely anonymous and impersonal forces which they put into action....

[T]he... Intichiuma... [consists of] rites destined to assure the fecundity of the animal or vegetable species which serves the clan as totem. This species is the pre-eminently sacred thing; in it is incarnated that which we have been able to call, by metaphor, the totemic divinity. Yet we have seen that to perpetuate itself it has need of the aid of men. It is they who dispense the life of the new generation each year; without them, it would never be born. If they stopped celebrating the Intichiuma, the sacred beings would disappear from the face of the earth. So in one sense, it is from men that they get their existence; yet in another way, it is from them that men get theirs; for after they have once arrived at maturity, it is from them that men acquire the force needed to support and repair their spiritual beings. Thus we are able to say that men make their gods, or, at least, make them live; but at the same time, it is from them that they live themselves.

~

The only way of renewing the collective representations which relate to sacred beings is to retemper them in the very source of the religious life, that is to say, in the assembled groups. Now the emotions aroused by these periodical crises through which external things pass induce the men who witness them to assemble, to see what should be done about it. But by the very fact of uniting, they are mutually comforted; they find a remedy because they seek it together. The common faith becomes reanimated quite naturally in the heart of this reconstituted group; it is born again because it again finds those very conditions in which it was born in the first place. After it has been restored, it easily triumphs over all the private doubts which may have arisen in individual minds....

So we must be careful not to believe... that the cult was founded solely for the benefit of men and that the gods have nothing to do with it: they have no less need of it than their worshippers. Of course men would be unable to live without gods, but, on the other hand, the gods would die if their cult were not rendered.... The things which the worshipper really gives his gods are not the foods which he places upon the altars, nor the blood which he lets flow from his veins: it is his thought.... The rule *do ut des,* by which the principle of sacrifice has sometimes been defined,...only expresses in an explicit way the very mechanism of the sacrificial system and, more generally, of the whole positive cult....

But this...will appear still more natural to us, and we shall understand its meaning and the reason for its existence still better if, carrying our analysis still farther and substituting for the religious symbols the realities which they represent, we investigate how these behave in the rite. If, as we have attempted to establish, the sacred principle is nothing more nor less than society transfigured and personified, it should be possible to interpret the ritual in lay and social terms....

[T]he religious ceremonies...put the group into action; the groups assemble to celebrate them. So their first effect is to bring individuals together, to multiply the relations between them and to make them more intimate with one another. By this very fact, the contents of their consciousnesses is changed. On ordinary days, it is utilitarian and individual avocations which take the greater part of the attention. Every one attends to his own personal business....On feast days, on the contrary, these preoccupations are necessarily eclipsed; being essentially profane, they are excluded from these sacred periods. At this time, their thoughts are centered upon their common beliefs, their common traditions, the memory of their great ancestors, the collective ideal of which they are the incarnation; in a word, upon social things. Even the material interests which these great religious ceremonies are designed to satisfy concern the public order and are therefore social. Society as a whole is interested that the harvest be abundant, that the rain fall at the right time and not excessively, that the animals reproduce regularly. So it is society that is in the foreground of every consciousness; it dominates and directs all conduct; this is equivalent to saying that it is more living and active, and consequently more real, than in profane times....

The essential constituent of the cult is the cycle of feasts which return regularly at determined epochs. We are now able to understand whence this tendency towards periodicity comes; the rhythm which the religious life follows only expresses the rhythm of the social life, and results from it. Society is able to revivify the sentiment it has of itself only by assembling. But it cannot be assembled all the time. The exigencies of life do not allow it to remain in congregation indefinitely; so it scatters, to assemble anew when it again feels the need of this. It is to these necessary alternations that the regular alternations of sacred and profane times correspond.

⌒

Piacular Rituals: Loss and Mourning

Howsoever much they may differ from one another in the nature of the gestures they imply, the positive rites which we have been passing under review have one common characteristic: they are all performed in a state of confidence, joy and even enthusiasm.... Men celebrate them with confidence, joyfully anticipating the happy event which they prepare and announce. Whatever movements men perform participate in this same state of mind: of course, they are marked with the gravity which a religious solemnity always supposes, but this gravity excludes neither animation nor joy.

These are all joyful feasts. But there are sad celebrations as well, whose object is either to meet a calamity, or else merely to commemorate and deplore it. These rites have a special aspect, which we are going to attempt to characterize and explain. It is the more necessary to study them by themselves since they are going to reveal a new aspect of the religious life to us.

We propose to call the ceremonies of this sort piacular. The term *piaculum* has the advantage that while it suggests the idea of expiation, it also has a much more extended signification. Every misfortune, everything of evil omen, everything that inspires sentiments of sorrow or fear necessitates a *piaculum* and is therefore called piacular. So this word seems to be very well adapted for designating the rites which are celebrated by those in a state of uneasiness or sadness.

Mourning offers us a first and important example of piacular rites.

⌒

[Piacular] rites belong to a very different type from those which we have studied hitherto.... Instead of happy dances, songs and dramatic representations which distract and relax the mind, they are tears and groans and, in a word, the most varied manifestations of agonized sorrow and a sort of mutual pity, which occupy the whole scene.... Here ... dejection, cries and tears are the rule. The ascetic tortures himself in order to prove, in his own eyes and those of his fellows, that he is above suffering. During mourning, men injure themselves to prove that they suffer. By all these signs, the characteristic traits of the piacular rites are to be recognized.

But how are they to be explained?

One initial fact is constant: mourning is not the spontaneous expression of individual emotions. If the relations weep, lament, mutilate themselves, it is not because they feel themselves personally affected by the death of their kinsman. Of course, it may be that in certain particular cases, the chagrin expressed is really felt. But it is more generally the case that there is no connection between the sentiments felt and the gestures made by the actors in the rite.... One weeps, not simply because he is sad, but because he is forced to weep. It is a ritual attitude which he is forced to adopt out of respect for custom, but which is, in a large measure, independent of his affective state....

Whence comes this obligation?

Ethnographers and sociologists are generally satisfied with the reply which the natives themselves give to this question. They say that the dead wish to be lamented, that by refusing them the tribute of sorrow which is their right, men offend them, and that the only way of preventing their anger is to conform to their will.

But this mythological interpretation merely modifies the terms of the problem, without resolving it; it is still necessary to explain why the dead imperatively reclaim the mourning....

[M]ythical explanations express the idea which the native has of the rite, and not the rite itself. So we may set them aside and face the reality which they translate, though disfiguring it in doing so. If mourning differs from the other forms of the positive cult, there is one feature in which it resembles them: it, too, is made up out of collective ceremonies which produce a state of effervescence among those who take part in them. The sentiments aroused are different; but the arousal is the same. So it is presumable that the explanation of the joyous rites is capable of being applied to the sad rites, on condition that the terms be transposed.

When some one dies, the family group to which he belongs feels itself lessened and, to react against this loss, it assembles. A common misfortune has the same effects as the approach of a happy event: collective sentiments are renewed which then lead men to seek one another and to assemble together. We have even seen this need for concentration affirm itself with a particular energy: they embrace one another, put their arms round one another, and press as close as possible to one another. But the affective state in which the group then happens to be only reflects the circumstances through which it is passing. Not only do the relatives, who are effected the most directly, bring their own personal sorrow to the assembly, but the society exercises a moral pressure over its members, to put their sentiments in harmony with the situation. To allow them to remain indifferent to the blow which has fallen upon it and diminished it, would be equivalent to proclaiming that it does not hold the place in their hearts which is due it; it would be denying itself. A family which allows one of its members to die without being wept for shows by that very fact that it lacks moral unity and cohesion: it abdicates; it renounces its existence. An individual, in his turn, if he is strongly attached to the society of which he is a member, feels that he is morally held to participating in its sorrows and joys; not to be interested in them would be equivalent to breaking the bonds uniting him to the group; it would be renouncing all desire for it and contradicting himself....

We see that this explanation of mourning completely leaves aside all ideas of souls or spirits. The only forces which are really active are of a wholly impersonal nature: they are the emotions aroused in the group by the death of one of its members. But the primitive does not know the psychical mechanism from which these practices result. So when he tries to account for them, he is obliged to forge a wholly different explanation. All he knows is that he must painfully mortify himself...

The foundation of mourning is the impression of a loss which the group feels when it loses one of its members. But this very impression results in bringing individuals together, in putting them into closer relations with one another, in associating them all in the same mental state, and therefore in disengaging a sensation of comfort which compensates the original loss. Since they weep together, they hold to one another and the group is not weakened, in spite of the blow which has fallen upon it. Of course they have only sad emotions in common, but communicating in sorrow is still communicating, and every communion of mind, in whatever form it may be made, raises the social vitality. The exceptional violence of the manifestations by which the common pain is necessarily and obligatorily expressed even testifies to the fact that at this moment, the society is more alive and active than ever. In fact, whenever the social sentiment is painfully wounded, it reacts with greater force than ordinarily: one never holds so closely to his family as when it has just suffered. This surplus energy effaces the more completely the effects of the interruption which was felt at first, and thus dissipates the feeling of coldness which death always brings with it. The group feels its strength gradually returning to it; it begins to hope and to live again.

$\sim$

Conclusion

At the beginning of this work we announced that the religion whose study we were taking up contained within it the most characteristic elements of the religious life. The exactness of this proposition may now be verified. Howsoever simple the system which we have studied may be, we have found within it all the great ideas and the principal ritual attitudes which are at the basis of even the most advanced religions: the division of things into sacred and profane, the notions of the soul, of spirits, of mythical personalities, and of a national and even international divinity, a negative cult with ascetic practices which are its exaggerated form, rites of oblation and communion, imitative rites, commemorative rites and expiatory rites; nothing essential is lacking. We are thus in a position to hope that the results at which we have arrived are not peculiar to totemism alone, but can aid us in an understanding of what religion in general is.

It may be objected that one single religion, whatever its field of extension may be, is too narrow a base for such an induction. We have not dreamed for a moment of ignoring the fact that an extended verification may add to the authority of a theory, but it is equally true that when a law has been proven by one well-made experiment, this proof is valid universally. If in one single case a scientist succeeded in finding out the secret of the life of even the most protoplasmic creature that can be imagined, the truths thus obtained would be applicable to all living beings, even the most advanced. Then if, in our studies of these very humble societies, we have really succeeded in discovering some of the elements out of which the most fundamental religious notions are made up, there is no reason for not extending the most general results of our researchers to other religions.... If among certain peoples the ideas of sacredness, the soul and God are to be explained sociologically, it should be presumed scientifically that, in principle, the same explanation is valid for all the peoples among whom these same ideas are found with the same essential characteristics. Therefore, supposing that we have not been deceived, certain at least of our conclusions can be legitimately generalized. The moment has come to disengage these. And an induction of this sort, having at its foundation a clearly defined experiment, is less adventurous than many summary generalizations which, while attempting to reach the essence of religion at once, without resting upon the careful analysis of any religion in particular, greatly risk losing themselves in space.

The theorists who have undertaken to explain religion in rational terms have generally seen in it before all else a system of ideas, corresponding to some determined object. This object has been conceived in a multitude of ways: nature, the infinite, the unknowable, the ideal, etc.; but these differences matter but little. In any case, it was the conceptions and beliefs which were considered as the essential elements of religion. As for the rites, from this point of view they appear to be only an external translation, contingent and material, of these internal states which alone pass as having any intrinsic value. This conception is so commonly held that generally the disputes of which religion is the theme turn about the question whether it can conciliate itself with science or not, that is to say, whether or not there is a place beside our scientific knowledge for another form of thought which would be specifically religious.

But the believers, the men who lead the religious life and have a direct sensation of what it really is, object to this way of regarding it, saying that it does not correspond to their daily experience. In fact, they feel that the real function of religion is not to make us think, to enrich our knowledge, nor to add to the conceptions which we owe to science others of another origin and another character, but rather, it is to make us act, to aid us to believe. The believer who has communicated with his god is not merely a man who sees new truths of which the unbeliever is ignorant; he is a man who is *stronger*. He feels within him more force, either to endure the trials of existence, or to conquer them. It is as though he were raised above the miseries of the world, because he is raised above his condition as a mere man; he believes that he is saved from evil, under whatever form he may conceive this evil.…

Our entire study rests upon this postulate that the unanimous sentiment of the believers of all times cannot be purely illusory. Together with a recent apologist of the faith [William James: ed.] we admit that these religious beliefs rest upon a specific experience whose demonstrative value is, in one sense, not one bit inferior to that of scientific experiments, though different from them. We, too, think that "a tree is known by its fruits," and that fertility is the best proof of what the roots are worth. But from the fact that a "religious experience," if we choose to call it this, does exist and that it has a certain foundation—and, by the way, is there any experience which has none?—it does not follow that the reality which is its foundation conforms objectively to the idea which believers have of it. The very fact that the fashion in which it has been conceived has varied infinitely in different times is enough to prove that none of these conceptions express it adequately. If a scientist states it as an axiom that the sensations of heat and light which we feel correspond to some objective cause, he does not conclude that this is what it appears to the senses to be. Likewise, even if the impressions which the faithful feel are not imaginary, still they are in no way privileged intuitions; there is no reason for believing that they inform us better upon the nature of their object than do ordinary sensations upon the nature of bodies and their properties. In order to discover what this object consists of, we must submit them to an examination and elaboration analogous to that which has substituted for the sensuous idea of the world another which is scientific and conceptual.

This is precisely what we have tried to do, and we have seen that this reality, which mythologies have represented under so many different forms, but which is the universal and eternal objective cause of these sensations *sui generis* out of which religious experience is made, is society. We have shown what moral forces it develops and how it awakens this sentiment of a refuge, of a shield and of a guardian support which attaches the believer to his cult. It is that which raises him outside himself; it is even that which made him. For that which makes a man is the totality of the intellectual property which constitutes civilization, and civilization is the work of society. Thus is explained the preponderating role of the cult in all religions, whichever they may be. This is because society cannot make its influence felt unless it is in action, and it is not in action unless the individuals who compose it are assembled together and act in common. It is by common action that it takes consciousness of itself and realizes its position; it is before all else an active co-operation. The collective ideas and sentiments are even possible only owing to these exterior movements which symbolize them, as we have established. Then it is action which dominates the religious life, because of the mere fact that it is society which is its source. . . .

In summing up, then, it may be said that nearly all the great social institutions have been born in religion. Now in order that these principle aspects of the collective life may have commenced by being only varied aspects of the religious life, it is obviously necessary that the religious life be the eminent form and, as it were, the concentrated expression of the whole collective life. If religion has given birth to all that is essential in society, it is because the idea of society is the soul of religion.

$\sim$

Religion and Science

Thus there is something eternal in religion which is destined to survive all the particular symbols in which religious thought has successively enveloped itself. There can be no society which does not feel the need of upholding and reaffirming at regular intervals the collective sentiments and the collective ideas which make its unity and its personality. Now this moral remaking cannot be achieved except by the means of reunions, assemblies and meetings where the individuals, being closely united to one another, reaffirm in common their common sentiments; hence come ceremonies which do not differ from regular religious ceremonies, either in their object, the results which they produce, or the processes employed to attain these results. What essential difference is there between an assembly of Christians celebrating the principal dates of the life of Christ, or of Jews remembering the exodus from Egypt or the promulgation of the decalogue, and a reunion of citizens commemorating the promulgation of a new moral or legal system or some great event in the national life?

If we find a little difficulty to-day in imagining what these feasts and ceremonies of the future could consist in, it is because we are going through a stage of transition and moral mediocrity. The great things of the past which filled our fathers with enthusiasm do not excite the same ardour in us, either because they have come into common usage to such an extent that we are unconscious of them, or else because they no longer answer to our actual aspirations; but as yet there is nothing to replace them.... In a word, the old gods are growing old or already dead, and others are not yet born. This is what rendered vain the attempt of Comte with the old historic souvenirs artificially revived: it is life itself, and not a dead past which can produce a living cult. But this state of incertitude and confused agitation cannot last for ever. A day will come when our societies will know again those hours of creative effervescence, in the course of which new ideas arise and new formulae are found which serve for a while to guide humanity.... We have already seen how the French Revolution established a whole cycle of holidays to keep the principles with which it was inspired in a state of perpetual youth.... There are no gospels which are immortal, but neither is there any reason for believing that humanity is incapable of inventing new ones....

It is said that science denies religion in principle. But religion exists; it is a system of given facts; in a word, it is a reality. How could science deny this reality? Also, in so far as religion is action, and in so far as it is a means of making men live, science could not take its place, for even if this expresses life, it does not create it; it may well seek to explain the faith, but by that very act it presupposes it. Thus there is no conflict except on one limited point. Of the two functions which religion originally fulfilled, there is one, and only one, which tends to escape it more and more: that is the speculative function. That which science refuses to grant to religion is not its right to exist, but its right to dogmatize upon the nature of things and the special competence which it claims for itself for knowing man and the world....

We have said that there is something eternal in religion: it is the cult and the faith. Men cannot celebrate ceremonies for which they see no reason, nor can they accept a faith which they in no way understand. To spread itself or merely to maintain itself, it must be justified, that is to say, a theory must be made of it. A theory of this sort must undoubtedly be founded upon the different sciences, from the moment when these exist; first of all, upon the social sciences, for religious faith has its origin in society; then upon psychology, for society is a synthesis of human consciousness; and finally upon the sciences of nature, for man and society are a part of the universe and can be abstracted from it only artificially. But howsoever important these facts taken from the constituted sciences may be, they are not enough; for faith is before all else an impetus to action, while science, no matter how far it may be pushed, always remains at distance from this. Science is fragmentary and incomplete; it advances but slowly and is never finished; but life cannot wait. The theories which are destined to make men live and act are therefore obliged to pass science and complete it prematurely....

But if the fundamental notions of science are of a religious origin, how has religion been able to bring them forth? At first sight, one does not see what relations there can be between religion and logic. Or, since the reality which religious thought expresses is society, the question can be stated in the following terms, which make the entire difficulty appear even better: what has been able to make social life so important a source of the logical life? ...

Logical thought is made up of concepts. Seeking how society can have played a role in the genesis of logical thought thus reduces itself to seeking how it can have taken a part in the formation of concepts. . . .

A concept is not my concept; I hold it in common with other men, or, in any case, can communicate it to them. It is impossible for me to make a sensation pass from my consciousness into that of another: it holds closely to my organism and personality and cannot be detached from them. All that I can do is to invite others to place themselves before the same object as myself and to leave themselves to its action. On the other hand, conversation and all intellectual communication between men is an exchange of concepts. The concept is essentially impersonal representation; it is through it that human intelligences communicate.

The nature of the concept, thus defined, bespeaks its origin. If it is common to all, it is the work of the community. Since it bears the mark of no particular mind, it is clear that it was elaborated by a unique intelligence, where all others meet each other, and after a fashion, come to nourish themselves.

$\sim$

We are now able to see what the part of society in the genesis of logical thought is. This is possible only from the moment when, above the fugitive conceptions which they owe to sensuous experience, men have succeeded in conceiving a whole world of stable ideas, the common ground of all intelligences. In fact, logical thinking is always impersonal thinking. . . . It is under the form of collective thought that impersonal thought is for the first time revealed to humanity; we can not see by what other way this revelation could have been made. From the mere fact that society exists, there is also, outside of the individual sensations and images, a whole system of representations which enjoy marvellous properties. By means of them, men understand each other and intelligences grasp each other. They have within them a sort of force or moral ascendancy, in virtue of which they impose themselves upon individual minds. Hence the individual at least obscurely takes account of the fact that above his private ideas, there is a world of absolute ideas according to which he must shape his own; he catches a glimpse of a whole intellectual kingdom in which he participates, but which is greater than he. This is the first intuition of the realm of truth.

$\sim$

In summing up, then, we must say that society is not at all the illogical or a-logical, incoherent and fantastic being which it has often been considered. Quite on the contrary, the collective consciousness is the highest form of the psychic life, since it is the consciousness of the consciousnesses. Being placed outside of and above individual and local contingencies, it sees things only in their permanent and essential aspects, which it crystallizes into communicable ideas. At the same time that it sees from above, it sees farther; at every moment of time, it embraces all known reality; that is why it alone can furnish the mind with the moulds which are applicable to the totality of things and which make it possible to think of them. They translate the ways of being which are found in all the stages of reality but which appear in their full clarity only at the summit, because the extreme complexity of the psychic life which passes there necessitates a greater development of consciousness. Attributing social origins to logical thought is not debasing it or diminishing its value or reducing it to nothing more than a system of artificial combinations; on the contrary, it is relating it to a cause which implies it naturally....

Thus it is not at all true that between science one the one hand, and morals and religion on the other, there exists that sort of antinomy which has so frequently been admitted, for the two forms of human activity really come form one and the same source.... Rational thinking is thinking according to the laws which are imposed upon all reasonable beings; acting morally is conducting one's self according to those maxims which can be extended without contradiction to all wills. In other words, science and morals imply that the individual is capable of raising himself above his own peculiar point of view and of living an impersonal life. In fact, it cannot be doubted that this is a trait common to all the higher forms of thought and action....

Perhaps some will be surprised to see us connect the most elevated forms of thought with society: the cause appears quite humble, in consideration of the value which we attribute to the effect.... But attributing to society this preponderating role in the genesis of our nature is not denying this creation; for society has a creative power which no other observable being can equal.... A society is the most powerful combination of physical and moral forces of which nature offers us an example. Nowhere else is an equal richness of different materials, carried to such a degree of concentration, to be found. Then it is not surprising that a higher life disengages itself which, by reacting upon the elements of which it is the product, raises them to a higher plane of existence and transforms them.

Thus sociology appears destined to open a new way to the science of man.... [F]rom the moment when it is recognized that above the individual there is society, and that this is not a nominal being created by reason, but a system of active forces, a new manner of explaining men becomes possible.

5

Karl Marx: Religion as Agent of Economic Oppression

No theorist has written about religion with greater passion—or deeper animosity—than Karl Marx (1818–1883), the German social critic who in the mid-nineteenth century advanced the cause of revolutionary Communism. In his day, these radical ideas left Marx a solitary prophet, revered by associates, but hunted by authorities and eventually exiled to a life of study in London at his chosen desk in the British Library. Yet within a few decades after his death in 1883, all of that would change—dramatically. Marx's communist ideas appealed to discontented intellectuals across Europe, and in Russia they won a convert in Vladimir Lenin, architect of the Bolshevik Revolution of 1917—the upheaval that brought the death of the Czar and founded the Soviet Socialist Republics. A generation later, an army of rural peasants led by another charismatic Marxist, Mao Zedong, achieved a comparable victory in China, the most populous land on the globe. In each case, Marx's original, militant atheism and strident socio-economic attack on religion figured large in the revolutionary agenda.

Marx was born into a large Jewish family in the Rhineland city of Trier. His father had undergone a Christian conversion, but Marx entertained no such thought. Despite marriage to the daughter of a Christian nobleman, he stood resolute in a fiercely combative form of atheism. At the University of Berlin, Marx studied under Georg Wilhelm Friedrich Hegel, the most eminent German philosopher of the day. Unlike Hegel, an idealist who stressed mind over matter, Marx joined a circle of young thinkers who saw matter as primary. They insisted that material forces drive all of history; ideas merely reflect the material conditions that determine them.

Marx had hoped for a university post, but his radical ideas made that impossible, so he turned to journalism, writing first for a German newspaper, then moving to Paris, where he read French theorists (including those who influenced Durkheim) and produced several of his most significant early writings. In *On the Jewish Question* (1843), *Toward a Critique of*

Hegel's Philosophy of Law: Introduction (1843), *Economic and Philosophic Manuscripts* (1844), and *The Holy Family* (1845), he developed ideas that were decisive for the rest of his life. At this time also he met and formed a lifelong partnership with Frederick Engels, a German factory owner's son who lived in England. In 1848, Engels and Marx together published the *Communist Manifesto,* their revolutionary call to arms. Its opening paragraph announced the first principle of all revolutionary socialism: "The history of all hitherto existing society is the history of class struggle." Everywhere in history, they insisted, we meet with one unvarying fact. There are the rich, who own the "means of production," and the poor, who own nothing and only provide labor for the rich. The rich live in luxury; the poor struggle to survive. These two classes have lived in a perpetual state of hidden or open warfare.

For Marx and Engels, the root of this enduring injustice is not hard to discover. In the primitive cultures of early humanity all goods were held in common; each person cared for all in shared equality. This idyllic world was destroyed, however, by the poisonous notion of private property. Once this idea took root, the perverse habit of personally acquiring things replaced the practice of using them in common. The sinister idea of selling to others—for a profit—replaced the ideal of sharing with others as they need. Thus arose the great social divide between "haves" and "have nots," between the rich and the poor, between the bourgeoisie, who own the farms and factories, and the proletariat, who own nothing and are condemned to work for those who do. In his great study *Das Kapital* (1867) Marx developed a technical economic theory for his judgments on society. He expounded a labor-theory of value, arguing that by their efforts workers actually put a surplus of value into the things they make, only to see it stolen from them in the form of profits taken by the landlord, prince, or (in modern times) the bourgeois factory owner. It is this "theft of surplus value" that forms the perpetual crime of the rich— and gives justice to violent revolutionary action by the poor.

The surprising thing, in light of this bitter social division, is not that there have been revolutions in history, but that they have not been more frequent. In explaining this fact Marx introduces a critical distinction between what he calls the material base of society and its cultural superstructure. Societies of all ages have seen the need for elaborate "superstructures" of cultural institutions—the state, systems of law, officially sanctioned armies or police, entertainments like the arts and literature, and the moral precepts promoted by philosophy and especially religion. Most people see these enterprises as good things, says Marx, but they are wrong. The chief and only reason for this elaborate superstructure is to anchor the corrupt social order. And religion is, if anything, the chief offender. Like the state and the police, its purpose is to defend the unjust order at all costs, to denounce as immoral any action of the poor to right the injustice. Like art and literature, religion also employs its skills of persuasion and of distraction to deflect and defuse the anger of the poor and suffocate their urge to revolt.

To explain this point about religion, Marx turned to a second German philosopher, Ludwig Feuerbach, who had said the figure of "God" is a fantasy that human beings create out of their own ideals. Marx read Feuerbach and agreed with him completely. Religion, he asserted defiantly, is "the opium of the people." It is, inescapably, a system of perverse and pernicious fantasies, a kind of narcotic that fills the minds of the poor with illusory ideas of a Heaven in the next life, all the better to distract them from acting against the very real oppressions of the present life.

Marx, finally, was not content just to advance these ideas; he insisted that they be acted upon. "The philosophers have only *interpreted* the world, in various ways," he wrote, "the point, however, is to *change* it." This deeply held axiom has made Marxism much more than just a theory about society and religion. Its commitment is to a militant agenda of violent revolution and complete social transformation. In the past century, especially, Marxism has offered the world less a theory of religion than a total system of thought and action that itself resembles a religion, complete with its own sacred texts and temples, saints and sacraments, missionaries, martyrs, and prophecies.

Though references to religion are frequent in Marx's writing, he chose not to offer a sustained theoretical discussion of the subject. Some of Engels' analyses, however, are more extensive. So this chapter offers a mixed set of selections: two brief declarations by Marx, including the famous passage which describes religion as the "opium of the people"; a selection from the now-famous *Manifesto,* the joint effort of Marx and Engels; two further brief discussions by Engels, including his notable account of religion and rebellion in the Peasants' War during the age of the Protestant Reformation; and finally, a short essay by Lenin that articulates his version of the Marxist critique, previous to the brutal Russian assault upon the Orthodox Church under his successor Josef Stalin.

Toward a Critique of Hegel's Philosophy of Law: Introduction

In this work and most others, Marx writes in a style dense with metaphors, word-plays, and rhetorical flourishes that make his argument difficult for the uninitiated reader to access. Even so, the point of his remarks, summarized in the famous phrase dismissing religion as the "opium of the people," can hardly be missed.

For Germany the *criticism of religion* is in the main complete, and criticism of religion is the premise of all criticism.

The *profane* existence of error is discredited after its *heavenly oratio pro aris et focis* [prayer for altars and hearths: ed.] has been disproved. Man, who looked for a superhuman being in the fantastic reality of heaven and found nothing there but the *reflection* of himself, will no longer be disposed to find but the *semblance* of himself, only an inhuman being, where he seeks and must seek his true reality.

The basis of irreligious criticism is: *Man makes religion,* religion does not make man. Religion is the self-consciousness and self-esteem of man who has either not yet found himself or has already lost himself again. But *man* is no abstract being encamped outside the world. Man is *the world of man,* the state, society. This state, this society, produce religion, an *inverted world-consciousness,* because they are an *inverted world.* Religion is the general theory of that world, its encyclopaedic compendium, its logic in a popular form, its spiritualistic *point d'honneur,* its enthusiasm, its moral sanction, its solemn complement, its universal source of consolation and justification. It is the *fantastic realization* of the human essence because the *human essence* has no true reality. The struggle against religion is therefore indirectly a fight against *the world* of which religion is the spiritual *aroma.*

Religious distress is at the same time the *expression* of real distress and also the *protest* against real distress. Religion is the sigh of the oppressed creature, the heart of a heartless world, just as it is the spirit of spiritless conditions. It is the *opium* of the people.

To abolish religion as the *illusory* happiness of the people is to demand their *real* happiness. The demand to give up illusions about the existing state of affairs is the *demand to give up a state of affairs which needs illusions.* The criticism of religion is therefore *in embryo the criticism of the vale of tears,* the *halo* of which is religion. Criticism has torn up the imaginary flowers from the chain not so that man shall wear the unadorned, bleak chain but so that he will shake off the chain and pluck the living flower. The criticism of religion disillusions man to make him think and act and shape his reality like a man who has been disillusioned and has come to reason, so that he will revolve round himself and therefore round his true sun. Religion is only the illusory sun which revolves round man as long as he does not revolve round himself.

The *task of history,* therefore, once *the world beyond the truth* has disappeared, is to establish the *truth of this world.* The immediate *task of philosophy,*

FROM volume 3 of Karl Marx and Friedrich Engels, *Collected Works,* copyright 1975, Progress Publishers. Printed with permission of International Publishers, New York, New York.

which is at the service of history, once the *holy form* of human self-estrangement has been unmasked, is to unmask self-estrangement in its *unholy forms*. Thus the criticism of heaven turns into the criticism of the earth, the *criticism of religion* into the *criticism of law* and the *criticism of theology* into the *criticism of politics*.

⌒

The evident proof of the radicalism of German theory, and hence of its practical energy, is that it proceeds from a resolute *positive* abolition of religion. The criticism of religion ends with the teaching that *man is the highest being for man,* hence with the *categorical imperative to overthrow all relations* in which man is a debased, enslaved, forsaken, despicable being, relations which cannot be better described than by the exclamation of a Frenchman when it was planned to introduce a tax on dogs: Poor dogs! They want to treat you like human beings!

Even historically, theoretical emancipation has specific practical significance for Germany. For Germany's *revolutionary* past is theoretical, it is the *Reformation*. As the revolution then began in the brain of the *monk,* so now it begins in the brain of the *philosopher*.

Luther, we grant, overcame the bondage of *piety* by replacing it by the bondage of *conviction*. He shattered faith in authority because he restored the authority of faith. He turned priests into laymen because he turned laymen into priests. He freed man from outer religiosity because he made religiosity the inner man. He freed the body from chains because he enchained the heart.

But if Protestantism was not the true solution it was at least the true setting of the problem. It was no longer a case of the layman's struggle against the *priest outside himself* but of his struggle against his *own priest inside himself,* his *priestly nature.* And if the Protestant transformation of the German laymen into priests emancipated the lay popes, the *princes,* with the whole of their priestly clique, the privileged and philistines, the philosophical transformation of priestly Germans into men will emancipate the *people.* But *secularisation* will not stop at the *pillaging of churches* practised mainly by hypocritical Prussia any more than emancipation stops at princes. The Peasant War, the most radical fact of German history, came to grief because of theology. Today, when theology itself has come to grief, the most unfree fact of German history, our *status quo,* will be shattered against philosophy.

⌒

Where, then, is the *positive* possibility of . . . emancipation?

Answer: In the formation of a class with radical chains, a class of civil society which is not a class of civil society, an estate which is the dissolution of all estates, a sphere which has a universal character by its universal suffering and claims no *particular right* because *no particular wrong* but *wrong generally* is perpetrated against it; which can no longer invoke a *historical* but only a *human* title; which does not stand in any one-sided antithesis to the consequences but in an all-round antithesis to the premises of the...state; a sphere, finally, which cannot emancipate itself without emancipating itself from all other spheres of society and thereby emancipating all other spheres of society, which, in a word, is the *complete loss* of man and hence can win itself only through the *complete rewinning of man.* This dissolution of society as a particular estate is the *proletariat.* The proletariat is coming into being...only as a result of the rising *industrial* development. For it is not the *naturally arising* poor but the *artificially impoverished,* not the human masses mechanically oppressed by the gravity of society but the masses resulting from the *drastic dissolution* of society, mainly of the middle estate, that form the proletariat....

By proclaiming the *dissolution of the hitherto existing world order* the proletariat merely states *the secret of its own existence,* for it *is in fact* the dissolution of that world order. By demanding the *negation of private property,* the proletariat merely raises to the rank of a *principle of society* what society has made the principle of the *proletariat,* what, without its own co-operation, is already incorporated in it as the negative result of society. In regard to the world which is coming into being the proletarian then finds himself possessing the same right as the *German king* in regard to the world which has come into being when he calls the people *his* people as he calls the horse *his* horse. By declaring the people his private property the king simply states that the property owner is king.

As philosophy finds its *material* weapons in the proletariat, so the proletariat finds its *spiritual* weapons in philosophy. And once the lightning of thought has squarely struck this ingenuous soil of the people the emancipation...into *human beings* will take place.

Let us sum up the result:

The only *practically* possible liberation...is liberation that proceeds from the standpoint of *the* theory which proclaims man to be the highest being for man. In Germany emancipation from the *Middle Ages* is possible only as emancipation from the *partial* victories over the Middle Ages as well. In Germany *no* kind of bondage can be broken without breaking *every* kind of bondage. [E]*mancipation*...is the emancipation of the human being. The *head* of this emancipation is *philosophy,* its *heart* is the *proletariat.* Philosophy cannot be made a reality without the abolition of the proletariat, the proletariat cannot be abolished without philosophy being made a reality.

The Communism of the *Rheinischer Beobachter*

This short selection, more journalistic and less philosophical in nature, records an indictment less of religion than specifically of the crimes and injustices of the Christian religion.

The social principles of Christianity have now had eighteen hundred years to be developed, and need no further development....

The social principles of Christianity justified the slavery of antiquity, glorified the serfdom of the Middle Ages and are capable, in case of need, of defending the oppression of the proletariat, even if with somewhat doleful grimaces.

The social principles of Christianity preach the necessity of a ruling and an oppressed class, and, for the latter all they have to offer is the pious wish that the former may be charitable.

The social principles of Christianity place the...compensation for all infamies in heaven, and thereby justify the continuation of these infamies on earth.

The social principles of Christianity declare all the vile acts of the oppressors against the oppressed to be either a just punishment for original sin and other sins, or trials which the Lord, in his infinite wisdom, ordains for the redeemed.

The social principles of Christianity preach cowardice, self-contempt, abasement, submissiveness and humbleness, in short, all the qualities of the rabble, and the proletariat, which will not permit itself to be treated as rabble, needs its courage, its self-confidence, its pride and its sense of independence even more than its bread.

The social principles of Christianity are sneaking and hypocritical, and the proletariat is revolutionary.

So much for the social principles of Christianity.

The Communist Manifesto

The "Manifesto" is of course the most famous of the combined efforts of Marx and Engels. As a defiant call to social revolution, it primarily addresses economic and political issues, but the selection below strikes out as well at cultural and religious forms of oppression.

FROM volume 6 of Karl Marx and Friedrich Engels, *Collected Works*, copyright 1976 Progress Publishers. Printed with permission of International Publishers, New York, New York.

In the conditions of the proletariat, those of old society at large are already virtually swamped. The proletarian is without property; his relation to his wife and children has no longer anything in common with the bourgeois family relations; modern industrial labour, modern subjection to capital, the same in England as in France, in America as in Germany, has stripped him of every trace of national character. Law, morality, religion, are to him so many bourgeois prejudices, behind which lurk in ambush just as many bourgeois interests.

All the preceding classes that got the upper hand, sought to fortify their already acquired status by subjecting society at large to their conditions of appropriation....

And here it becomes evident, that the bourgeoisie is unfit any longer to be the ruling class in society, and to impose its conditions of existence upon society as an over-riding law. It is unfit to rule because it is incompetent to assure an existence to its slave within his slavery, because it cannot help letting him sink into such a state, that it has to feed him, instead of being fed by him. Society can no longer live under this bourgeoisie, in other words, its existence is no longer compatible with society.

~

You are horrified at our intending to do away with private property. But in your existing society, private property is already done away with for nine-tenths of the population; its existence for the few is solely due to its non-existence in the hands of those nine-tenths. You reproach us, therefore, with intending to do away with a form of property, the necessary condition for whose existence is the non-existence of any property for the immense majority of society.

In one word, you reproach us with intending to do away with your property. Precisely so; that is just what we intend....

Communism deprives no man of the power to appropriate the products of society; all that it does is to deprive him of the power to subjugate the labour of others by means of such appropriation.

It has been objected that upon the abolition of private property all work will cease, and universal laziness will overtake us.

According to this, bourgeois society ought long ago to have gone to the dogs through sheer idleness; for those of its members who work, acquire nothing, and those who acquire anything, do not work....

All objections urged against the Communistic mode of producing and appropriating material products, have, in the same way, been urged against the Communistic modes of producing and appropriating intellectual products. Just as, to the bourgeois, the disappearance of class property is the disappearance of production itself, so the disappearance of class culture is to him identical with the disappearance of all culture.

That culture, the loss of which he laments, is, for the enormous majority, a mere training to act as a machine.

But don't wrangle with us so long as you apply, to our intended abolition of bourgeois property, the standard of your bourgeois notions of freedom, culture, law, &c. Your very ideas are but the outgrowth of the conditions of your bourgeois production and bourgeois property, just as your jurisprudence is but the will of your class made into a law for all, a will, whose essential character and direction are determined by the economical conditions of existence of your class.

The selfish misconception that induces you to transform into eternal laws of nature and of reason, the social forms springing from your present mode of production and form of property—historical relations that rise and disappear in the progress of production—this misconception you share with every ruling class that has preceded you. What you see clearly in the case of ancient property, what you admit in the case of feudal property, you are of course forbidden to admit in the case of your own bourgeois form of property.

Abolition of the family! Even the most radical flare up at this infamous proposal of the Communists.

On what foundation is the present family, the bourgeois family, based? On capital, on private gain. But this state of things finds its complement in the practical absence of the family among the proletarians, and in public prostitution.

The bourgeois family will vanish as a matter of course when its complement vanishes, and both will vanish with the vanishing of capital. Do you charge us with wanting to stop the exploitation of children by their parents? To this crime we plead guilty.

But you will say, we destroy the most hallowed of social relations, when we replace home education by social.

And your education! Is not that also social, and determined by the social conditions under which you educate by the intervention, direct or indirect, of society, by means of schools &c.? The Communists have not invented the intervention of society in education; they do but seek to…rescue education from the influence of the ruling class.

The bourgeois clap-trap about the family and education, about the hallowed co-relation of parent and child, becomes all the more disgusting, the more, by the action of Modern Industry, all family ties among the proletarians are torn asunder, and their children transformed into simple articles of commerce and instruments of labour….

The Communists are further reproached with desiring to abolish countries and nationality.

The working men have no country. We cannot take from them what they have not got. Since the proletariat must first of all acquire political supremacy, must rise to be the leading class of the nation, must constitute itself *the* nation, it is so far, itself national, though not in the bourgeois sense of the word. . . .

The charges against Communism made from a religious, a philosophical, and, generally, from an ideological standpoint, are not deserving of serious examination.

Does it require deep intuition to comprehend that man's ideas, views and conceptions, in one word, man's consciousness, changes with every change in the conditions of his material existence, in his social relations and in his social life?

What else does the history of ideas prove, than that intellectual production changes its character in proportion as material production is changed? The ruling ideas of each age have ever been the ideas of its ruling class.

When people speak of ideas that revolutionise society, they do but express the fact, that within the old society, the elements of a new one have been created, and that the dissolution of the old ideas keeps even pace with the dissolution of the old conditions of existence.

When the ancient world was in its last throes, the ancient religions were overcome by Christianity. When Christian ideas succumbed in the 18th century to rationalist ideas, feudal society fought its death battle with the then revolutionary bourgeoisie. The ideas of religious liberty and freedom of conscience merely gave expression to the sway of free competition within the domain of knowledge.

"Undoubtedly," it will be said, "religious, moral, philosophical and juridical ideas have been modified in the course of historical development. But religion, morality, philosophy, political science, and law, constantly survived this change.

"There are, besides, eternal truths, such as Freedom, Justice, etc., that are common to all states of society. But Communism abolishes eternal truths, it abolishes all religion and all morality, instead of constituting them on a new basis; it therefore acts in contradiction to all past historical experience."

What does this accusation reduce itself to? The history of all past society has consisted in the development of class antagonisms, antagonisms that assumed different forms at different epochs.

But whatever form they may have taken, one fact is common to all past ages, *viz.*, the exploitation of one part of society by the other. No wonder, then, that the social consciousness of past ages, despite all the multiplicity and variety it displays, moves within certain common forms, or general ideas, which cannot completely vanish except with the total disappearance of class antagonisms.

The Communist revolution is the most radical rupture with traditional property relations; no wonder that its development involves the most radical rupture with traditional ideas. . . .

When, in the course of development, class distinctions have disappeared, and all production has been concentrated in the hands of a vast association of the whole nation, the public power will lose its political character. Political power, properly so called, is merely the organized power of one class for oppressing another. If the proletariat during its contest with the bourgeoisie is compelled, by the force of circumstances, to organize itself as a class, if, by means of a revolution, it makes itself the ruling class, and, as such, sweeps away by force the old conditions of production, then it will, along with these conditions, have swept away the conditions for the existence of class antagonisms and of classes generally, and will thereby have abolished its own supremacy as a class.

In place of the old bourgeois society, with its classes and class antagonisms, we shall have an association, in which the free development of each is the condition of the free development of all.

~

In short, the Communists everywhere support every revolutionary movement against the existing social and political order of things.

In all these movements they bring to the front, as the leading question in each, the property question, no matter what its degree of development at the time.

Finally, they labour everywhere for the union and agreement of the democratic parties of all countries.

The Communists disdain to conceal their views and aims. They openly declare that their ends can be attained only by the forcible overthrow of all existing social conditions. Let the ruling classes tremble at a Communistic revolution. The proletarians have nothing to lose but their chains. They have a world to win.

Working Men of All Countries Unite!

The Peasant War in Germany

Marxists found an early form of their revolutionary agenda played out in the revolutionary "Peasant War" sparked by the Protestant Reformation. Here Engels draws a sharp contrast between Martin Luther, the "betrayer" of the social revolution he might well have led, and his radical opponent Thomas Münzer, the hero of the proletarian cause and the only reformer true to its revolutionary ideals.

FROM: Frederick Engels, *The Peasant War in Germany*, chapter 11. In Karl Marx and Frederick Engels, *Marx and Engels on Religion*. Introduction by Reinhold Niebuhr. Reprinted from the edition of 1957. Moscow: The Foreign Languages Publishing House. New York: Shocken Books, Inc. [1850] 1964.

In spite of the latest experiences, the German ideology [prevalent thinking: ed.] still sees nothing except violent theological bickering in the
struggles that ended the Middle Ages. If only the people of that time, say our
home-bred historians and sages, had come to an understanding concerning
heavenly things, there would have been no ground whatever to quarrel over
earthly affairs. These ideologists are gullible enough to accept unquestioningly
all the illusions that an epoch makes about itself or that ideologists of some
epoch make about that epoch....

[T]he so-called religious wars of the sixteenth century involved primarily...material class interests; those were class wars just as the later internal col-
lisions in England and France were....

The Middle Ages had...wiped the old [Roman: ed.] civilization, the old
philosophy, politics and jurisprudence off the slate, to begin anew in everything. The only thing they kept from the old shattered world was Christianity
and a number of half-ruined towns divested of all their civilization. As a consequence, just as in every primitive stage of development, the clergy obtained
a monopoly on intellectual education, and education itself became essentially
theological. In the hands of the clergy politics and jurisprudence, much like all
other sciences, remained mere branches of theology, and were treated according
to the principles prevailing in the latter. Church dogmas were at the same time
political axioms, and Bible quotations had the force of law in any court. Even as
a special estate of jurists was taking shape, jurisprudence long remained under
the tutelage of theology. And this supremacy of theology in the entire realm of
intellectual activity was at the same time an inevitable consequence of the place
held by the Church as the most general synthesis and sanction of the existing
feudal domination.

It is clear that under the circumstances, all the generally voiced attacks
against feudalism were above all attacks against the Church, and all social and
political, revolutionary doctrines were necessarily at the same time and mainly
theological heresies. The existing social conditions had to be stripped of their
halo of sanctity before they could be attacked....

The town heresy—and that was the actual official heresy of the Middle
Ages—was directed primarily against the clergy, whose wealth and political
importance it attacked. Just as the present-day bourgeoisie demands a "*gou-
vernement à bon marché*" (cheap government), the mediaeval burghers chiefly
demanded an "*église à bon marché*" (cheap church). Reactionary in form, like
any heresy that sees only degeneration in the further development of church
and dogma, the burgher heresy demanded the revival of the simple Early Christian Church constitution and abolition of exclusive priesthood. This cheap
arrangement would have eliminated monks, prelates, and the Roman court,
in short, everything in the Church that was expensive. The towns, republics

themselves, albeit under the protection of monarchs, first enunciated in general terms through their attacks upon the Papacy that a republic was the normal form of bourgeois rule....

The heresy that directly expressed the peasant and plebeian demands, and almost invariably accompanied an insurrection, was of a totally different nature. Though it shared all the demands of burgher heresy with regard to the clergy, the Papacy, and revival of the early Christian Church constitution, it also went infinitely further. It demanded the restoration of early Christian equality among members of the community and the recognition of this equality as a prescript for the burgher world as well. From "equality of the children of God" it inferred civil equality, and partly even equality of property. Equality of nobleman and peasant, of patrician, privileged burgher and plebeian, abolition of the *corvée* (unpaid labor: ed.), ground-rents, taxes, privileges, and at least the most crying differences in property—those were demands advanced with more or less determination as natural implications of the early Christian doctrine....

At that time the plebeians were the only class that stood outside the existing official society. They stood outside both the feudal and the burgher associations. They had neither privileges nor property; they did not even have the kind of property the peasant or petty burgher had, weighed down as it was with burdensome taxes. They were unpropertied and rightless in every respect; their living conditions never even brought them into direct contact with the existing institutions, which ignored them completely. They were a living symptom of the decay of the feudal and guild-burgher society and at the same time the first precursors of the modern bourgeois society.

This violent anticipation of coming historical developments, easily explained by the living conditions of the plebeians, is first observed in Germany, in Thomas Münzer and his party.... Only in the teachings of Münzer did these communist strains express the aspirations of a real fraction of society. He was the first to formulate them with a certain definiteness, and since him they have been observed in every great popular upheaval....

Luther and Münzer each fully represented his party by his doctrine as well as by his character and actions....

Martin Luther

When in 1517 Luther first opposed the dogmas and statutes of the Catholic Church, his opposition by no means possessed a definite character.... At that early stage all the oppositional elements had to be united, the most aggressive revolutionary energy displayed, and the sum of the existing heresies against the Catholic orthodoxy had to find a protagonist....

Luther's lightning struck home. The entire German people was set in motion. On the one hand, peasants and plebeians saw the signal to revolt in his appeals against the clergy and in his preaching of Christian freedom; and on the other, he was joined by the moderate burghers and a large section of the lesser nobility, and even princes were drawn into the current. The former believed the day had come to wreak vengeance upon all their oppressors, the latter only wished to break the power of the clergy, the dependence upon Rome and the Catholic hierarchy, and to enrich themselves on the confiscation of church property.

~

When the Peasant War broke out Luther strove to adopt a mediatory attitude in regions where the nobility and the princes were mostly Catholic. He resolutely attacked the governments. He said they were to blame for the rebellion because of their oppression; it was not the peasants, but God himself, who rose against them. Yet, on the other hand, he said, the revolt was ungodly, and contrary to the Gospel. In conclusion he called upon both parties to yield and reach a friendly settlement.

But in spite of these well-meaning mediatory offers, the revolt spread swiftly and even involved Protestant regions dominated by Lutheran princes, lords and towns, rapidly outgrowing the "circumspect" burgher reform. The most determined group of the insurgents under Münzer made its headquarters in Luther's immediate proximity in Thuringia. A few more successes, and the whole of Germany would be in flames, Luther surrounded and perhaps piked as a traitor, and the burgher reform swept away by the tide of a peasant-plebeian revolution. There was no more time for circumspection. All the old animosities were forgotten in the face of the revolution. Burger and prince, noble and clergyman, Luther and the Pope, all joined hands "against the murderous and plundering peasant hordes."

"They must be knocked to pieces, strangled and stabbed, covertly and overtly, by everyone who can, just as one must kill a mad dog!" Luther cried. "Therefore, dear sirs, help here, save there, stab, knock, strangle them everyone who can, and should you lose your life, bless you, no better death can you ever attain." ...

Luther had put a powerful weapon into the hands of the plebeian movement by translating the Bible. Through the Bible he contrasted the feudalized Christianity of his day with the unassuming Christianity of the first century, and the decaying feudal society with a picture of a society that knew nothing of the complex and artificial feudal hierarchy. The peasants had made extensive use of this instrument against the princes, the nobility, and the clergy. Now Luther turned it against them, extracting from the Bible a real hymn to the God-ordained authorities such as no bootlicker of absolute monarchy had ever been able to achieve. Princedom by the grace of God, resigned obedience, even serfdom, were sanctioned with the aid of the Bible. Not the peasant revolt alone, but Luther's own mutiny against ecclesiastical and secular authority was thereby disavowed; and not only the popular movement, but the burgher movement as well, were betrayed to the princes....

Thomas Münzer

Let us now compare the plebeian revolutionary Münzer, with Luther, the burgher reformist.

Thomas Münzer was born at *Stolberg*, in the Harz, in 1498. His father is said to have died on the scaffold, a victim of the tyranny of the Count of Stolberg. At the age of fifteen Münzer organized a secret union at a Halle school against the Archbishop of Magdeburg and the Roman Church in general. His learning in the theology of his time brought him an early doctor's degree and the position of chaplain in a Halle nunnery. Here he treated the church dogmas and rites with the greatest contempt. At mass he omitted the words of the transubstantiation, and ate, as Luther said, the almighty gods unconsecrated.... He preached in the neighbourhood with great success. In 1520 he went to Zwickau as the first evangelical preacher....

In 1522 he became preacher at Allstedt, in Thuringia. Here he started with reforming the cult. Even before Luther dared to go so far, he entirely discarded the Latin language and ordered the entire Bible, and not only the prescribed Sunday Gospels and epistles, to be read to the people. At the same time, he organized propaganda in his locality. People flocked to him from all directions, and Allstedt soon became the centre of the popular anti-priest movement for the whole of Thuringia.

Münzer was as yet a theologian before everything else. He still directed his attacks almost exclusively against the priests. He did not, however, preach quiet debate and peaceful progress, as Luther was already then doing, but continued Luther's earlier violent sermons, calling upon the princes of Saxons and the people to rise in arms against the Roman priests.

"Does not Christ say, 'I came not to bring peace, but the sword'? What must you (the princes of Saxony) do with that sword? Only one thing if you wish to be the servants of God, and that is to drive out and destroy the evil ones who stand in the way of the Gospel. Christ ordered very earnestly (Luke, 19, 27): 'Bring hither mine enemies and slay them before me.'"...

Münzer, whose ideas became ever more sharply defined and bolder, now broke resolutely away from the burgher Reformation, and henceforth became an outright political agitator.

His philosophico-theological doctrine attacked all the main points not only of Catholicism, but of Christianity generally. Under the cloak of Christian forms he preached a kind of pantheism, which curiously resembles modern speculative contemplation and at times even approaches atheism. He repudiated the Bible both as the only and the infallible revelation. The real and living revelation, he said, was reason, a revelation which has always existed among all peoples at all times. To hold up the Bible against reason, he maintained, was to kill the spirit by the letter, for the Holy Spirit of which the Bible speaks is not something that exists outside; the Holy Spirit is our reason. Faith is nothing else but reason come to life in man, and pagans could therefore also have faith. Through this faith, through reason come to life, man became godlike and blessed. Heaven is, therefore, not a thing of another world, and is to be sought in this life and it is the task of believers to establish this Heaven, the kingdom of God, here on earth. Just as there is no Heaven in the beyond, there is also no Hell and no damnation. Similarly, there is no devil but man's evil lusts and greed. Christ was a man as we are, a prophet and a teacher, and his Eucharist is a mere commemoration meal wherein bread and wine are consumed without any mystic garnishing.

Münzer preached these doctrines mostly cloaked in the same Christian phraseology under which the new philosophy had to hide for some time. But the arch heretical fundamental idea is easily discerned in all his writings, and he obviously took the biblical cloak much less in earnest than many a disciple of Hegel in modern times. And yet three hundred years separate Münzer from modern philosophy.

Münzer's political doctrine followed his revolutionary religious conceptions very closely, and just as his theology overstepped the current conceptions of his time, so his political doctrine went beyond the directly prevailing social and political conditions. Just as Münzer's religious philosophy approached atheism, so his political programme approached communism, and even on the eve of the February Revolution, there was more than one modern communist sect that had not such a well-stocked theoretical arsenal as was "Münzer's" in the sixteenth century. This programme... demanded the immediate establishment of the kingdom of God, of the prophesied millennium, by... abolishing all the institutions that conflicted with this allegedly early-Christian, but, in fact, very novel church. By the kingdom of God Münzer understood a society in which there would be no class differences or private property and no state authority independent of or foreign to the members of society. All the existing authorities, insofar as they refused to submit and join the revolution, were to be overthrown, all work and all property shared in common, and complete equality introduced....

His sermons became still more militant and revolutionary. He thundered forth against the princes, the nobility and the patricians with a passion that equalled the fervour of his attacks upon the clergy. He depicted the prevailing oppression in fiery colours, and countered it with his dream-vision of the millennium of social republican equality. He published one revolutionary pamphlet after another and sent emissaries in all directions, while personally organizing the union in Allstedt and its vicinity.

The first fruit of this propaganda was the destruction of the Marienkapelle at Mellerbach near Allstedt, according to the command of the Bible (Deut. 7, 6): "Ye shall destroy their altars, and break down their images and burn their graven images with fire." ... Münzer maintained that ungodly rulers, especially priests and monks, who treated the Gospel as heresy, should be killed, and referred to the New Testament for confirmation. The ungodly had no right to live save by the mercy of God's elect. If the princes would not exterminate the ungodly, God would take their sword from them, *because the entire community had the power of the sword.* The princes and lords are the prime movers of usury, thieving and robbery; they take all creatures into their private possession—the fish in the water, the birds in the air, and the plants in the soil—and still preach to the poor the commandment, "Thou shalt not steal," while they themselves take everything they find, rob and oppress the peasant and the artisan; but when one of the latter commits the slightest transgression, he has to hang....

Münzer's writings were ... censored by the ducal government in Weimar. But he paid no heed to this order. He lost no time in publishing a highly seditious paper in the imperial city of Mühlhausen, ... which ended with the following words: "All the world must suffer a big jolt. There will be such a game that the ungodly will be thrown off their seats, and the downtrodden will rise."

Thomas Münzer, "the man with the hammer," wrote the following motto on the title page: "Behold, I have put my words in thy mouth. I have this day set thee over the nations and over the kingdoms to root out, and to pull down, and to destroy, and to throw down, to build, and to plant...."

Münzer's breach with Luther and his party had long been an accomplished fact....

But when Münzer's ... revolutionary brochure appeared, Luther openly denounced him. In his *Letter to the Princes of Saxony against the Rebellious Spirit,* he declared Münzer to be an instrument of Satan, and demanded of the princes to intervene and drive the instigators of the upheaval out of the country, since they did not confine themselves to preaching their evil doctrine, but incited to insurrection, to violent action against the authorities....

In the meantime, the growing unrest among the peasants and plebeians had made Münzer's propaganda work incomparably easier. In the Anabaptists he found invaluable agents for that purpose. This sect, which had no definite dogmas, held together only by its common opposition to all ruling classes and by the common symbol of the second baptism, ascetic in their mode of living, untiring, fanatical and intrepid in carrying on propaganda, had grouped itself more and more closely around Münzer. Made homeless by persecutions, its members wandered all over Germany and carried everywhere word of the new teaching, in which Münzer had made their own demands and wishes clear to them. Countless Anabaptists were put on the rack, burned or otherwise executed, but the courage and endurance of these emissaries were unshakeable, and the success of their activities amidst the rapidly growing unrest of the people was enormous. Thus, on his flight from Thuringia, Münzer found the ground prepared wherever he turned.

Near Nuremberg, where Münzer first went, a peasant revolt had been nipped in the bud a month before. Münzer conducted his propaganda clandestinely; people soon appeared who defended his most audacious theological propositions on the non-obligatory nature of the Bible and the meaninglessness of the sacraments, who declared Christ a mere man, and the power of the secular authorities ungodly. "There is Satan stalking, the Spirit of Allstedt!" Luther exclaimed....

Now he [Münzer: ed.] went via Swabia to Alsace, then to Switzerland, and then back to the Upper Black Forest... This propaganda tour of Münzer's unquestionably and substantially contributed to the establishment of the people's party, to a clear formulation of its demands and to the final general outbreak of the insurrection in April 1525. This trip particularly brought out the dual effect of Münzer's activities—on the one hand, on the people, whom he addressed in the only language they could then understand, that of religious prophecy; and, on the other hand, on the initiated, to whom he could disclose his ultimate aims. Even before his journey he had assembled in Thuringia a group of resolute men from among the people and the lower clergy, whom he had put at the head of his secret society. Now he became the soul of the entire revolutionary movement in South-Western Germany, organized ties between Saxony and Thuringia through Franconia and Swabia as far as Alsace and the Swiss border.... The bloody persecutions undertaken everywhere by the alarmed princes and lords against this new plebeian heresy, contributed not a little to fan the spirit of rebellion and consolidate the ranks of the society.

Luther and Münzer Compared

We... see how truly the character and behaviour of the two party leaders reflected the attitude of their respective parties, how Luther's indecision and fear of the movement, which was assuming serious proportions, and his cowardly servility to the princes, fully corresponded to the hesitant and ambiguous policy of the burghers, and how Münzer's revolutionary energy and resolution was reproduced among the most advanced section of the plebeians and peasants. The only difference was that while Luther confined himself to expressing the conceptions and wishes of the majority of his class and thereby won an extremely cheap popularity among it, Münzer, on the contrary, went far beyond the immediate ideas and demands of the plebeians and peasants, and first organized a party of the elite of the then existing revolutionary elements, which, inasmuch as it shared his ideas and energy, was never more than a small minority of the insurgent masses.

On Historical Materialism

Engels carries his historical argument into his own time in the following text, which defends Marx's "historical materialism," in the context of pungent observations on English society and religion. The discussion is taken from the introduction to the pamphlet, Socialism: Utopian and Scientific, *which was derived from a set of earlier articles published in a German periodical* Vorwärts. *The pamphlet was published in 1880 in French and in 1892 in this English version.*

This book defends what we call "historical materialism," and the word materialism grates upon the ears of the immense majority of British readers. "Agnosticism" might be tolerated, but materialism is utterly inadmissible....

～

But England has been "civilised."... The exhibition of 1851 sounded the knell of English insular exclusiveness. England became gradually internationalised, in diet, in manners, in ideas; so much so that I begin to wish that some English manners and customs had made as much headway on the Continent as other Continental habits have made here. Anyhow, the introduction and spread of salad oil (before 1851 known only to the aristocracy) has been accompanied by a fatal spread of Continental scepticism in matters religious, and it has come to this, that agnosticism, though not yet considered "the thing" quite as much as the Church of England, is yet very nearly on a par, as far as respectability goes, with Baptism, and decidedly ranks above the Salvation Army....

FROM: Frederick Engels, "On Historical Materialism." In Karl Marx, *Selected Works,* Volume 1. 2 volumes. New York: Prepared by the Marx-Engels-Lenin Institute, Moscow. New York: International Publishers, [1892] 1949.

What, indeed, is agnosticism, but, to use an expressive Lancashire term, "shamefaced" materialism? The agnostic's conception of nature is materialistic throughout. The entire natural world is governed by law, and absolutely excludes the intervention of action from without. But, he adds, we have no means either of ascertaining or of disproving the existence of some supreme being beyond the known universe. Now, this might hold good at the time when Laplace, to Napoleon's question, why in the great astronomer's *Mécanique céleste* the Creator was not even mentioned, proudly replied: "*Je n'avais pas besoin de cette hypothèse.*" ["I have no need of that hypothesis.": ed.] But nowadays, in our evolutionary conception of the universe, there is absolutely no room for either a creator or a ruler; and to talk of a supreme being shut out from the whole existing world implies a contradiction in terms, and as it seems to me, a gratuitous insult to the feelings of religious people. . . .

～

I hope even British respectability will not he overshocked if I use, in English, as well as in so many other languages the term "historical materialism," to designate that view of the course of history, which seeks the ultimate cause and the great moving power of all important historic events in the economic development of society, in the changes in the modes of production and exchange, in the consequent division of society into distinct classes, and in the struggles of these classes against one another.

This indulgence will perhaps be accorded to me all the sooner if I show that historical materialism may be of advantage even to British respectability. I have mentioned the fact that, about forty or fifty years ago, any cultivated foreigner settling in England was struck by what he was then bound to consider the religious bigotry and stupidity of the English respectable middle class. I am now going to prove that the respectable English middle class of that time was not quite as stupid as it looked to the intelligent foreigner. Its religious leanings can be explained.

When Europe emerged from the Middle Ages, the rising middle class of the towns constituted its revolutionary element. It had conquered a recognised position within medieval feudal organisation, but this position, also, had become too narrow for its expansive power. The development of the middle class, the bourgeoisie, became incompatible with the maintenance of the feudal system; the feudal system, therefore, had to fall.

But the great international centre of feudalism was the Roman Catholic Church. It united the whole of feudalised Western Europe. . . . It surrounded feudal institutions with the halo of divine consecration. It had organised its own hierarchy on the feudal model, and, lastly, it was itself by far the most powerful feudal lord, holding, as it did, fully one-third of the soil of the Catholic world. Before profane feudalism could be successfully attacked in each country and in detail, this, its sacred central organisation, had to be destroyed.

Moreover, parallel with the rise of the middle class went on the great revival of science; astronomy, mechanics, physics, anatomy, physiology, were again cultivated. And the bourgeoisie, for the development of its industrial production, required a science which ascertained the physical properties of natural objects and the modes of action of the forces of nature. Now up to then science had but been the humble handmaid of the Church, had not been allowed to overstep the limits set by faith, and for that reason had been no science at all. Science rebelled against the Church; the bourgeoisie could not do without science, and, therefore, had to join in the rebellion.

The above, though touching but two of the points where the rising middle class was bound to come into collision with the established religion, will be sufficient to show, first, that the class most directly interested in the struggle against the pretensions of the Roman Church was the bourgeoisie; and second, that every struggle against feudalism, at that time, had to take on a religious disguise, had to be directed against the Church in the first instance. But if the universities and the traders of the cities started the cry, it was sure to find, and did find, a strong echo in the masses of the country people, the peasants, who everywhere had to struggle for their very existence with their feudal lords, spiritual and temporal.

The Three Bourgeois Revolutions

The long fight of the bourgeoisie against feudalism culminated in three great decisive battles.

The first was what is called the Protestant Reformation in Germany. The war-cry raised against the Church by Luther was responded to by two insurrections of a political nature: first, that of the lower nobility under Franz von Sickingen (1523), then the great Peasants' War, 1525. Both were defeated....

But where Luther failed, Calvin won the day. Calvin's creed was one fit for the boldest of the bourgeoisie of his time.... Calvin's church constitution was thoroughly democratic and republican; and where the kingdom of God was republicanised, could the kingdoms of this world remain subject to monarchs, bishops and lords? While German Lutheranism became a willing tool in the hands of princes, Calvinism founded a republic in Holland and active republican parties in England, and, above all, Scotland.

In Calvinism, the second great bourgeois upheaval found its doctrine ready cut and dried. This upheaval took place in England [the English Civil

War 1642–51, also known as "The Great Rebellion": ed.] The middle class of the towns brought it on, and the yeomanry of the country districts fought it out. Curiously enough, in all the three great bourgeois risings, the peasantry furnishes the army that has to do the fighting; and the peasantry is just the class that, the victory once gained, is most surely ruined by the economic consequences of that victory. A hundred years after Cromwell, the yeomanry of England had almost disappeared. Anyhow, had it not been for that yeomanry and for the plebeian element in the towns, the bourgeoisie alone would never have fought the matter out to the bitter end, and would never have brought Charles I to the scaffold....

Well, upon this excess of revolutionary activity there necessarily followed the inevitable reaction which in its turn went beyond the point where it might have maintained itself. After a series of oscillations, the new centre of gravity was at last attained and became a new starting point. The grand period of English history, known to respectability under the name of "the Great Rebellion," and the struggles succeeding it, were brought to a close by the comparatively puny event entitled by Liberal historians, "the Glorious Revolution."...

The compromise of 1689 was, therefore, easily accomplished. The political spoils...were left to the great landowning families, provided the economic interests of the financial, manufacturing and commercial middle class were sufficiently attended to. And these economic interests were at that time powerful enough to determine the general policy of the nation....

[T]he English bourgeoisie now had to take a part in keeping down the "lower orders," the great producing mass of the nation, and one of the means employed for that purpose was the influence of religion.

There was another fact that contributed to strengthen the religious leanings of the bourgeoisie. That was the rise of materialism in England. This new doctrine not only shocked the pious feelings of the middle class; it announced itself as a philosophy only fit for scholars and cultivated men of the world, in contrast to religion which was good enough for the uneducated masses, including the bourgeoisie....

In the meantime materialism passed from England to France....In France, too, it remained at first an exclusively aristocratic doctrine. But soon its revolutionary character asserted itself. The French materialists did not limit their criticism to matters of religious belief; they extended it to whatever scientific tradition or political institution they met with; and to prove the claim of their doctrine to universal application, they took the shortest cut, and boldly applied it to all subjects of knowledge in the giant work after which they were named—the *Encyclopedie*....The Great French Revolution was the third uprising of the bourgeoisie, but the first that had entirely cast off the religious cloak and was fought out on undisguised political lines; it was the first, too, that was really fought out up to the destruction of one of the combatants, the aristocracy, and the complete triumph of the other, the bourgeoisie.... In France the revolution constituted a complete breach with the traditions of the past; it cleared out the very last vestiges of feudalism, and created in the *Code Civil* a masterly adaptation of the old Roman law—that almost perfect expression of of the juridical relations corresponding to the economic stage called by Marx the production of commodities—to modern capitalistic conditions....

[I]f materialism became the creed of the French Revolution, the God-fearing English bourgeois held all the faster to his religion. Had not the reign of terror in Paris proved what was the upshot, if the religious instincts of the masses were lost? The more materialism spread from France to neighbouring countries, and was reinforced by similar doctrinal currents, notably by German philosophy, the more in fact, materialism and free thought generally became, on the Continent, the necessary qualifications of a cultivated man, the more stubbornly the English middle class stuck to its manifold religious creeds. These creeds might differ from one another, but they were, all of them, distinctly religious, Christian creeds....

Then came the Continental revolutions of February and March 1848, in which the working people played such a prominent part, and, at least in Paris, put forward demands which were certainly inadmissible from the point of view of capitalist society. And then came the general reaction. First the defeat of the Chartists on the 10th April, 1848, then the crushing of the Paris workingmen's insurrection in June of the same year, then the disasters of 1849 in Italy, Hungary, South Germany, and at last the victory of Louis Bonaparte over Paris, 2nd December, 1851. For a time, at least, the bugbear of working class pretensions was put down, but at what cost! If the British bourgeois had been convinced before of the necessity of maintaining the common people in a religious mood, how much more must he feel that necessity after all these experiences? Regardless of the sneers of his Continental compeers, he continued to spend thousands and tens of thousands, year after year, upon the evangelisation of the lower orders; not content with his own native religious machinery, he appealed to...the greatest organiser in existence of religion as a trade, and imported from America revivalism, Moody and Sankey, and the like; and, finally, he accepted the dangerous aid of the Salvation Army, which revives the propaganda of early Christianity, appeals to the poor as the elect, fights capitalism in a religious way, and thus fosters an element of early Christian class antagonism, which one day may become troublesome to the well-to-do people who now find the ready money for it.

∽

But the English middle class...had shared their power but reluctantly with the working class. They had learnt...what that *puer robustus sed malitiosus* [robust but roguish child: ed.],...the people, is capable of....Now, if ever, the people must be kept in order by moral means, and the first and foremost of all moral means of action upon the masses is and remains—religion. Hence the parson's majorities on the School Boards, hence the increasing self-taxation of the bourgeoisie for the support of all sorts of revivalism, from ritualism to the Salvation Army. And now came the triumph of British respectability over the free thought and religious laxity of the Continental bourgeois. The workmen of France and Germany had become rebellious. They were thoroughly infected with socialism, and, for very good reasons, were not at all particular as to the legality of the means by which to secure their own ascendency. The *puer robustus,* here, turned from day to day more *malitiosus.* Nothing remained to the French and German bourgeoisie as a last resource but to silently drop their free thought, as a youngster, when sea-sickness creeps upon him, quietly drops the burning cigar he brought swaggeringly on board; one by one, the scoffers turned pious in outward behaviour, spoke with respect of the Church, its dogmas and rites, and even conformed with the latter as far as could not be helped....They had come to grief with materialism. "*Die Religion muss dem Volk erhalten werden,*"—religion must be kept alive for the people—that was the only and the last means to save society from utter ruin. Unfortunately for themselves, they did not find this out until they had done their level best to break up religion for ever. And now it was the turn of the British bourgeois to sneer and to say: "Why, you fools, I could have told you that two hundred years ago!"

The Proletarian Revolution to Come

However, I am afraid neither the religious stolidity of the British, nor the...conversion of the Continental bourgeois will stem the rising proletarian tide. Tradition is a great retarding force, is the *vis inertiae* [force of inertia: ed.] of history, but, being merely passive, is sure to be broken down; and thus religion will be no lasting safeguard to capitalist society. If our juridical, philosophical and religious ideas are the more or less remote offshoots of the economic relations prevailing in a given society, such ideas cannot, in the long run, withstand the effects of a complete change in these relations. And, unless we believe in supernatural revelation, we must admit that no religious tenets will ever suffice to prop up a tottering society.

In fact, in England too, the working people have begun to move again. They are, no doubt, shackled by traditions of various kinds....But for all that the English working class is moving....It moves, like all things in England, with a slow and measured step.... It has now shaken out of their torpor the unskilled labourers of the East End of London, and we all know what a splendid impulse these fresh forces have given it in return. And if the pace of the movement is not up to the impatience of some people, let them not forget that it is the working class which keeps alive the finest qualities of the English character, and that, if a step in advance is once gained in England, it is, as a rule, never lost afterwards....

But the triumph of the European working class does not depend upon England alone. It can only be secured by the cooperation of, at least, England, France and Germany. In both the latter countries the working class movement is well ahead of England. In Germany it is even within measurable distance of success. The progress it has there made during the last twenty-five years is unparalleled. It advances with ever increasing velocity.... Four hundred years ago, Germany was the starting point of the first upheaval of the European middle class; as things are now, is it outside the limits of possibility that Germany will be the scene, too, of the first great victory of the European proletariat?

Socialism and Religion

Vladimir Ilych Lenin, architect of the Bolshevik Revolution in Russia, was more activist than theorist. But in this short magazine article, written more than a decade before the tumultuous overthrow of the czar in 1917, he reaffirms Marx's disdain for faith and articulates his own views on religion, the state, and the Communist party.

Present-day society is wholly based on the exploitation of the vast masses of the working class by a tiny minority of the population, the class of the landowners and that of the capitalists. It is a slave society, since the "free" workers, who all their life work for the capitalists, are "entitled" only to such means of subsistence as are essential for the maintenance of slaves who produce profit, for the safeguarding and perpetuation of capitalist slavery.

The economic oppression of the workers inevitably calls forth and engenders every kind of political oppression and social humiliation, the coarsening and darkening of the spiritual and moral life of the masses.... Religion is one of the forms of spiritual oppression which everywhere weighs down heavily upon the masses of the people, over burdened by their perpetual work for others, by

---

FROM: Vladimir Ilych Lenin, "Socialism and Religion." In *Novaya Zhizn,* No. 28, December 3, 1905. In Volume 10 of *Lenin Collected Works.* Moscow: Progress Publishers, 1965.

want and isolation. Impotence of the exploited classes in their struggle against the exploiters just as inevitably gives rise to the belief in a better life after death as impotence of the savage in his battle with nature gives rise to belief in gods, devils, miracles, and the like. Those who toil and live in want all their lives are taught by religion to be submissive and patient while here on earth, and to take comfort in the hope of a heavenly reward. But those who live by the labour of others are taught by religion to practise charity while on earth, thus offering them a very cheap way of justifying their entire existence as exploiters and selling them at a moderate price tickets to well-being in heaven. Religion is opium for the people. Religion is a sort of spiritual booze, in which the slaves of capital drown their human image, their demand for a life more or less worthy of man.

But a slave who has become conscious of his slavery and has risen to struggle for his emancipation has already half ceased to be a slave. The modern class-conscious worker, reared by large-scale factory industry and enlightened by urban life, contemptuously casts aside religious prejudices, leaves heaven to the priests and bourgeois bigots, and tries to win a better life for himself here on earth. The proletariat of today takes the side of socialism, which enlists science in the battle against the fog of religion, and frees the workers from their belief in life after death by welding them together to fight in the present for a better life on earth.

Religion must be declared a private affair. In these words socialists usually express their attitude towards religion. But the meaning of these words should be accurately defined to prevent any misunderstanding. We demand that religion be held a private affair so far as the state is concerned. But by no means can we consider religion a private affair so far as our Party is concerned. Religion must be of no concern to the state, and religious societies must have no connection with governmental authority. Everyone must be absolutely free to profess any religion he pleases, or no religion whatever, i.e., to be an atheist, which every socialist is, as a rule. Discrimination among citizens on account of their religious convictions is wholly intolerable. Even the bare mention of a citizen's religion in official documents should unquestionably be eliminated. No subsidies should be granted to the established church nor state allowances made to ecclesiastical and religious societies. These should become absolutely free associations of like-minded citizens, associations independent of the state. Only the complete fulfilment of these demands can put an end to the shameful and accursed past when the church lived in feudal dependence on the state, and Russian citizens lived in feudal dependence on the established church, when medieval, inquisitorial laws (to this day remaining in our criminal codes and on our statute-books) were in existence and were applied, persecuting men for their belief or disbelief, violating men's consciences, and linking cozy government jobs and government-derived incomes with the dispensation of this or that dope by the established church. Complete separation of Church and State is what the socialist proletariat demands of the modern state and the modern church.

The Russian revolution must put this demand into effect as a necessary component of political freedom. In this respect, the Russian revolution is in a particularly favourable position, since the revolting officialism of the police-ridden feudal autocracy has called forth discontent, unrest and indignation even among the clergy. However abject, however ignorant Russian Orthodox clergymen may have been, even they have now been awakened by the thunder of the downfall of the old, medieval order in Russia. Even they are joining in the demand for freedom, are protesting against bureaucratic practices and officialism, against the spying for the police imposed on the "servants of God." We socialists must lend this movement our support, carrying the demands of honest and sincere members of the clergy to their conclusion, making them stick to their words about freedom, demanding that they should resolutely break all ties between religion and the police. Either you are sincere, in which case you must stand for the complete separation of Church and State and of School and Church, for religion to be declared wholly and absolutely a private affair. Or you do not accept these consistent demands for freedom, in which case you evidently are still held captive by the traditions of the inquisition, in which case you evidently still cling to your cozy government jobs and government-derived incomes, in which case you evidently do not believe in the spiritual power of your weapon and continue to take bribes from the state. And in that case the class-conscious workers of all Russia declare merciless war on you.

So far as the party of the socialist proletariat is concerned, religion is not a private affair. Our Party is an association of class-conscious, advanced fighters for the emancipation of the working class. Such an association cannot and must not be indifferent to lack of class-consciousness, ignorance or obscurantism in the shape of religious beliefs. We demand complete disestablishment of the Church so as to be able to combat the religious fog with purely ideological and solely ideological weapons, by means of our press and by word of mouth. But we founded our association, the Russian Social-Democratic Labour Party, precisely for such a struggle against every religious bamboozling of the workers. And to us the ideological struggle is not a private affair, but the affair of the whole Party, of the whole proletariat.

If that is so, why do we not declare in our Programme that we are atheists? Why do we not forbid Christians and other believers in God to join our Party?

The answer to this question will serve to explain the very important difference in the way the question of religion is presented by the bourgeois democrats and the Social-Democrats.

Our Programme is based entirely on the scientific, and moreover the materialist, world-outlook. An explanation of our Programme, therefore, necessarily includes an explanation of the true historical and economic roots of the religious fog. Our propaganda necessarily includes the propaganda of atheism; the publication of the appropriate scientific literature, which the autocratic feudal government has hitherto strictly forbidden and persecuted, must now form one of the fields of our Party work. We shall now probably have to follow the advice Engels once gave to the German Socialists: to translate and widely disseminate the literature of the eighteenth-century French Enlighteners and atheists.

But under no circumstances ought we to fall into the error of posing the religious question in an abstract, idealistic fashion, as an "intellectual" question unconnected with the class struggle, as is not infrequently done by the radical-democrats from among the bourgeoisie. It would be stupid to think that, in a society based on the endless oppression and coarsening of the worker masses, religious prejudices could be dispelled by purely propaganda methods. It would be bourgeois narrow-mindedness to forget that the yoke of religion that weighs upon mankind is merely a product and reflection of the economic yoke within society. No number of pamphlets and no amount of preaching can enlighten the proletariat, if it is not enlightened by its own struggle against the dark forces of capitalism. Unity in this really revolutionary struggle of the oppressed class for the creation of a paradise on earth is more important to us than unity of proletarian opinion on paradise in heaven.

That is the reason why we do not and should not set forth our atheism in our Programme; that is why we do not and should not prohibit proletarians who still retain vestiges of their old prejudices from associating themselves with our Party. We shall always preach the scientific world-outlook, and it is essential for us to combat the inconsistency of various "Christians." But that does not mean in the least that the religious question ought to be advanced to first place, where it does not belong at all; nor does it mean that we should allow the forces of the really revolutionary economic and political struggle to be split up on account of third-rate opinions or senseless ideas, rapidly losing all political importance, rapidly being swept out as rubbish by the very course of economic development.

Everywhere the reactionary bourgeoisie has concerned itself, and is now beginning to concern itself in Russia, with the fomenting of religious strife—in order thereby to divert the attention of the masses from the really important and fundamental economic and political problems, now being solved in practice by the all-Russian proletariat uniting in revolutionary struggle. This reactionary policy of splitting up the proletarian forces, which today manifests itself mainly in Black-Hundred pogroms, may tomorrow conceive some more subtle forms. We, at any rate, shall oppose it by calmly, consistently and patiently preaching proletarian solidarity and the scientific world-outlook—a preaching alien to any stirring up of secondary differences.

The revolutionary proletariat will succeed in making religion a really private affair, so far as the state is concerned. And in this political system, cleansed of medieval mildew, the proletariat will wage a broad and open struggle for the elimination of economic slavery, the true source of the religious humbugging of mankind.

6

William James: The Testimony of Religious Experience

William James (1842–1910) was born into one of the most illustrious families in American intellectual life. His father, Henry James Sr., was independently wealthy and religiously eccentric—an amateur theologian dismissive of churches and drawn to the Swedish mystic and visionary Emanuel Swedenborg. His younger brother, the novelist Henry James, Jr., is one of the great names in American literature; his sister Alice, a diarist who chronicled the habits and lives of the social and cultural elite at the turn of the twentieth century. Because the family traveled often to Europe, the James children were educated in a manner that was unconventional and unusually cosmopolitan. In his early adult years, William struggled to cope with a variety of physical ailments and did battle with depression, nearly coming to suicide. He fought a continuing battle with both types of affliction until he reached his thirties.

In 1861 James began studies in the natural sciences at Harvard; a few years later he turned to medicine, but his program of study there was interrupted several times by smallpox and other illnesses, by travel to Germany to study other subjects, and by new struggles with the mental condition he described as his "soul sickness." For a time after his return from Europe he remained house-bound as a semi-invalid. In the 1870s, however, he experienced a strong recovery, which came in part from reading the works of Charles Renouvier, a disciple of Immanuel Kant, and in part from his marriage, in 1878, to Alice Gibbons, a woman who would prove to be an ideal partner. James' emotional problems were at least partly intellectual—tied to the pessimistic doctrines of determinism he encountered in both the sciences and philosophy. In the work of Renouvier, however, he found an optimistic thinker and a persuasive defense of the freedom of the will. Under this influence, he committed himself firmly to the idea of human freedom; and his energies soon revived. In addition, his scholarly interests began to turn from physiology to psychology—or more precisely, to psychology anchored in the empirical method of the physical sciences. The rest of his career was devoted to the emerging field of psychology and the application of its findings in the realms of philosophy and religion.

While at Harvard, James participated in regular discussions with a group of eminent Bostonians who came to call themselves The Metaphysical Club. They included his Harvard colleague and philosopher Charles Sanders Pierce, Supreme Court Justice Oliver Wendell Holmes, and others, all of whom kept him closely attuned to wider cultural, intellectual, and social issues and their converse with matters both scientific and psychological. Toward the end of the 1870s, James began work on a book designed as a general introduction to psychology. Over twelve years it grew, and gradually grew more, until it came to two large volumes. *The Principles of Psychology,* the masterwork of his chosen discipline, appeared in 1890. In this, and all of his work, he embraced the theory advanced by his colleague C. S. Pierce that came to be known as pragmatism. Pierce held that what we call the truth of our ideas and beliefs must be measured in terms of their value, or usefulness, to the individual who embraces them. Since the ultimate nature of the world is a subject open to a continuous revision of our understanding, based on acquisition of greater knowledge drawn from new experiences, it is pointless for any person, at any given moment, to claim that what we currently know is some kind of fixed, eternal truth. The rational thing, accordingly, is to replace this absolute ideal with a functional one. We should regard as true those beliefs which enable us, as living organisms, to function well. The test of truth is its pragmatism, its usefulness. This philosophical-psychological precept bore a natural compatibility with the evolutionary idea of "survival of the fittest" in the sphere of biology. Just as those organisms most suited to their environment survive, so those ideas that deserve to survive are those that contribute most to the health of the mind.

This precept is what guided James when he agreed to give the prestigious Gifford Lectures in Edinburgh (1901–02), dedicated to expounding the claims of religion by appeal only to natural evidence, rather than supernatural revelation. After their presentation, James published them under the title *Varieties of Religious Experience.* Over the years this seminal work has acquired the status of a touchstone in the study of religion—comparable in its way to *The Principles of Psychology* in the science of the mind. Throughout its pages, James employs his empirical method to strong effect, carefully assembling scores of personal accounts (mostly, but not exclusively, Western) into a broad inventory of human encounters with the divine. For him such experiences furnish the definition of religion: "the feelings, acts, and experiences of individual men in their solitude, so far as they apprehend themselves in relation to whatever they may consider the divine." In the course of his expounding on these experiences, James offers distinctions and analyses that have become standard points of reference in the discussions of later theorists. He offers his well-known distinction between optimistic and pessimistic personalities: what he calls the "religion of healthy mindedness" on the one hand and the religion of the "sick soul" on the other. He examines the nature and stages of conversion and describes the features and virtues of the religious saint, the exemplar of the pious life for all others. He explores as well the forms and features of mysticism. The sequence of passages reproduced below follows the main line of exposition in *Varieties,* as James takes it to the conclusion that not only in mysticism, but in all religious experience, there is real and personal truth to be found in a continuous engagement "with a wider self through which saving experiences come." This conviction that for every individual there is both truth and personal value in religious experience serves for James as a main point of departure from the theories of Freud, Durkheim, and Marx. Against reductionist efforts to "explain away" the claims of belief, he is prepared to say that there is "a positive content of religious experience which, it seems to me, *is literally and objectively true as far as it goes.*"

Whether the empirical method of the *Varieties* entirely justifies the claims James makes for his sources is a question his readers must decide anew as they encounter him. Certainly, James himself was fully persuaded. Most religious impulses, he contends, call us into the realm of the mystical and the supernatural. And in so far as that is the region in which our ideal impulses originate, "we belong to it in a more intimate sense than that in which we belong to the visible world, for we belong in the most intimate sense wherever our ideals belong."

Religion Defined: For Present Purposes

The sequence of selections below traces the main path of James' argument, starting from his definitions of terms and topic and proceeding through the discussions of "healthy mindedness" and the "sick" soul, the nature of conversion, saintliness and its attributes, mysticism, the uses of philosophy, and the "pragmatic" criterion by which the value of religious experiences is to be judged.

Most books on the philosophy of religion try to begin with a precise definition of what its essence consists of. Some of these would-be definitions may possibly come before us in later portions of this course, and I shall not be

---

FROM: *The Varieties of Religious Experience: A Study in Human Nature.* The Gifford Lectures, 1901–02. Amherst, New York: Prometheus Books, [1902] 2002.

pedantic enough to enumerate any of them to you now. Meanwhile the very fact that they are so many and so different from one another is enough to prove that the word "religion" cannot stand for any single principle or essence, but is rather a collective name....

[A]lthough it would indeed be foolish to set up an abstract definition against all comers, yet this need not prevent me from taking my own narrow view of what religion shall consist of *for the purpose of these lectures,* or, out of the many meanings of the word, from choosing the one meaning in which I wish to interest you particularly, and proclaiming arbitrarily that when I say "religion" I mean *that.* This, in fact, is what I must do, and I will now preliminarily seek to mark out the field I choose.

One way to mark it out easily is to say what aspects of the subject we leave out. At the outset we are struck by one great partition which divides the religious field. On the one side of it lies institutional, on the other personal religion.... [O]ne branch of religion keeps the divinity, another keeps man most in view. Worship and sacrifice, procedures for working on the dispositions of the deity, theology and ceremony and ecclesiastical organization, are the essentials of religion in the institutional branch. Were we to limit our view to it, we should have to define religion as an external art, the art of winning the favor of the gods. In the more personal branch of religion it is on the contrary the inner dispositions of man himself which form the centre of interest, his conscience, his deserts, his helplessness, his incompleteness. And although the favor of God...is still an essential feature of the story, and theology plays a vital part therein, yet the acts to which this sort of religion prompts us are personal not ritual acts, the individual transacts the business by himself alone, and the ecclesiastical organization, with its priests and sacraments and other go-betweens, sinks into an altogether secondary place. The relation goes direct from heart to heart, from soul to soul, between man and his maker.

Now in these lectures I propose to ignore the institutional branch entirely, to say nothing of the ecclesiastical organization, to consider as little as possible the systematic theology and the ideas about the gods themselves, and to confine myself as far as I can to personal religion pure and simple....

I am willing to accept almost any name for the personal religion of which I propose to treat. Call it conscience or morality, if you yourselves prefer, and not religion—under either name it will be equally worthy of our study....

In one sense at least the personal religion will prove itself more fundamental than either theology or ecclesiasticism. Churches, when once established, live at second-hand upon tradition; but the *founders* of every church owed their power originally to the fact of their direct personal communion with the divine. Not only the superhuman founders, the Christ, the Buddha, Mahomet, but all the originators of Christian sects have been in this case;—so personal religion should still seem the primordial thing, even to those who continue to esteem it incomplete.

There are, it is true, other things in religion chronologically more primordial than personal devoutness in the moral sense. Fetishism and magic seem to have preceded inward piety historically—at least our records of inward piety do not reach back so far. And if fetishism and magic be regarded as stages of religion, one may say that personal religion in the inward sense and the genuinely spiritual considerations which it founds are phenomena of secondary or even tertiary order. But, quite apart from the fact that many anthropologists—for instance, Jevons and Frazer—expressly oppose "religion" and "magic" to each other, it is certain that the whole system of thought which leads to magic, fetishism, and the lower superstitions may just as well be called primitive science as called primitive religion. The question thus becomes a verbal one again; and our knowledge of all those early stages of thought and feeling is in any case so conjectural and imperfect that farther discussion would not be worth while.

Religion, therefore, as I now ask you arbitrarily to take it, shall mean for us *the feelings, acts, and experiences of individual men in their solitude, so far as they apprehend themselves to stand in relation to whatever they may consider the divine.* Since the relation may be either moral, physical, or ritual, it is evident that out of religion in the sense in which we take it, theologies, philosophies, and ecclesiastical organizations may secondarily grow. In these lectures, however, . . . the immediate personal experiences will amply fill our time, and we shall hardly consider theology or ecclesiasticism at all.

We escape much controversial matter by this arbitrary definition of our field. But, still, a chance of controversy comes up over the word "divine," if we take it in the definition in too narrow a sense. There are systems of thought which the world usually calls religious, and yet which do not positively assume a God. Buddhism is in this case. Popularly, of course, the Buddha himself stands in place of a God; but in strictness the Buddhistic system is atheistic. Modern transcendental idealism, Emersonianism, for instance, also seems to let God evaporate into abstract Ideality. Not a deity *in concreto,* not a superhuman person, but the immanent divinity in things, the essentially spiritual structure of the universe, is the object of the transcendentalist cult.

∼

There must be something solemn, serious, and tender about any attitude which we denominate religious. If glad, it must not grin or snicker; if sad, it must not scream or curse. It is precisely as being *solemn* experiences that I wish to interest you in religious experiences. So I propose—arbitrarily again, if you please—to narrow our definition once more by saying that the word "divine," as employed therein, shall mean for us not merely the primal and enveloping and real, for that meaning if taken without restriction might well prove too broad. The divine shall mean for us only such a primal reality as the individual feels impelled to respond to solemnly and gravely, and neither by a curse nor a jest.

◡

If religion is to mean anything definite for us, it seems to me that we ought to take it as meaning this added dimension of emotion, this enthusiastic temper of espousal, in regions where morality strictly so called can at best but bow its head and acquiesce. It ought to mean nothing short of this new reach of freedom for us, with the struggle over, the keynote of the universe sounding in our ears, and everlasting possession spread before our eyes.

This sort of happiness in the absolute and everlasting is what we find nowhere but in religion. It is parted off from all mere animal happiness, all mere enjoyment of the present, by that element of solemnity of which I have already made so much account. Solemnity is a hard thing to define abstractly, but certain of its marks are patent enough. A solemn state of mind is never crude or simple—it seems to contain a certain measure of its own opposite in solution. A solemn joy preserves a sort of bitter in its sweetness; a solemn sorrow is one to which we intimately consent.

◡

Two Temperaments: Healthy-Mindedness and the "Sick Soul"

If, then, we give the name of healthy-mindedness to the tendency which looks on all things and sees that they are good, we find that we must distinguish between a more involuntary and a more voluntary or systematic way of being healthy-minded. In its involuntary variety, healthy-mindedness is a way of feeling happy about things immediately. In its systematical variety, it is an abstract way of conceiving things as good. Every abstract way of conceiving things selects some one aspect of them as their essence for the time being, and disregards the other aspects. Systematic healthy-mindedness, conceiving good as the essential and universal aspect of being, deliberately excludes evil from its field of vision....

In all this I say nothing of any mystical insight or persuasion that the total frame of things absolutely must be good. Such mystical persuasion plays an enormous part in the history of the religious consciousness, and we must look at it later with some care. But we need not go so far at present. More ordinary non-mystical conditions of rapture suffice for my immediate contention. All invasive moral states and passionate enthusiasms make one feelingless to evil in some direction....

The systematic cultivation of healthy-mindedness as a religious attitude is therefore consonant with important currents in human nature, and is anything but absurd. In fact, we all do cultivate it more or less, even when our professed theology should in consistency forbid it. We divert our attention from disease and death as much as we can...

The advance of liberalism, so-called, in Christianity, during the past fifty years, may fairly be called a victory of healthy-mindedness within the church over the morbidness with which the old hell-fire theology was more harmoniously related. We have now whole congregations whose preachers, far from magnifying our consciousness of sin, seem devoted rather to making little of it. They ignore, or even deny, eternal punishment, and insist on the dignity rather than on the depravity of man. They look at the continual preoccupation of the old-fashioned Christian with the salvation of his soul as something sickly and reprehensible rather than admirable.... I am not asking whether or not they are right, I am only pointing out the change.

The persons to whom I refer have still retained for the most part their nominal connection with Christianity, in spite of their discarding of its more pessimistic theological elements. But in that "theory of evolution" which, gathering momentum for a century, has within the past twenty-five years swept so rapidly over Europe and America, we see the ground laid for a new sort of religion of Nature, which has entirely displaced Christianity from the thought of a large part of our generation. The idea of a universal evolution lends itself to a doctrine of general meliorism and progress which fits the religious needs of the healthy-minded so well that it seems almost as if it might have been created for their use. Accordingly we find "evolutionism" interpreted thus optimistically and embraced as a substitute for the religion they were born in, by a multitude of our contemporaries....

∽

Let us now say good-by for a while to all this way of thinking, and turn towards those persons who cannot so swiftly throw off the burden of the consciousness of evil, but are congenitally fated to suffer from its presence. Just as we saw that in healthy-mindedness there are shallower and profounder levels..., so also are there different levels of the morbid mind, and the one is much more formidable than the other. There are people for whom evil means only a mal-adjustment with *things,* a wrong correspondence of one's life with the environment.... But there are others for whom evil is no mere relation of the subject to particular outer things, but something more radical and general, a wrongness or vice in his essential nature, which no alteration of the environment, or any superficial rearrangement of the inner self, can cure, and which requires supernatural remedy.

∽

Arrived at this point, we can see how great an antagonism may naturally arise between the healthy-minded way of viewing life and the way that takes all this experience of evil as something essential. To this latter way, the morbid-minded way, as we might call it, healthy-mindedness pure and simple seems unspeakably blind and shallow. To the healthy-minded way, on the other hand, the way of the sick soul seems unmanly and diseased.... [W]ith their manufacture of fears, and preoccupation with every unwholesome kind of misery, there is something almost obscene about these children of wrath and cravens of a second birth....

In our own attitude, not yet abandoned, of impartial onlookers, what are we to say of this quarrel? It seems to me that we are bound to say that morbid-mindedness ranges over the wider scale of experience, and that its survey is the one that overlaps. The method of averting one's attention from evil, and living simply in the light of good is splendid as long as it will work.... But it breaks down impotently as soon as melancholy comes; and even though one be quite free from melancholy one's self, there is no doubt that healthy-mindedness is inadequate as a philosophical doctrine, because the evil facts which it refuses positively to account for are a genuine portion of reality; and they may after all be the best key to life's significance, and possibly the only openers of our eyes to the deepest levels of truth.

The normal process of life contains moments... in which radical evil gets its innings and takes its solid turn. The lunatic's visions of horror are all drawn from the material of daily fact. Our civilization is founded on the shambles, and every individual existence goes out in a lonely spasm of helpless agony.... To believe in the carnivorous reptiles of geologic times is hard for our imagination.... Yet there is no tooth in any one of those museum-skulls that did not... hold fast to the body struggling in despair of some fated living victim....

[S]ince the evil facts are as genuine parts of nature as the good ones, the philosophic presumption should be that they have some rational significance, and that systematic healthy-mindedness, failing as it does to accord to sorrow, pain, and death any positive and active attention whatever, is formally less complete than systems that try at least to include these elements in their scope.

The completest religions would therefore seem to be those in which the pessimistic elements are best developed. Buddhism, of course, and Christianity are the best known to us of these. They are essentially religions of deliverance: the man must die to an unreal life before he can be born into the real life. In my next lecture, I will try to discuss some of the psychological conditions of this second birth. Fortunately from now onward we shall have to deal with more cheerful subjects than those which we have recently been dwelling on.

The Divided Self, and the Process of Its Unification

The last lecture was a painful one, dealing as it did with evil as a pervasive element of the world we live in. At the close of it we were brought into full view of the contrast between the two ways of looking at life which are characteristic respectively of what we called the healthy-minded, who need to be born only once, and of the sick souls, who must be twice-born in order to be happy. The result is two different conceptions of the universe of our experience. In the religion of the once-born the world is a sort of rectilinear or one-storied affair, whose accounts are kept in one denomination, whose parts have just the values which naturally they appear to have, and of which a simple algebraic sum of pluses and minuses will give the total worth. Happiness and religious peace consist in living on the plus side of the account. In the religion of the twice-born, on the other hand, the world is a double-storied mystery. Peace cannot be reached by the simple addition of pluses and elimination of minuses from life. Natural good is not simply insufficient in amount and transient, there lurks a falsity in its very being....

In their extreme forms, of pure naturalism and pure salvationism, the two types are violently contrasted; though here as in most other current classifications, the radical extremes are somewhat ideal abstractions, and the concrete human being whom we oftenest meet are intermediate varieties and mixtures. Practically, however, you all recognize the difference: you understand, for example, the disdain of the Methodist convert for the mere sky-blue healthy-minded moralist; and you likewise enter into the aversion of the latter to what seems to him the diseased subjectivism of the Methodist, dying to live, as he calls it, and making of paradox and the inversion of natural appearances the essence of God's truth.

～

Now in all of us, however constituted, but to a degree the greater in proportion as we are intense and sensitive and subject to diversified temptations..., does the normal evolution of character chiefly consist in the straightening out and unifying of the inner self. The higher and the lower feelings, the useful and the erring impulses, begin by being a comparative chaos within us—they must end by forming a stable system of functions in right subordination. Unhappiness is apt to characterize the period of order-making and struggle. If the individual be of tender conscience and religiously quickened, the unhappiness will take the form of moral remorse and compunction, of feeling inwardly vile and wrong, and of standing in false relations to the author of one's being and appointer of one's spiritual fate. This is the religious melancholy and "conviction of sin" that have played so large a part in the history of Protestant Christianity.

The man's interior is a battle-ground for what he feels to be two deadly hostile selves, one actual, the other ideal.

◦

Conversion

To be converted, to be regenerated, to receive grace, to experience religion, to gain an assurance, are so many phrases which denote the process, gradual or sudden, by which a self hitherto divided, and consciously wrong inferior and unhappy, becomes unified and consciously right superior and happy, in consequence of its firmer hold upon religious realities. This at least is what conversion signifies in general terms, whether or not we believe that a direct divine operation is needed to bring such a moral change about.

◦

Let us hereafter, in speaking of the hot place in a man's consciousness, the group of ideas to which he devotes himself, and from which he works, call it *the habitual centre of his personal energy*. It makes a great difference to a man whether one set of his ideas, or another, be the centre of his energy; and it makes a great difference, as regards any set of ideas which he may possess, whether they become central or remain peripheral in him. To say that a man is "converted" means, in these terms, that religious ideas, previously peripheral in his consciousness, now take a central place, and that religious aims form the habitual centre of his energy.

◦

[T]here are two things in the mind of the candidate for conversion: first, the present incompleteness or wrongness, the "sin" which he is eager to escape from; and, second, the positive ideal which he longs to compass. Now with most of us the sense of our present wrongness is a far more distinct piece of our consciousness than is the imagination of any positive ideal we can aim at. In a majority of cases, indeed, the "sin" almost exclusively engrosses the attention, so that conversion is "*a process of struggling away from sin rather than of striving towards righteousness.*" A man's conscious wit and will, so far as they strain towards the ideal, are aiming at something only dimly and inaccurately imagined. Yet all the while the forces of mere organic ripening within him are going on towards their own prefigured result, and his conscious strainings are letting loose subconscious allies behind the scenes, which in their way work towards rearrangement; and the rearrangement towards which all these deeper forces tend is pretty surely definite, and definitely different from what he consciously conceives and determines....

"Man's extremity is God's opportunity" is the theological way of putting this fact of the need of self-surrender; whilst the physiological way of stating it would be, "Let one do all in one's power, and one's nervous system will do the rest." Both statements acknowledge the same fact.

To state it in terms of our own symbolism: When the new centre of personal energy has been subconsciously incubated so long as to be just ready to open into flower, "hands off" is the only word for us, it must burst forth unaided!

We have used the vague and abstract language of psychology. But since, in any terms, the crisis described is the throwing of our conscious selves upon the mercy of powers which, whatever they may be, are more ideal than we are actually, and make for our redemption, you see why self-surrender has been and always must be regarded as the vital turning-point of the religious life, so far as the religious life is spiritual and no affair of outer works and ritual and sacraments.

～

The characteristics of the affective experience...can be easily enumerated, though it is probably difficult to realize their intensity, unless one have been through the experience one's self.

The central one is the loss of all the worry, the sense that all is ultimately well with one, the peace, the harmony, *the willingness to be,* even though the outer conditions should remain the same.... A passion of willingness, of acquiescence, of admiration, is the glowing centre of this state of mind. The second feature is the sense of perceiving truths not known before. The mysteries of life become lucid...; and often, nay usually, the solution is more or less unutterable in words. But these more intellectual phenomena may be postponed until we treat of mysticism.

A third peculiarity of the assurance state is the objective change which the world often appears to undergo. "An appearance of newness beautifies every object," the precise opposite of that other sort of newness, that dreadful unreality and strangeness in the appearance of the world, which is experienced by melancholy patients, and of which you may recall my relating some examples. This sense of clean and beautiful newness within and without is one of the commonest entries in conversion records. Jonathan Edwards thus describes it in himself:—

"After this my sense of things gradually increased and became more and more lively, and had more of that inward sweetness. The appearance of everything was altered; there seemed to be, as it were, a calm sweet cast, or appearance of divine glory, in almost everything. God's excellency, his wisdom, his purity and love, seemed to appear in everything; in the sun, moon, and stars;

in the clouds and blue sky; in the grass, flowers, and trees; in the water and all nature; which used greatly to fix my mind. And scarce anything, among all the works of nature, was so sweet to me as thunder and lightning.... Before, I used to be uncommonly terrified with thunder, and to be struck with terror when I saw a thunderstorm rising; but now, on the contrary, it rejoices me."

$\sim$

Saintliness

We may now turn from...psychological generalities to...fruits of the religious state....The man who lives in his religious centre of personal energy, and is actuated by spiritual enthusiasms, differs from his previous carnal self in perfectly definite ways. The new ardor which burns in his breast consumes in its glow the lower "noes" which formerly beset him, and keeps him immune against infection from the entire groveling portion of his nature. Magnanimities once impossible are now easy; paltry conventionalities and mean incentives once tyrannical hold no sway. The stone wall inside of him has fallen, the hardness in his heart has broken down. The rest of us can, I think, imagine this by recalling our state of feeling in those temporary "melting moods" into which either the trials of real life, or theatre, or a novel sometimes throw us....With most of us the customary hardness quickly returns, but not so with saintly persons. Many saints, even as energetic ones as Teresa and Loyola, have possessed what the church traditionally reveres as a special grace, the so-called gift of tears. In these persons the melting mood seems to have held almost uninterrupted control.

$\sim$

The collective name for the ripe fruits of religion in a character is Saintliness. The saintly character is the character for which spiritual emotions are the habitual centre of the personal energy; and there is a certain composite photograph of universal saintliness, the same in all religions, of which the features can easily be traced.

They are these:—

1. A feeling of being in a wider life than that of this world's selfish little interests; and a conviction, not merely intellectual, but as it were sensible, of the existence of an Ideal Power. In Christian saintliness this power is always personified as God; but abstract moral ideals, civic or patriotic utopias, or inner visions of holiness or right may also be felt as the true lords and enlargers of our life, in ways which I described in the lecture on the Reality of the Unseen.

2. A sense of the friendly continuity of the ideal power with our own life, and a willing self-surrender to its control.
3. An immense elation and freedom, as the outlines of the confining self-hood melt down.
4. A shifting of the emotional centre towards loving and harmonious affections, towards "yes, yes," and away from "no," where the claims of the non-ego are concerned.

These fundamental inner conditions have characteristic practical consequences, as follows:—

a. *Asceticism.*—The self-surrender may become so passionate as to turn into self-immolation. It may then so overrule the ordinary inhibitions of the flesh that the saint finds positive pleasure in sacrifice and asceticism, measuring and expressing as they do the degree of his loyalty to the higher power.

b. *Strength of Soul.*—The sense of enlargement of life may be so uplifting that personal motives and inhibitions, commonly omnipotent, become too insignificant for notice, and new reaches of patience and fortitude open out. Fears and anxieties go, and blissful equanimity takes their place. Come heaven, come hell, it makes no difference now!

c. *Purity.*—The shifting of the emotional centre brings with it, first, increase of purity. The sensitiveness to spiritual discords is enhanced, and the cleansing of existence from brutal and sensual elements becomes imperative. Occasions of contact with such elements are avoided: the saintly life must deepen its spiritual consistency and keep unspotted from the world. In some temperaments this need of purity of spirit takes an ascetic turn, and weaknesses of the flesh are treated with relentless severity.

d. *Charity.*—The shifting of the emotional centre brings, secondly, increase of charity, tenderness for fellow-creatures. The ordinary motives to antipathy, which usually set such close bounds to tenderness among human beings, are inhibited. The saint loves his enemies, and treats loathsome beggars as his brothers.

～

The Value of Saintliness

We have now passed in review the more important of the phenomena which are regarded as fruits of genuine religion and characteristics of men who are devout. Today we have changed our attitude from that of description to that of appreciation; we have to ask whether the fruits in question can help us to judge the absolute value of what religion adds to human life. Were I to parody Kant, I should say that a "Critique of pure Saintliness" must be our theme.

If, in turning to this theme, we could descend upon our subject from above like Catholic theologians, with our fixed definitions of man and man's perfection and our positive dogmas about God, we should have an easy time of it. Man's perfection would be the fulfillment of his end; and his end would be union with his maker.... The absolute significance and value of any bit of religious experience we might hear of would thus be given almost mathematically into our hands.

If convenience were everything, we ought now to grieve at finding ourselves cut off from so admirably convenient a method as this. But we did cut ourselves off from it deliberately in those remarks which you remember we made, in our first lecture, about the empirical method; and it must be confessed that after that act of renunciation we can never hope for clean-cut and scholastic results. We can not divide man sharply into an animal and a rational part. We cannot distinguish natural from supernatural effects; nor among the latter know which are favors of God, and which are counterfeit operations of the demon. We have merely to collect things together without any special *a priori* theological system, and out of an aggregate of piecemeal judgments as to the value of this and that experience ... decide that *on the whole* one type of religion is approved by its fruits, and another type condemned. "On the whole,"—I fear we shall never escape complicity with that qualification, so dear to your practical man, so repugnant to your systematizer! ...

Abstractly, it would seem illogical to try to measure the worth of a religion's fruits in merely human terms of value. How *can* you measure their worth without considering whether the God really exists who is supposed to inspire them? If he really exists, then all the conduct instituted by men to meet his wants must necessarily be a reasonable fruit of his religion,—it would be unreasonable only in case he did not exist. If, for instance, you were to condemn a religion of human or animal sacrifices by virtue of your subjective sentiments, and if all the while a deity were really there demanding such sacrifices, you would be making a theoretical mistake by tacitly assuming that the deity must be non-existent; you would be setting up a theology of your own as much as if you were a scholastic philosopher.

To this extent, to the extent of disbelieving peremptorily in certain types of deity, I frankly confess that we must be theologians....

But such common-sense prejudices and instincts are themselves the fruit of an empirical evolution.... After an interval of a few generations the mental climate proves unfavorable to notions of the deity which at an earlier date were perfectly satisfactory: the older gods have fallen below the common secular level, and can no longer be believed in. Today a deity who should require bleeding sacrifices to placate him would be too sanguinary to be taken seriously. Even if powerful historical credentials were put forward in his favor, we would not look at them....

The deity to whom the prophets, seers, and devotees who founded the particular cult bore witness was worth something to them personally. They could use him. He guided their imagination, warranted their hopes, and controlled their will.... [T]hey chose him for the value of the fruits he seemed to them to yield. It was in this way that the Greek and Roman gods ceased to be believed in by educated pagans; it is thus that we ourselves judge of the Hindu, Buddhist, and Mohammedan theologies; Protestants have so dealt with Catholic notions of deity, and liberal Protestants with older Protestant notions; it is thus that Chinamen judge of us, and that all of us now living will be judged by our descendants. When we cease to admire or approve what the definition of a deity implies, we end by deeming that deity incredible.

Few historic changes are more curious than these mutations of theological opinion.... We shall see examples of it from the annals of Catholic saintship which make us rub our Protestant eyes. Ritual worship in general appears to the modern transcendentalist, as well as to the ultra-puritanic type of mind, as if addressed to a deity of an almost absurdly childish character, taking delight in toy-shop furniture, tapers and tinsel, costume and mumbling and mummery, and finding his "glory" incomprehensibly enhanced thereby,—just as on the other hand the formless spaciousness of pantheism appears quite empty to ritualistic natures, and the gaunt theism of evangelical sects seems intolerably bald and chalky and bleak....

So far, then, although we are compelled, whatever may be our pretensions to empiricism, to employ some sort of a standard of theological probability of our own whenever we assume to estimate the fruits of other men's religion, yet this very standard has been begotten out of the drift of common life. It is the voice of human experience within us, judging and condemning all gods that stand athwart the pathway along which it feels itself to be advancing....

If we pass from disbeliefs to positive beliefs, it seems to me that there is not even a formal inconsistency to be laid against our method. The gods we stand by are the gods we need and can use, the gods whose demands on us are reinforcements of demand on ourselves and on one another. What I then propose to do is, briefly stated, to test saintliness by common sense, to use human standards to help us decide how far the religious life commends itself as an ideal kind of human activity. If it commends itself, then any theological belief that may inspire it, in so far forth will stand accredited. If not, then they will be discredited, and all without reference to anything but human working principles. It is but the elimination of the humanly unfit, and the survival of the humanly fittest, applied to religious beliefs; and if we look at history candidly and without prejudice, we have to admit that no religion has ever in the long run established or proved itself in any other way. Religions have *approved* themselves; they have ministered to sundry vital needs which they found reigning. When they violated other needs too strongly, or when other faiths came which served the same needs better, the first religions were supplanted.

The needs were always many, and the tests were never sharp.... No religion has ever yet owed its prevalence to "apodictic certainty." In a later lecture I will ask whether objective certainty can ever be added by theological reasoning to a religion that already empirically prevails....

The mere outward form of inalterable certainty is so precious to some minds that to renounce it explicitly is for them out of the question. They will claim it even where the facts most patently pronounce its folly. But the safe thing is surely to recognize that all insights of creatures of a day like ourselves must be provisional. The widest of critics is an altering being, subject to the better insight of the morrow, and right at any moment, only "up to date" and "on the whole." When larger ranges of truth open, it is surely best to be able to open ourselves to their reception, unfettered by our previous pretensions....

The fact of diverse judgments about religious phenomena is therefore entirely unescapable, whatever may be one's own desire to attain the irreversible. But apart from that fact, a more fundamental question awaits us, the question whether men's opinions ought to be expected to be absolutely uniform in this field. Ought all men to have the same religion? Ought they to approve the same fruits and follow the same leadings? Are they so like in their inner needs that, for hard and soft, for proud and humble, for strenuous and lazy, for healthy-minded and despairing, exactly the same religious incentives are required?...

I am well aware of how anarchic much of what I say may sound. Expressing myself thus abstractly and briefly, I may seem to despair of the very notion of truth. But I beseech you to reserve your judgment until we see it applied to the details which lie before us. I do indeed disbelieve that we or any other mortal men can attain on a given day to absolutely incorrigible and unimprovable truth about such matters of fact as those with which religions deal. But I reject this dogmatic ideal not out of perverse delight in intellectual instability. I am no lover of disorder and doubt as such. Rather do I fear to lose truth by this pretension to possess it already wholly. That we can gain more and more of it by moving always in the right direction, I believe as much as anyone, and I hope to bring you all to my way of thinking before the termination of these lectures. Till then, do not, I pray you, harden your minds irrevocably against the empiricism which I profess.

I will waste no more words, then, in abstract justification of my method, but seek immediately to use it upon the facts.

In critically judging of the value of religious phenomena, it is very important to insist on the distinction between religion as an individual personal function, and religion as an institutional, corporate, or tribal product. I drew this distinction, you may remember, in my second lecture. A survey of history shows us that, as a rule, religious geniuses attract disciples, and produce groups of sympathizers. When these groups get strong enough to "organize" themselves, they become ecclesiastical instrumentations with corporate ambitions of their own....

But in this course of lectures ecclesiastical institutions hardly concern us at all. The religious experience which we are studying is that which lives itself out within the private breast. First-hand individual experience of this kind has always appeared as a heretical sort of innovation to those who witnessed its birth. Naked comes it into the world and lonely; and it has always, for a time at least, driven him who had it into the wilderness, often into the literal wilderness out of doors, where the Buddha, Jesus, Mohammed, St. Francis, George Fox, and so many others had to go....

A genuine first-hand experience...is bound to be a heterodoxy to its witnesses, the prophet appearing as a mere lonely madman. If his doctrine prove contagious enough to spread to any others, it becomes a definite and labeled heresy. But if it then still prove contagious enough to triumph over persecution, it becomes itself an orthodoxy; and when a religion has become an orthodoxy, its day of inwardness is over: the spring is dry; the faithful live at second hand exclusively and stone the prophets in their turn. The new church, in spite of whatever human goodness may foster, can be henceforth counted on as a staunch ally in every attempt to stifle the spontaneous religious spirit, and to stop all later bubblings of the fountain from which in purer days it drew its own supply of inspiration....

The plain fact is that men's minds are built, as has been often said, in watertight compartments. Religious after as fashion, they yet have many other things in them beside their religion, and unholy entanglements and associations inevitably obtain. The basenesses so commonly charged to religion's account are thus, almost all of them, not chargeable at all to religion proper, but rather to religion's wicked practical partner, the spirit of corporate dominion. And the bigotries are most of them in their turn chargeable to religion's wicked intellectual partner, the spirit of dogmatic dominion, the passion for laying down the law in the form of an absolutely closed-in theoretic system. The ecclesiastical spirit in general is the sum of these spirits of dominion; and I beseech you never to confound the phenomena of mere tribal or corporate psychology which it presents with those manifestations of the purely interior life which are the exclusive object of our study....

∼

In a general way, then, and "on the whole," our abandonment of theological criteria, and our testing of religion by practical common sense and the empirical method, leave it in possession of its towering place in history. Economically, the saintly group of qualities is indispensable to the world's welfare. The great saints are immediate successes; the smaller ones are at least heralds and harbingers, and they may be leavens also, of a better mundane order. Let us be saints, then, if we can, whether or not we succeed visibly and temporally. But in our father's house are many mansions, and each of us must discover for himself the kind of religion and the amount of saintship which best comports with what he believes to be his powers and feels to be his truest mission and vocation. There are no successes to be guaranteed and no set orders to be given to individuals, so long as we follow the methods of empirical philosophy.

This is my conclusion so far. I know that on some of your minds it leaves a feeling of wonder that such a method should have been applied to such a subject, and this in spite of all those remarks about empiricism which I made.... How, you say, can religion, which believes in two worlds and an invisible order, be estimated by the adaptation of its fruits to this world's order alone? It is its *truth*, not its utility, you insist, upon which our verdict ought to depend. If religion is true, its fruits are good fruits, even though in this world they should prove uniformly ill adapted and full of naught but pathos. It goes back, then, after all, to the question of the truth of theology. The plot inevitably thickens upon us; we cannot escape theoretical considerations. I propose, then, that to some degree we face the responsibility. Religious persons have often, though not uniformly, professed to see truth in a special manner. That manner is known as mysticism. I will consequently now proceed to treat at some length of mystical phenomena, and after that, though more briefly, I will consider religious philosophy.

Mysticism

Over and over again in these lectures I have raised points and left them open and unfinished until we should have come to the subject of Mysticism. Some of you, I fear, may have smiled as you noted my reiterated postponements. But now the hour has come when mysticism must be faced in good earnest, and those broken threads wound up together. One may say truly, I think, that personal religious experience has it root and centre in mystical states of consciousness; so for us, who in these lectures are treating personal experience as the exclusive subject of our study, such state of consciousness ought to form the vital chapter from which the other chapters get their light. Whether my treatment of mystical states will shed more light or darkness, I do not know, for my own constitution shuts me out from their enjoyment almost entirely, and I can speak of them only at second hand. But though forced to look upon the subject so externally, I will be as objective and receptive as I can; and I think I shall at least succeed in convincing you of the reality of the states in question, and of the paramount importance of their function.

First of all, then, I ask, What does the expression "mystical state of consciousness" mean? How do we part off mystical states from other states?

The words "mysticism" and "mystical" are often used as terms of mere reproach, to throw at any opinion which we regard as vague and vast and sentimental, and without base in either facts or logic. For some writers a "mystic" is any person who believes in thought-transference, or spirit-return. Employed in this way the word has little value: there are too many ambiguous synonyms. So, to keep it useful by restricting it, I will do what I did in the case of the word "religion," and simply propose to your four marks which, when an experience has them, may justify us in calling it mystical for the purpose of the present lectures. In this way we shall save verbal disputation, and the recriminations that generally go therewith.

1. *Ineffability.*—The handiest of the marks by which I classify a state of mind as mystical is negative. The subject of it immediately says that it defies expression, that no adequate report of its contents can be given in the words. It follows from this that its quality must be directly experienced; it cannot be imparted or transferred to others. In this peculiarity mystical states are more like states of feeling than like states of intellect. No one can make clear to another who has never had a certain feeling, in what the quality or worth of it consists. One must have musical ears to know the value of a symphony; one must have been in love one's self to understand a lover's state of mind. Lacking the heart or ear, we cannot interpret the musician or the lover justly, and are even likely to consider him weak-minded or absurd. The mystic finds that most of us accord to his experiences an equally incompetent treatment.

2. *Noetic quality.*—Although so similar to states of feeling, mystical states seem to those who experience them to be also states of knowledge. They are states of insight into depths of truth unplumbed by the discursive intellect. They are illuminations, revelations, full of significance and importance, all inarticulate though they remain; and as a rule they carry with them a curious sense of authority for after-time.

These two characters will entitle any state to be called mystical, in the sense in which I use the word. Two other qualities are less sharply marked but are usually found. These are:—

3. *Transiency.*—Mystical states cannot be sustained for long. Except in rare instances, half an hour, or at most an hour or two, seems to be the limit beyond which they fade into the light of common day. Often, when

faded, their quality can but imperfectly be reproduced in memory; but when they recur it is recognized; and from one recurrence to another, it is susceptible of continuous development in what is felt as inner richness and importance.

4. *Passivity.*—Although the oncoming of mystical states may be facilitated by preliminary voluntary operations, as by fixing the attention, or going through certain bodily performances, or in other ways which manuals of mysticism prescribe; yet when the characteristic sort of consciousness once has set in, the mystic feels as if his own will were in abeyance, and indeed sometimes as if he were grasped and held by a superior power....

These four characteristics are sufficient to mark out a group of states of consciousness peculiar enough to deserve a special name and to call for careful study.

⁓

I have now sketched with extreme brevity and insufficiency, but as fairly as I am able in the time allowed, the general traits of the mystic range of consciousness. *It is on the whole pantheistic and optimistic, or at least the opposite of pessimistic. It is anti-materialistic, and harmonizes best with twice-bornness and so-called other-worldly states of mind."*...

The mystic is... *invulnerable,* and must be left, whether we relish it or not, in undisturbed enjoyment of his creed. Faith, says Tolstoy, is that by which men live. And faith-state and mystic state are practically convertible.

But I now proceed to add that mystics have no right to claim that we ought to accept the deliverance of their peculiar experiences, if we are ourselves outsiders and feel no private call thereto. The utmost they can ever ask from us in this life is to admit that they establish a presumption. They form a consensus and have an unequivocal outcome; and it would be odd, mystics might say, if such a unanimous type of experience should prove to be altogether wrong....

But even this presumption from the unanimity of mystics is far from being strong.... The classic religious mysticism, it now must be confessed, is only a "privileged case." It is an *extract,* kept true to type by the selection of the fittest specimens and their preservation in "schools." It is carved out from a much larger mass; and if we take the larger mass as seriously as religious mysticism has historically taken itself, we find that supposed unanimity largely disappears. To begin with, even religious mysticism itself, the kind that accumulates traditions and makes schools, is much less unanimous than I have allowed. It has been both ascetic and antinomianly self-indulgent within the Christian church. It is dualistic in Sankhya, and monistic in Vedanta philosophy. I called it pantheistic; but the great Spanish mystics are anything but pantheists. They are with few exceptions non-metaphysical minds, for whom "the category of personality" is absolute. The "union" of man with God is for them much more like an occasional miracle than like an original identity. How different again, apart from the happiness common to all, is the mysticism of Walt Whitman…and other naturalistic pantheists, from the more distinctively Christian sort. The fact is that the mystical feeling of enlargement, union, and emancipation has no specific intellectual content whatever of its own. It is capable of forming matrimonial alliances with material furnished by the most diverse philosophies and theologies, provided only they can find a place in their framework for its peculiar emotional mood. We have no right, therefore, to invoke its prestige as distinctly in favor of any special belief, such as that in absolute idealism, or in the absolute monistic identity, or in the absolute goodness, of the world. It is only relatively in favor of all these things—it passes out of common human consciousness in the direction in which they lie.

～

In this shape, I think, we have to leave the subject. Mystical states indeed wield no authority due simply to their being mystical states. But the higher ones among them point in directions to which the religious sentiments even of non-mystical men incline. They tell of the supremacy of the ideal, of vastness, of union, of safety, and of rest. They offer us *hypotheses,* hypotheses which we may voluntarily ignore, but which as thinkers we cannot possibly upset. The supernaturalism and optimism to which they would persuade us may, interpreted in one way or another, be after all the truest insights into the meaning of this life.

～

Philosophy

The subject of Saintliness left us face to face with the question, Is the sense of the divine presence a sense of anything objectively true? We turned first to mysticism for an answer, and found that although mysticism is entirely willing to corroborate religion, it is too private (and also too various) in its utterances to be able to claim a universal authority. But philosophy publishes results which claim to be universally valid if they are valid at all, so we now turn with our question to philosophy. Can philosophy stamp a warrant of veracity upon the religious man's sense of the divine?

～

The arguments for God's existence have stood for hundreds of years with the waves of unbelieving criticism breaking against them, never totally discrediting them in the ears of the faithful, but on the whole slowly and surely washing out the mortar from between their joints. If you have a God already whom you believe in, these arguments confirm you. If you are atheistic, they fail to set you right. The proofs are various. The "cosmological" one, so-called, reasons from the contingence of the world to a First Cause which must contain whatever perfections the world itself contains. The "argument from design" reasons, from the fact that Nature's laws are mathematical, and her parts benevolently adapted to each other, that this cause is both intellectual and benevolent. The "moral argument" is that the moral law presupposes a lawgiver. The "argument ex consensu gentium" [from the consent of the nations: ed.] is that the belief in God is so widespread as to be grounded in the rational nature of man, and should therefore carry authority with it.

As I just said, I will not discuss these arguments technically. The bare fact that all idealists since Kant have felt entitled either to scout or to neglect them shows that they are not solid enough to serve as religion's all-sufficient foundation. Absolutely impersonal reasons would be in duty bound to show more general convincingness. Causation is indeed too obscure a principle to bear the weight of the whole structure of theology.

∼

The Continental schools of philosophy have too often overlooked the fact that man's thinking is organically connected with his conduct. It seems to me to be the chief glory of English and Scottish thinkers to have kept the organic connection in view. The guiding principle of British philosophy has in fact been that every difference must *make* a difference, every theoretical difference somewhere issue in a practical difference, and that the best method of discussing points of theory is to begin ascertaining what practical difference would result from one alternative or the other being true. . . . This is the characteristic English way of taking up a question. . . .

An American philosopher of eminent originality, Mr. Charles Sanders Pierce, has rendered thought a service by disentangling from the particulars of its application the principle by which these men were instinctively guided, and by singling it out as fundamental and giving to it a Greek name. He calls it the principle of *pragmatism,* and he defends it somewhat as follows:—

Thought in movement has for its only conceivable motive the attainment of belief, or thought at rest. Only when our thought about a subject has found its rest in belief can our action on the subject firmly and safely begin. Beliefs, in short, are rules for action; and the whole function of thinking is but one step in the production of active habits. If there were any part of a thought that made no difference in the thought's practical consequences, then that part would be no proper element of the thought's significance. To develop a thought's meaning we need therefore only determine what conduct it is fitted to produce; the conduct is for us its sole significance; and the tangible fact at the root of all our thought-distinctions is that there is no one of them so fine as to consist in anything but a possible difference of practice. To attain perfect clearness in our thoughts of an object, we need then only consider what sensations, immediate or remote, we are conceivably to expect from it, and what conduct we must prepare in case the object should be true. Our conception of these practical consequences is for us the whole of our conception of the object, so far as that conception has positive significances at all.

This is the principal of Pierce, the principle of pragmatism. Such a principle will help us on this occasion to decide, among the various attributes set down in the scholastic inventory of God's perfection, whether some be not far less significant than others.

If, namely, we apply the principle of pragmatism to God's metaphysical attributes, strictly so called, as distinguished from his moral attributes, I think that, even were we forced by a coercive logic to believe them, we still should have to confess them to be destitute of all intelligible significance. Take God's aseity, for example; or his necessariness; his immateriality; his "simplicity" or superiority to the kind of inner variety and succession which we find in finite beings, his indivisibility, and lack of inner distinctions of being and actuality, and the rest. . . .

For my own part, although I dislike to say aught that may grate upon tender associations, I must frankly confess that even though these attributes were faultlessly deduced, I cannot conceive of its being the smallest consequence to us religiously that any one of them should be true. . . .

So much for the metaphysical attributes of God! From the standpoint of practical religion, the metaphysical monster which they offer to our worship is an absolutely worthless invention of the scholarly mind.

What shall we now say of the attributes called moral? Pragmatically, they stand on an entirely different footing. They positively determine fear and hope and expectation, and are foundations for the saintly life. It needs but a glance at them to show how great is their significance.

God's holiness, for example: being holy, God can will nothing but the good. Being omnipotent, he can secure its triumph. Being omniscient, he can see us in the dark. Being just, he can punish us for what he sees. Being loving, he can pardon too. Being unalterable, we can count on him securely. These qualities enter into connection with our life, it is highly important that we should be informed concerning them. That God's purpose in creation should be the manifestation of his glory is also an attribute which has definite relations to our practical life. Among other things it has given a definite character to worship in all Christian countries.

$\sim$

Let me close, then, by briefly enumerating what she [philosophy: ed.] *can* do for religion. If she will abandon metaphysics and deduction for criticism and induction, and frankly transform herself from theology into science of religions, she can make herself enormously useful.

The spontaneous intellect of man always defines the divine which it feels in ways that harmonize with its temporary intellectual prepossessions. Philosophy can by comparison eliminate the local and the accidental from these definitions....

Sifting out in this way unworthy formulations, she can leave a residuum of conceptions that at least are possible. With these she can deal as *hypotheses,* testing them in all the manners, whether negative or positive, by which hypotheses are ever tested. She can reduce their number, as some are found more open to objection.... As a result, she can offer mediation between different believers, and help to bring about consensus of opinion. She can do this the more successfully, the better she discriminates the common and essential from the individual and local elements of the religious beliefs which she compares.

I do not see why a critical Science of Religions of this sort might not eventually command as general a public adhesion as is commanded by a physical science.... [A]s the science of optics has to be fed in the first instance, and continually verified later, by facts experienced by seeing persons; so the science of religions would depend for its original material on facts of personal experience, and would have to square itself with personal experience through all its critical reconstructions. It could never get away from concrete life, or work in a conceptual vacuum. It would forever have to confess, as every science confesses, that the subtlety of nature flies beyond it, and that its formulas are but approximations....

Other Characteristics

We have wound our way back, after our excursion through mysticism and philosophy, to where we were before: the uses of religion, its uses to the individual who has it, and the uses of the individual himself to the world, are the best arguments that truth is in it. We return to the empirical philosophy: the true is what works well, even though the qualification "on the whole" may always have to be added. In this lecture we must revert to description again, and finish our picture of the religious consciousness by a word about some of its other characteristic elements.

～

When, in addition to...phenomena of inspiration, we take religious mysticism into the account, when we recall the striking and sudden unifications of a discordant self which we saw in conversion, and when we review the extravagant obsessions of tenderness, purity, and self-severity met with in saintliness, we cannot, I think, avoid the conclusion that in religion we have a department of human nature with unusually close relations to the transmarginal or subliminal region. If the word "subliminal" is offensive to any of you, as smelling too much of psychical research or other aberrations, call it by any other name you please, to distinguish it from the level of full sunlit consciousness. Call this latter the A-region of personality, if you care to, and call the other the B-region. The B-region, then, is obviously the larger part of each of us, for it is the abode of everything that is latent and the reservoir of everything that passes unrecorded or unobserved. It contains, for example, such things as all our momentarily inactive memories, and it harbors the springs of all our obscurely motived passions, impulses, likes, dislikes, and prejudices. Our intuitions, hypotheses, fancies, superstitions, persuasions, convictions, and in general all our non-rational operations, come from it. It is the source of our dreams, and apparently they may return to it. In it arise whatever mystical experiences we may have, and our automatisms, sensory or motor; our life in hypnotic and "hypnoid" conditions, if we are subjects to such conditions; our delusions, fixed ideas, and hysterical accidents, if we are hysteric subjects; our supra-normal cognitions, if such there be, and if we are telepathic subjects. It is also the fountain-head of much that feeds our religion. In persons deep in the religious life, as we have now abundantly seen,—and this is my conclusion,—the door into this region seems unusually wide open; at any rate, experiences making their entrance through that door have had emphatic influence in shaping religious history.

With this conclusion I turn back and close the circle which I opened in my first lecture, terminating thus the review which I then announced of inner religious phenomena as we find them in developed and articulate human individuals. I might easily, if the time allowed, multiply both my documents and my discriminations, but a broad treatment is, I believe, in itself better, and the most important characteristics of the subject lie, I think, before us already. In the next lecture, which is also the last one, we must try to draw the critical conclusions which so much material may suggest.

Conclusions

The material of our study of human nature is now spread before us; and in this parting hour, set free from the duty of description, we can draw our theoretical and practical conclusions. In my first lecture, defending the empirical method, I foretold that whatever conclusions we might come to could be reached by spiritual judgments only, appreciations of the significance for life of religion, taken "on the whole." Our conclusions cannot be as sharp as dogmatic conclusions would be, but I will formulate them, when the time comes, as sharply as I can.

Summing up in the broadest possible way the characteristics of the religious life, as we have found them, it includes the following beliefs:—

1. That the visible world is part of a more spiritual universe from which it draws its chief significance;
2. That union or harmonious relation with that higher universe is our true end;
3. That prayer or inner communion with the spirit thereof—be that spirit "God" or "law"—is a process wherein work is really done, and spiritual energy flows in and produces effects, psychological or material, within the phenomenal world.

Religion includes also the following psychological characteristics:—

4. A new zest which adds itself like a gift to life, and takes the form either of lyrical enchantment or of appeal to earnestness and heroism.
5. An assurance of safety and a temper of peace, and, in relation to others, a preponderance of loving affections.

〜

The pivot round which the religious life, as we have traced it, revolves, is the interest of the individual in his private personal destiny. Religion, in short, is a monumental chapter in the history of human egotism. The gods believed in—whether by crude savages or by men disciplined intellectually—agree with each other in recognizing personal calls. Religious thought is carried on in terms of personality, this being, in the world of religion, the one fundamental fact. Today, quite as much as at any previous age, the religious individual tells you that the divine meets him on the basis of his personal concerns.

Science, on the other hand, has ended by utterly repudiating the personal point of view. She catalogues her elements and records her laws indifferent as to what purpose may be shown forth by them, and constructs her theories quite careless of their bearing on human anxieties and fates. Though the scientist may individually nourish a religion, and be a theist in his irresponsible hours, the days are over when it could be said that for Science herself the heavens declare the glory of God and the firmament showeth his handiwork....The God whom science recognizes must be a God of universal laws exclusively....He cannot accommodate his processes to the convenience of individuals....Our private selves...weigh nothing and determine nothing in the world's irremediable currents of events.

You see how natural it is, from this point of view, to treat religion as a mere survival, for religion does in fact perpetuate the traditions of the most primeval thought. To coerce the spiritual powers, or to square them and get them on our side, was, during enormous tracts of time, the one great object in our dealings with the natural world. For our ancestors, dreams, hallucinations, revelations, and cock-and-bull stories were inextricably mixed with facts. Up to a comparatively recent date such distinctions as those between what has been verified and what is only conjectured, between the impersonal and the personal aspects of existence, were hardly suspected or conceived.... Truth was what had not yet been contradicted, most things were taken into the mind from the point of view of their human suggestiveness, and the attention confined itself exclusively to the aesthetic and dramatic aspects of events.

How indeed could it be otherwise?... How could the richer animistic aspects of Nature ... fail to have been first singled out and followed by philosophy as the more promising avenue to the knowledge of Nature's life? Well, it is still in these richer animistic and dramatic aspects that religion delights to dwell. It is the terror and beauty of phenomena, the "promise" of the dawn and of the rainbow, the "voice" of the thunder, the "gentleness" of the summer rain, the "sublimity" of the stars, and not the physical laws which these things follow, by which the religious mind still continues to be most impressed....

Pure anachronism! says the survival-theory;—anachronism for which deanthropomorphization of the imagination is the remedy required. The less we mix the private with the cosmic, the more we dwell in universal and impersonal terms, the truer heirs of science become.

In spite of the appeal which this impersonality of the scientific attitude makes to a certain magnanimity of temper, I believe it to be shallow, and I can now state my reason in comparatively few words. The reason is that, so long as we deal with the cosmic and the general, we deal only with symbols of reality, but *as soon as we deal with private and personal phenomena as such, we deal with realities in the completest sense of the term....*

That unsharable feeling which each one of us has of the pinch of his individual destiny as he privately feels it rolling out on fortune's wheel may be disparaged for its egotism, may be sneered at as unscientific, but it is the one thing that fills up the measure of our concrete actuality, and any would-be existent that should lack such a feeling, or its analogue, would be a piece of reality only half made up.

If this be true, it is absurd for science to say that the egotistic elements of experience should be suppressed. The axis of reality runs solely through the egotistic places....

You see now why I have been so individualistic throughout these lectures, and why I have seemed so bent on rehabilitating the element of feeling in religion and subordinating its intellectual part. Individuality is founded on feeling; and the recesses of feeling, the darker, blinder strata of character, are the only places in the world in which we catch real fact in the making, and directly perceive how events happen, and how work is actually done. Compared with this world of living individualized feelings, the world of generalized objects which the intellect contemplates is without solidity or life....

Let us agree, then, that Religion, occupying herself with personal destinies and keeping thus in contact with the only absolute realities which we know, must necessarily play an eternal part in human history. The next thing to decide is what she reveals about those destinies, or whether indeed she reveals anything distinct enough to be considered a general message to mankind. We have done as you see, with our preliminaries, and our final summing up can now begin....

I am expressly trying to reduce religion to its lowest admissible terms, to that minimum, free from individualistic excrescences, which all religions contain as their nucleus, and on which it may be hoped that all religious persons may agree. That established, we should have a result which might be small, but would at least be solid; and on it and round it the ruddier additional beliefs on which the different individuals make their venture might be grafted, and flourish as richly as you please.

~

We must next pass beyond the point of view of merely subjective utility, and make inquiry into the intellectual content [of religion: ed.] itself.

First, is there, under all the discrepancies of the creeds, a common nucleus to which they bear their testimony unanimously?

And second, ought we to consider the testimony true? I will take up the first question first, and answer it immediately in the affirmative. The warring gods and formulas of the various religions do indeed cancel each other, but there is a certain uniform deliverance in which religions all appear to meet. It consists of two parts:—

1. An uneasiness; and
2. Its solution.

1. The uneasiness, reduced to its simplest terms, is a sense that there is *something wrong about us* as we naturally stand.
2. The solution is a sense that *we are saved from the wrongness* by making proper connection with the higher powers.

In those more developed minds which alone we are studying, the wrongness takes a moral character, and the salvation takes a mystical tinge. I think we shall keep well within the limits of what is common to all such minds if we formulate the essence of their religious experience in terms like these:—

The individual, so far as he suffers from his wrongness and criticises it, is to that extent consciously beyond it, and in at least possible touch with something higher, if anything higher exist. Along with the wrong part there is thus a better part of him, even though it may be but a most helpless germ. With which part he should identify his real being is by no means obvious at this stage; but when stage 2 (the stage of solution or salvation) arrives, the man identifies his real being with the germinal higher part of himself; and does so in the following way. *He becomes conscious that this higher part is conterminous and continuous with a MORE of the same quality, which is operative in the universe outside of him, and which he can keep in working touch with, and in a fashion get on board of and save himself when all his lower being has gone to pieces in the wreck.*

It seems to me that all the phenomena are accurately describable in these very simple general terms. They allow for the divided self and the struggle; they involve the change of personal centre and the surrender of the lower self; they express the appearance of exteriority of the helping power and yet account for our sense of union with it; and they fully justify our feelings of security and joy. There is probably no autobiographic document, among...those which I have quoted, to which the description will not well apply. One need only add such specific details as will adapt it to various theologies and various personal temperaments, and one will then have the various experiences reconstructed in their individual forms.

So far, however, as this analysis goes, the experiences are only psychological phenomena. They possess, it is true, enormous biological worth. Spiritual strength really increases in the subject when he has them, a new life opens for him, and they seem to him a place of conflux where the forces of two universes meet; and yet this may be nothing but his subjective fancy, in spite of the effects produced. I now turn to my second question: What is the objective "truth" of their content?

The part of the content concerning which the question of truth most pertinently arises is that "MORE of the same quality" with which our own higher self appears in the experience to come into harmonious working relation. Is such a "more" merely our own notion, or does it really exist? If so, in what shape does it exist? Does it act, as well as exist? And in what form should we conceive of that "union" with it of which religious geniuses, are so convinced?...

The "more," as we called it, and the meaning of our "union" with it, form the nucleus of our inquiry. Into what definite description can these words be translated, and for what definite facts do they stand? It would never do for us to place ourselves offhand at the position of a particular theology, the Christian theology, for example, and proceed immediately to define the "more" as Jehovah, and the "union" as his imputation to us of the righteousness of Christ. That would be unfair to other religions, and, from our present standpoint at least, would be an over-belief.

We must begin by using less particularized terms; and, since one of the duties of the science of religions is to keep religion in connection with the rest of science, we shall do well to seek first of all a way of describing the "more," which psychologists may also recognize as real. The subconscious self is nowadays a well-accredited psychological entity; and I believe that in it we have exactly the mediating term required. Apart from all religious considerations, there is actually and literally more life in our total soul than we are at any time aware of....

Let me then propose, as an hypothesis, that whatever it may be on its *farther* side, the "more" with which in religious experience we feel ourselves connected is on its *hither* side the subconscious continuation of our conscious life. Starting thus with a recognized psychological fact as our basis, we seem to preserve a contact with "science" which the ordinary theologian lacks. At the same time the theologian's contention that the religious man is moved by an external power is vindicated, for it is one of the peculiarities of invasions from the subconscious region to take on objective appearances, and to suggest to the Subject an external control. In the religious life the control is felt as "higher"; but since on our hypothesis it is primarily the higher faculties of our own hidden mind which are controlling, the sense of union with the power beyond us is a sense of something, not merely apparently, but literally true.

This doorway into the subject seems to me the best one for a science of religions, for it mediates between a number of different points of view. Yet it is only a doorway, and difficulties present themselves as soon as we step through it, and ask how far our transmarginal consciousness carries us if we follow it on its remoter side. Here the over-beliefs begin: here mysticism and the conversion-rapture and Vedantism and transcendental idealism bring in their monistic interpretations and tell us that the finite self rejoins the absolute self, for it was always one with God and identical with the soul of the world. Here the prophets of all the different religions come with their visions, voices, raptures, and other openings, supposed by each to authenticate his own peculiar faith....

Disregarding the over-beliefs, and confining ourselves to what is common and generic, we have *in the fact that the conscious person is continuous with a wider self through which saving experiences come,* a positive content of religious experience which, it seems to me, *is literally and objectively true as far as it goes.* If I now proceed to state my own hypothesis about the farther limits of this extension of our personality, I shall be offering my own over-belief—though I know it will appear a sorry under-belief to some of you—for which I can only bespeak the same indulgence which in a converse case I should accord to yours....

God is the natural appellation, for us Christians at least, for the supreme reality, so I will call this higher part of the universe by the name of God. We and God have business with each other; and in opening ourselves to his influence our deepest destiny is fulfilled. The universe, at those parts of it which our personal being constitutes, takes a turn genuinely for the worse or for the better in proportion as each one of us fulfills or evades God's demands. As far as this goes I probably have you with me, for I only translate into schematic language what I may call the instinctive belief of mankind: God is real since he produces real effects....

That the God with whom, starting from the hither side of our own extra-marginal self, we come at its remoter margin into commerce should be the absolute world-ruler, is of course a very considerable over-belief. Over-belief as it is, though, it is an article of almost every one's religion. Most of us pretend in some way to prop it upon our philosophy, but the philosophy itself is really propped upon this faith. What is this but to say that Religion, in her fullest exercise of function, is not a mere illumination of facts already elsewhere given, not a mere passion, like love, which views things in a rosier light. It is indeed that, as we have seen abundantly. But it is something more, namely, a postulator of new facts as well. The world interpreted religiously is not the materialistic world over again, with an altered expression; it must have, over and above the altered expression, a natural constitution different at some point from that which a materialistic world would have. It must be such that different events can be expected in it, different conduct must be required.

This thoroughly "pragmatic" view of religion has usually been taken as a matter of course by common men. They have interpolated divine miracles into the field of nature, they have built a heaven out beyond the grave. It is only transcendentalist metaphysicians who think that, without adding any concrete details to Nature, or subtracting any, but by simply calling it the expression of absolute spirit, you make it more divine just as it stands.

I believe the pragmatic way of taking religion to be the deeper way. It gives it body as well as soul, it makes it claim, as everything real must claim, some characteristic realm of fact as its very own. What the more characteristically divine facts are, apart from the actual inflow of energy in the faith-state and the prayer-state, I know not. But the over-belief on which I am ready to make my personal venture is that they exist. The whole drift of my education goes to persuade me that the world of our present consciousness is only one out of many worlds of consciousness that exist, and that those other worlds must contain experiences which have a meaning for our life also; and that although in the main their experiences and those of this world keep discrete, yet the two become continuous at certain points, and higher energies filter in. By being faithful in my poor measure to this over-belief, I seem to myself to keep more sane and true. I *can,* of course, put myself into the sectarian scientist's attitude, and imagine vividly that the world of sensations and of scientific laws and objects may be all. But whenever I do this, I hear that inward monitor of which W. K. Clifford once wrote, whispering the word "bosh!" Humbug is humbug, even though it bear the scientific name, and the total expression of human experience, as I view it objectively, invincibly urges me beyond the narrow "scientific" bounds. Assuredly, the real world is of a different temperament,—more intricately built than physical science allows. So my objective and my subjective conscience both hold me to the over-belief which I express. Who knows whether the faithfulness of individuals here below to their own poor over-beliefs may not actually help God in turn to be more effectively faithful to his own greater tasks?

If asked just where the differences in fact which are due to God's existence come in, I should have to say that in general I have no hypothesis to offer beyond what the phenomenon of "prayerful communion," especially when certain kinds of incursion from the subconscious region take part in it, immediately suggests. The appearance is that in this phenomenon something ideal, which in one sense is part of ourselves and in another sense is not ourselves, actually exerts an influence, raises our centre of personal energy, and produces regenerative effects unattainable in other ways. If, then, there be a wider world of being than that of our every-day consciousness, if in it there be forces whose effects on us are intermittent, if one facilitating condition of the effects be the openness of the "subliminal" door, we have the elements of a theory to which the phenomena of religious life lend plausibility. I am so impressed by the importance of these phenomena that I adopt the hypothesis which they so naturally suggest. At these places at least, I say, it would seem as though transmundane energies, God, if you will, produced immediate effects within the natural world to which the rest of experience belongs.

The difference in natural "fact" which most of us would assign as the first difference which the existence of a God ought to make would, I imagine, be personal immortality. Religion, in fact, for the great majority of our own race *means* immortality, and nothing else. God is the producer of immortality; and whoever has doubts of immortality is written down as an atheist without farther trial.... I sympathize with the urgent impulse to be present ourselves, and in the conflict of impulses, both of them so vague yet both of them noble, I know not how to decide. It seems to me that it is eminently a case for facts to testify....

Meanwhile the practical needs and experiences of religion seem to me sufficiently met by the belief that beyond each man and in a fashion continuous with him there exists a larger power which is friendly to him and to his ideals. All that the facts require is that the power should be both other and larger than our conscious selves. Anything larger will do, if only it be large enough to trust for the next step. It need not be infinite, it need not be solitary. It might conceivably even be only a larger and more godlike self, of which the present self would then be but the mutilated expression, and the universe might conceivably be a collection of such selves, of different degrees of inclusiveness, with no absolute unity realized in it at all. . . .

Common sense is less sweeping in its demands than philosophy or mysticism have been wont to be, and can suffer the notion of this world being partly saved and partly lost. The ordinary moralistic state of mind makes the salvation of the world conditional upon the success with which each unit does its part. . . . For practical life at any rate, the *chance* of salvation is enough. No fact in human nature is more characteristic than its willingness to live on a chance. The existence of the chance makes the difference . . . between a life of which the keynote is resignation and a life of which the keynote is hope.

7

Rudolf Otto: Religion and the Sense of the "Numinous"

Rudolf Otto (1869–1937) was a German theologian and historian of religions who, like William James, took keen interest in the character of human religious experience, particularly its unique emotional elements and aspects. Born into a prosperous family from the village of Peine near Hanover, Otto studied at the Universities of Erlangen and Göttingen, earning his doctorate with a first thesis on aspects of the theology of Martin Luther and a second on the philosopher Immanuel Kant—two figures formative of modern German religious and intellectual life. Subsequently he became a professor at the University of Breslau and later at the Divinity School of historic Marburg University. Alongside his scholarly work, he took a vigorous interest in German politics and university administration.

Though a devout Protestant Christian, Otto developed a wide appreciation of religious sentiments and beliefs across cultures. In his scholarly endeavors he gave special attention to the practice of mysticism in both Western and Eastern civilizations. Shortly before World War I he embarked on a two-year tour of the Middle East and Asia that included stays in Egypt, North Africa, India, China, and Japan. He mastered Sanskrit, the language of India's sacred texts, some of which he translated, while also producing comparative studies of Hinduism and Christianity, and of European and Indian forms of religious thought and devotional practice. His comparative study of Catholic mysticism in the Christian Middle Ages and Hinduism's great medieval philosopher-mystic Shankara (700–750 C.E.) was a rich, subtle, and original inquiry. Few scholars of our day—or his—could lay claim to the demanding linguistic and historical skills needed to undertake it.

Otto was considerably influenced by the work of Friedrich Schleiermacher, the German theologian from the turn of the nineteenth century whose famous *Speeches on Religion* (1799) had traced all of religion to the human "feeling of absolute dependence." He found that Schleiermacher's formulation resonated not only with his own religious experience, but also with his studies of Luther and Christian theology, as well as his encounters with Indian and Asiatic spirituality. It was this conviction that led him to the most important book of his career: a relatively brief, but highly original and provocative study published in 1915 under the title *Das Heilige*—translated into English as *The Idea of the Holy*. The subtitle described the book as "An Inquiry into the Non-Rational Factor in the Idea of the Divine and Its Relation to the Rational." By this Otto did not mean to say that religious belief is somehow irrational, or even less rational than other human beliefs; rather, that religion is rooted in an utterly distinctive feeling, or emotional intuition, which he described as a sense of the "numinous"—an adjective created from the Latin word *numen*, meaning a "spirit" or a "divinity."

Otto draws further on Latin terminology to describe the two key aspects of the numinous; it is, he says, a sense of a something "wholly other" than our world that is best depicted in Latin as a *mysterium* that is both *tremendum et fascinans*. In moments of encounter with the numinous, and quite beyond the concepts we use to describe it, we find ourselves overtaken by the paradoxical twin sentiments of fear and fascination. We are terrified, but also captivated. Cultures and faiths differ in the conceptual formulas they adopt—Jehovah, Creator God, many gods, Brahman, Allah, the Tao—to frame a rational understanding of the divine. But what they all may be found to share—beside and beyond the rational concepts used to describe their belief—is a sense of the immense unworldly mystery that elicits in us the sentiments of dread and desire.

The selection provided here includes both the arresting early chapters of *The Idea of the Holy*, where Otto first outlines the nature of the numinous, and a later chapter where he develops its logical and theological implications. In the course of the discussions that explore this idea, Otto draws extensively on analogies from events in ordinary life—intimations of things weird or uncanny, perceptions of ghosts or fairies and angels or demons, and encounters with the sublime in nature, in literature, and in music. These experiences faintly resemble the sense of the numinous, but of course they are not the same. On the contrary, Otto maintains, religious experience is of a kind unlike any other; it is something completely (in another Latin phrase) *sui generis*: a thing entirely of its own kind.

The claim that religious experience is something *sui generis* is what has made Otto's book so provocative over the near-century since its publication. In stiff opposition to the reductionism of Freud, Durkheim, and Marx, Otto draws also on the psychology of religious experience to make an argument somewhat similar to that of James but in terms clearly less modest and more assertive. He does not just proceed empirically. He argues the case categorically (using concepts drawn from the philosophy of Immanuel Kant). The religious sensibility, he insists, is intrinsically independent and autonomous. By way of analogies and images, we can try to explain it, but we will fail utterly if we seek, as do reductionist theories, to explain it away. It is this assertive protest and defense of a distinctively religious experience against the dominant reductionisms of the age that has made *Das Heilige* one of the most widely translated and internationally influential books on religion in the twentieth century.

Chapter I
The Rational and the Non-Rational

In these early chapters of Das Heilige *Otto outlines the uniquely distinctive features in the human sense of the "numinous," as it apprehends the holy in its stark and majestic otherness. In the later chapter, he argues for this kind of experience as* sui generis—*something uniquely "of its own kind," and thus not reducible to experiences or causes of other kinds.*

It is essential to every theistic conception of God, and most of all to the Christian, that it designates and precisely characterizes deity by the attributes spirit, reason, purpose, good will, supreme power, unity, selfhood. The nature of God is thus thought of by analogy with our human nature of reason and personality; only, whereas in ourselves we are aware of this as qualified by restriction and limitation, as applied to God the attributes we use are "completed," i.e. constitute clear and definite *concepts*: they can be grasped by the intellect; they can be analysed by thought; they can even admit of definition. An object that can thus be thought conceptually may be termed *rational*. The nature of deity described in the attributes above mentioned is, then, a rational nature; and a religion which recognizes and maintains such a view of God is in so far a "rational" religion. Only on such terms is *belief* possible in contrast to mere *feeling*. And of Christianity at least it is false that "feeling is all, the name but sound and smoke" [Goethe in *Faust*: ed.];—where "name" stands for conception or thought. Rather we count this the very mark and criterion of a religion's high rank and superior value—that it should have no lack of *conceptions* about God;

FROM: *The Idea of the Holy: An Inquiry into the Non-Rational Factor in the Idea of the Divine and Its Relation to the Rational.* Translated by John W. Harvey. New York: Oxford University Press, © 1958 [1915; Eng. Tr. 1923]. Reprinted by permission of Oxford University Press, England.

that it should admit knowledge—the knowledge that comes by faith—of the transcendent in terms of conceptual thought, whether those already mentioned or others which continue and develop them. Christianity not only possesses such conceptions but possesses them in unique clarity and abundance, and this is, though not the sole or even the chief, yet a very real sign of its superiority over religions of other forms and at other levels. This must be asserted at the outset and with the most positive emphasis.

But, when this is granted, we have to be on our guard against an error which would lead to a wrong and one-sided interpretation of religion. This is the view that the essence of deity can be given completely and exhaustively in such "rational" attributions as have been referred to above and in others like them. It is not an unnatural misconception. We are prompted to it by the traditional language of edification, with its characteristic phraseology and ideas; by the learned treatment of religious themes in sermon and theological instruction; and further even by our Holy Scriptures themselves. In all these cases the "rational" element occupies the foreground, and often nothing else seems to be present at all. But this is after all to be expected. All language, in so far as it consists of words, purports to convey ideas or concepts;—that is what language means;—and the more clearly and unequivocally it does so, the better the language. And hence expositions of religious truth in language inevitably tend to stress the "rational" attributes of God.

But though the above mistake is thus a natural one enough, it is none the less seriously misleading. For so far are these "rational" attributes from exhausting the idea of deity, that they in fact imply a non-rational or supra-rational Subject of which they are predicates. They are "essential" (and not merely "accidental") attributes of that subject, but they are also, it is important to notice, *synthetic* essential attributes. That is to say, we have to predicate them of a subject which they qualify, but which in its deeper essence is not, nor indeed can be, comprehended in them; which rather requires comprehension of a quite different kind. Yet, though it eludes the conceptual way of understanding, it must be in some way or other within our grasp, else absolutely nothing could be asserted of it. And even mysticism, in speaking of it as . . . the ineffable, does not really mean to imply that absolutely nothing can be asserted of the object of the religious consciousness; otherwise, mysticism could exist only in unbroken silence, whereas what has generally been a characteristic of the mystics is their copious eloquence.

Here for the first time we come up against the contrast between rationalism and profounder religion, and with this contrast and its signs we shall be repeatedly concerned in what follows. We have here in fact the first and most distinctive mark of rationalism, with which all the rest are bound up. It is not that which is commonly asserted, that rationalism is the denial, and its opposite the affirmation, of the miraculous. That is manifestly a wrong or at least a very superficial distinction. For the traditional theory of the miraculous as a the occasional breach in the causal nexus in nature by a Being who himself instituted and must therefore be master of it—this theory is itself as massively "rational" as it is possible to be. Rationalists have often enough acquiesced in the possibility of the miraculous in this sense; they have even themselves contributed to frame a theory of it;—whereas anti-rationalists have been often indifferent to the whole controversy about miracles. The difference between rationalism and its opposite is to be found elsewhere. It resolves itself rather into a peculiar difference of *quality* in the mental attitude and emotional content of the religious life itself. All depends upon this: in our idea of God is the non-rational overborne, even perhaps wholly excluded, by the rational? Or conversely, does the non-rational itself preponderate over the rational? Looking at the matter thus, we see that the common dictum, that orthodoxy itself has been the mother of rationalism, is in some measure well founded. It is not simply that orthodoxy was preoccupied with doctrine and the framing of dogma, for these have been no less a concern of the wildest mystics. It is rather that orthodoxy found in the construction of dogma and doctrine no way to do justice to the non-rational aspect of its subject. So far from keeping the non-rational element in religion alive in the heart of the religious experience, orthodox Christianity manifestly failed to recognize its value, and by this failure gave to the idea of God a one-sidedly intellectualistic and rationalistic interpretation.

This bias to rationalization still prevails, not only in theology but in the science of comparative religion in general, and from top to bottom of it. The modern students of mythology, and those who pursue research into the religion of "primitive man" and attempt to reconstruct the "bases" or "sources" of religion, are all victims to it. Men do not, of course, in these cases employ those lofty "rational" concepts which we took as our point of departure; but they tend to take these concepts and their gradual "evolution" as setting the main problem of their inquiry, and fashion ideas and notions of lower value, which they regard as paving the way for them. It is always in terms of concepts and ideas that the subject is pursued, "natural" ones, moreover, such as have a place in the general sphere of man's ideational life, and are not specifically "religious." And then with a resolution and cunning which one can hardly help admiring, men shut their eyes to that which is quite unique in the religious experience, even in its most primitive manifestations. But it is rather a matter for astonishment than for admiration! For if there be any single domain of human experience that presents us with something unmistakably specific and unique, peculiar to itself, assuredly it is that of the religious life. In truth the enemy has often a keener vision in this matter than either the champion of religion or the neutral and professedly impartial theorist. For the adversaries on their side know very well that the entire "pother about mysticism" has nothing to do with "reason" and "rationality."

And so it is salutary that we should be incited to notice that religion is not exclusively contained and exhaustively comprised in any series of "rational" assertions; and it is well worth while to attempt to bring the relation of the different "moments" of religion to one another clearly before the mind, so that its nature may become more manifest.

This attempt we are now to make with respect to the quite distinctive category of the holy or sacred.

Chapter II
"Numen" and the "Numinous"

"Holiness"—"the holy"—is a category of interpretation and valuation peculiar to the sphere of religion. It is, indeed, applied by transference to another sphere—that of ethics—but it is not itself derived from this. While it is complex, it contains a quite specific element or "moment," which sets it apart from "the rational" in the meaning we gave to that word above, and which remains inexpressible—ἄρρητον or *ineffabile* [beyond words: ed.]—in the sense that it completely eludes apprehension in terms of concepts. The same thing is true (to take a quite different region of experience) of the category of the beautiful.

Now these statements would be untrue from the outset if "the holy" were merely what is meant by the word, not only in common parlance, but in philosophical, and generally even in theological usage. The fact is we have come to use the words "holy," "sacred" (*heilig*) in an entirely derivative sense, quite different from that which they originally bore. We generally take "holy" as meaning "completely good"; it is the absolute moral attribute, denoting the consummation of moral goodness...

But this common usage of the term is inaccurate. It is true that all this moral significance is contained in the word "holy," but it includes in addition—as even we cannot but feel—a clear overplus of meaning, and this it is now our task to isolate. Nor is this merely a later or acquired meaning; rather, "holy," or at least the equivalent words in Latin and Greek, in Semitic and other ancient languages, denoted first and foremost *only* this overplus: if the ethical element was present at all, at any rate it was not original and never constituted the whole meaning of the word. Any one who uses it today does undoubtedly always feel "the morally good" to be implied in "holy"; and accordingly in our inquiry into that element which is separate and peculiar to the idea of the holy it will be useful, at least for the temporary purpose of the investigation, to invent a special term to stand for "the holy" *minus* its moral factor...and, as we can now add, minus its "rational" aspect altogether.

It will be our endeavour to suggest this unnamed Something to the reader as far as we may, so that he may himself feel it. There is no religion in which it does not live as the real innermost core, and without it no religion would be worthy of the name. It is pre-eminently a living force in the Semitic religions, and of these again in none has it such vigour as in that of the Bible. Here, too, it has a name of its own, viz. the Hebrew (*qadosh*) to which the Greek (ἅγιος) and the Latin *sanctus,* and, more accurately still, *sacer,* are the corresponding terms. It is not, of course, disputed that these terms in all three languages connote, as part of their meaning, *good, absolute goodness,* when, that is, the notion has ripened and reached the highest stage in its development. And we then use the word "holy" to translate them. But this "holy" then represents the gradual shaping and filling in with ethical meaning, or what we shall call the "schematization," of what was a unique original feeling-response, which can be in itself ethically neutral and claims consideration in its own right. And when this moment or element first emerges and begins its long development, all those expressions (*qadosh*, ἅγιος, *sacer,* &c.) mean beyond all question something quite other than "the good." This is universally agreed by contemporary criticism, which rightly explains the rendering of *qadosh* by "good" as a mistranslation and unwarranted "rationalization" or "moralization" of the term.

Accordingly, it is worth while, as we have said, to find a word to stand for this element in isolation, this "extra" in the meaning of "holy" above the meaning of goodness. By means of a special term we shall the better be able, first, to keep the meaning clearly apart and distinct, and second to apprehend and classify connectedly whatever subordinate forms or stages of development it may show. For this purpose I adopt a word coined from the Latin *numen. Omen* has given us "ominous," and there is no reason why from *numen* we should not similarly form a word "numinous." I shall speak, then, of a unique "numinous" category of value and of a definitely "numinous" state of mind, which is always found wherever the category is applied. This mental state is perfectly *sui generis* and irreducible to any other; and therefore, like every absolutely primary and elementary datum, while it admits of being discussed, it cannot be strictly defined. There is only one way to help another to an understanding of it. He must be guided and led on by consideration and discussion of the matter through the ways of his own mind, until he reach the point at which "the numinous" in him perforce begins to stir, to start into life and into consciousness. We can co-operate in this process by bringing before his notice all that can be found in other regions of the mind, already known and familiar, to resemble, or again to afford some special contrast to, the particular experience we wish to elucidate. Then we must add: "This X of ours is not precisely *this* experience, but akin to this one and the opposite of that other. Cannot you now realize for yourself what it is?" In other words, our *X* cannot, strictly speaking, be taught, it can only be evoked, awakened in mind; as everything that comes "of the spirit" must be awakened.

Chapter III
The Elements in the "Numinous"

Creature-Feeling

The reader is invited to direct his mind to a moment of deeply-felt religious experience, as little as possibly qualified by other forms of consciousness. Whoever cannot do this, whoever knows no such moments in his experience, is requested to read no farther; for it is not easy to discuss questions of religious psychology with one who can recollect the emotions of his adolescence, the discomforts of indigestion, or, say, social feeling, but cannot recall any intrinsically religious feeling. We do not blame such an one, when he tries for himself to advance as far as he can with the help of such principles of explanation as he knows, interpreting "aesthetics" in terms of sensuous pleasure, and "religion" as a function of the gregarious instinct and social standards, or as something more primitive still. But the artist, who for his part has an intimate personal knowledge of the distinctive element in the aesthetic experience, will decline his theories with thanks, and the religious man will reject them even more uncompromisingly.

Next, in the probing and analysis of such states of the soul as that of solemn worship, it will be well if regard be paid to what is unique in them rather than to what they have in common with other similar states. To be *rapt* in worship is one thing; to be morally *uplifted* by the contemplation of a good deed is another; and it is not to their common features, but to those elements of emotional content peculiar to the first that we would have attention directed as precisely as possible. As Christians we undoubtedly here first meet with feelings familiar enough in a weaker form in other departments of experience, such as feelings of gratitude, trust, love, reliance, humble submission, and dedication. But this does not by any means exhaust the content of religious worship. Not in any of these have we got the special features of the quite unique and incomparable experience of solemn worship. In what does this consist?

Schleiermacher has the credit of isolating a very important element in such an experience. This is the "feeling of dependence." But this important discovery of Schleiermacher is open to criticism in more than one respect.

In the first place, the feeling or emotion which he really has in mind in this phrase is in its specific quality not a "feeling of dependence" in the "natural" sense of the word. As such, other domains of life and other regions of experience than the religious occasion the feeling, as a sense of personal insufficiency and impotence, a consciousness of being determined by circumstances and environment. The feeling of which Schleiermacher wrote has an undeniable analogy with these states of mind: they serve as an indication to it, and its nature may be elucidated by them, so that, by following the direction in which they point, the feeling itself may be spontaneously felt. But the feeling is at the same time also qualitatively different from such analogous states of mind. Schleiermacher himself, in a way, recognizes this by distinguishing the feeling of pious or religious dependence from all other feelings of dependence. His mistake is in making the distinction merely that between "absolute" and "relative" dependence, and therefore a difference of degree and not of intrinsic quality. What he overlooks is that, in giving the feeling the name "feeling of dependence" at all, we are really employing what is no more than a very close analogy. Anyone who compares and contrasts the two states of mind introspectively will find out, I think, what I mean. It cannot be expressed by means of anything else, just because it is so primary and elementary a datum in our physical life, and therefore only definable through itself. It may perhaps help him if I cite a well-known example, in which the precise "moment" or element of religious feeling of which we are speaking is most actively present. When Abraham ventures to plead with God for the men of Sodom, he says (Gen. xviii. 27): "Behold now, I have taken upon me to speak unto the Lord, which am but dust and ashes." There you have a self-confessed "feeling of dependence," which is yet at the same time far more than, and something other than, *merely* a feeling of dependence. Desiring to give it a name of its own, I propose to call it "creature-consciousness" or creature-feeling. It is the emotion of a creature, submerged and overwhelmed by its own nothingness in contrast to that which is supreme above all creatures.

It is easily seen that, once again, this phrase, whatever it is, is not a *conceptual* explanation of the matter. All that this new term, "creature-feeling," can express, is the note of submergence into nothingness before an overpowering, absolute might of some kind; whereas everything turns upon the *character* of this overpowering might, a character which cannot be expressed verbally, and can only be suggested indirectly through the tone and content of a man's feeling-response to it. And this response must be directly experienced in oneself to be understood.

We have now to note a second defect in the formulation of Schleiermacher's principle. The religious category discovered by him, by whose means he professes to determine the real content of the religious emotion, is merely a category of *self*-valuation, in the sense of self-depreciation. According to him the religious emotion would be directly and primarily a sort of *self*-consciousness, a feeling concerning oneself in a special, determined relation, viz. one's dependence. Thus, according to Schleiermacher, I can only come upon the very fact of God as the result of an inference, that is, by reasoning to a cause beyond myself to account for my "feeling of dependence." But this is entirely opposed to the psychological facts of the case. Rather, the "creature-feeling" is itself a first subjective concomitant and effect of another feeling-element, which casts it like a shadow, but which in itself indubitably has immediate and primary reference to an object outside the self.*

Now this object is just what we have already spoken of as "the numinous." For the "creature-feeling" and the sense of dependence to arise in the mind the "numen" must be experienced as present, a *numen praesens,* as is in the case of Abraham. There must be felt a something "numinous," something bearing the character of a "numen," to which the mind turns spontaneously; or (which is the same thing in other words) these feelings can only arise in the mind as accompanying emotions when the category of "the numinous" is called into play.

The numinous is thus felt as objective and outside the self. We have now to inquire more closely into its nature and the modes of its manifestation.

---

* This is so manifestly borne out by experience that it must be about the first thing to force itself upon the notice of psychologists analysing the facts of religion. There is a certain naïveté in the following passage from William James's *Varieties of Religious Experience* (p. 58), where, alluding to the origin of the Grecian representations of the gods, he says: "As regards the origin of the Greek gods, we need not at present seek an opinion. But the whole array of our instances leads to a conclusion something like this: It is as if there were in the human consciousness *a sense of reality, a feeling of objective presence,* a *perception* of what we may call 'something there,' more deep and more general than any of the special and particular "senses" by which the current psychology supposes existent realities to be originally revealed." (The italics are James's own.) James is debarred by his empiricist and pragmatist standpoint from coming to a recognition of faculties of knowledge and potentialities of thought in the spirit itself, and he is therefore obliged to have recourse to somewhat singular and mysterious hypotheses to explain this fact. But he grasps the fact itself clearly enough and is sufficient of a realist not to explain it away. But this "feeling of reality," the feeling of a "numinous" *object* objectively given, must be posited as a primary immediate datum of consciousness, and the "feeling of dependence" is then a consequence, following very closely upon it, viz. a depreciation of the *subject* in his own eyes. The latter presupposes the former.

Chapter IV
"Mysterium Tremendum"

The Analysis of "Tremendum"

We said above that the nature of the numinous can only be suggested by means of the special way in which it is reflected in the mind in terms of feeling. "Its nature is such that it grips or stirs the human mind with this and that determinate affective state." We have now to attempt to give a further indication of these determinate states. We must once again endeavour, by adducing feelings akin to them for the purpose of analogy or contrast, and by the use of metaphor and symbolic expressions, to make the states of mind we are investigating ring out, as it were, of themselves.

Let us consider the deepest and most fundamental element in all strong and sincerely felt religious emotion. Faith unto salvation, trust, love—all these are there. But over and above these is an element which may also on occasion, quite apart from them, profoundly affect us and occupy the mind with a well-nigh bewildering strength. Let us follow it up with every effort of sympathy and imaginative intuition wherever it is to be found, in the lives of those around us, in sudden, strong ebullitions of personal piety and the frames of mind such ebullitions evince, in the fixed and ordered solemnities of rites and liturgies, and again in the atmosphere that clings to old religious monuments and buildings, to temples and to churches. If we do so we shall find we are dealing with something for which there is only one appropriate expression, "*mysterium tremendum*." The feeling of it may at times come sweeping like a gentle tide, pervading the mind with a tranquil mood of deepest worship. It may pass over into a more set and lasting attitude of the soul, continuing, as it were, thrillingly vibrant and resonant, until at last it dies away and the soul resumes its "profane," non-religious mood of everyday experience. It may burst in sudden eruption up from the depths of the soul with spasms and convulsions, or lead to the strangest excitements, to intoxicated frenzy, to transport, and to ecstasy. It has its wild and demonic forms and can sink to an almost grisly horror and shuddering. It has its crude, barbaric antecedents and early manifestations, and again it may be developed into something beautiful and pure and glorious. It may become the hushed, trembling, and speechless humility of the creature in the presence of—whom or what? In the presence of that which is a *mystery* inexpressible and above all creatures.

It is again evident at once that here too our attempted formulation by means of a concept is once more a merely negative one. Conceptually *mysterium* denotes merely that which is hidden and esoteric, that which is beyond conception or understanding, extraordinary and unfamiliar. The term does not define the object more positively in its qualitative character. But though what is enunciated in the word is negative, what is meant is something absolutely and intensely positive. This pure positive we can experience in feelings, feelings which our discussion can help to make clear to us, in so far as it arouses them actually in our hearts.

1. The Element of Awefulness.

To get light upon the positive "*quale*" of the object of these feelings, we must analyse more closely our phrase *mysterium tremendum,* and we will begin first with the adjective.

Tremor is in itself merely the perfectly familiar and "natural" emotion of *fear*. But here the term is taken, aptly enough but still only by analogy, to denote a quite specific kind of emotional response, wholly distinct from that of being afraid, though it so far resembles it that the analogy of fear may be used to throw light upon its nature. There are in some languages special expressions which denote, either exclusively or in the first instance, this 'fear' that is more than fear proper. The Hebrew *hiqdish* (hallow) is an example. To "keep a holy thing in the heart" means to mark it off by a feeling of peculiar dread, not to be mistaken for any ordinary dread, that is, to appraise it by the category of the numinous. But the Old Testament throughout is rich in parallel expressions for this feeling. Specially noticeable is the *emah* of Yahweh ("fear of God"), which Yahweh can pour forth, dispatching almost like a daemon, and which seizes upon a man with paralyzing effect. It is closely related to the δεῖμα πανικόν of the Greeks. Compare Exod. xxiii. 27: "I will send my fear before thee, and will destroy all the people to whom thou shalt come..."; also Job ix. 34; xiii. 21 ("let not his fear terrify me"; "let not thy dread make me afraid"). Here we have a terror fraught with an inward shuddering such as not even the most menacing and overpowering created thing can instil. It has something spectral in it....

Not only is the saying of Luther, that the natural man cannot fear God perfectly, correct from the standpoint of psychology, but we ought to go farther and add that the natural man is quite unable even to "shudder" (*grauen*) or feel horror in the real sense of the word. For "shuddering" is something more than "natural," ordinary fear. It implies that the mysterious is already beginning to loom before the mind, to touch the feelings. It implies the first application of a category of valuation which has no place in the everyday natural world of ordinary experience, and is only possible to a being in whom has been awakened a mental predisposition, unique in kind and different in a definite way from any "natural" faculty. And this newly-revealed capacity, even in the crude and violent manifestations which are all it at first evinces, bears witness to a completely new function of experience and standard of valuation, only belonging to the spirit of man.

Before going on to consider the elements which unfold as the *"tremendum"* develops, let us give a little further consideration to the first crude, primitive forms in which this "numinous dread" or *awe* shows itself. It is the mark which really characterizes the so-called "religion of primitive man," and there it appears as "daemonic dread." This crudely naïve and primordial emotional disturbance, and the fantastic images to which it gives rise, are later overborne and ousted by more highly developed forms of the numinous emotion, with all its mysteriously impelling power. But even when this has long attained its higher and purer mode of expression it is possible for the primitive types of excitation that were formerly a part of it to break out in the soul in all their original naïveté and so to be experienced afresh. That this is so is shown by the potent attraction again and again exercised by the element of horror and "shudder" in ghost stories, even among persons of high all-round education. It is a remarkable fact that the physical reaction to which this unique "dread" of the uncanny gives rise is also unique, and is not found in the case of any "natural" fear or terror. We say: "my blood ran icy cold," and "my flesh crept." The "cold blood" feeling may be a symptom of ordinary, natural fear, but there is something non-natural or supernatural about the symptom of "creeping flesh." And any one who is capable of more precise introspection must recognize that the distinction between such a "dread" and natural fear is not simply one of degree and intensity. The awe or "dread" *may* indeed be so overwhelmingly great that it seems to penetrate to the very marrow, making the man's hair bristle and his limbs quake. But it may also steal upon him almost unobserved as the gentlest of agitations, a mere fleeting shadow passing across his mood. It has therefore nothing to do with intensity, and no natural fear passes over into it merely by being intensified. I may be beyond all measure afraid and terrified without there being even a trace of the feeling of uncanniness in my emotion.

We should see the facts more clearly if psychology in general would make a more decisive endeavour to examine and classify the feelings and emotions according to their qualitative differences. But the far too rough division of elementary feelings in general into pleasures and pains is still an obstacle to this. In point of fact "pleasures" no more than other feelings are differentiated merely by degrees of intensity: they show very definite and specific differences. It makes a specific difference to the condition of mind whether the soul is merely in a state of pleasure, or joy, or aesthetic rapture, or moral exaltation, or finally in the religious bliss that may come in worship. Such states certainly show resemblances one to another, and on that account can legitimately be brought under a common class-concept ("pleasure"), which serves to cut them off from other psychical functions, generically different. But this class-concept, so far from turning the various subordinate species into merely different degrees of the same thing, can do nothing at all to throw light upon the essence of each several state of mind which it includes.

Though the numinous emotion in its completest development shows a world of difference from the mere "daemonic dread," yet not even at the highest level does it belie its pedigree or kindred. Even when the worship of "daemons" has long since reached the higher level of worship of "gods," these gods still retain as *numina* something of the "ghost" in the impress they make on the feelings of the worshipper, viz. the peculiar quality of the "uncanny" and "aweful," which survives with the quality of exaltedness and sublimity or is symbolized by means of it. And this element, softened though it is, does not disappear even on the highest level of all, where the worship of God is at its purest. Its disappearance would be indeed an essential loss. The "shudder" reappears in a form ennobled beyond measure where the soul, held speechless, trembles inwardly to the farthest fibre of its being. It invades the mind mightily in Christian worship with the words: "Holy, holy, holy"; it breaks forth from the hymn of Tersteegen:

> God Himself is present:
> Heart, be stilled before Him:
> Prostrate inwardly adore Him.

The "shudder" has here lost its crazy and bewildering note, but not the ineffable something that holds the mind. It has become mystical awe, and sets free as its accompaniment, reflected in self-consciousness, that "creature-feeling" that has already been described as the feeling of personal nothingness and submergence before the awe-inspiring object directly experienced.

The referring of this feeling of numinous *tremor* to its object in the numen brings into relief a property of the latter . . . which has been the occasion of many difficulties . . . from its puzzling and baffling nature. This is the ὀργή (*orgé*), the Wrath of Yahweh, which recurs in the New Testament as ὀργή θεοῦ ["wrath of God": ed.], and which is clearly analogous to the idea occurring in many religions of a mysterious *ira deorum*. To pass through the Indian Pantheon of gods is to find deities who seem to be made up altogether out of such an ὀργή; and even the higher Indian gods of grace and pardon have frequently, besides their merciful, their "wrath" form. But as regards the "wrath of Yahweh," the strange features about it have for long been a matter for constant remark. In the first place, it is patent from many passages of the Old Testament that this "wrath" has no concern whatever with moral qualities. There is something very baffling in the way in which it "is kindled" and manifested. It is, as has been well said, "like a hidden force of nature," like stored-up electricity, discharging itself upon anyone who comes too near. It is "incalculable" and "arbitrary." Anyone who is accustomed to think of deity only by its rational attributes must see in this "wrath" mere caprice and willful passion. But such a view would have been emphatically rejected by the religious men of the Old Covenant, for to them the Wrath of God, so far from being a diminution of His Godhead, appears as a natural expression of it, an element of "holiness" itself, and a quite indispensable one. And in this they are entirely right. This ὀργή is nothing but the *tremendum* itself, apprehended and expressed by the aid of a naïve analogy from the domain of natural experience, in this case from the ordinary passional life of men. But naïve as it may be, the analogy is most disconcertingly apt and striking; so much so that it will always retain its value and for us no less than for the men of old to be an inevitable way of expressing one element in the religious emotion.…

It will be again at once apparent that in the use of this word we are not concerned with a genuine intellectual "concept," but only with a sort of illustrative substitute for a concept. "Wrath" here is the "ideogram" of a unique emotional moment in religious experience, a moment whose singularly *daunting* and awe-inspiring character must be gravely disturbing to those persons who will recognize nothing in the divine nature but goodness, gentleness, love, and a sort of confidential intimacy, in a word, only those aspects of God which turn towards the world of men.

This ὀργή is thus quite wrongly spoken of as "natural" wrath: rather it is an entirely non- or super-natural, i.e. numinous, quality. The rationalization process takes place when it begins to be filled in with the elements derived from the moral reason: righteousness in requital, and punishment for moral transgression. But it should be noted that the idea of the wrath of God in the Bible is always a synthesis, in which the original is combined with the later meaning that has come to fill it in. Something supra-rational throbs and gleams, palpable and visible, in the "wrath of God," prompting to a sense of "terror" that no "natural" anger can arouse.…

2. The Element of "Overpoweringness" ("Majestas").

We have been attempting to unfold the implications of that aspect of the *mysterium tremendum* indicated by the adjective, and the result so far may be summarized in two words, constituting, as before, what may be called an "ideogram," rather than a concept proper, viz. "absolute unapproachability."

It will be felt at once that there is yet a further element which must be added, that, namely, of "might," "power," "absolute overpoweringness." We will take to represent this the term *majestas*, majesty—the more readily because anyone with a feeling for language must detect a last faint trace of the numinous still clinging to the word. The *tremendum* may then be rendered more adequately *tremenda majestas*, or "aweful majesty." This second element of majesty may continue to be vividly preserved, where the first, that of unapproachability, recedes and dies away, as may be seen, for example, in mysticism. It is especially in relation to this element of majesty or absolute overpoweringness that the creature-consciousness, of which we have already spoken, comes upon the scene, as a sort of shadow or subjective reflection of it. Thus, in contrast to "the overpowering" of which we are conscious as an object over against the self, there is the feeling of one's own submergence, of being but "dust and ashes" and nothingness. And this forms the numinous raw material for the feeling of religious humility. . . .

The difference between the "feeling of dependence" of Schleiermacher and that which finds typical utterance in the words of Abraham already cited might be expressed as that between the consciousness of *createdness* and the consciousness of *creaturehood*. In the one case you have the creature as the work of the divine creative act; in the other, impotence and general nothingness as against overpowering might, dust and ashes as against "majesty." In the one case you have the fact of having been created; in the other, the status of the creature. And as soon as speculative thought has come to concern itself with this latter type of consciousness—as soon as it has come to analyse this "majesty"—we are introduced to a set of ideas quite different from those of creation or preservation. We come upon the ideas, first, of the annihilation of self, and then, as its complement, of the transcendent as the sole and entire reality. These are the characteristic notes of mysticism in all its forms, however otherwise various in content. For one of the chiefest and most general features of mysticism is just this *self-depreciation* (so plainly parallel to the case of Abraham), the estimation of the self, of the personal "I," as something not perfectly or essentially real, or even as mere nullity, a self-depreciation which comes to demand its own fulfillment in practice in rejecting the delusion of selfhood, and so makes for the annihilation of the self. And on the other hand mysticism leads to a valuation of the transcendent object of its reference as that which through plenitude of being stands supreme and absolute, so that the finite self contrasted with it becomes conscious even in its nullity that "I am naught, Thou art all." There is no thought in this of any causal relation between God, the creator, and the self, the creature. The point from which speculation starts is not a "consciousness of absolute dependence"—of myself as a result and effect of a divine cause—for that would in point of fact lead to insistence upon the reality of the self; it starts from a consciousness of the absolute superiority or supremacy of a power other than myself, and it is only as it falls back upon ontological terms to achieve its end—terms generally borrowed from natural science—that that element of the *tremendum*, originally apprehended as "plenitude of power," becomes transmuted into "plenitude of being."

This leads again to the mention of mysticism. No mere inquiry into the genesis of a thing can throw any light upon its essential nature, and it is hence immaterial to us how mysticism historically arose. But essentially mysticism is the stressing to a very high degree, indeed the overstressing, of the non-rational or supra-rational elements in religion; and it is only intelligible when so understood. The various phases and factors of the non-rational may receive varying emphasis, and the type of mysticism will differ according as some or others fall into the background. What we have been analysing, however, is a feature that recurs in all forms of mysticism everywhere, and it is nothing but the "creature-consciousness" stressed to the utmost and to excess, the expression meaning, if we may repeat the contrast already made, not "feeling of our createdness" but "feeling of our creaturehood," that is, the consciousness of the littleness of every creature in face of that which is above all creatures.

A characteristic common to all types of mysticism is the *Identification,* in different degrees of completeness, of the personal self with the transcendent Reality. This identification has a source of its own, with which we are not here concerned, and springs from "moments" of religious experience which would require separate treatment. "Identification" alone, however, is not enough for mysticism; it must be Identification with the Something that is at once absolutely supreme in power and reality and wholly non-rational. And it is among the mystics that we must encounter this element of religious consciousness....

3. The Element of 'Energy' or Urgency.

There is, finally, a third element comprised in those of *tremendum* and *majestas,* awefulness and majesty, and this I venture to call the "urgency" or "energy" of the numinous object. It is particularly vividly perceptible in the ὀργή or "wrath"; and it everywhere clothes itself in symbolical expressions— vitality, passion, emotional temper, will, force, movement, excitement, activity, impetus. These features are typical and recur again and again from the daemonic level up to the idea of the "living" God. We have here the factor that has everywhere more than any other prompted the fiercest opposition to the "philosophic" God of mere rational speculation, who can be put into a definition. And for their part the philosophers have condemned these expressions of the energy of the numen, whenever they are brought on to the scene, as sheer anthropomorphism. In so far as their opponents have for the most part themselves failed to recognize that the terms they have borrowed from the sphere of human conative and affective life have merely value as analogies, the philosophers are right to condemn them. But they are wrong, in so far as, this error notwithstanding, these terms stood for a genuine aspect of the divine nature—its non-rational aspect—a due consciousness of which served to protect religion itself from being "rationalized" away.

For wherever men have been contending for the "living" God or for voluntarism, there, we may be sure, have been non-rationalists fighting rationalists and rationalism. It was so with Luther in his controversy with Erasmus; and

Luther's *omnipotentia Dei* in his *De Servo Arbitrio* is nothing but the union of "majesty"—in the sense of absolute supremacy—with this "energy," in the sense of a force that knows not stint nor stay, which is urgent, active, compelling, and alive. In mysticism, too, this element of "energy" is a very living and vigorous factor, at any rate in the "voluntaristic" mysticism, the mysticism of love, where it is very forcibly seen in that "consuming fire" of love whose burning strength the mystic can hardly bear, but begs that the heat that has scorched him may be mitigated, lest he be himself destroyed by it. And in this urgency and pressure the mystic's "love" claims a perceptible kinship with the ὀργή itself, the scorching and consuming wrath of God; it is the same "energy," only differently directed. "Love," says one of the mystics, "is nothing else than quenched wrath." ...

Chapter V
The Analysis of "Mysterium"

Ein Begriffener Gott ist kein Gott.
"A God Comprehended is No God." (Tersteegen)

We gave the object to which the numinous consciousness is directed the name *mysterium tremendum*, and we then set ourselves first to determine the meaning of the adjective *tremendum*—which we found to be itself only justified by analogy—because it is more easily analysed than the substantive idea *mysterium*. We have now to turn to this, and try, as best we may, by hint and suggestion, to get to a clearer apprehension of what it implies.

4. The "Wholly Other".

It might be thought that the adjective itself gives an explanation of the substantive; but this is not so. It is not merely analytical; it is a synthetic attribute to it; i.e. *tremendum* adds something not necessarily inherent in *mysterium*. It is true that the reactions in consciousness that correspond to the one readily and spontaneously overflow into those that correspond to the other; in fact, anyone sensitive to the use of words would commonly feel that the idea of "mystery" (*mysterium*) is so closely bound up with its synthetic qualifying attribute "aweful" (*tremendum*) that one can hardly say the former without catching an echo of the latter, "mystery" almost of itself becoming "aweful mystery" to us. But the passage from the one idea to the other need not by any means be always so easy. The elements of meaning implied in "awefulness" and "mysteriousness" are in themselves definitely different. The latter may so far preponderate in the religious consciousness, may stand out so vividly, that in comparison with it the former almost sinks out of sight; a case which again could be clearly exemplified from some forms of mysticism. Occasionally, on the other hand, the reverse happens, and the *tremendum* may in turn occupy the mind without the *mysterium*. This latter, then, needs special consideration on its own account. We need an expression for the mental reaction peculiar to it; and here, too, only one word seems appropriate, though, as it is strictly applicable only to a "natural" state of mind, it has here meaning only by analogy: it is the word "stupor." *Stupor* is plainly a different thing from *tremor*; it signifies blank wonder, an astonishment that strikes us dumb, amazement absolute. Taken, indeed, in its purely natural sense, *mysterium* would first mean merely a secret or a mystery in the sense of that which is alien to us, uncomprehended and unexplained; and so far *mysterium* is itself merely an ideogram, an analogical notion taken from the natural sphere, illustrating, but incapable of exhaustively rendering, our real meaning. Taken in the religious sense, that which is "mysterious" is—to give it perhaps the most striking expression—the "wholly other"..., that which is quite beyond the sphere of the usual, the intelligible, and the familiar, which therefore falls quite outside the limits of the "canny," and is contrasted with it, filling the mind with blank wonder and astonishment.

This is already to be observed on the lowest and earliest level of the religion of primitive man, where the numinous consciousness is but an inchoate stirring of the feelings. What is really characteristic of this stage is *not*—as the theory of Animism would have us believe—that men are here concerned with curious entities, called "souls" or "spirits," which conceptions are rather one and all early models of "rationalizing" a precedent experience, to which they are subsidiary. They are attempts in some way or other, it little matters how, to guess the riddle it propounds, and their effect is at the same time always to weaken and deaden the experience itself. They are the source from which springs, not religion, but the rationalization of religion, which often ends by constructing such a massive structure of theory and such a plausible fabric of interpretation, that the "mystery" is frankly excluded. Both imaginative "myth," when developed into a system, and intellectualist Scholasticism, when worked out to its completion, are methods by which the fundamental fact of religious experience is, as it were, simply rolled out so thin and flat as to be finally eliminated altogether.

Even on the lowest level of religious development the essential characteristic is therefore to be sought elsewhere than in the appearance of "spirit" representations. It lies rather, we repeat, in a peculiar "moment" of consciousness, to wit, the *stupor* before something "wholly other," whether such another be named "spirit" or "daemon" or "deva," or be left without any name. Nor does it make any difference in this respect whether, to interpret and preserve their apprehension of this "other," men coin original imagery of their own or adapt imaginations drawn from the world of legend, the fabrications of fancy apart from and prior to any stirrings of daemonic dread....

[T]his feeling or consciousness of the "wholly other" will attach itself to, or sometimes be indirectly aroused by means of, objects which are already puzzling upon the "natural" plane, or are of a surprising or astounding character; such as extraordinary phenomena or astonishing occurrences or things in inanimate nature, in the animal world, or among men. But here once more we are dealing with a case of association between things specifically different—the "numinous" and the "natural" moments of consciousness—and not merely with the gradual enhancement of one of them—the "natural"—till it becomes the other. As in the case of "natural fear" and "daemonic dread" already considered, so here the transition from natural to daemonic amazement is not a mere matter of degree. But it is only with the latter that the complementary expression *mysterium* perfectly harmonizes, as will be felt perhaps more clearly in the case of the adjectival form "mysterious." No one says, strictly and in earnest, of a piece of clockwork that is beyond his grasp, or of a science that he cannot understand: "That is 'mysterious' to me."

It might be objected that the mysterious is something which is and remains absolutely and invariably beyond our understanding, whereas that which merely eludes our understanding for a time but is perfectly intelligible in principle should be called, not a "mystery," but merely a "problem." But this is by no means an adequate account of the matter. The truly "mysterious" object is beyond our apprehension and comprehension, not only because our knowledge has certain irremovable limits, but because in it we come upon something inherently "wholly other," whose kind and character are incommensurable with our own, and before which we therefore recoil in a wonder that strikes us chill and numb.

This may be made still clearer by a consideration of that degraded offshoot and travesty of the genuine "numinous" dread or awe, the fear of ghosts. Let us try to analyse this experience. We have already specified the peculiar feeling-element of "dread" aroused by the ghost as that of "grue," grisly horror. Now this "grue" obviously contributes something to the attraction which ghost-stories exercise, in so far, namely, as the relaxation of tension ensuing upon our release from it relieves the mind in a pleasant and agreeable way. So far, however, it is not really the ghost itself that gives us pleasure, but the fact that we are rid of it. But obviously this is quite insufficient to explain the ensnaring attraction of the ghost-story. The ghost's real attraction rather consists in this, that of itself and in an uncommon degree it entices the imagination, awakening strong interest and curiosity; it is the weird thing itself that allures the fancy. But it does this, not because it is "something long and white" (as someone once defined a ghost), not yet through any of the positive and conceptual attributes which fancies about ghosts have invented, but because it is a thing that "doesn't really exist at all," the "wholly other," something which has no place in our scheme of reality but belongs to an absolutely different one, and which at the same time arouses an irrepressible interest in the mind.

But that which is perceptibly true in the fear of ghosts, which is, after all, only a caricature of the genuine thing, is in a far stronger sense true of the "daemonic" experience itself, of which the fear of ghosts is a mere off-shoot. And while, following this main line of development, this element in the numinous consciousness, the feeling of the "wholly other," is heightened and clarified, its higher modes of manifestation come into being, which set the numinous object in contrast not only to everything wonted and familiar (i.e. in the end, to nature in general), thereby turning it into the "supernatural," but finally to the world itself, and thereby exalt it to the "supramundane," that which is above the whole world-order.

In mysticism we have in the "beyond"...again the strongest stressing and over-stressing of those non-rational elements which are already inherent in all religion. Mysticism continues to its extreme point this contrasting of the numinous object (the numen), as the "wholly other," with ordinary experience. Not content with contrasting it with all that is of nature or this world, mysticism concludes by contrasting it with Being itself and all that "is," and finally actually calls it "that which is nothing." By this "nothing" is meant not only that of which nothing can be predicated, but that which is absolutely and intrinsically other than and opposite of everything that is and can be thought. But while exaggerating to the point of paradox this *negation* and contrast—the only means open to conceptual thought to apprehend the *mysterium*—mysticism at the same time retains the *positive quality* of the "wholly other" as a very living factor in its over-brimming religious emotion.

But what is true of the strange "nothingness" of our mystics holds good equally of the..."void" and "emptiness" of the Buddhist mystics. This aspiration for the "void" and for becoming void, no less than the aspiration of our western mystics for "nothing" and for becoming nothing, must seem a kind of lunacy to anyone who has no inner sympathy for the esoteric language and ideograms of mysticism, and lacks the matrix from which these come necessarily to birth. To such an one Buddhism itself will be simply a morbid sort of pessimism. But in fact the "void" of the eastern, like the "nothing" of the western, mystic is a numinous ideogram of the "wholly other."

These terms "supernatural" and "transcendent" give the appearance of positive attributes, and, as applied to the mysterious, they appear to divest the *mysterium* of its originally negative meaning and to turn it into an affirmation. On the side of conceptual thought this is nothing more than appearance, for it is obvious that the two terms in question are merely negative and exclusive attributes with reference to "nature" and the world or cosmos respectively. But on the side of the feeling-content it is otherwise; that *is* in very truth positive in the highest degree, though here too, as before, it cannot be rendered explicit in conceptual terms. It is through this positive feeling-content that the concepts of the "transcendent" and "supernatural" become forthwith designations for a unique "wholly other" reality and quality, something of whose special character we can *feel*, without being able to give it clear conceptual expression.

Chapter VI
5. The Element of Fascination

The qualitative *content* of the numinous experience, to which "the mysterious" stands as *form*, is in one of its aspects the element of daunting "awefulness" and "majesty," which has already been dealt with in detail; but it is clear that it has at the same time another aspect, in which it shows itself as something uniquely attractive and *fascinating*.

These two qualities, the daunting and the fascinating, now combine in a strange harmony of contrasts, and the resultant dual character of the numinous consciousness, to which the entire religious development bears witness... is at once the strangest and most noteworthy phenomenon in the whole history of religion. The daemonic-divine object may appear to the mind an object of horror and dread, but at the same time it is no less something that allures with a potent charm, and the creature, who trembles before it, utterly cowed and cast down, has always at the same time the impulse to turn to it, nay even to make it somehow his own. The "mystery" is for him not merely something to be wondered at but something that entrances him; and beside that in it which bewilders and confounds, he feels a something that captivates and transports him with a strange ravishment, rising often enough to the pitch of dizzy intoxication; it is the Dionysiac-element in the numen.

The ideas and concepts which are the parallels or "schemata" on the rational side of this non-rational element of "fascination" are love, mercy, pity, comfort; these are all "natural" elements of the common physical life, only they are here thought as absolute and in completeness. But important as these are for the experience of religious bliss or felicity, they do not by any means exhaust it. It is just the same as with the opposite experience of religious infelicity—the experience of the ὀργή or "wrath" of God:—both alike contain fundamentally non-rational elements. Bliss or beatitude is more, far more, than the mere natural feeling of being comforted, of reliance, of the joy of love, however these may be heightened and enhanced. Just as "wrath," taken in a purely rational or a purely ethical sense, does not exhaust that profound element of *awefulness* which is locked in the mystery of deity, so neither does "graciousness" exhaust the profound element of *wonderfulness* and rapture which lies in the mysterious beatific experience of deity. The term "grace" may indeed be taken as its aptest designation, but then only in the sense in which it is really applied in the language of the mystics, and in which not only the "gracious intent" but "something more" is meant by the word. This "something more" has its antecedent phases very far back in the history of religions.

It may well be possible, it is even probable, that in the first stage of its development the religious consciousness started with only one of its poles—the "daunting" aspect of the numen—and so at first took shape only as "daemonic dread." But if this did not point to something beyond itself, if it were not but one "moment" of a completer experience, pressing up gradually into consciousness, then no transition would be possible to the feelings of positive self-surrender to the numen. The only type of worship that could result from this "dread" alone would be that of…expiation and propitiation, the averting or the appeasement of the "wrath" of the numen. It can never explain how it is that "the numinous" is the object of search and desire and yearning, and that too for its own sake and not only for the sake of the aid and backing that men expect from it in the natural sphere. It can never explain how this takes place, not only in the forms of "rational" religious worship, but in those queer "sacramental" observances and rituals and procedures of communion in which the human being seeks to get the numen into his possession.

Religious practice may manifest itself in those normal and easily intelligible forms which occupy so prominent a place in the history of religion, such forms as propitiation, petition, sacrifice, thanksgiving &c. But besides these there is a series of strange proceedings which are constantly attracting greater and greater attention, and in which it is claimed that we may recognize, besides mere religion in general, the particular roots of mysticism. I refer to those numerous curious modes of behaviour and fantastic forms of medication, by means of which the primitive religious man attempts to master "the mysterious," and to fill himself and even to identify himself with it. These modes of behaviour fall apart into two classes. On the one hand the "magical" identification of the self with the numen proceeds by means of various transactions, at once magical and devotional in character—by formula, ordination, adjuration, consecration, exorcism, &c.: on the other hand are the "shamanistic" ways of procedure, possession, indwelling, self-fulfilment in exaltation and ecstasy. All these have, indeed, their starting-points simply in magic, and their intention at first was certainly simply to appropriate the prodigious force of the numen for the natural ends of man. But the process does not rest there. Possession of and by the numen becomes an end in itself; it begins to be sought for its own sake; and the wildest and most artificial methods of asceticism are put into practice to attain it. In a word, the *vita religiosa* begins; and to remain in these strange and bizarre states of numinous possession becomes a good in itself, even a way of salvation, wholly different from the profane goods pursued by means of magic. Here, too, commences the process of development by which the experience is matured and purified, till finally it reaches its consummation in the sublimest and purest states of the "life within the Spirit" and in the noblest mysticism. Widely various as these states are in themselves, yet they have this element in common, that in them the *mysterium* is experienced in its essential, positive, and specific character, as something that bestows upon man a beatitude beyond compare, but one whose real nature he can neither proclaim in speech nor conceive in thought, but may know only by a direct and living experience. It is a bliss which embraces all those blessings that are indicated or suggested in positive fashion by any "doctrine of salvation," and it quickens all of them through and through; but these do not exhaust it. Rather by its all-pervading, penetrating glow it makes of these very blessings more than the intellect can conceive in them or affirm of them. It gives the peace that passes understanding, and of which the tongue can only stammer brokenly. Only from afar, by metaphors and analogies, do we come to apprehend what it is in itself, and even so our notion is but inadequate and confused.

"Eye hath not seen, nor ear heard, neither have entered into the heart of man, the things which God hath prepared for them that love him." Who does not feel the exalted sound of these words and the "Dionysiac" element of transport and fervour in them? It is instructive that in such phrases as these, in which consciousness would fain put its highest consummation into words, "all images fall away" and the mind turns from them to grasp expressions that are purely negative. And it is still more instructive that in reading and hearing such words their merely negative character simply is not noticed; that we can let whole chains of such negations enrapture, even intoxicate us, and that entire hymns—and deeply impressive hymns—have been composed, in which there is really nothing positive at all! All this teaches us the independence of the positive content of this experience from the implications of its overt conceptual expression, and how it can be firmly grasped, thoroughly understood, and profoundly appreciated, purely in, with, and from the feeling itself.

Mere love, mere trust, for all the glory and happiness they bring, do not explain to us that moment of rapture that breathes in our tenderest and most heart-felt hymns of salvation, as also in ... eschatological hymns of longing. ...

This is where the living "something more" of the *fascinans,* the element of fascination, is to be found. It lives no less in those tense extollings of the blessing of salvation, which recur in all religions of salvation, and stand in such remarkable contrast to the relatively meager and frequently childish import of that which is revealed in them by concept or by image. Everywhere salvation is something whose meaning is often very little apparent, is even wholly obscure, to the "natural" man; on the contrary, *so far as he understands it,* he tends to find it highly tedious and uninteresting, sometimes downright distasteful and repugnant to his nature, as he would, for instance, find the beatific vision of God in our own doctrine of salvation.... "So far as he understands," be it noted; but then he does not understand it in the least. Because he lacks the inward teaching of the Spirit, he must needs confound what is offered him as an expression for the experience of salvation—a mere ideogram of what is felt, whose import it hints at by analogy—with "natural" concepts, as though it were itself just such an one. And so he "wanders ever farther from the goal."

It is not only in the religious feeling of longing that the moment of fascination is a living factor. It is already alive and present in the moment of "solemnity," both in the gathered concentration and humble submergence of private devotion, when the mind is exalted to the holy, and in the common worship of the congregation, where this is practised with earnestness and deep sincerity, as, it is to be feared, is with us a thing rather desired than realized. It is this and nothing else that in the solemn moment can fill the soul so full and keep it so inexpressibly tranquil. Schleiermacher's assertion is perhaps true of it, as of the numinous consciousness in general, viz. that it cannot really occur alone on its own account, or except combined and penetrated with rational elements. But, if this be admitted, it is upon other grounds than those adduced by Schleiermacher; while, on the other hand, it may occupy a more or less predominant place and lead to states of calm...as well as of transport, in which it *almost* of itself wholly fits the soul. But in all the manifold forms in which it is aroused in us, whether in eschatological promise of the coming kingdom of God and the transcendent bliss of paradise, or in the guise of an entry into that beatific reality that is "above the world"; whether it comes first in expectancy or pre-intimation or in a present experience ("When I but *have* Thee, I ask no question of heaven and earth"); in all these forms, outwardly diverse but inwardly akin, it appears as a strange and mighty propulsion towards an ideal good known only to religion and in its nature fundamentally non-rational, which the mind knows of in yearning and presentiment, recognizing it for what it is behind the obscure and inadequate symbols which are its only expression. And this shows that above and beyond our rational being lies hidden the ultimate and highest part of our nature, which can find no satisfaction in the mere allaying of the needs of our sensuous, psychical or intellectual impulses and cravings. The mystics called it the basis or ground of the soul.

We saw that in the case of the element of the mysterious the "wholly other" led on to the supernatural and transcendent and that above these appeared the "beyond"...of mysticism, through the non-rational side of religion being raised to its highest power and stressed to excess. It is the same in the case of the element of "fascination"; here, too, is possible a transition into mysticism. At its highest point of stress the fascinating becomes the "overabounding," "exuberant," the mystical "moment" which exactly corresponds…to…the other line of approach, and which is to be understood accordingly. But while this feeling of the "over-abounding" is specially characteristic of mysticism, a trace of it survives in all truly felt states of religious beatitude, however restrained and kept within measure by other factors. This is seen most clearly from the psychology of those great experiences—of grace, conversion, second birth—in which the religious experience appears in its pure intrinsic nature and in heightened activity, so as to be more clearly grasped than in the less typical form of piety instilled by education. The hard core of such experiences in their Christian form consists of the redemption from guilt and bondage to sin, and we shall have presently to see that this also does not occur without a participation of non-rational elements. But leaving this out of account, what we have here to point out is the unutterableness of what has been yet genuinely experienced, and how such an experience may pass into blissful excitement, rapture, and exaltation verging often on the bizarre and the abnormal. This is vouched for by the autobiographical testimony of the "converted" from St. Paul onward. William James has collected a great number of these, without, however, himself noticing the non-rational element that thrills in them.…

"O that I could tell you what the heart feels, how it burns and is consumed inwardly! Only, I find no words to express it. I can but say: Might but one little drop of what I feel fall into Hell, Hell would be transformed into a Paradise." So says St. Catherine of Genoa; and all the multitude of her spiritual kindred testify to the same effect.

What we Christians know as the experiences of grace and the second birth have their parallels also in the religions of high spiritual rank beyond the borders of Christianity. Such are the breaking out of the saving "Bodhi," the opening of the "heavenly eye," which is victorious over the darkness of nescience and shines out in an experience with which no other can be measured. And in all these the entirely non-rational and specific element in the beatific experience is immediately noticeable. The qualitative character of it varies widely in all these cases, and is again in them all very different from its parallels in Christianity; still in all it is very similar in intensity, and in all it is a "salvation" and an absolute "fascination," which in contrast to all that admits of "natural" expression or comparison is deeply imbued with the "over-abounding" ("exuberant") nature of the numen.

And this is also entirely true of the rapture of Nirvana, which is only in appearance a cold negative state. It is only conceptually that "Nirvana" is a negation; it is felt in consciousness as in the strongest degree positive; it exercises a "fascination" by which its votaries are as much carried away as are the Hindu or the Christian by the corresponding objects of their worship. I recall vividly a conversation I had with a Buddhist monk. He had been putting before me methodically and pertinaciously the arguments for the Buddhist "theology of negation," the doctrine of Anātman and "entire emptiness." When he had made an end, I asked him, what then Nirvana itself is; and after a long pause came at last the single answer, low and restrained: "Bliss—unspeakable." And the hushed restraint of that answer, the solemnity of his voice, demeanour, and gesture, made more clear what was meant than the words themselves.

And so we maintain, on the one hand...that the divine is indeed the highest, strongest, best, loveliest, and dearest that man can think of; but we assert on the other...that God is not *merely* the ground and superlative of all that can be thought; He is in Himself a subject on His own account in Himself.

∼

In the adjective δεινός the Greek language possesses a word peculiarly difficult to translate, and standing for an idea peculiarly difficult to grasp in all its strange variations. And if we ask whence this difficulty arises, the answer is plain; it is because δεινός is simply the numinous (mostly of course at a lower level, in an arrested form, attenuated by rhetorical or poetic usage). Consequently δεινός is the equivalent of...*tremendus*. It may mean evil or imposing, potent and strange, queer and marvelous, horrifying and fascinating, divine and daemonic, and a source of "energy."...[O]ur language has no term that can isolate distinctly and gather into one word the total numinous impression a thing may make on the mind. The nearest that German can get to it is in the expression *das Ungeheure* (monstrous), while the English "weird" is perhaps the closest rendering possible....

The German *ungeheuer* is not by derivation simply "huge," in quantity or quality;—this, its common meaning, is in fact a rationalizing interpretation of the real idea; it is that which is not *geheuer,* i.e. approximately, the *uncanny*—in a word, the numinous.... If this, its fundamental meaning, be really and thoroughly felt in consciousness, then the word could be taken as a fairly exact expression for the numinous in its aspects of mystery, awefulness, majesty, augustness, and "energy"; nay, even the aspect of fascination is dimly felt in it.

The variations of meaning in the German word *ungeheuer* can be well illustrated from Goethe. He, too, uses the word first to denote the huge in size—what is too vast for our faculty of space-perception, such as the immeasureable vault of the night sky. In other passages the word retains its original non-rational colour more markedly; it comes to mean the uncanny, the fearful, the dauntingly "other" and incomprehensible, that which arouses in us *stupor*...; and finally, in the wonderful words of Faust which I have put at the beginning of this book, it becomes an almost exact synonym for our "numinous" under all its aspects....

> Awe is the best part of man; howe'er the world's
> Misprizing of the feeling would prevent us,
> Deeply we feel, once gripped, the weird Portentous.

~

Chapter XVII
The Holy as an *A Priori* Category

We conclude, then, that not only the rational but also the non-rational elements of the complex category of "holiness" are *a priori* elements and each in the same degree. Religion is not in vassalage either to morality or teleology, *ethos* or *telos*, and does not draw its life from postulates; and its non-rational content has, no less than its rational, its own independent roots in the hidden depths of the spirit itself.

But the same *a priori* character belongs, in the third place, to the *connexion* of the rational and the non-rational elements in religion, their inward and necessary union. The histories of religion recount indeed, as though it were something axiomatic, the gradual interpenetration of the two, the process by which "the divine" is charged and filled out with ethical meaning. And this process is, in fact, *felt* as something axiomatic, something whose inner necessity we feel to be self-evident. But then this inward self-evidence is a problem in itself; we are forced to assume an obscure, *a priori* knowledge of the necessity of this synthesis, combining rational and non-rational. For it is not by any means a *logical* necessity. How should it be logically inferred from the still "crude," half-daemonic character of a moon-god or a sun-god or a numen attached to some locality, that he is a guardian and guarantor of the oath and of honourable dealing, of hospitality, of the sanctity of marriage, and of duties to tribe and clan? How should it be inferred that he is a god who decrees happiness and misery, participates in the concerns of the tribe, provides for its well-being, and directs the course of destiny and history? Whence comes this most surprising of all the facts in the history of religion, that beings, obviously born originally of horror and terror, become *gods*—beings to whom men pray, to whom they confide their sorrow or their happiness, in whom they behold the origin and the sanction of morality, law, and the whole canon of justice? And how does all this come about in such a way that, when once such ideas have been aroused, it is understood at once as the plainest and most evident of axioms, that so it must be?

Socrates, in Plato's *Republic,* ii. 382 E, says: "God, then, is single and true in deed and word, and neither changes himself nor deceives others...." Adeimantos answers him: "So too is it apparent to me, now that you say it." The most interesting point in this passage is not the elevation and purity of the conception of God, nor yet the lofty rationalization and moralization of it here enunciated, but, on the side of Socrates, the apparently "dogmatic" tone of his pronouncement—for he does not spend the least pains in demonstrating it—and, on the side of Adeimantos, the ingenuous surprise and, at the same time, the confident assurance with which he admits a truth novel to him. And his assent is such as implies convincement; he does not simply believe Socrates; he sees clearly for himself the truth of his words. Now this is the criterion for all *a priori* knowledge, namely, that, so soon as an assertion has been clearly expressed and understood, knowledge of its truth comes into mind with the certitude of first-hand insight. And what passed here between Socrates and Adeimantos has been repeated a thousand times in the history of religions. Amos, also, says something new when he proclaims Yahweh as the God of inflexible, universal, and absolute righteousness, and yet this is a novelty that he neither proves nor justifies by an appeal to authorities. He appeals to *a priori* judgements, viz. to the religious conscience itself, and this in truth bears witness to his message.

Luther, again, recognizes and maintains such an *a priori* knowledge of the divine nature. His rage against the "whore Reason" leads him, to be sure, usually to utterances in the opposite sense, such as the following:

> It is a knowledge *a posteriori,* in that we look at God from without, at His works and His government, as one looketh at a castle or house from without and thereby feeleth (*spüret*) the lord or householder thereof. But *a priori* from within hath no wisdom of men yet availed to discover what and of what manner of being is God as He is in Himself or in His inmost essence, nor can any man know nor say aught thereof, but they to whom it has been revealed by the Holy Ghost.

Here Luther overlooks the fact that a man must "feel" or detect the "householder" *a priori* or not at all. But in other passages he himself allows the general human reason to possess many true cognitions of what "God is in Himself or in His inmost essence." ...

It is the same experience which missionaries have so often undergone. Once enunciated and understood, the ideas of the unity and goodness of the divine nature often take a surprisingly short time to become firmly fixed in the hearer's mind, if he show any susceptibility for religious feeling. Frequently, thereupon, the hearer adapts the religious tradition that has hitherto been his to the new meaning he has learned. Or, where resistance is offered to the new teaching, it is yet often noticeably in the face of pressure the other way from the man's own conscience. Such experiences have been made known to me by missionaries ... and it would be interesting to make a collection of them, both in regard to the general question of the *a priori* factors in religion, and especially as throwing light upon the *a priori* knowledge of the essential interdependence of the rational and the non-rational elements in the idea of God. For this the history of religion is itself an almost unanimous witness. Incomplete and defective as the process of moralizing the "numina" may often have been throughout the wide regions of primitive religious life, everywhere there are traces of it to be found. And wherever religion, escaping from its first crudity of manifestation, has risen to a higher type, this process of synthesis has in all cases set in and continued more and more positively. And this is all the more remarkable when one considers at what widely different dates the imaginative creation of the figures of gods had its rise in different cases, and under what diverse conditions of race, natural endowment, and social and political structure its evolution proceeded. All this points to the existence of *a priori* factors universally and necessarily latent in the human spirit: those, in fact, which we can find directly in our own religious consciousness, when we, too, like Adeimantos, naïvely and spontaneously concur with Socrates' saying, as with an axiom whose truth we have seen for ourselves: "God is single, and true in deed and word."

As the rational elements, following *a priori* principles, come together in the historical evolution of religions with the non-rational, they serve to "schematize" these. This is true, not only in general of the relation of the rational aspect of "the holy," taken as a whole, to its non-rational, taken as a whole, but also in detail of the several constituent elements of the two aspects. The *tremendum,* the daunting and repelling moment of the numinous, is schematized by means of the rational ideas of justice, moral will, and the exclusion of what is opposed to morality; and schematized thus, it becomes the holy "wrath of God," which Scripture and Christian preaching alike proclaim. The *fascinans,* the attracting and alluring moment of the numinous, is schematized by means of the ideas of goodness, mercy, love, and, so schematized, becomes all that we mean by Grace, that term so rich in import, which unites with the holy wrath in a single "harmony of contrasts," and like it is, from the numinous strain in it, tinged with mysticism. The "moment" *mysteriosum* is schematized by the *absoluteness* of all rational attributes applied to the Deity. Probably the correspondence here implied—between "the mysterious" and the *absoluteness* of all rational attributes—will not appear at first sight so immediately evident as in the two foregoing cases, within wrath and grace. None the less it is a very exact correspondence. God's rational attributes can be distinguished from like attributes applied to the created spirit by being not relative, as those are, but absolute. Human love is relative, admitting of degrees, and it is the same with human knowledge and human goodness. God's love and knowledge and goodness, on the other hand, and all else that can be asserted of Him in conceptual terms, are formally absolute. The *content* of the attributes is the same; it is an *element of form* which marks them apart as attributes of God. But such an element of form is also the "mysterious" as such: it is...the formal aspect of the "wholly other." But to this plain correspondence of the two things, "the mysterious" and the absoluteness of rational attributes, a further one must be added. Our understanding can only compass the relative. That which is in contrast absolute, though it may in a sense be *thought,* cannot be *thought home, thought out*; it is within the reach of our conceiving, but it is beyond the grasp of our comprehension. Now, though this does not make what is "absolute" itself genuinely "mysterious,"...it does make it a genuine *schema* of "the mysterious." The absolute exceeds our power to comprehend; the mysterious wholly eludes it. The absolute is that which surpasses the limits of our understanding, not through its actual qualitative character, for that is familiar to us, but through its formal character. The mysterious, on the other hand, is that which lies altogether outside what can be thought, and is, alike in form, quality, and essence, the utterly and "wholly other." We see, then, that in the case of the moment of "mystery," as well as those of "awefulness" and "fascination," there is an exact correspondence between the non-rational element and its rational *schema,* and one that admits of development.

By the continual living activity of its non-rational elements a religion is guarded from passing into "rationalism." By being steeped in and saturated with rational elements it is guarded from sinking into fanaticism or mere mysticality, or at least from persisting in these, and is qualified to become a religion for all civilized humanity. The degree in which both rational and non-rational elements are jointly present, united in healthy and lovely harmony, affords a criterion to measure the relative rank of religions—and one, too that is specifically religious. Applying this criterion, we find that Christianity, in this as in other respects, stands out in complete superiority over all its sister religions. The lucid edifice of its clear and pure conceptions, feelings, and experiences is built up on a foundation that goes far deeper than the rational. Yet the non-rational is only the basis, the setting, the woof in the fabric, ever preserving for Christianity its mystical depth, giving religion thereby the deep undertones and heavy shadows of mysticism, without letting it develop into a mere rank growth of mysticality. And thus Christianity, in the healthily proportioned union of its elements, assumes an absolutely classical form and dignity, which is only the more vividly attested in consciousness as we proceed honestly and without prejudice to set it in its place in the comparative study of religions. Then we shall recognize that in Christianity an element of man's spiritual life, which yet has its analogies in other fields, has for the first time come to maturity in a supreme and unparalleled way.

8

Max Weber: Religion
and Culture Interwoven

Maximilian "Max" Weber (1864–1920) was a German cultural theorist of exceptionally wide learning, which he combined with a keen interest in comparative analysis and conceptual generalization. With Durkheim, he is counted by many as one of the twin founders of modern academic sociology. That accolade is deserved certainly, but the great breadth of Weber's analyses, probing law and economics, as well as religion, social behavior and structures, political theory, the arts, and intellectual history, place him equally close to Marx in both the scope of his interests and scale of his achievement, though he was of course nearly two generations younger. Weber was raised in Berlin, the eldest son of Max Weber Sr., a well-connected lawyer and member of the German Parliament, who frequently hosted at his residence the leading scholars, thinkers, and government officials of the day. For his gifted son, the animated debates and informed conversation of these household guests furnished an education that rivaled anything the formalities of the classroom could offer. Even so, he excelled in scholarship from an early age. In 1884, he followed a path similar to that of Marx, entering the University of Berlin, where he combined studies in economic and social history with training in law. In time, he wrote dissertations on Roman agriculture and on medieval business, acquiring along the way an extensive knowledge of Western civilization in almost all of its main aspects—religion not least among them.

After choosing the academy over career options in either politics or law, Weber quickly involved himself in the German *Methodenstreit,* a learned scholarly debate over proper methods that raged among historians and economists at the time. In these discussions, he endorsed the principle of *Verstehen* (German for "understanding"), which emphasized the importance of human intentions and actions alongside impersonal structures and forces in explaining historical events. He also stressed the importance of formalized general categories—what he called "Ideal Types"—as critical to comparative historical and sociological thinking. These theoretical works offered an early measure of the young Weber's analytical talents and formidable work ethic. To his academic peers, he was a portrait of intellectual promise, destined for a glittering career in politics or the academy.

Early into this career, however, Weber suffered a mysterious emotional collapse, most likely brought on by personal issues in his parental family, and possibly his marriage. Unable to teach, he felt compelled to resign a position he had acquired at Heidelberg University and to continue his work—what there was of it—as a strictly private scholar, relying on family resources to support himself. In time he began to recover and accepted the post of editor at an important journal, *The Archive for Social Science and Social Policy*. There in 1904–05 he published a pair of provocative articles under the title "The Protestant Ethic and the Spirit of Capitalism." In these studies he sought to account for a profound change in attitudes that transformed both the economy and society of the Western world. He argues that the "spirit" of modern capitalism, which consists of a positive attitude toward both work and wealth, can be traced ultimately to a new religious ethic introduced by the two foremost theologians of the Protestant reformation, the German monk Martin Luther and the French lawyer-theologian John Calvin. As much as any other factor, it was their new system of religious teachings that—indirectly—created today's complex socioeconomic systems, anchored in the profit motive and free markets in goods and services, and sent into eclipse the agrarian social order that had been in place since time immemorial. In brief, Protestantism transformed Europe from a collection of farms to a center of burgeoning commerce.

This provocative argument—known today as "the Weber thesis"—stirred a vigorous debate that has continued to the present day. One part of that debate, often unnoticed, is clearly relevant to the enterprise of explaining religion. It becomes apparent as soon as we set Weber's thesis beside those of Freud, Durkheim, and Marx. In each of their cases, as noted, the theorist explains religious belief by "reducing" it to something else, some other cause that is more basic and fundamental. They account for religious ideas and actions as the result of some other cause—something more real and more basic, of which they are the mere expression, or effect. It was discomfort with this approach that elicited the appeals by James and Otto, each in his way, to the independent validity of religious experience. Weber proceeds differently but comes to a not dissimilar conclusion. In framing an argument that draws jointly on the history, theology, and psychology of early Protestantism, he finds at least one crucial cause-and-effect connection that moves in a direction exactly opposite to reductionist expectation. In Europe's economic revolution, religious ideas and attitudes are the causes; the social and economic changes are the effects. For Weber, we can-not escape the fact that human cultural actions and institutions are ines-capably complex and multidimensional; explaining them requires recourse to multiple interacting causes, conditions, and influences that never move in just one direction.

After *The Protestant Ethic,* Weber turned with increasing interest to the wider role of religion in economic and social life, always guided by his working theorem of multi-layered causation. In his landmark study *Econ-omy and Society,* into which he put years of labor, he included a large sec-tion on religion, published in the English-speaking world after his death as *Sociology of Religion.* This discussion includes some of Weber's most intricate analyses and influential ideas: on the types of religious leader-ship, the shaping role of social classes and groups, the influence of dif-fering doctrines of salvation, and the engagements of religion with other spheres of life, such as the arts and sexual mores. A sample of these discus-sions appears in the second of the selections provided here. It shows that although he opposed reductionist theories, Weber did not do so simplis-tically. Often, he recognized, the train of causes and conditions moves in both directions; religion both shapes, and is in turn shaped by, such things as social attachments within a class or a status group, economic pressures, forms of leadership, and mere historical circumstance or coincidence.

Most of Weber's research on these themes had been completed by 1914, when World War I intruded on German academic life. Neither the text of the *Sociology of Religion* nor the rest of *Economy and Society* would see publication until after the fighting ended—and his own untimely death two years later. Meanwhile, despite the uncertainties of the war years, Weber set himself a final ambitious plan: to produce a magisterial series of comparative studies under the title of "The Economic Ethic of World Religions." This was a truly daunting enterprise—global in its scope and complexity. His aim was to explore the crucial role of the great religious belief systems in the development of economic practices, social structures, and cultural institutions. Eight volumes were projected. *The Protestant Ethic* would stand as the first, followed by studies of Asian-Oriental reli-gions and further volumes on what Weber called the great Western salva-tion religions—Judaism, Christianity, and Islam. Of these, only three were completed when he died, suddenly, of pneumonia in 1920 at the age of 56. They include *The Religion of China* (1916) and *The Religion of India* (1917), which examined both Hinduism and Buddhism, as well as *Ancient Judaism* (1919). Among them, Weber included two thoughtful general essays—one as an introduction, the other a "Midpoint Reflection"—which offer some of his most thoughtful comparative analyses. The final two selections are drawn from these essays, which explicate some of his typologies and distinctions as applied to society and spirituality in the civilizations of both the East and the West.

The Protestant Ethic and the Spirit of Capitalism

In this selection, Weber contends that, indirectly and even unintentionally, the religious ideas of two Protestant theologians in the sixteenth century, Martin Luther and John Calvin, were crucial to the economic revolution that ended the Middle Ages and gave shape to the modern world.

In the title of this study is used the somewhat pretentious phrase, the *spirit* of capitalism. What is to be understood by it? The attempt to give anything like a definition of it brings out certain difficulties which are in the very nature of this type of investigation. If any object can be found to which this term can be applied with any understandable meaning, it can only be an historical individual, i.e. a complex of elements associated in historical reality which we unite into a conceptual whole from the standpoint of their cultural significance.

~

[T]he *summum bonum* [Latin: "highest good": ed.] of this ethic, the earning of more and more money, combined with the strict avoidance of all spontaneous enjoyment of life, is above all completely devoid of any eudoemonistic, not to say hedonistic, admixture. It is thought of so purely as an end in itself, that from the point of view of the happiness of, or utility to, the single individual, it appears entirely transcendental and absolutely irrational. Man is dominated by the making of money, by acquisition as the ultimate purpose of his life. Economic acquisition is no longer subordinated to man as the means for the satisfaction of his material needs. This reversal of what we should call the natural relationship, so irrational from a naive point of view, is evidently as definitely a leading principle of capitalism as it is foreign to all peoples not under capitalistic influence. At the same time it expresses a type of feeling which is closely connected with certain religious ideas. If we thus ask, why should "money be made out of men," Benjamin Franklin...answers in his autobiography with a quotation from the Bible, which his strict Calvinistic father drummed into him

FROM Weber, Max. *The Protestant Ethic and the Spirit of Capitalism.* 1ˢᵗ edition, © 1977. Reprinted by permission of Pearson Education, Inc., Upper Saddle River, NJ.

again and again in his youth: "Seest thou a man diligent in his business? He shall stand before kings" (Prov. xxii. 29). The earning of money within the modern economic order is, so long as it is done legally, the result and the expression of virtue and proficiency in a calling; and this virtue and proficiency are, as it is now not difficult to see, the real Alpha and Omega of Franklin's ethic. . . .

And in truth this peculiar idea, so familiar to us to-day, but in reality so little a matter of course, of one's duty in a calling, is what is most characteristic of the social ethic of capitalistic culture, and is in a sense the fundamental basis of it. It is an obligation which the individual is supposed to feel and does feel towards the content of his professional activity. . . .

[A] manner of life so well adapted to the peculiarities of capitalism . . . had to originate somewhere, and not in isolated individuals alone, but as a way of life common to whole groups of men. This origin is what really needs explanation. Concerning the doctrine of the more naive historical materialism [the creed of Marx and Engels: ed.], that such ideas originate as a reflection or superstructure of economic situations, we shall speak in more detail below. At this point it will suffice for our purpose to call attention to the fact that without doubt, in the country of Benjamin Franklin's birth (Massachusetts), the spirit of capitalism (in the sense we have attached to it) was present before the capitalistic order. There were complaints of a peculiarly calculating sort of profit-seeking in New England, as distinguished from other parts of America, as early as 1632. . . . In this case the causal relation is certainly the reverse of that suggested by the materialistic standpoint.

But the origin and history of such ideas is much more complex than the theorists of the superstructure suppose. The spirit of capitalism, in the sense in which we are using the term, had to fight its way to supremacy against a whole world of hostile forces. A state of mind such as that expressed in the passages we have quoted from Franklin, and which called forth the applause of a whole people, would both in ancient times and in the Middle Ages have been proscribed as the lowest sort of avarice and as an attitude entirely lacking in self-respect. . . .

⁓

The ideal type of the capitalistic entrepreneur . . . avoids ostentation and unnecessary expenditure, as well as conscious enjoyment of his power, and is embarrassed by the outward signs of the social recognition which he receives. His manner of life is, in other words, often . . . distinguished by a certain ascetic tendency, as appears clearly enough in the sermon of Franklin which we have quoted. It is, namely, by no means exceptional, but rather the rule, for him to have a sort of modesty. . . . He gets nothing out of his wealth for himself, except the irrational sense of having done his job well.

But it is just that which seems to the pre-capitalistic man so incomprehensible and mysterious, so unworthy and contemptible. That anyone should be able to make it the sole purpose of his life-work, to sink into the grave weighed down with a great material load of money and goods, seems to him explicable only as the product of a perverse instinct....

[T]hat the conception of money-making as an end in itself to which people were bound, as a calling, was contrary to the ethical feelings of whole epochs, it is hardly necessary to prove.... [T]he feeling was never quite overcome, that activity directed to acquisition for its own sake...was to be tolerated only because of the unalterable necessities of life in this world....

[T]he dominant doctrine rejected the spirit of capitalistic acquisition as *turpitudo* [wrongdoing: ed.], or at least could not give it a positive sanction. An ethical attitude like that of Ben Franklin would have been unthinkable.... Quite considerable sums, as the sources show, went at the death of rich people to religious institutions as conscience money, at times even back to former debtors as *usura* [borrowings: ed.] which had been unjustly taken from them.... Here the either non-moral or immoral character of their action in the opinion of the participants themselves comes clearly to light.

Now how could activity, which was at best ethically tolerated, turn into a calling...? The fact to be explained historically is that in the most highly capitalistic centre of that time, in Florence of the fourteenth and fifteenth centuries...this attitude was considered ethically unjustifiable, or at best to be tolerated. But in the backwoods small bourgeois circumstances of Pennsylvania in the eighteenth century..., where only the earliest beginnings of banking were to be found, the same thing was considered the essence of moral conduct, even commanded in the name of duty. To speak here of a reflection of material conditions in the ideal superstructure would be patent nonsense. What was the background of ideas which could account for the sort of activity apparently directed toward profit alone as a calling toward which the individual feels himself to have an ethical obligation? For it was this idea which gave the way of life of the new entrepreneur its ethical foundation and justification.

～

Luther's Concept of "Calling"

The conception of the calling...brings out that central dogma of all Protestant denominations.... The only way of living acceptably to God was not to surpass worldly morality in monastic asceticism, but solely through the fulfilment of the obligations imposed upon the individual by his position in the world. That was his calling.

Luther developed the conception in the course of the first decade of his activity as a reformer. At first, quite in harmony with the prevailing tradition of the Middle Ages, as represented, for example, by Thomas Aquinas, he thought of activity in the world as a thing of the flesh.... But with the development of the conception of *sola fide* [by faith alone: ed.] in all its consequences..., the calling grew in importance. The monastic life is not only quite devoid of value as a means of justification before God, but he [Luther: ed.] also looks upon its renunciation of the duties of this world as the product of selfishness, withdrawing from temporal obligations. In contrast, labour in a calling appears to him as the outward expression of brotherly love.... [T]here remains, more and more strongly emphasized, the statement that the fulfilment of worldly duties is under all circumstances the only way to live acceptably to God. It and it alone is the will of God, and hence every legitimate calling has exactly the same worth in the sight of God.

That this moral justification of worldly activity was one of the most important results of the Reformation, especially of Luther's part in it, is beyond doubt, and may even be considered a platitude....

The effect of the Reformation as such was only that, as compared with the Catholic attitude, the moral emphasis on and the religious sanction of, organized worldly labour in a calling was mightily increased. The way in which the concept of the calling, which expressed this change, should develop further depended upon the religious evolution which now took place in the different Protestant Churches.

$\sim$

[F]or Luther the concept of the calling remained traditionalistic. His calling is something which a man has to accept as a divine ordinance, to which he must adapt himself. This aspect outweighed the other idea, which was also present, that work in the calling was a, or rather *the*, task set by God. And in its further development, orthodox Lutheranism emphasized this aspect still more. Thus, for the time being, the only ethical result was negative; worldly duties were no longer subordinated to ascetic ones; obedience to authority and the acceptance of things as they were, were preached.... That was precisely because he could not but suspect the tendency to ascetic self-discipline of leading to salvation by works, and hence he and his Church were forced to keep it more and more in the background.

Thus the mere idea of the calling in the Lutheran sense is at best of questionable importance for the problems in which we are interested.... It is thus well for us next to look into those forms in which a relation between practical life and a religious motivation can be more easily perceived than in Lutheranism. We have already called attention to the conspicuous part played by Calvinism and the Protestant sects in the history of capitalistic development. As Luther found a different spirit at work in Zwingli than in himself, so did his spiritual successors in Calvinism....

A purely superficial glance shows that there is here [in Calvinism: ed.] quite a different relationship between the religious life and earthly activity than in either Catholicism or Lutheranism....

Calvin and the Calvinist Doctrine of Election

We ... take as our starting-point in the investigation of the relationship between the old Protestant ethic and the spirit of capitalism the works of Calvin, of Calvinism, and the other Puritan sects. But it is not to be understood that we expect to find any of the founders or representatives of these religious movements considering the promotion of what we have called the spirit of capitalism as in any sense the end of his life-work.... The salvation of the soul and that alone was the centre of their life and work. Their ethical ideals and the practical results of their doctrines were all based on that alone, and were the consequences of purely religious motives. We shall thus have to admit that the cultural consequences of the Reformation were to a great extent, perhaps in the particular aspects with which we are dealing predominantly, unforeseen and even unwished-for results of the labours of the reformers. They were often far removed from or even in contradiction to all that they themselves thought to attain....

[I]t may at once be definitely stated, no attempt is made to evaluate the ideas of the Reformation in any sense, whether it concern their social or their religious worth. We have continually to deal with aspects of the Reformation which must appear to the truly religious consciousness as incidental and even superficial. For we are merely attempting to clarify the part which religious forces have played in forming the developing web of our specifically worldly modern culture, in the complex interaction of innumerable different historical factors. We are thus inquiring only to what extent certain characteristic features of this culture can be imputed to the influence of the Reformation. At the same time we must free ourselves from the idea that it is possible to deduce the Reformation, as a historically necessary result, from certain economic changes. Countless historical circumstances, which cannot be reduced to any economic law, and are not susceptible of economic explanation of any sort, especially purely political processes, had to concur in order that the newly created Churches should survive at all. On the other hand, however, we have no intention whatever of maintaining such a foolish and doctrinaire thesis as that the spirit of capitalism (in the provisional sense of the term explained above) could only have arisen as the result of certain effects of the Reformation, or even that capitalism as an economic system is a creation of the Reformation. In itself, the fact that certain important forms of capitalistic business organization are known to be considerably older than the Reformation is a sufficient refutation of such a claim.

On the contrary, we only wish to ascertain whether and to what extent religious forces have taken part in the qualitative formation and the quantitative expansion of that spirit over the world.... In view of the tremendous confusion of interdependent influences between the material basis, the forms of social and political organization, and the ideas current in the time of the Reformation, we can only proceed by investigating whether and at what points certain correlations between forms of religious belief and practical ethics can be worked out. At the same time we shall as far as possible clarify the manner and the general direction in which, by virtue of those relationships, the religious movements have influenced the development of material culture. Only when this has been determined with reasonable accuracy can the attempt be made to estimate to what extent the historical development of modern culture can be attributed to those religious forces and to what extent to others.

$$\sim$$

Calvinism was the faith over which the great political and cultural struggles of the sixteenth and seventeenth centuries were fought in the most highly developed countries, the Netherlands, England, and France. To it we shall hence turn first. At that time, and in general even today, the doctrine of predestination was considered its most characteristic dogma.... If now we ... inquire into the significance which is to be attributed to that dogma by virtue of its cultural and historical consequences, it must certainly be rated very highly.... Again and again it was looked upon as the real element of political danger in Calvinism and attacked as such by those in authority. The great synods of the seventeenth century, above all those of Dordrecht and Westminster, besides numerous smaller ones, made its elevation to canonical authority the central purpose of their work. It served as a rallying-point to countless heroes of the church militant.... We cannot pass it by, and since today it can no longer be assumed as known to all educated men, we can best learn its content from the authoritative words of the Westminster Confession of 1647, which in this regard is simply repeated by both Independent and Baptist creeds...

"Chapter III (of God's Eternal Decree), No. 3. By the decree of God, for the manifestation of His glory, some men and angels are predestinated unto everlasting life, and others foreordained to everlasting death.

"No. 5. Those of mankind that are predestined unto life, God before the foundation of the world was laid, according to his eternal and immutable purpose, and the secret counsel and good pleasure of His will, hath chosen in Christ unto everlasting glory, out of His mere free grace and love, without any foresight of faith or good works, or perseverance in either of them..., and all to the praise of His glorious grace.".....

"Though I may be sent to Hell for it, such a God will never command my respect," was Milton's well-known opinion of the doctrine. But we are here concerned not with the evaluation, but the historical significance of the dogma. We can only briefly sketch the question of how the doctrine originated and how it fitted into the framework of Calvinistic theology....

With Calvin the *decretum horribile* ["horrific decree": ed.] is derived not, as with Luther, from religious experience, but from the logical necessity of his thought; therefore its importance increases with every increase in the logical consistency of that religious thought. The interest of it is solely in God, not in man; God does not exist for men, but men for the sake of God. All creation, including of course the fact, as it undoubtedly was for Calvin, that only a small proportion of men are chosen for eternal grace, can have any meaning only as means to the glory and majesty of God.... We know only that a part of humanity is saved, the rest damned.... The Father in heaven of the New Testament, so human and understanding, who rejoices over the repentance of a sinner as a woman over the lost piece of silver she has found, is gone. His place has been taken by a transcendental being, beyond the reach of human understanding, who with His quite incomprehensible decrees has decided the fate of every individual and regulated the tiniest details of the cosmos from eternity....

In what was for the man of the age of the Reformation the most important thing in life, his eternal salvation, he was forced to follow his path alone to meet a destiny which had been decreed for him from eternity. No one could help him. No priest, for the chosen one can understand the word of God only in his own heart. No sacraments had been ordained by God for the increase of his glory.... No Church, for...the membership of the external Church included the doomed. Finally, even no God. For even Christ had died only for the elect.... This, the complete elimination of salvation through the Church and the sacraments...was what formed the absolutely decisive difference from Catholicism.

That great historic process in the development of religions, the elimination of magic from the world which had begun with the old Hebrew prophets and, in conjunction with Hellenistic scientific thought, had repudiated all magical means to salvation as superstition and sin, came here to its logical conclusion. The genuine Puritan even rejected all signs of religious ceremony at the grave and buried his nearest and dearest without song or ritual in order that no superstition, no trust in the effects of magical and sacramental forces on salvation, should creep in.

There was not only no magical means of attaining the grace of God for those to whom God had decided to deny it, but no means whatever.... In striking contrast to Lutheranism, this attitude toward life was also connected with the quiet disappearance of the private confession...from all the regions of fully developed Calvinism. That was an occurrence of the greatest importance.... The means to a periodical discharge of the emotional sense of sin was done away with.

Of the consequences for the ethical conduct of everyday life we speak later. But for the general religious situation of a man the consequences are evident. In spite of the necessity of membership in the true Church for salvation, the Calvinist's intercourse with his God was carried on in deep spiritual isolation....

It seems at first a mystery how the undoubted superiority of Calvinism in social organization can be connected with this tendency to tear the individual away from the closed ties with which he is bound to this world. But, however strange it may seem, it follows from the peculiar form which the Christian brotherly love was forced to take under the pressure of the inner isolation of the individual through the Calvinistic faith. In the first place it follows dogmatically. The world exists to serve the glorification of God and for that purpose alone. The elected Christian is in the world only to increase this glory of by fulfilling His commandments to the best of his ability....

Election and the Ethic of "Worldly Asceticism"

The question, Am I one of the elect? must[a] sooner or later have arisen for every believer and have forced all other interests into the background. And how can I be sure of this state of grace? For Calvin himself this was not a problem. He felt himself to be a chosen agent of the Lord, and was certain of his own salvation. Accordingly, to the question of how the individual can be certain of his own election, he has at bottom only the answer that we should be content with the knowledge that God has chosen and depend further only on that implicit trust in Christ which is the result of true faith. He rejects in principle the assumption that one can learn from the conduct of others whether they are chosen or damned. It is an unjustifiable attempt to force God's secrets. The elect differ externally in this life in no way from the damned.... The elect thus are and remain God's invisible Church.

Quite naturally this attitude was impossible for his followers... and, above all, for the broad mass of ordinary men.... So, wherever the doctrine of predestination was held, the question could not be suppressed whether there were any infallible criteria by which membership in the *electi* could be known....

It was impossible, at least so far as the question of a man's own state of grace arose, to be satisfied with Calvin's trust in the testimony of the expectant faith resulting from grace.... Above all, practical pastoral work, which had immediately to deal with all the suffering caused by the doctrine, could not be satisfied. It met these difficulties in various ways. So far as predestination was not reinterpreted, toned down, or fundamentally abandoned, two principal, mutually connected, types of pastoral advice appear. On the one hand it is held to be an absolute duty to consider oneself chosen, and to combat all doubts as temptations of the devil, since lack of self-confidence is the result of insufficient faith, hence of imperfect grace... In the place of the humble sinners to whom Luther promises grace if they trust themselves to God in penitent faith are bred those self-confident saints whom we can rediscover in the hard Puritan merchants of the heroic age of capitalism and in isolated instances down to the present. On the other hand, in order to attain that self-confidence intense worldly activity is recommended as the most suitable means. It and it alone disperses religious doubts and gives the certainty of grace.

That worldly activity should be considered capable of this achievement, that it could, so to speak, be considered the most suitable means of counteracting feelings of religious anxiety, finds its explanation in the fundamental peculiarities of religious feeling in the Reformed Church....

The typical religion of the Reformed Church... has from the beginning repudiated... purely inward emotional piety.... A real penetration of the human soul by the divine was made impossible by the absolute transcendentality of God compared to the flesh.... The community of the elect with their God could only take place and be perceptible to them in that God worked (*operatur*) through them and that they were conscious of it. That is, their action originated from the faith caused by God's grace, and this faith in turn justified itself by the quality of that action. Deep-lying differences of the most important conditions of salvation which apply to the classification of all practical religious activity appear here. The religious believer can make himself sure of his state of grace either in that he feels himself to be the vessel of the Holy Spirit or the tool of the divine will. In the former case his religious life tends to mysticism and emotionalism, in the latter to ascetic action; Luther stood close to the former type, Calvinism belonged definitely to the latter....

If we now ask further, by what fruits the Calvinist thought himself able to identify true faith? The answer is: by a type of Christian conduct which served to increase the glory of God.... It was through the consciousness that his conduct... rested on a power within himself working for the glory of God; that it is not only willed of God but rather done by God that he attained the highest good towards which this religion strove, the certainty of salvation..... Thus, however useless good works might be as a means of attaining salvation..., they are indispensable as a sign of election. They are the technical means, not of purchasing salvation, but of getting rid of the fear of damnation....

In practice this means that God helps those who help themselves. Thus the Calvinist, as it is sometimes put, himself creates his own salvation, or, as would be more correct, the conviction of it. But this creation cannot, as in Catholicism, consist in a gradual accumulation of individual good works to one's credit, but rather in a systematic self-control which at every moment stands before the inexorable alternative, chosen or damned. This brings us to a very important point in our investigation.

[A] more intensive form of the religious valuation of moral action than that to which Calvinism led its adherents has perhaps never existed. But what is important for the practical significance of this sort of salvation by works must be sought in a knowledge of the particular qualities which characterized their type of ethical conduct and distinguished it from the everyday life of an average Christian of the Middle Ages. The difference may well be formulated as follows: the normal mediaeval Catholic layman lived ethically, so to speak, from hand to mouth. In the first place he conscientiously fulfilled his traditional duties. But beyond that minimum his good works did not necessarily form a connected, or at least not a rationalized, system of life, but rather remained a succession of individual acts....

The rationalization of the world, the elimination of magic as a means to salvation, the Catholics had not carried nearly so far as the Puritans (and before them the Jews) had done. To the Catholic the absolution of his Church was a compensation for his own imperfections. The priest was a magician who performed the miracle of transubstantiation, and who held the key to eternal life in his hand. One could turn to him in grief and penitence. He dispensed atonement, hope of grace, certainty of forgiveness, and thereby granted release from that tremendous tension to which the Calvinist was doomed by an inexorable fate, admitting of no mitigation. For him such friendly and human comforts did not exist. He could not hope to atone for hours of weakness or thoughtlessness by increased good will at other times, as the Catholic or even the Lutheran could. The God of Calvinism demanded of his believers not single good works, but a life of good works combined into a unified system. There was no place for the very human Catholic cycle of sin, repentance, atonement, release, followed by renewed sin....

The moral conduct of the average man was thus deprived of its planless and unsystematic character and subjected to a consistent method for conduct as a whole.... [O]nly by a fundamental change in the whole meaning of life at every moment and in every action could the effects of grace transforming a man from the *status naturae* ["state of nature"] to the *status gratiae* ["state of grace"] be proved.

The life of the saint was directed solely toward a transcendental end, salvation. But precisely for that reason it was thoroughly rationalized in this world and dominated entirely by the aim to add to the glory of God on earth.... It was this rationalization which gave the Reformed faith its peculiar ascetic tendency, and is the basis of both its relationship to and its conflict with Catholicism....

[A]ctive self-control...was...the most important practical ideal of Puritanism. In the deep contempt with which the cool reserve of its adherents is contrasted, in the reports of the trials of its martyrs, with the undisciplined blustering of the noble prelates and officials can be seen that respect for quiet self-control which still distinguishes the best type of English or American gentleman today. To put it in our terms: The Puritan, like every rational type of asceticism, tried to enable man to maintain and act upon his constant motives, especially those which it taught him itself, against the emotions. In this formal psychological sense of the term it tried to make him into a personality. Contrary to many popular ideas, the end of this asceticism was to be able to lead an alert, intelligent life: the most urgent task the destruction of spontaneous, impulsive enjoyment, the most important means was to bring order into the conduct of its adherents. All these important points are emphasized in the rules of Catholic monasticism as strongly as in the principles of conduct of the Calvinists....

But in the course of its development Calvinism added something positive to this, the idea of the necessity of proving one's faith in worldly activity. Therein it gave...religiously inclined people a positive incentive to asceticism. By founding its ethic in the doctrine of predestination, it substituted for the spiritual aristocracy of the monks outside of and above the world the spiritual aristocracy of the predestined saints of God within the world. It was an aristocracy which...was divided from the eternally damned remainder of humanity by a more impassable and in its invisibility more terrifying gulf, than separated the monk of the Middle Ages from the rest of the world about him, a gulf which penetrated all social relations with its sharp brutality. This consciousness of divine grace of the elect and holy was accompanied by an attitude toward the sin of one's neighbor, not of sympathetic understanding based on consciousness of one's own weakness, but of hatred and contempt for him as an enemy of God bearing signs of eternal damnation.

～

As he observed his own conduct the later Puritan also observed that of God and saw His finger in all the details of life. And contrary to the strict doctrine of Calvin, he always knew why God took this or that measure. The process of sanctifying life could thus almost take on the character of a business enterprise. A thoroughgoing Christianization of the whole of life was the consequence of this methodical quality of ethical conduct into which Calvinism...forced men. That this rationality was decisive in its influence on practical life must always be borne in mind in order rightly to understand the influence of Calvinism....

～

Calvinist Asceticism and Capitalism

It is our next task to follow out the results of the Puritan idea of calling in the business world, now that the above sketch has attempted to show its religious foundations. With all the differences of detail and emphasis which these different ascetic movements [Calvinist, Pietist, Methodist, and Baptist: ed.] show in the aspects with which we have been concerned, much the same characteristics are present and important in all of them. But for our purposes the decisive point was, to recapitulate, the conception of the state of religious grace, common to all the denominations, as a status which marks off its possessor from the degradation of the flesh, from the world....

From that followed for the individual an incentive methodically to supervise his own state of grace in his own conduct, and thus to penetrate it with asceticism. But, as we have seen, this ascetic conduct meant a rational planning of the whole of one's life in accordance with God's will.... The religious life of the saints, as distinguished from the natural life, was—the most mportant point—no longer lived outside of the world in monastic communities, but within the world and its institutions. This rationalization of conduct within this world, but for the sake of the world beyond, was the consequence of the concept of calling of ascetic Protestantism.

Christian asceticism, at first fleeing from the world into solitude, had already ruled the world which it had renounced from the monastery and through the Church. But it had, on the whole, left the naturally spontaneous character of daily life in the world untouched. Now it strode into the marketplace of life, slammed the door of the monastery behind it, and undertook to penetrate just that daily routine of life with its methodicalness, to fashion it into a life in the world, but neither of nor for this world.

～

In the Puritan concept of the calling the emphasis is always placed on this methodical character of worldly asceticism, not...on the acceptance of the lot which God has irretrievably assigned to man....

It is true that the usefulness of a calling, and thus its favour in the sight of God, is measured primarily in moral terms, and thus in terms of the importance of the goods produced in it for the community. But a further, and, above all, in practice the most important, criterion is found in private profitableness. For if that God, whose hand the Puritan sees in all the occurrences of life, shows one of his elect a chance of profit, he must do it with a purpose. Hence the faithful Christian must follow the call by taking advantage of the opportunity....

Wealth is thus bad ethically only in so far as it is a temptation to idleness and sinful enjoyment of life, and its acquisition is bad only when it is with the purpose of later living merrily and without care. But as a performance of duty in a calling it is not only morally permissible, but actually enjoined. The parable of the servant who was rejected because he did not increase the talent which was entrusted to him seemed to say so directly. To wish to be poor was, it was often argued, the same as wishing to be unhealthy; it is objectionable as a glorification of works and derogatory to the glory of God. Especially begging, on the part of one able to work, is not only the sin of slothfulness, but a violation of the duty of brotherly love according to the Apostle's own word.

~

Although we cannot here enter upon a discussion of the influence of Puritanism in all these directions, we should call attention to the fact that the toleration of pleasure in cultural goods...certainly always ran up against one characteristic limitation: they must not cost anything. Man is only a trustee of the goods which have come to him through God's grace. He must, like the servant in the parable, give an account of every penny entrusted to him, and it is at least hazardous to spend any of it for a purpose which does not serve the glory of God but only one's own enjoyment. What person, who keeps his eyes open, has not met representatives of this viewpoint even in the present? The idea of man's duty to his possessions, to which he subordinates himself as an obedient steward, or even as an acquisitive machine, bear with chilling weight on his life. The greater the possessions the heavier...the feeling of responsibility for them, for holding them undiminished for the glory of God and increasing them by restless effort. The origin of this type of life also extends...back to the Middle Ages. But it was in the ethic of Protestantism that it first found a consistent ethical foundation. Its significance for the development of capitalism is obvious.

This worldly Protestant asceticism, as we may recapitulate up to this point, acted powerfully against the spontaneous enjoyment of possessions; it restricted consumption, especially of luxuries. On the other hand, it had the psychological effect of freeing the acquisition of good from the inhibitions of traditionalistic ethics. It broke the bonds of the impulse of acquisition in that it not only legalized it, but (in the sense discussed) looked upon it as directly willed by God....

[A]sceticism looked upon the pursuit of wealth as an end in itself as highly reprehensible; but the attainment of it as a fruit of labor in a calling was a sign of God's blessing. And even more important: the religious valuation of restless, continuous, systematic work in a worldly calling, as the highest means to asceticism, and at the same time the surest and most evident proof of rebirth and genuine faith, must have been the most powerful conceivable lever for the expansion of that attitude toward life which we here have called the spirit of capitalism.

When the limitation of consumption is combined with the release of acquisitive activity, the inevitable practical result in obvious: accumulation of capital through ascetic compulsion to save. The restraints which were imposed upon the consumption of wealth naturally served to increase it by making possible the productive investment of capital. How strong this influence was is not, unfortunately, susceptible of exact statistical demonstration. In New England the connection is... evident.... But also in Holland, which was really only dominated by strict Calvinism for seven years, the greater simplicity of life in the more seriously religious circles, in combination with great wealth, led to an excessive propensity to accumulation....

As far as the influence of the Puritan outlook extended, under all circumstances—and this is, of course, much more important than the mere encouragement of capital accumulation—it favoured the development of a rational bourgeois economic life; it was the most important, and above all the only consistent influence in the development of that life. It stood at the cradle of the modern economic man.

~

What the great religious epoch of the seventeenth century bequeathed to its utilitarian successor was... above all an amazingly good, we may even say a pharisaically good, conscience in the acquisition of money, so long as it took place legally....

A specifically bourgeois economic ethic had grown up. With the consciousness of standing in the fullness of God's grace and being visibly blessed by Him, the bourgeois business man, as long as he remained within the bounds of formal correctness, as long as his moral conduct was spotless and the use to which he put his wealth was not objectionable, could follow his pecuniary interests as he would and feel that he was fulfilling a duty in doing so. The power of religious asceticism provided him in addition with sober, conscientious, and unusually industrious workmen, who clung to their work as to a life purpose willed by God.

Finally, it gave him the comforting assurance that the unequal distribution of the goods of this world was a special dispensation of Divine Providence.... This formulation of a leading idea of capitalistic economy later entered into the current theories of the productivity of low wages....

Now naturally the whole ascetic literature of almost all denominations is saturated with the idea that faithful labour, even at low wages, on the part of those whom life offers no other opportunities, is highly pleasing to God. In this respect Protestant Asceticism added in itself nothing new. But it not only deepened this idea most powerfully, it also created the force which was alone decisive for its effectiveness: the psychological sanction of it through the conception of this labour as a calling, as the best, often in the last analysis the only means of attaining certainty of grace. And on the other hand it legalized the exploitation of this specific willingness to work, in that it also interpreted the employer's business activity as a calling. It is obvious how powerfully the exclusive search for the Kingdom of God only through fulfillment of duty in the calling, and the strict asceticism which Church discipline naturally imposed, especially on the propertyless classes, was bound to affect the productivity of labour in the capitalistic sense of the word. The treatment of labour as a calling became as characteristic of the modern worker as the corresponding attitude toward acquisition of the business man....

One of the fundamental elements of the spirit of modern capitalism, and not only of that but of all modern culture: rational conduct on the basis of the idea of the calling, was born—that is what this discussion has sought to demonstrate—from the spirit of Christian asceticism....

The Puritan wanted to work in a calling; we are forced to do so. For when asceticism was carried out of monastic cells into everyday life, and began to dominate worldly morality, it did its part in building the tremendous cosmos of the modern economic order. This order is now bound to the technical and economic conditions of machine production which today determine the lives of all the individuals who are born into this mechanism, not only those directly concerned with economic acquisition, with irresistible force. Perhaps it will so determine them until the last ton of fossilized coal is burnt. In [theologian Richard: ed] Baxter's view the care for external goods should only lie on the shoulders of the "saint like a light cloak, which can be thrown aside at any moment." But fate decreed that the cloak should become an iron cage.

Since asceticism undertook to remodel the world and to work out its ideals in the world, material goods have gained an increasing and finally inexorable power over the lives of men as at no previous period in history. Today the spirit of religious asceticism—whether finally, who knows?—has escaped from the cage. But victorious capitalism, since it rests on mechanical foundations, needs its support no longer....

No one knows who will live in this cage in the future, or whether at the end of this tremendous development entirely new prophets will arise, or there will be a great rebirth of old ideas and ideals, or, if neither, mechanized petrification, embellished with a sort of compulsive self-importance. For of the last stage of cultural development, it might well be truly said: "Specialists without spirit, sensualists without heart; this nullity imagines that it has attained a level of civilization never before achieved."

But this brings us to the world of judgments of value and of faith, with which this purely historical discussion need not be burdened....

Here we have only attempted to trace the fact and the direction of its influence to their motives in one, though a very important point. But it would also further be necessary to investigate how Protestant Asceticism was in turn influenced in its development and its character by the totality of social conditions, especially economic. The modern man is in general, even with the best will, unable to give religious ideas a significance for culture and national character which they deserve. But it is, of course, not my aim to substitute for a one-sided materialistic an equally one-sided spiritualistic causal interpretation of culture and of history. Each is equally possible, but each, if it does not serve as the preparation, but as the conclusion of an investigation, accomplishes equally little in the interest of historical truth.

The Sociology of Religion

Weber here discusses, from a sociological perspective, the differences between the practitioner of magic, the institutionalized office of the priest, and the charismatic figure of the religious prophet; he also outlines two different types of prophecy.

[T]he "priesthood" [is]...something distinct from "practitioners of magic."...Following the distinction between "cult" and "sorcery," one may contrast those professional [priestly: ed.] functionaries who influence the gods by means of worship with those magicians who coerce demons by magical means; but in many great religions, including Christianity, the concept of the priest includes such magical qualification....

It is more correct for our purpose, in order to do justice to the diverse and mixed manifestations of this phenomenon, to set up as the crucial feature of the priesthood the specialization of a particular group of persons in the continuous operation of a cultic enterprise, permanently associated with particular norms, places and times, and related to specific social groups. There can be no priesthood without a cult, although there may well be a cult without a specialized priesthood. The latter was the case in China, where state officials and the heads of households exclusively conducted the services of the official gods and the ancestral spirits....
[M]agicians may wield considerable power, and their essentially magical celebrations may play a central role in the life of their people. Yet they lack a continuously operative cult, and so the term "priests" cannot be applied to them.

FROM *The Sociology of Religion* by Max Weber. Copyright © 1956 by J.C.B. Mohr (Paul Siebeck). English translation by Ephraim Fischoff © 1963, 1991 by Beacon Press. Reprinted by permission of Beacon Press, Boston.

A rationalization of metaphysical views and a specifically religious ethic are usually missing in the case of a cult without priests, as in the case of a magician without a cult. The full development of both a metaphysical rationalization and a religious ethic requires an independent and professionally trained priesthood, permanently occupied with the cult and with the practical problems involved in the cure of souls. Consequently, ethics developed into something quite different from a metaphysically rationalized religion in classic Chinese thought, by reason of the absence of an independent priesthood; and this also happened with the ethics of ancient Buddhism, which lacked both cult and priesthood....

However, not every priesthood developed what is distinctively new as against magic: a rational metaphysic and religious ethic. Such developments generally presupposed the operation of one or both of two forces outside the priesthood: *prophets,* the bearers of metaphysical or religious-ethical revelation, and the *laity,* the non-priestly devotees of the cult....

Whether one should at all try to influence a particular god or demon by coercion or by entreaty is the most basic question, and the answer to it depends only upon proven effect. As the magician must keep up his charisma, so too the god must continually demonstrate his prowess. Should the effort to influence a god prove to be permanently inefficacious, then it is concluded that either the god is impotent or the correct procedure of influencing him is unknown, and he is abandoned. In China, to this day, a few striking successes suffice to enable a god to acquire prestige and power (*shen, ling*), thereby winning a sizeable circle of devotees. The emperor, as the representative of his subjects vis-à-vis the heavens, provides the gods with titles and other distinctions whenever they have proven their capacity. Yet a few striking disappointments subsequently will suffice to empty a temple forever. Conversely, the historical accident that Isaiah's steadfast prophecy actually came to fulfillment—God would not permit Jerusalem to fall into the hands of the Assyrian hordes, if only the Judean king remained firm—provided the subsequently unshakeable foundation for the position of this god and his prophets.

∼

Prophet versus Priest and Magician

What is a prophet from the perspective of sociology?...

We shall understand "prophet" to mean a purely individual bearer of charisma, who by virtue of his mission proclaims a religious doctrine or divine commandment. No radical distinction will be drawn between a "renewer of religion" who preaches an older revelation, actual or supposititious, and a "founder of religion" who claims to bring completely new deliverances. The two types merge into one another. In any case, the formation of a new religious community need not be the result of doctrinal preaching by prophets, since it may be produced by the activities of non-prophetic reformers. Nor shall we be concerned in this context with the question whether the followers of a prophet are more attracted to his person, as in the cases of Zoroaster, Jesus, and Muhammad, or to his doctrine, as in the cases of Buddha and the prophets of Israel.

For our purposes here, the personal call is the decisive element distinguishing the prophet from the priest. The latter lays claim to authority by virtue of his service in a sacred tradition, while the prophet's claim is based on personal revelation and charisma. It is no accident that almost no prophets have emerged from the priestly class. As a rule, the Indian teachers of salvation were not Brahmins, nor were the Israelite prophets priests. Zoroaster's case is exceptional in that there exists a possibility that he may have descended from the hieratic nobility. The priest, in clear contrast, dispenses salvation by virtue of his office. Even in cases in which personal charisma may be involved, it is the hierarchical office that confers legitimate authority upon the priest as a member of an organized enterprise of salvation.

But the prophet, like the magician, exerts his power simply by virtue of his personal gifts. Unlike the magician, however, the prophet claims definite revelations, and the core of his mission is doctrine or commandment, not magic. Outwardly, at least, the distinction is fluid, for the magician is frequently a knowledgeable expert in divination, and sometimes in this alone. At this stage, revelation functions continuously as oracle or dream interpretation. Without prior consultation with the magician, no innovations in social relations could be adopted in primitive times. To this day, in certain parts of Australia, it is the dream revelations of magicians that are set before the councils of clan heads for adoption, and it is a mark of secularization that this practice is receding.

On the other hand, it was only under very unusual circumstances that a prophet succeeded in establishing his authority without charismatic authentication, which in practice meant magic. At least the bearers of new doctrine practically always needed such validation. It must not be forgotten for an instant that the entire basis of Jesus' own legitimation, as well as his claim that he and only he knew the Father and that the way to God led through faith in him alone, was the magical charisma he felt within himself. It was doubtless this consciousness of power, more than anything else, that enabled him to traverse the road of the prophets. During the apostolic period of early Christianity and thereafter the figure of the wandering prophet was a constant phenomenon. There was always required of such prophets a proof of their possession of particular gifts of the spirit, of special magical or ecstatic abilities.

Prophets very often practiced divination as well as magical healing and counseling. This was true, for example, of the prophets (*nabi, nebiim*) so frequently mentioned in the Old Testament, especially in the prophetic books and Chronicles. But what distinguishes the prophet, in the sense that we are employing the term, from the types just described is an economic factor, i.e., that his *prophecy is unremunerated*. . . . This criterion of gratuitous service also distinguishes the prophet from the priest. The typical prophet propagates ideas for their own sake and not for fees, at least not in any obvious or regulated form. The provisions enjoining the non-remunerative character of prophetic propaganda have taken various forms. Thus developed the carefully cultivated postulate that the apostle, prophet, or teacher of ancient Christianity must not "trade on" his religious proclamations. Also, limitations were set upon the length of the time he could enjoy the hospitality of his friends. The Christian prophet was enjoined to live by the labor of his own hands or, as among the Buddhists, only from alms which he had not specifically solicited. These injunctions were repeatedly emphasized in the Pauline epistles, and in another form in the Buddhist monastic regulations. The dictum "whosoever will not work, shall not eat" applied to missionaries; however, the prophesying free of charge is, of course, one of the chief reasons for the success of prophetic propaganda itself.

~

Ethical and Exemplary Prophecy

[T]here remain only two kinds of prophets in our sense, one represented most clearly by the Buddha, the other with especial clarity by Zoroaster and Muhammad. The prophet may be primarily, as in the last cases, an instrument for the proclamation of a god and his will, be this a concrete command or an abstract norm. Preaching as one who has received a commission from god, he demands obedience as an ethical duty. This type we shall term the "ethical prophet." On the other hand, the prophet may be an exemplary man who, by his personal example, demonstrates to others the way to religious salvation, as in the case of the Buddha. The preaching of this type of prophet says nothing about a divine mission or an ethical duty of obedience, but rather directs itself to the self-interest of those who crave salvation, recommending to them the same path as he himself traversed. Our designation for this second type is that of the "*exemplary prophet.*"

The exemplary type is particularly characteristic of prophecy in India, although there have been a few manifestations of it in China (e.g., Lao Tzu) and the Near East. On the other hand, the ethical type is confined to the Near East, regardless of racial differences there. For neither the Vedas nor the classical books of the Chinese...makes it appear at all probable that prophecy of the ethical type, such as developed in the Near East or Iran, could ever have arisen in India or China. The decisive reason for this is the absence of a personal, transcendental, and ethical god. In India this concept was found only in a sacramental and magical form, and then only in the later and popular faiths. But in the religions of those social strata within which the decisive prophetic conceptions of Mahavira and Buddha were developed, ethical prophecy appeared only intermittently and was constantly subjected to reinterpretations in the direction of pantheism. In China the notion of ethical prophecy was altogether lacking in the ethics of the stratum that exercised the greatest influence in the society....

As far as purely religious factors are concerned, it was decisive for both India and China that the conception of a rationally regulated world had its point of origin in the ceremonial order of sacrifices, on the unalterable sequence of which everything depended: especially the indispensable regularity of meteorological processes; in animistic terms, what was involved here was the normal activity or inactivity of the spirits and demons. According to both classical and heterodox Chinese views, these processes were held to be insured by the ethically proper conduct of government that followed the correct path of virtue, the Tao; without this everything would fail, even according to Vedic doctrine. Thus, in India and China, Rita and Tao respectively represented similar superdivine, impersonal forces.

On the other hand, the personal, transcendental and ethical god is a Near-Eastern concept. It corresponds so closely to that of an allpowerful mundane king with his rational bureaucratic regime that a causal connection can scarcely be denied....

The Nature of Prophetic Revelation: The World As a Meaningful Totality

Regardless of whether a particular religious prophet is predominantly of the ethical or predominantly of the exemplary type, prophetic revelation involves for both the prophet himself and for his followers—and this is the element common to both varieties—a unified view of the world derived from a consciously integrated meaningful attitude toward life. To the prophet, both the life of man and the world, both social and cosmic events, have a certain systematic and coherent meaning, to which man's conduct must he oriented if it is to bring salvation, and after which it must be patterned in an integrally meaningful manner. Now the structure of this meaning may take varied forms, and it may weld together into a unity motives that are logically quite heterogeneous. The whole conception is dominated, not by logical consistency, but by practical valuations. Yet it always denotes, regardless of any variations in scope and in measure of success, an effort to systematize all the manifestations of life; that is, to organize practical behavior into a direction of life, regardless of the form it may assume in any individual case. Moreover, this meaning always contains the important religious conception of the world as a cosmos which is challenged to produce somehow a "meaningful," ordered totality, the particular manifestations of which are to be measured and evaluated according to this postulate.

The conflict between empirical reality and this conception of the world as a meaningful totality, which is based on a religious postulate, produces the strongest tensions in man's inner life as well as in his external relationship to the world. To be sure, this problem is by no means dealt with in prophecy alone. Both priestly wisdom and secular philosophy, the intellectualist as well as the popular varieties, are somehow concerned with it. The ultimate question of all metaphysics has always been something like this: if the world as a whole and life in particular were to have a meaning, what might it be, and how would the world have to look to correspond to it?

The Social Psychology of the World Religions

Using his method of "Ideal Types," Weber here expands on the two main forms of prophecy: "exemplary," which is characteristic of Asian religions, and "emissary," or "ethical," which is more distinctively Western. The discussion then moves to distinctions between "virtuoso" and "mass" religiosity, between a "sect" and a "church," and between "mysticism" and "asceticism." Finally, Weber outlines what is perhaps the best known of all his typologies: the division of religious—like social—authority into three forms: charismatic, traditional, and bureaucratic, or "legal."

[T] here has always existed the possibility—even though in greatly varying measure—of letting an *ethical* and rational regulation of life arise. This may occur by the linkage of such an ethic to the tendency of technological and economic rationalism. Such regulation has not been able to make headway against traditions which, in the main, were magically stereotyped. But where prophecy has provided a religious basis, this basis could be one of two

---

FROM chapter 9, "The Social Psychology of the World Religions," in *From Max Weber: Essays in Sociology.* Translated and edited by H. H. Gerth and C. Wright Mills. New York: Oxford University Press, [1915] © 1946. Reprinted by permission of Oxford University Press, England.

fundamental types of prophecy which we...repeatedly discuss: "exemplary" prophecy, and "emissary" [or "ethical" as Weber refers to it in the selection previous: ed.] prophecy.

Exemplary prophecy points out the path of salvation by exemplary living, usually by a contemplative and apathetic-ecstatic life. The emissary type of prophecy addresses its *demands* to the world in the name of a god. Naturally these demands are ethical; and they are often of an active ascetic character....

In the missionary [i.e., emissary, or ethical: ed.] prophecy the devout have not experienced themselves as vessels of the divine but rather as instruments of a god. This emissary prophecy has had a profound elective affinity to a special conception of God: the conception of a supra-mundane, personal, wrathful, forgiving, loving, demanding, punishing Lord of Creation. Such a conception stands in contrast to the supreme being of exemplary prophecy. As a rule, though by no means without exception, the supreme being of an exemplary prophecy is an impersonal being because, as a static state, he is accessible only by means of contemplation. The conception of an active God, held by emissary prophecy, has dominated the Iranian and Mid-Eastern religions and the Occidental religions which are derived from them. The conception of a supreme and static being, held by exemplary prophecy, has come to dominate Indian and Chinese religiosity....

"Virtuoso" and "Mass" Religiosity; "Church" and "Sect"

The empirical fact, important for us, that men are *differently qualified* in a religious way stands at the beginning of the history of religion. This fact had been dogmatized in the sharpest rationalist form in the "particularism of grace," embodied in the doctrine of predestination by the Calvinists. The sacred values that have been most cherished, the ecstatic and visionary capacities of shamans, sorcerers, ascetics, and pneumatics of all sorts, could not be attained by everyone. The possession of such faculties is a "charisma," which, to be sure, might be awakened in some but not in all. It follows from this that all intensive religiosity has a tendency toward a sort of *status stratification,* in accordance with differences in the charismatic qualifications. "Heroic" or "virtuoso" religiosity is opposed to mass religiosity. By "mass" we understand those who are religiously "unmusical"; we do not, of course, mean those who occupy an inferior position in the secular status order. In this sense, the status carriers of a virtuoso religion have been the...religious status group...who were expressly recognized in the congregation as a special "estate";...all genuine "sects"—that is, sociologically speaking, associations that accept only religiously qualified persons in their midst; and finally, monk communities all over the world.

Now, every hierocratic and official authority of a "church"—that is, a community organized by officials into an institution which bestows gifts of grace—fights principally against all virtuoso-religion and against its autonomous development. For the church, being the holder of institutionalized grace, seeks to organize the religiosity of the masses and to put its own officially monopolized and mediated sacred values in the place of the autonomous and religious status qualifications of the religious virtuosos. By its nature...the church must be "democratic" in the sense of making the sacred values generally accessible. This means that the church stands for a universalism of grace and for the ethical sufficiency of all those who are enrolled under its institutional authority....As with hierocracy, every full-grown political bureaucracy is necessarily and in a quite similar sense "democratic"—namely, in the sense of leveling and of fighting against status privileges that compete with its power.

The most varied compromises have resulted from this struggle between officialdoms and the virtuosos. These struggles have not always been official but they have always existed at least covertly. Thus, the religiosity of the Ulema [Muslim council of leaders: ed.]stood against the religiosity of the Dervishes [mystics: ed.]; the early Christian bishops against the pneumatics and heroist sectaries....The religious virtuosos saw themselves compelled to adjust their demands to the possibilities of the religiosity of everyday life in order to gain and to maintain ideal and material mass-patronage. The nature of their concessions has naturally been of primary significance for the way in which they have religiously influenced everyday life. In almost all Oriental religions, the virtuosos allowed the masses to remain stuck in magical tradition. Thus, the influence of religious virtuosos has been infinitely smaller than was the case where religion has undertaken ethically and generally to rationalize everyday life....Besides the relations between the religiosity of the virtuosos and the religion of the masses, which finally resulted from this struggle, the peculiar nature of the concrete religiosity of the virtuosos has been of decisive importance for the development of the way of life of the masses. This virtuoso religiosity has therefore also been important for the economic ethic of the respective religion. The religion of the virtuoso has been the genuinely "exemplary" and practical religion. According to the way of life his religion prescribed to the virtuoso, there have been various possibilities of establishing a rational ethic of everyday life....

Wherever the sacred values and the redemptory means of a virtuoso religion bore a contemplative...character, there has been no bridge between religion and the practical action of the workaday world. In such cases, the economy and all other action in the world has been considered religiously inferior, and no psychological motives for worldly action could be derived from the attitude cherished as the supreme value. In their innermost beings, contemplative and ecstatic religions have been rather specifically hostile to economic life.... Mystic...and ecstatic experiences...lead away from everyday life and from all expedient conduct....With such religions, a deep abyss separates the way of life of the laymen from that of the community of virtuosos. The...virtuoso is directly worshipped as a Saint, or at least laymen buy his blessing and his magical powers as a means of promoting mundane success or religious salvation. As the peasant was to the landlord, so the layman was to the Buddhist and Jainist bhikshu [monk: ed.]: ultimately, mere sources of tribute. Such tribute allowed the virtuosos to live entirely for religious salvation without themselves performing profane work, which always would endanger their salvation....For action in this world remained in principle religiously insignificant; and compared with the desire for the religious end, action lay in the very opposite direction.

In the end, the charisma of the pure "mystic" serves only himself. The charisma of the genuine magician serves others.

Things have been quite different where the religiously qualified virtuosos have combined into an ascetic sect, striving to mould life in this world according to the will of a god. To be sure, two things were necessary before this could happen in a genuine way. First, the supreme and sacred value must not be of a contemplative nature; it must not consist of a union with a supra-mundane being who, in contrast to the world, lasts forever....For these ways always lie apart from everyday life and beyond the real world and lead away from it. Second, such a religion must, so far as possible, have given up the purely magical or sacramental character of the means of grace. For these means always devalue action in this world..., and they link the decision about salvation to the success of processes which are not of a rational everyday nature.

When religious virtuosos have combined into an active asceticist sect, two aims a are completely attained: the disenchantment of the world and the blockage of the path to salvation by a flight from the world. The path to salvation is turned away from a contemplative "flight from the world" and towards an active ascetic "work in this world." If one disregards the small rationalist sects, such as are found all over the world, this has been attained only in the great church and sect organizations of Occidental and asceticist Protestantism. The quite distinct and the purely historically determined destinies of Occidental religions have co-operated in this matter. Partly, the social environment exerted an influence, above all, the environment of the stratum that was decisive for the development of such religion. Partly, however—and just as strongly—the intrinsic character of Christianity exerted an influence: the supra-mundane God....

The religious virtuoso can be placed in the world as the instrument of a God and cut off from all magical means of salvation. At the same time, it is imperative for the virtuoso that he "prove" himself before God, as being called *solely* through the ethical quality of his conduct in this world. This actually means that he "prove" himself to himself as well. No matter how much the "world" as such is religiously devalued and rejected as being creatural and a vessel of sin, yet psychologically the world is all the more affirmed as the theatre of God-willed activity in one's worldly "calling." For this inner-wordly asceticism rejects the world in the sense that it despises and taboos the values of dignity and beauty, of the beautiful frenzy and the dream, purely secular power, and the purely worldly pride of the hero. Asceticism outlawed these values as competitors of the kingdom of God. Yet precisely because of this rejection, asceticsim did not fly from the world, as did contemplation. Instead, asceticism has wished to rationalize the world ethically in accordance with with God's commandments. It has therefore remained oriented towards the world....In inner-worldly asceticism, the grace and the chosen state of the religiously qualified man prove themselves in everyday life. To be sure, they do so not in the everyday life as given, but in the methodical and rationalized routine-activities of workaday life in the service of the Lord. Rationally raised into a vocation, everyday conduct becomes the locus for proving one's state of grace. The Occidental sects of the religious virtuosos have fermented the methodical rationalization of conduct, including economic conduct. These sects have not constituted valves for the longing to escape from the senselessness of work in the world, as did the Asiastic communities of the ecstatics: contemplative...or apathetic.

The most varied transitions and combinations are found between the polar opposites of "exemplary" and "emissary" prophecy. Neither religions nor men are open books. They have been historical rather than logical or even psychological constructions without contradiction....In religious matters "consistency" has been the exception and not the rule. The ways and means of salvation are also psychologically ambiguous. The search for God of the early Christian monk as well as of the Quaker contained very strong contemplative elements. Yet the total content of their religions and, above all, their supra-mundane God of creation and their way of making sure of their states of grace again and again directed them to the course of action. On the other hand, the Buddhist monk was also active, but his activities were withdrawn from any consistent rationalization *in this world*; his quest for salvation was ultimately oriented to the flight from the "wheel" of the rebirths....

We shall not accumulate more examples here, as we wish to consider the great religions separately. In no respect can one simply integrate various world religions into a chain of types, each of them signifying a new "stage." All the great religions are historical individualities of a highly complex nature; taken all together, they exhaust only a few of the possible combinations that could conceivably be formed from the very numerous individual factors to be considered in such historical combinations.

Three Forms of Religious Authority

1. [T]he term "charisma" shall be understood to refer to an *extraordinary* quality of a person, regardless of whether this quality is actual, alleged, or presumed. "Charismatic authority," hence, shall refer to a rule over men, whether predominantly external or predominantly internal, to which the governed submit because of their belief in the extraordinary quality of the specific *person*. The magical sorcerer, the prophet, the leader of hunting and booty expeditions, the warrior chieftain, the so-called "Caesarist" ruler, and, under certain conditions, the personal head of a party are such types of rulers for their disciples, followings, enlisted troops, parties, et cetera. The legitimacy of their rule rests on the belief in and the devotion to the extraordinary, which is valued because it goes beyond the normal human qualities, and which was originally valued as supernatural. The legitimacy of charismatic rule thus rests upon the belief in magical powers, revelations and hero worship. The source of these beliefs is the "proving" of the charismatic quality through miracles, through victories and other successes, that is, through the welfare of the governed. Such beliefs and the claimed authority resting on them therefore disappear, or threaten to disappear, as soon as proof is lacking and as soon as the charismatically qualified person appears to be devoid of his magical power or forsaken by his god. Charismatic rule is not managed according to general norms, either traditional or rational, but, in principle, according to concrete revelations and inspirations, and in this sense, charismatic authority is "irrational." It is "revolutionary" in the sense of not being bound to the existing order: "It is written—but I say unto you...!"

2. "Traditionalism"... shall refer to the psychic attitude-set for the habitual workaday and to the belief in the everyday routine as an inviolable norm of conduct. Domination that rests upon this basis, that is, upon piety for what actually, allegedly, or presumably has always existed, will be called "traditionalist authority."

Patriarchalism is by far the most important type of domination the legitimacy of which rests upon tradition. Patriarchalism means the authority of the father, the husband, the senior of the house, the sib elder over the members of the household and sib; the rule of the master and patron over bondsmen, serfs, freed men; of the lord over the domestic servants and household officials; of the prince over house- and court-officials, nobles of office, clients, vassals; of the patrimonial lord and sovereign prince (*Landesvater*) over the "subjects."...

3. Throughout early history, charismatic authority, which rests upon a belief in the sanctity or the value of the extraordinary, and traditionalist (patriarchical) domination, which rests upon a belief in the sanctity of everyday routines, divided the most important authoritative relations between them. The bearers

of charisma, the oracles of prophets, or the edicts of charismatic war lords alone could integrate "new" laws into the circle of what was upheld by tradition. Just as revelation and the sword were the two extraordinary powers, so were they the two typical innovators. In typical fashion, however, both succumbed to routinization as soon as their work was done.

With the death of the prophet or the war lord the question of successorship arises. This question can be solved by . . . a selection in terms of charismatic qualification; or the question can be solved by the sacramental substantiation of charisma, the successor being designated by consecration, as is the case in hierocratic or apostolic succession; or the belief in the charismatic qualification of the charismatic leader's sib can lead to a belief in hereditary charisma, as represented by hereditary kingship and hereditary hierocracy. With these routinizations, *rules* in some form always come to govern. The prince or the hierocrat no longer rules by virtue of purely personal qualities, but by virtue of acquired or inherited qualities, or because he has been legitimized by an act of charismatic election. The process of routinization, and thus traditionalization, has set in.

Perhaps it is even more important that when the organization of authority becomes permanent, the staff supporting the charismatic ruler becomes routinized. The ruler's disciples, apostles, and followers became priests, feudal vassals and, above all, officials. The original charismatic community lived communistically off donations, alms, and the booty of war: they were thus specifically alienated from the economic order. . . . The staff derived its legitimate power in greatly varying stages of appropriation. . . . As a rule, this meant that princely prerogatives became *patrimonial* in nature. Patrimonialism can also develop from pure patriarchalism through the disintegration of the patriarchical master's strict authority. . . .

With the triumph of *formalistic* juristic rationalism, the legal type of domination appeared in the Occident. . . . Bureaucratic rule was not and is not the only variety of legal authority, but it is the purest. The modern state and municipal official, the modern Catholic priest and chaplain, the officials and employees of modern banks and of large capitalist enterprises represent, as we have already mentioned, the most important types of this domination.

The following characteristic must be considered decisive for our terminology: in legal authority, submission does not rest upon the belief and devotion to charismatically gifted persons, like prophets and heroes, or upon sacred tradition, or upon piety toward a personal lord and master. . . . Rather, submission under legal authority is based upon an impersonal bond to the generally defined and functional "duty of office." The official duty—like the corresponding right to exercise authority: the "jurisdictional competency"—is fixed by rationally established norms, by enactments, decrees, and regulations. . . .

Religious Rejections of the World and Their Directions

In this reflective essay, written as an interlude in the series of studies on "The Economic Ethic of the World's Religions," Weber applies his method of Ideal Types to compare the divergent religious ideals of "asceticism" and "mysticism."

We have had repeatedly to use the terms "asceticism" and "mysticism" as polar concepts. In order to elucidate this terminology we shall here further differentiate these terms.

In our introductory comments we contrasted, as abnegations of the world, the active asceticism that is a God-willed *action* of the devout who are God's tools, and, on the other hand, the contemplative *possession* of the holy, as found in mysticism. Mysticism intends a state of "possession," not action, and the individual is not a tool but a "vessel" of the divine. Action in the world must thus appear as endangering the absolutely irrational and other-worldly religious state. Active asceticism operates within the world; rationally active asceticism, in mastering the world, seeks to tame what is creatural and wicked through work in a worldly "vocation" (inner-worldly asceticism). Such asceticism contrasts radically with mysticism, if the latter draws the full conclusion of fleeing from the world (contemplative flight from the world).

The contrast is tempered, however, if active asceticism confines itself to keeping down and to overcoming creatural wickedness in the actor's own nature. For then it enhances the concentration on the firmly established God-willed and active redemptory accomplishments to the point of avoiding any action in the orders of the world (asceticist flight from the world). Thereby active asceticism in external bearing comes close to contemplative flight from the world.

The contrast between asceticism and mysticism is also tempered if the contemplative mystic does not draw the conclusion that he should flee from the world, but, like the inner-worldly asceticist, remain in the orders of the world (inner-worldly mysticism).

In both cases the contrast can actually disappear in practice and some combination of both forms of the quest for salvation may occur. But the contrast may continue to exist even under the veil of external similarity. For the true mystic the principle continues to hold: the creature must be silent so that God may speak.

FROM chapter 13, "Religious Rejections of the World and Their Directions," in *From Max Weber: Essays in Sociology*. Translated and edited by H. H. Gerth and C. Wright Mills. New York: Oxford University Press, [1915] © 1946. Reprinted by permission of Oxford University Press, England.

He "is" in the world and externally "accommodates" to its orders, but only in order to gain a certainty of his state of grace in opposition to the world by resisting the temptation to take the ways of the world seriously. As we can see with Lao-tse, the typical attitude of the mystic is one of a specifically broken humility, a minimization of action, a sort of religious incognito existence in the world. He proves himself *against* the world, against his action in the world. Inner-worldly asceticism, on the contrary, proves itself *through* action. To the inner-worldly asceticist the conduct of the mystic is an indolent enjoyment of self; to the mystic the conduct of the (inner worldly active) asceticist is an entanglement in the godless ways of the world combined with complacent self-righteousness. With that "blissful bigotry," usually ascribed to the typical Puritan, inner-worldly asceticism executes the positive and divine resolutions whose ultimate meaning remains concealed. Asceticism executes these resolutions as given in the God-ordained rational orders of the creatural. To the mystic, on the contrary, what matters for his salvation is only the grasping of the ultimate and completely irrational meaning through mystic experience. The forms in which both ways of conduct flee from the world can be distinguished by similar confrontations....

Directions of the Abnegation of the World

We have said that these modes of behavior, once developed into a methodical way of life, formed the nucleus of asceticism as well as of mysticism, and that they originally grew out of magical presuppositions. Magical practices were engaged in, either for the sake of awakening charismatic qualities or for the sake of preventing evil charms....

The magician has been the historical precursor of the prophet, of the exemplary as well as of the emissary prophet and savior. As a rule the prophet and the savior have legitimized themselves through the possession of a magical charisma. With them, however, this has been merely a means of securing recognition and followers for the exemplary significance, the mission, or the savior quality of their personalities. For the substance of the prophecy or of the savior's commandment is to direct a way of life to the pursuit of a sacred value. Thus understood, the prophecy or commandment means, at least relatively, to systematize and rationalize the way of life, either in particular points or totally. The latter has been the rule with all true "religions of salvation," that is, with all religions that hold out deliverance from suffering to their adherents. This is more likely to be the case the more sublimated, the more inward, and the more principled the essence of suffering is conceived. For then it is important to put the follower into a *permanent* state which makes him inwardly safe against suffering. Formulated abstractly, the rational aim of redemption religion has been to secure for the saved a holy state, and thereby a habitude that assures salvation. This takes the place of an acute and extraordinary, and thus a holy, state which is transitorily attained by means of orgies [in Weber's usage, ecstatic experiences: ed.], asceticism, or contemplation.

Now if a religious community emerges in the wake of a prophecy or of the propaganda of a savior, the control of regular conduct first falls into the hands of the charismatically qualified successors, pupils, disciples of the prophet or of the savior. Later, under certain very regularly recurrent conditions..., this task falls into the hands of a priestly, hereditary, or official hierocracy. Yet, as a rule, the prophet or the savior personally has stood in opposition to the traditional hierocratic powers of magicians or of priests. He has set his personal charisma against their dignity consecrated by tradition in order to break their power or force them to his service.

~

The Economic Sphere

The tension between brotherly religion and the world has been most obvious in the economic sphere....

The dependence of religious communities themselves, and of their propaganda and maintenance, upon economic means, and their accommodation to cultural needs and the everyday interests of the masses, have compelled them to enter compromises of which the history of the interdiction of interests is but one example. Yet, ultimately no genuine religion of salvation has overcome the tension between their religiosity and a rational economy.

Externally, the ethic of religious virtuosos has touched this tense relation in the most radical fashion: by rejecting the possession of economic goods. The ascetic monk has fled from the world by denying himself individual property; his existence has rested entirely upon his own work; and, above all, his needs have been correspondingly restricted to what was absolutely indispensable. The paradox of all rational asceticism, which in an identical manner has made monks in all ages stumble, is that rational asceticism itself has created the very wealth it rejected. Temples and monasteries have everywhere become the very *loci* of rational economies.

Contemplative seclusion as a principle has only been able to establish the rule that the propertyless monk must enjoy only what nature and men voluntarily offer: berries, roots, and free alms. Labor was something which distracted the monk from concentration upon the contemplated value of salvation. Yet even contemplative seclusion has made its compromises by establishing districts for begging, as in India.

There have been only two consistent avenues for escaping the tension between religion and the economic world in a principled and *inward* manner: First, the paradox of the Puritan ethic of "vocation." As a religion of virtuosos, Puritanism renounced the universalism of love, and rationally routinized all work in this world into serving God's will and testing one's state of grace....

Mysticism is the other consistent avenue by which the tension between economics and religion has been escaped. This way is represented quite purely in the mystic's "benevolence," which does not at all enquire into the man to whom and for whom it sacrifices. Ultimately, mysticism is not interested in his person. Once and for all, the benevolent mystic gives his shirt when he is asked for his coat, by anybody who accidentally happens to come his way—and merely because he happens to come his way.

9

Mircea Eliade: Religion as Response to the Sacred

Both Otto and James offered early resistance to reductionism, mainly by anchoring the claims of religion in the emotions, in personal experiences that of themselves certify their "truth," or value. In their view, the religious heart has reasons which the reasoning of others cannot explain away. In his quite different way, Max Weber came to a similar verdict, finding religious ideas and behaviors as much an agent in shaping society as society is in shaping religion. But none of these dissents was as assertive as others still to come. In the years before and during World War II, new challenges to the ways of Freud, Durkheim, and Marx were coming into place, although their full impact would not be felt until the postwar era. The most emphatic of these new voices appeared from an unexpected place—and person. Mircea Eliade (1907–1986), a humanist scholar born and educated in Romania, brought a revisionist perspective out of Central Europe into the discussion. His thinking was informed less by the new social sciences than by his own wide-ranging comparative study of religions—and a personal sensibility shaped by both the Orthodox Christianity of his homeland and the spirituality of India, into which he apprenticed himself early in life.

Eliade was a man of multiple talents and diverse intellectual engagements—a truly multicultural scholar, fluent in several European languages and well versed in more than a few others. Born in Bucharest in 1907, he had been a retiring, bookish child, who developed early interests in mythology, literature, and the arts. He himself wrote so assiduously—fiction, opinions, book reviews, magazine and newspaper pieces—that already at the age of eighteen he could celebrate with friends the appearance of his one hundredth publication. After studies at the University of Bucharest and in Italy, he traveled to India, where he was deeply affected by the devout sensibility—what he called the "archaic," or "cosmic" religion—of its rural peasants, who found an eternal meaning in nature's unbroken cycle of life, death, and renewal. Returning to Romania, he continued his comparative studies, later acquiring a university post in Paris, where his international stature as a historian and theorist of religions steadily grew. In the prime of his career, he crossed the Atlantic and settled at the University of Chicago, where he took a prestigious Chair in its Divinity School. From that post, he tutored a full generation of scholars, now active across the spectrum of American universities and colleges.

Eliade affirmed two principles as basic to all his inquiries. The first— directly opposed to reductionist theory—was what he called the independence, or "autonomy" of religion. Religious activity, he insisted, must be grasped "at its own level," not explained as a mere by-product of social, psychological, or other conditions. Such thinking, he contended, misreads religion fundamentally by missing "the one unique and irreducible element in it—the element of the sacred." The second principle, which pertained to scholarly method, joined history with what can be best called "phenomenology." Eliade recognized that much of the study of religion is simply the study of history—inquiry into past human events, ideas, and achievements. But he stressed also that history needs a complement in phenomenology (from the Greek *phenomenon,* an "appearance"), which is the effort to place these human activities within certain general forms, or fixed patterns, that can be discerned by the trained observer. Like the axioms of geometry, and similar to Weber's "ideal types," these phenomenological categories can be applied to the actions, institutions, or ideas of any culture or tradition, enabling us to compare, contrast, connect, or distinguish them across all times and places.

Chief among these patterns is the set of paired opposites that define the Sacred and the Profane. This is of course the same formula we saw Emile Durkheim employ to distinguish social concerns from private and personal ones. Eliade endorses it, but chooses to employ it quite differently. Archaic peoples, he says, define the sacred as the sphere not of society, but of the supernatural—the realm beyond earthly life, full of changeless perfection, order, power, and beauty: the dwelling place of the ancestors and the gods. The profane, by contrast, is not just the personal, but the entire changeable, chaotic, often dreary realm of ordinary human earthly life, stained by struggle and suffering and bordered by death. One of Eliade's most well-known books in English, *The Sacred and the Profane* (1959), seeks to show how this cosmic contrast between the sacred and the profane deeply engages the archaic mind. This book furnishes the first of the selections below, which explains how, in early and traditional cultures, nearly every important endeavor is governed by precepts, or modeled on patterns, which derive from the sacred—the realm of the divine, the home of the gods. The center of a tribal community, for example, often may be marked with a pole, or tree, that rises skyward, linking the earthly community to heaven and the gods. Such a pole more than marks a place at the village center; it also serves as a symbol of the *axis mundi* (in Latin: "axle of the world"), a fixed point around which the entire cosmos is ordered.

Because the realm of the sacred is so utterly unlike that of the profane world, it can only be described indirectly, through the suggestive effect of images and symbols. They are the language of religion. In *Patterns in Comparative Religion,* one of two important works he published in 1949, Eliade makes it his mission to expound and interpret the symbolic world of archaic peoples. He considers such things as the symbolism of sky and storm gods and of sun and savior divinities, the imagery of the moon and the waters, the themes of renewal in the widespread mythologies of the world, and the great variety of other meanings that are invested by cultures of the most varied kinds in natural objects and processes seen as symbolic expressions of the sacred. The selection from *Patterns* provided here illustrates in detail how Eliade proceeds with one of his analyses, exploring the ways of the religious imagination as it seeks to convey the sacred through the profane.

Eliade's other signature work is *The Myth of the Eternal Return: Or, Cosmos and History,* also published in 1949. This study centers as well on the idea of the sacred, but more particularly as it affects archaic attitudes toward time and history. In archaic cultures, he argues, life in history is seen as a kind of "fall" from perfection—a profound loss, or separation, from the gods. People accordingly live with a deep "nostalgia for Paradise," a longing to abolish ordinary history—all of history—and make an eternal return to the beginning of time, where they can "live in the world as it came from the Creator's hands, fresh, pure, and strong." Among others, Buddhist and Hindu doctrines of rebirth show that this sense of loss and longing was spread as widely in the great civilizations of East as it was in the classical civilizations of the West and tribal cultures across the globe. It was a sentiment one could even describe as universal, were it not for the unusual case of the ancient Hebrews. For in their sacred Pentateuch and in the oracles of their monotheistic prophets—Amos, Isaiah, and others—they articulated the theology of a sole, sovereign god who had chosen them to carry out his purposes *in* history, rather than to escape from it. This new religious vision, which passed also into Christianity, effected a decisive turn away from the archaic belief in the myth of the eternal return. For Jews, meaning was to be found in the plan God unfolds for, and within, historical time, not in the human longing to withdraw from it. The appearance of this new, distinctively Jewish-Christian sensibility formed what may be called the first—but not the only—great transformation in the religious history of humanity. For in its wake—and especially within the very civilization created by Judaism and Christianity, the modern West—has come a second revolution, now underway. That is the secular rejection of all religion, a revolt, largely among modern intellectual elites, which contends that we no longer have need of the sacred at all, either within history or outside of it. Such thinking holds that we create our own meaning, without sacred archetypes; it insists that we live exclusively in historical time—in the profane world—with no prospect of eternal return. Throughout his career, Eliade remained uneasy about this new nonreligious frame of mind, and unsure whether humanity really can live meaningfully within it. He was deeply suspicious of purely secular ideologies—communism, nationalism, capitalism, and fascism. And he was keen to notice how in secular society, the avenues of film and fiction, art and literature, sports, games, and entertainment all offer "nostalgias" of their own as escapes from the numbing, dreary routines of modern life. The passage provided here from *The Myth of the Eternal Return* exhibits this other face of Eliade, the historian of religions as contemporary cultural critic. In the inner reaches of his own soul, he resonated deeply with the archaic mind and its hope of eternal return. The modern secular sensibility troubled him, and to the end of his life he persisted in deep doubt that a civilization wholly without religion could promise its people a framework of values any more fulfilling than those that since time immemorial guided archaic cultures to a willing and worshipful embrace of the sacred.

The Sacred and the Profane

In this short book, designed to introduce the key elements of his approach, Eliade describes the mentality of archaic cultures and draws extensively on his comparative study of world religions for examples and illustrations.

The extraordinary interest aroused all over the world by Rudolf Otto's *Das Heilige* (The Sacred), published in 1917, still persists. Its success was certainly due to the author's new and original point of view. Instead of studying the *ideas* of God and religion, Otto undertook to analyze the modalities of *the religious experience*. Gifted with great psychological subtlety, and thoroughly

EXCERPT FROM *The Sacred and the Profane: The Nature of Religion* by Mircea Eliade, copyright © 1957 by Rowohlt Taschenbuch Verlag GmbH. English translation copyright © 1959 and renewed 1987 by Harcourt, Inc. Reprinted by permission of the publisher.

prepared by his twofold training as theologian and historian of religions, he succeeded in determining the content and specific characteristics of religious experience. Passing over the rational and speculative side of religion, he concentrated chiefly on its irrational aspect. For Otto had read Luther and had understood what the "living God" meant to a believer. It was not the God of the philosophers—of Erasmus, for example; it was not an idea, an abstract notion, a mere moral allegory. It was a terrible *power,* manifested in the divine wrath.

In *Das Heilige* Otto sets himself to discover the characteristics of this frightening and irrational experience. He finds the *feeling of terror* before the sacred, before the awe-inspiring mystery (*mysterium tremendum*), the majesty (*majestas*) that emanates an overwhelming superiority of power; he finds *religious fear* before the fascinating mystery (*mysterium fascinans*) in which perfect fullness of being flowers. Otto characterizes all these experiences as numinous (from Latin *numen,* god), for they are induced by the revelation of an aspect of divine power. The numinous presents itself as something "wholly other" (*ganz andere*), something basically and totally different. It is like nothing human or cosmic; confronted with it, man senses his profound nothingness, feels that he is only a creature, or, in the words in which Abraham addressed the Lord "but dust and ashes" (Genesis, 18, 27).

The sacred always manifests itself as a reality of a wholly different order from "natural" realities. It is true that language naively expresses the *tremendum,* or the *majestas,* or the *mysterium fascinans* by terms borrowed from the world of nature or from man's secular mental life. But we know that this analogical terminology is due precisely to human inability to express the *ganz andere*; all that goes beyond man's natural experience, language is reduced to suggesting by terms taken from that experience.

After forty years, Otto's analyses have not lost their value; readers of this book will profit by reading and reflecting on them. But in the following pages we adopt a different perspective. We propose to present the phenomenon of the sacred in all its complexity, and not only in so far as it is *irrational.* What will concern us is not the relation between the rational and the nonrational elements of religion but the *sacred in its entirety.* The first possible definition of the sacred is that it is *the opposite of the profane.* The aim of the following pages is to illustrate and define this opposition between sacred and profane.

When the Sacred Manifests Itself

Man becomes aware of the sacred because it manifests itself, shows itself, as something wholly different from the profane. To designate the *act of manifestation* of the sacred, we have proposed the term *hierophany.* It is a fitting term, because it does not imply anything further; it expresses no more than is implicit in its etymological content, *i.e.*, that *something sacred shows itself to us*. It could be said that the history of religions—from the most primitive to the most highly developed—is constituted by a great number of hierophanies, by manifestations of sacred realities. From the most elementary hierophany— *e.g.*, manifestation of the sacred in some ordinary object, a stone or a tree—to the supreme hierophany (which, for a Christian, is the incarnation of God in Jesus Christ) there is no solution of continuity. In each case we are confronted by the same mysterious act—the manifestation of something of a wholly different order, a reality that does not belong to our world, in objects that are an integral part of our natural "profane" world.

The modern Occidental experiences a certain uneasiness before many manifestations of the sacred. He finds it difficult to accept the fact that, for many human beings, the sacred can be manifested in stones or trees, for example. But as we shall soon see, what is involved is not a veneration of the stone in itself, a cult of the tree in itself. The sacred tree, the sacred stone are not adored as stone or tree; they are worshipped precisely because they are *hierophanies*, because they show something that is no longer stone or tree but the sacred, the *ganz andere*.

It is impossible to overemphasize the paradox represented by every hierophany, even the most elementary. By manifesting the sacred, any object becomes *something else,* yet it continues to remain *itself,* for it continues to participate in its surrounding cosmic milieu. A *sacred* stone remains a *stone*; apparently (or, more precisely, from the profane point of view), nothing distinguishes it from all other stones. But for those to whom a stone reveals itself as sacred, its immediate reality is transmuted into a supernatural reality. In other words, for those who have a religious experience all nature is capable of revealing itself as cosmic sacrality. The cosmos in its entirety can become a hierophany.

The man of the archaic societies tends to live as much as possible *in* the sacred or in proximity to consecrated objects. The tendency is perfectly understandable, because, for primitives as for the man of all pre-modern societies, the *sacred* is equivalent to a *power,* and in the last analysis, to *reality.* The sacred is saturated with being. Sacred power means reality and at the same time enduringness and efficacity. The polarity sacred–profane is often expressed as an opposition between *real* and *unreal* or pseudoreal. (Naturally, we must not expect to find the archaic languages in possession of this philosophical terminology, *real-unreal,* etc.; but we find the *thing.*) Thus it is easy to understand that religious man deeply desires *to be,* to participate in *reality,* to be saturated with power.

Our chief concern in the following pages will be to elucidate this subject— to show in what ways religious man attempts to remain as long as possible in a sacred universe, and hence what his total experience of life proves to be in comparison with the experience of the man without religious feeling, of the man who lives, or wishes to live, in a desacralized world. It should be said at once that the *completely* profane world, the wholly descralized cosmos, is a recent discovery in the history of the human spirit. It does not devolve upon us to show by what historical processes and as the result of what changes in spiritual attitudes and behavior modern man has desacralized his world and assumed a profane existence. For our purpose it is enough to observe that desacralization pervades the entire experience of the nonreligious man of modern societies and that, in consequence, he finds it increasingly difficult to rediscover the existential dimensions of religious man in the archaic societies.

Two Modes of Being in the World

The abyss that divides the two modalities of experience—sacred and profane—will be apparent when we come to describe sacred space and the ritual building of the human habitation, or the varieties of the religious experience of time, or the relations of religious man to nature and the world of tools, or the consecration of human life itself, the sacrality with which man's vital functions (food, sex, work and so on) can be charged. Simply calling to mind what the city or the house, nature, tools, or work have become for modern and nonreligious man will show with the utmost vividness all that distinguishes such a man from a man belonging to any archaic society, or even from a peasant of Christian Europe. For modern consciousness, a physiological act—eating, sex, and so on—is in sum only an organic phenomenon.... But for the primitive, such an act is never simply physiological; it is, or can become, a sacrament, that is, a communion with the sacred.

The reader will very soon realize that *sacred* and *profane* are two modes of being in the world, two existential situations assumed by man in the course of his history. These modes of being in the world are not of concern only to the history of religions or to sociology; they are not the object only of historical, sociological, or ethnological study. In the last analysis, the *sacred* and *profane* modes of being depend upon the different positions that man has conquered in the cosmos; hence they are of concern both to the philosopher and to anyone seeking to discover the possible dimensions of human existence.

It is for this reason that, though he is a historian of religions, the author of this book proposes not to confine himself only to the perspective of his particular science. The man of the traditional societies is admittedly a *homo religiosus,* but his behavior forms part of the general behavior of mankind and hence is of concern to philosophical anthropology, to phenomenology, to psychology.

The better to bring out the specific characteristics of life in a world capable of becoming sacred, I shall not hesitate to cite examples from many religions belonging to different periods and cultures. Nothing can take the place of the example, the concrete fact. It would be useless to discuss the structure of sacred space without showing, by particular examples, how such a space is constructed and why it becomes qualitatively different from the profane space by which it is surrounded. I shall select such examples from among the Mesopotamians, the Indians, the Chinese, the Kwakiutl and other primitive peoples. From the historico-cultural point of view, such a juxtaposition of religious data pertaining to peoples so far removed in time and space is not without some danger. For there is always the risk of falling back into the errors of the nineteenth century and, particularly, of believing with Tylor or Frazer that the reaction of the human mind to natural phenomena is uniform. But the progress accomplished in cultural ethnology and in the history of religions has shown that this is not always true, that man's reactions to nature are often conditioned by his culture and hence, finally, by history.

But the important thing for our purpose is to bring out the specific characteristics of the religious experience, rather than to show its numerous variations and the differences caused by history. It is somewhat as if, in order to obtain a better grasp of the poetic phenomenon, we should have recourse to a mass of heterogeneous examples, and, side by side with Homer and Dante, quote Hindu, Chinese, and Mexican poems; that is, should take into consideration not only poetics possessing a historical common denominator (Homer, Vergil, Dante) but also creations that are dependent upon other aesthetics. From the point of view of literary history, such juxtapositions are to be viewed with suspicion; but they are valid if our object is to describe the poetic phenomenon as such, if we propose to show the essential difference between poetic language and the utilitarian language of everyday life.

The Sacred and History

Our primary concern is to present the specific dimensions of religious experience, to bring out the differences between it and profane experience of the world. I shall not dwell on the variations that religious experience of the world has undergone in the course of time. It is obvious, for example, that the symbolisms and cults of Mother Earth, of human and agricultural fertility, of the sacrality of woman, and the like, could not develop and constitute a complex religious system except through discovery of agriculture; it is equally obvious that a preagricultural society, devoted to hunting, could not feel the sacrality of Mother Earth in the same way or with the same intensity. Hence there are differences in religious experience explained by differences in economy, culture, and social organization—in short, by history. Nevertheless, between the nomadic hunters and the sedentary cultivators there is a similarity in behavior that seems to us infinitely more important than their differences: *both live in a sacralized cosmos,* both share in a cosmic sacrality manifested equally in the animal world and in the vegetable world. We need only compare their existential situations with that of a man of the modern societies, *living in a desacralized cosmos,* and we shall immediately be aware of all that separates him from them. At the same time we realize the validity of comparisons between religious facts pertaining to different cultures; all these facts arise from a single type of behavior, that of *homo religiosus....*

Sacred Space and Making the World Sacred

Homogeneity of Space and Heirophany

For religious man, space is not homogeneous; he experiences interruptions, breaks in it; some parts of space are qualitatively different from others. "Draw not nigh hither," says the Lord to Moses; "put off thy shoes from off thy feet, for the place whereon thou standest is holy ground" (Exodus, 3, 5). There is, then, a sacred space, and hence a strong, significant space; there are other spaces that are not sacred and so are without structure or consistency, amorphous. Nor is this all. For religious man, this spatial nonhomogeneity finds expression in the experience of an opposition between space that is sacred—the only *real* and *real-ly* existing space—and all other space, the formless expanse surrounding it.

It must be said at once that the religious experience of the nonhomogeneity of space is a primordial experience, homologizable to [able to be identified with: ed.] a founding of the world. It is not a matter of theoretical speculation, but of a primary religious experience that precedes all reflection on the world. For it is the break effected in space that allows the world to be constituted, because it reveals the fixed point, the central axis for all future orientation. When the sacred manifests itself in any hierophany, ... there is also revelation of an absolute reality, opposed to the nonreality of the vast surrounding expanse. The manifestation of the sacred ontologically founds the world. In the homogeneous and infinite expanse, in which no point of reference is possible and hence no *orientation* can be established, the hierophany reveals an absolute fixed point, a center.

So it is clear to what a degree the discovery—that is, the revelation—of a sacred space possesses existential value for religious man; for nothing can begin, nothing can be *done,* without a previous orientation—and any orientation implies acquiring a fixed point. It is for this reason that religious man has always sought to fix his abode at the "center of the world." *If the world is to be lived in,* it must be *founded*—and no world can come to birth in the chaos of the homogeneity and relativity of profane space. The discovery or projection of a fixed point—the center—is equivalent to the creation of the world....

For profane experience, on the contrary, space is homogeneous and neutral; no break qualitatively differentiates the various parts of its mass. Geometrical space can be cut and delimited in any direction; but no qualitative differentiation and, hence, no orientation are given by virtue of its inherent structure. We need only remember how a classical geometrician defines space....

[F]or the moment we will...confine ourselves to comparing the two experiences in question—that of sacred space and that of profane space....Revelation of a sacred space makes it possible to obtain a fixed point and hence to acquire orientation in the chaos of homogeneity, to "found the world" and to live in a real sense. The profane experience, on the contrary, maintains the homogeneity and hence the relativity of space. No *true* orientation is now possible, for the fixed point no longer enjoys a unique ontological status; it appears and disappears in accordance with the needs of the day. Properly speaking, there is no longer any world, there are only fragments of a shattered universe, an amorphous mass consisting of an infinite number of more or less neutral places in which man moves, governed and driven by the obligations of an existence incorporated into an industrial society.

Yet this experience of profane space still includes values that to some extent recall the nonhomogeneity peculiar to the religious experiences of space. There are, for example, privileged places, qualitatively different from all others—a man's birthplace, or the scenes of his first love, or certain places in the first foreign city he visited in youth. Even for the most frankly nonreligious man, all these places still retain an exceptional, a unique quality; they are the "holy places" of his private universe, as if it were in such spots that he had received the revelation of a reality *other* than that in which he participates through his ordinary daily life.

This example of crypto-religious behavior on profane man's part is worth noting. In the course of this book we shall encounter other examples of this sort of degradation and desacralization of religious values and forms of behavior. Their deeper significance will become apparent later.

Theophanies and Signs

To exemplify the nonhomogeneity of space as experienced by nonreligious man, we may turn to any religion. We will choose an example that is accessible to everyone—a church in a modern city. For a believer, the church shares in a different space from the street in which it stands. The door that opens on the interior of the church actually signifies a solution of continuity. The threshold that separates the two spaces also indicates the distance between two modes of being, the profane and the religious. The threshold is the limit, the boundary, the frontier that distinguishes and opposes two worlds—and at the same time the paradoxical place where those worlds communicate, where passage from the profane to the sacred world becomes possible.

A similar ritual function falls to the threshold of the human habitation, and it is for this reason that the threshold is an object of great importance. Numerous rites accompany passing the domestic threshold—a bow, a prostration, a pious touch of the hand, and so on. The threshold has its guardians—gods and spirits who forbid entrance both to human enemies and to demons and the powers of pestilence. It is on the threshold that sacrifices to the guardian divinities are offered....

What has been said will make it clear why the church shares in an entirely different space from the buildings that surround it. Within the sacred precincts the profane world is transcended. On the most archaic levels of culture this possibility of transcendence is expressed by various *images of an opening*; here, in the sacred enclosure, communication with the gods is made possible; hence there must be a door to the world above, by which the gods can descend to earth and man can symbolically ascend to heaven. We shall soon see that this was the case in many religions; properly speaking, the temple constitutes an opening in the upward direction and ensures communication with the world of the gods.

Every sacred space implies a hierophany, an irruption of the sacred that results in detaching a territory from the surrounding cosmic milieu and making it qualitatively different. When Jacob in his dream at Haran saw a ladder reaching to heaven, with angels ascending and descending on it, and heard the Lord speaking from above it, saying: "I am the Lord God of Abraham," he awoke and was afraid and cried out: "How dreadful is this place: this is none other but the house of God, and this is the gate of heaven." And he took the stone that had been his pillow, and set it up as a monument, and poured oil on the top of it. He called the place Beth-el, that is, house of God (Genesis, 28, 12–19). The symbolism implicit in the expression "gate of heaven" is rich and complex; the theophany that occurs in a place consecrates it by the very fact that it makes it open above—that is, in communication with heaven, the paradoxical point of passage from one mode of being to another. We shall soon see even clearer examples—sanctuaries that are "doors of the gods" and hence places of passage between heaven and earth.

Often there is no need for a theophany or hierophany properly speaking; some *sign* suffices to indicate the sacredness of a place. "According to the legend, the *marabout* [warrior-saint: ed.] who founded El-Hamel at the end of the sixteenth century stopped to spend the night near a spring and planted his stick in the ground. The next morning, when he went for it to resume his journey, he found that it had taken root and that buds had sprouted on it. He considered this a sign of God's will and settled in that place." In such cases the *sign*, fraught with religious meaning, introduces an absolute element and puts an end to relativity and confusion. *Something* that does not belong to this world has manifested itself apodictically and in so doing has indicated an orientation or determined a course of conduct....

These...examples have shown the different means by which religious man receives the revelation of a sacred place. In each case the hierophany has annulled the homogeneity of space and revealed a fixed point. But since religious man cannot live except in an atmosphere impregnated with the sacred, we must expect to find a large number of techniques for consecrating space. As we saw, the sacred is pre-eminently the *real*, at once power, efficacity, the source of life and fecundity. Religious man's desire to live *in the sacred* is in fact equivalent to his desire to take up his abode in objective reality, not to let himself be paralyzed by the never-ceasing relativity of purely subjective experiences, to live in a real and effective world, and not in an illusion....

Chaos and Cosmos

One of the outstanding characteristics of traditional societies is the opposition that they assume between their inhabited territory and the unknown and indeterminate space that surrounds it.... [I]f every inhabited territory is a cosmos, this is precisely because it was first consecrated, because, in one way or another, it is the work of the gods or is in communication with the world of the gods....

All this appears very clearly from the Vedic ritual for taking possession of a territory; possession becomes legally valid through the erection of a fire altar consecrated to Agni. "One says that one is installed when one has built a fire altar [*garhapatya*] and all those who build the fire altar are legally established" (*Shatapatha Brahmana*, VII, 1, 1, 1–4). By the erection of a fire altar Agni is made present, and communication with the world of the gods is ensured; the space of the altar becomes a sacred space. But the meaning of the ritual is far more complex, and if we consider all of its ramifications we shall understand why consecrating a territory is equivalent to making it a cosmos, to *cosmicizing* it. For, in fact, the erection of an altar to Agni is nothing but the reproduction—on the microcosmic scale—of the Creation.... The water in which the clay is mixed is assimilated to the primordial water; the clay that forms the base of the altar symbolizes the earth; the lateral walls represent the atmosphere, and so on. And the building of the altar is accompanied by songs that proclaim which cosmic region has just been created (*Shatapatha Brahmana* I, 9, 2, 29, etc.). Hence the erection of a fire altar—which alone validates taking possession of a new territory—is equivalent to a cosmogony.

An unknown, foreign, and unoccupied territory (which often means, "unoccupied by our people") still shares in the fluid and larval modality of chaos. By occupying it and, above all, by settling in it, man symbolically transforms it into a cosmos through a ritual repetition of the cosmogony. What is to become "our world" must first be "created," and every creation has a paradigmatic model—the creation of the universe by the gods. When the Scandinavian colonists took possession of Iceland (*land-nama*) and cleared it, they regarded the enterprise neither as an original undertaking nor as human and profane work. For them, their labor was only repetition of a primordial act, the transformation of chaos into cosmos by the divine act of creation. When they tilled the desert soil, they were in fact repeating the act of the gods who had organized chaos by giving it a structure, forms, and norms....

Consecration of Place = Repetition of the Cosmogony

It must be understood that the cosmicization of unknown territories is always a consecration; to organize a space is to repeat the paradigmatic work of the gods.... According to the traditions of an [Australian: ed.] Arunta tribe, the Achilpa, in mythical times the divine being Numbakula cosmicized their future territory, created their Ancestor, and established their institutions. From the trunk of a gum tree Numbakula fashioned the sacred pole (*kauwa-auwa*) and, after anointing it with blood, climbed it and disappeared into the sky. This pole represents a cosmic axis, for it is around the sacred pole that territory becomes habitable, hence is transformed into a world. The sacred pole consequently plays an important role ritually. During their wanderings the Achilpa always carry it with them and choose the direction they are to take by the direction toward which it bends. This allows them, while being continually on the move, to be always in "their world" and, at the same time, in communication with the sky into which Numbakula vanished.

For the pole to be broken denotes catastrophe; it is like "the end of the world," reversion to chaos. Spencer and Gillen report that once, when the pole was broken, the entire clan were in consternation; they wandered about aimlessly for a time, and finally lay down on the ground together and waited for death to overtake them.

This example admirably illustrates both the cosmological function of the sacred pole and its soteriological role. For on the one hand the *kauwa-auwa* reproduces the pole that Numbakula used to cosmicize the world, and on the other the Achilpa believed it to be the means by which they can communicate with the sky realm. Now, human existence is possible only by virtue of this permanent communication with the sky. The world of the Achilpa really becomes *their* world only in proportion as it reproduces the cosmos organized and sanctified by Numbakula. Life is not possible without an opening toward the transcendent; in other words, human beings cannot live in chaos. Once contact with the transcendent is lost, existence in the world ceases to be possible—and the Achilpa let themselves die....

The sacred pole of the Achilpa supports *their* world and ensures communication with the sky. Here we have the prototype of a cosmological image that has been very widely disseminated—the cosmic pillars that support heaven and at the same time open the road to the world of the gods....

The Center of the World

The cry of the Kwakiutl neophyte, "I am at the Center of the World!" at once reveals one of the deepest meanings of sacred space. Where the break-through from plane to plane has been effected by a hierophany, there too an opening has been made, either upward (the divine world) or downward (the underworld, the world of the dead). The three cosmic levels—earth, heaven, underworld—have been put in communication. As we just saw, this communication is sometimes expressed through the image of a universal pillar, *axis mundi,* which at once connects and supports heaven and earth and whose base is fixed in the world below (the infernal regions). Such a cosmic pillar can be only at the very center of the universe, for the whole of the habitable world extends around it. Here, then, we have a sequence of religious conceptions and cosmological images that are inseparably connected and form a system that may be called the "system of the world" prevalent in traditional societies: (*a*) a sacred place constitutes a break in the homogeneity of space; (*b*) this break is symbolized by an opening by which passage from one cosmic region to another is made possible (from heaven to earth and vice versa; from earth to the underworld); (*c*) communication with heaven is expressed by one or another of certain images, all of which refer to the *axis mundi:* pillar (cf. the *universalis columna*), ladder (cf. Jacob's ladder), mountain, tree, vine, etc.; (*d*) around this cosmic axis lies the world (= our world), hence the axis is located "in the middle," at the "naval of the earth"; it is the Center of the World.

Many different myths, rites, and beliefs are derived from this traditional "system of the world." They cannot all be mentioned here. Rather, we shall confine ourselves to a few examples, taken from various civilizations and particularly suited to demonstrate the role of sacred space in the life of traditional societies. Whether that space appears in the form of sacred precinct, a ceremonial house, a city, a world, we everywhere find the symbolism of the Center of the World; and it is this symbolism which, in the majority of cases, explains religious behavior in respect to the space in which one lives....

We shall begin with an example that has the advantage of immediately showing not only the consistency but also the complexity of this type of symbolism—the cosmic mountain.... [I]n a number of cultures we do in fact hear of such mountains, real or mythical, situated at the center of the world; examples are Meru in India, Haraberezaiti in Iran, the mythical "Mount of the Lands" in Mesopotamia, Gerizim in Palestine—which, moreover, was called the "naval of the earth." Since the sacred mountain is an *axis mundi* connecting earth with heaven, it in a sense touches heaven and hence marks the highest point in the world; consequently the territory that surrounds it, and that constitutes "our world," is held to be the highest among countries....

This same symbolism of the center explains other series of cosmological images and religious beliefs. Among these the most important are: (*a*) holy sites and sanctuaries are believed to be situated at the center of the world; (*b*) temples are replicas of the cosmic mountain and hence constitute the pre-eminent "link" between earth and heaven; (*c*) the foundations of temples descend deep into the lower regions. A few examples will suffice. After citing them, we shall attempt to integrate all these various aspects of the same symbolism; the remarkable consistency of these traditional conceptions of the world will then appear with greater clarity.

The capital of the perfect Chinese sovereign is located at the center of the world; there, on a day of the summer solstice, the gnomon must cast no shadow. It is striking that the same symbolism is found in regard to the Temple of Jerusalem; the rock on which it was built was the navel of the earth. The Icelandic pilgrim, Nicholas of Thverva, who visited Jerusalem in the twelfth century, wrote of the Holy Sepulcher: "The Center of the World is there; there, on the day of the summer solstice, the light of the Sun falls perpendicularly from Heaven." The same conception occurs in Iran; the Iranian land (*Airyanam Vaejah*) is the center and heart of the world. Just as the heart lies at the center of the body, "the land of Iran is more precious than all other countries because it is set at the middle of the world." This is why Shiz, the "Jerusalem" of the Iranians (for it lay at the center of the world) was held to be the original site of the royal power and, at the same time, the birthplace of Zarathustra....

"Our World" is Always Situated at the Center

...To us, it seems an inescapable conclusion that *the religious man sought to live as near as possible to the Center of the World*. He knew that his country lay at the midpoint of the earth; he knew too that his city constituted the navel of the universe, and, above all, that the temple or the palace were veritably Centers of the World. But he also wanted his own house to be at the Center and to be an *imago mundi*. And, in fact, as we shall see, houses are held to be at the Center of the World and, on the microcosmic scale, to reproduce the universe. In other words, the man of traditional societies could only live in a space opening upward, where the break in plane was symbolically assured and hence communication with the *other world,* the transcendental world, was ritually possible. Of course the sanctuary—the Center par excellence—was there, close to him, in the city, and he could be sure of communicating with the world of the gods simply by entering the temple. But he felt the need to live at the Center *always*—like the Achilpa, who, as we saw, always carried the sacred pole, the *axis mundi,* with them, so that they should never be far from the Center and should remain in communication with the supraterrestrial world. In short, whatever the dimensions of the space with which he is familiar and in which he regards himself as situated—his country, his city, his village, his house—religious man feels the need always to exist in a total and organized world, in a cosmos....

It follows that *every construction or fabrication has the cosmogony as paradigmatic model.* The creation of the world becomes the archetype of every creative human gesture, whatever its plane of reference may be. We have already seen that settling in a territory reiterates the cosmogony. Now that the cosmogonic value of the Center has become clear, we can still better understand why every human establishment repeats the creation of the world from a central point (the navel). Just as the universe unfolds from a center and stretches out toward the four cardinal points, the village comes into existence around an intersection. In Bali, as in some parts of Asia, when a new village is to be built the people look for a natural intersection, where two roads cross at right angles. A square constructed from a central point is an *imago mundi*. The division of the village into four sections—which incidentally implies a similar division of the community—corresponds to the division of the universe into four horizons. A space is often left empty in the middle of the village; there the ceremonial house will later be built, with its roof symbolically representing heaven (in some cases, heaven is indicated by the top of a tree or by the image of a mountain). At the other end of the same perpendicular axis lies the world of the dead, symbolized by certain animals (snake, crocodile, etc.) or by ideograms expressing darkness....

We are not surprised to find a similar concept in ancient Italy, and among the ancient Germans. In short, the underlying idea is both archaic and widely disseminated: from a center, the four horizons are projected in the four cardinal directions.... Similar ideas have been shown to explain the structure of Germanic villages and towns. In extremely varied cultural contexts, we constantly find the same cosmological schema and the same ritual scenario: *settling in a territory is equivalent to founding a world.*

Patterns in Comparative Religion

Among the many systems of symbols explored in this work, Eliade centers in these passages on the elaborate set of sacred associations connected with the moon in its multiple phases and aspects.

The Moon and Its Mystique

The Moon and Time

The sun is always the same, always itself, never in any sense "becoming." The moon, on the other hand, is a body which waxes, wanes and disappears, a body whose existence is subject to the universal law of becoming, of birth and death. The moon, like man, has a career involving tragedy, for its failing, like man's, ends in death. For three nights the starry sky is without a moon. But this "death" is followed by a rebirth: the "new moon." ...

This perpetual return to its beginnings, and this ever-recurring cycle make the moon *the* heavenly body above all others concerned with the rhythms of life. It is not surprising, then, that it governs all those spheres of nature that fall under the law of recurring cycles: waters, rain, plant life, fertility. The phases of the moon showed man time in the concrete sense—as distinct from astronomical time which certainly only came to be realized later. Even in the Ice Age the meaning of the moon's phases and their magic powers were clearly known. We find the symbolism of spirals, snakes and lightning—all of them growing out of the notion of the moon as the measure of rhythmic change and fertility—in the Siberian cultures of the Ice Age. Time was quite certainly measured everywhere by the phases of the moon. Even to-day there are nomad tribes living off what they can hunt and grow who use only the lunar calendar. The oldest Indo-Aryan root connected with the heavenly bodies is the one that means "moon": it is the root *me*, which in Sanskrit becomes *mami*, "I measure." The moon becomes the universal measuring gauge. All the words relating to the moon in the Indo-European languages come from that root....

Time as governed and measured by the phases of the moon might be called "living" time. It is bound up with the reality of life and nature, rain and the tides,

FROM *Patterns in Comparative Religion* by Mircea Eliade, translated by Rosemary Sheed, by permission of the University of Nebraska Press. © 1958 by Sheed and Ward, Inc.

the time of sowing, the menstrual cycle. A whole series of phenomena belonging to totally different "cosmic levels" are ordered according to the rhythms of the moon or are under their influence.... [F]rom the earliest times, certainly since the Neolithic Age, with the discovery of agriculture, the same symbolism has linked together the moon, the sea waters, rain, the fertility of women and of animals, plant life, man's destiny after death and the ceremonies of initiation....

The moon measures, but it also unifies. Its "forces" or rhythms are what one may call the "lowest common denominator" of an endless number of phenomena and symbols. The whole universe is seen as a pattern, subject to certain laws. The world is no longer an infinite space filled with the activity of a lot of disconnected autonomous creatures: within that space itself things can be seen to correspond and fit together. All this, of course, is not the result of a reasoned analysis of reality, but of an ever clearer intuition of it in its totality.... [T]here can be no symbol, ritual or myth of the moon that does not imply all the lunar values known at a given time. There can be no part without the whole. The spiral, for instance,... relates to the phases of the moon, but also includes erotic elements springing from the vulva-shell analogy, water elements (the moon=shell), and some to do with fertility (the double volute, horns and so on). By wearing a pearl as an amulet a woman is united to the powers of water (shell), the moon (the shell a symbol of the moon; created by the rays of the moon, etc.), eroticism, birth and embryology.... Vegetation, for instance, implies notions of death and rebirth, of light and darkness (as zones of the universe), of fecundity and abundance, and so on. There is no such thing as a symbol, emblem or power with only one kind of meaning. Everything hangs together, everything is connected, and makes up a cosmic whole.

The Coherence of All Lunar Epiphanies

Such a whole could certainly never be grasped by any mind accustomed to proceeding analytically. And even by intuition modern man cannot get hold of all the wealth of meaning and harmony that such a cosmic *reality* (or, in fact, sacred reality) involves in the primitive mind. To the primitive, a lunar symbol (an amulet or iconographic sign) does not merely contain in itself all the lunar forces at work on every level of the cosmos—but actually, by the power of the ritual involved, places the wearer himself at the center of those forces, increasing his vitality, making him more *real,* and guaranteeing him a happier state after death. It is important to keep stressing this fact that every religious act (that is, every act with a meaning) performed by primitive man has a character of *totality,* for there is always a danger of our looking upon the functions, powers and attributes of the moon as we discuss them in this chapter in an *analytic* and *cumulative* manner. We tend to divide what is and must remain a whole.

Where we use the words "because," and "therefore," the mind of the primitive man would phrase it perhaps as "in the same way" (for instance, I say: because the moon governs the waters, plants are subject to it, but it would be more correct to say: plants and the waters are subject to it *in the same way*...).

The "powers" of the moon are to be discovered not by means of a succession of analytical exercises, but by intuition; *it reveals itself* more and more fully. The analogies formed in the primitive mind are as it were orchestrated there by means of symbols; for instance, the moon appears and disappears; the snail shows and withdraws its horns; the bear appears and disappears with the seasons; thus, the snail becomes the scene of a lunar theophany, as in the ancient religion of Mexico in which the moon god, Tecciztecatl, is shown enclosed in a snail's shell; it also becomes an amulet, and so on....

The symbols which get their meaning from the moon *are* at the same time the moon. The spiral is both a lunar hierophany—expressing the light-darkness cycle—and a sign by which man can absorb the moon's powers into himself. Lightning, too, is a kratophany [expression of power: ed.] of the moon, for its brightness recalls that of the moon, and it heralds rain, which is governed by the moon. All these symbols, hierophanies, myths, rituals, amulets and the rest, which I call lunar to give them one convenient name, form a whole in the mind of the primitive; they are bound together by harmonies, analogies, and elements "held in common, like one great cosmic "net," a vast web in which every piece fits and nothing is isolated from the rest. If you want to express the multiplicity of lunar hierophanies in a single formula, you may say that they reveal life repeating itself rhythmically. All the values of the moon, whether cosmological, magic or religious, are explained by its modality of *being*: by the fact that it is "living," and inexhaustible in its own regeneration.... Man saw himself reflected in the "life" of the moon; not simply because his own life came to an end, like that of all organisms, but because his own thirst for regeneration, his hopes of a "rebirth," gained confirmation from the fact of there being always a new moon.

It does not matter to us a great deal whether, in the innumerable beliefs centring upon the moon, we are dealing with adoration of the moon itself, of a divinity inhabiting it, or of a mythical personification of it. Nowhere in the history of religions do we find an adoration of any natural object in itself. A sacred thing, whatever its form and substance, is sacred because it reveals or shares in ultimate *reality*. Every religious object is always an "incarnation" of something: of the *sacred*....It incarnates it by the quality of its being (as for instance, the sky, the sun, the moon or the earth), or by its form (that is symbolically: as with the spiral-snail), or by a hierophany (a *certain* stone, etc. becomes sacred; a certain object is "sanctified" or "consecrated" by a ritual, or by contact with another sacred object or person, and so on).

Consequently, the moon is no more adored in *itself* than any other object, but in what it reveals of the sacred, that is, in the power centred in it, in the inexhaustible life and reality that it manifests...To the primitive mind, I repeat, everything that had a meaning, everything connected with *absolute reality,* had sacred value. We can observe the religious character of the moon with as much precision on the symbolism of the pearl or of the lightning as we can by studying a lunar divinity like the Babylonian Sin or the goddess Hecate.

The Moon and the Waters

Both because they are subject to rhythms (rain and tides), and because they sponsor the growth of living things, waters are subject to the moon. "The moon is in the waters" and "rain comes from the moon."...

All the moon divinities preserve more or less obvious water attributes of functions. To certain American Indian tribes, the moon, or the moon god, is at the same time the god of water....The link between the moon and the tides which both the Greeks and the Celts observed, was also known to the Maoris of New Zealand and the Eskimos (whose moon divinities govern the tides.).

From the earliest times it was recognized that rainfall followed the phases of the moon. A whole series of mythical characters, belonging to cultures as varied as the Bushman, Mexican, Australian, Samoyed and Chinese, were marked by their power to cause rain and by having only one foot or only one hand....While the waters and the rain are governed by the moon, and normally follow a fixed order—that is, they follow the phases of the moon—all disasters connected with them, on the other hand, display the moon's other aspect, as the periodic destroyer of outworn "forms" and, we may say, of effecting regeneration on the cosmic scale.

Flood corresponds to the three days of darkness, or "death," of the moon. It is a cataclysm, but never a final one, for it takes place under the seal of the moon and the waters, which are pre-eminently the sign of growth and regeneration. A flood destroys simply because the "forms" are old and worn out, but it is always followed by a new humanity and a new history....The vast majority of deluge myths tell how a single individual survived, and how the new race was descended from him. This survivor—man or woman—occasionally marries a lunar animal, which thus becomes ancestor to the race....

Of the numerous variants on the Deluge myth we will look at one—an Australian version (that of the Kurnai tribe). One day all the waters were swallowed by an immense frog, Dak. In vain the parched animals tried to make her laugh. Not until the eel (or serpent) began to roll about and twist itself round did Dak burst out laughing, and the waters thus rushed out and produced the flood. The frog is a lunar animal, for a great many legends speak of a frog to be seen in the moon, and it is always present in the innumerable rites for inducing rain....

The Moon and Vegetation

That there was a connection between the moon, rain and plant life was realized before the discovery of agriculture. The plant world comes from the same source of universal fertility, and is subject to the same recurring cycles governed by the moon's movements. One Iranian text says that plants grow by its warmth. Some tribes in Brazil call it "mother of grasses" and in a great many places (Polynesia, Moluccas, Melanesia, China, Sweden, etc.) it is thought that grass grows on the moon....

The organic connection between the moon and vegetation is so strong that a very large number of fertility gods are also divinities of the moon; for instance the Egyptian Hathor, Ishtar the Iranian Anaitis, and so on. In almost all the gods of vegetation and fecundity there persist lunar attributes or powers—even when their divine "form" has become completely autonomous.... Dionysos is both moon-god and god of vegetation; Osiris possesses all these attributes—moon, water, plant life and agriculture. We can discern the moon-water-vegetation pattern particularly clearly in the religious nature of certain beverages of divine origin, such as the Indian *soma,* and the Iranian *haoma*; these were even personified into divinities—autonomous, though less important than the major gods of the Indo-Iranian pantheon. And in this divine liquor which confers immortality on all who drink it, we can recognize the sacredness that centers round the moon, water and vegetation.... It is supremely the "divine substance," for it transmutes life into absolute reality—or immortality. *Amrta,* ambrosia, *soma, haoma* and the rest all have a celestial prototype drunk only by gods and heroes.... Furthermore, these earthly drinks owe their potency to their corresponding celestial prototype. Sacred inebriation makes it possible to share—though fleetingly and imperfectly—in the divine mode of being; it achieves, in fact, the paradox of at once possessing the fullness of existence, and becoming; of being at once dynamic and static....

The Moon and Fertility

The fertility of animals, as well as that of plants, is subject to the moon. The relationship between the moon and fecundity occasionally becomes somewhat complicated owing to the appearance of new religious "forms"—like the Earth-Mother, and the various agricultural divinities. However, there is one aspect of the moon that remains permanently evident, however many religious syntheses have gone towards making up these new "forms"; and that is the prerogative of fertility, of recurring creation, of inexhaustible life. The horns of oxen, for instance, which are used to characterize the great divinities of fecundity, are an emblem of the divine *Magna Mater*. Wherever they are to be found in Neolithic cultures, either in iconography, or as part of idols in the form of oxen, they denote the presence of the Great Goddess of fertility. And a horn is always the image of the new moon. . . .

Certain animals become symbols or even "presences" of the moon because their shape or their behaviour is reminiscent of the moon's. So with the snail which goes in and out of its shell; the bear, which disappears in midwinter and reappears in the spring; the frog because it swells up, submerges itself, and later returns to the surface of the water; . . . the snake, because it appears and disappears, and because it has as many coils as the moon has days (this legend is also preserved in Greek tradition); or because it is "the husband of all women," or because it sloughs its skin (that is to say, is periodically reborn, is "immortal"), and so on. . . .

I can only mention here a few of the myths and symbols connected with the serpent, and only those which indicate its character of a lunar animal. In the first place, its connection with women and with fecundity: the moon is the source of all fertility, and also governs the menstrual cycle. It is personified as "the master of women." A great many peoples used to think—and some think it to this day—that the moon, in the form of a man, or a serpent, copulates with their women. That is why, among the Eskimos for instance, unmarried girls will not look at the moon for fear of becoming pregnant. The Australians believe that the moon comes down to earth in the form of a sort of Don Juan, makes women pregnant and then deserts them. . . . In Germany, France, Portugal and elsewhere, women used to be afraid that a snake would slip into their mouths when they were asleep, and they would become pregnant, particularly during menstruation. In India, when women wanted to have children, they adored a cobra. All over the East it was believed that Woman's first sexual contact was with a snake, at puberty or during menstruation. . . .

The Moon, Woman, and Snakes

The moon then can also be personified as reptile and masculine, but such personifications (which often break away from the original pattern and follow a path of their own in myth and legend), are still fundamentally based on the notion of the moon as source of living reality, and basis of all fertility and periodic regeneration. Snakes are thought of as producing children . . .

There are a great many different woman-snake relationships, but none of them can be fully explained by any purely erotic symbolism. The snake has a variety of meanings, and I think we must hold its "regeneration" to be one of the most important. The snake is an animal that "changes." . . .

The same central symbolism of fertility and regeneration governed by the moon, and bestowed by the moon itself or by forms the same in substance (*magna mater, terra mater*) explains the presence of snakes in the imagery and rites of the Great Goddesses of universal fertility. As an attribute of the Great

Goddess, the snake keeps its lunar character (of periodic regeneration) in addition to a telluric one.... Some races even believe that the earth and the moon are formed of the same substance. The Great Goddesses share as much in the sacred nature of the moon as in that of the earth. And because these goddesses are also funeral goddesses (the dead disappear into the ground or into the moon to be reborn and reappear under new forms), the snake becomes very specially the animal of death and burial, embodying the souls of the dead, the ancestor of the tribe, etc. And this symbolism of regeneration also explains the presence of snakes in initiation ceremonies.

Lunar Symbolism

What emerges fairly clearly from all this varied symbolism of snakes is their lunar character—that is, their powers of fertility, of regeneration, of immortality through metamorphosis. We could, of course, look at a series of their attributes or functions and conclude that all these various relationships and significations have developed one from another by some method of logical analysis. You can reduce any religious system to nothing by methodically breaking it down to its component parts and studying them. In reality, all the meanings in a symbol are present together, even when it may look as if only some of them are effective. The intuition of the moon as the measure of rhythms, as the source of energy, of life, and of rebirth, has woven a sort of web between the various levels of the universe, producing parallels, similarities and unities among vastly differing kinds of phenomena. It is not always easy to find the center of such a "web"; secondary centers will sometimes stand out, looking like the most important, or perhaps the oldest starting point....

Thus the whole pattern is moon-rain-fertility-woman-serpent-death-periodic-regeneration, but we may be dealing with one of the patterns within a pattern such as Serpent-Woman-Fertility, or Serpent-Rain-Fertility, or perhaps Woman-Serpent-Magic, and so on. A lot of mythology has grown up around these secondary "centers," and if one does not realize this, it may overshadow the original pattern, though that pattern is, in fact, fully implicated in even the tiniest fragments....

The Moon and Death

[T]he moon is the first of the dead. For three nights the sky is dark; but as the moon is reborn on the fourth night, so shall the dead achieve a new sort of existence. Death, as we shall see later, is not an extinction, but a change—and generally a provisional one—of one's level of existence. Death belongs to another kind of "life." And because what happens to the moon, and to the earth (for as people discovered the agricultural cycle they came to see the Earth as related to the Moon) proves that there is a "life in death" and gives the idea meaning, the dead either go to the moon or return to the underworld to be regenerated and to absorb the forces needed to start a new existence. That is why so many lunar divinities are in addition chthonian and funereal divinities (Min, Persephone, probably Hermes, and so on). And why, too, so many beliefs see the moon as the land of the dead. . . .

This journey to the moon after death was also preserved in highly developed cultures (India, Greece, Iran), but something else was added. To the Indians, it is the "path of the *manes*" *(pitryana)*, and souls reposed in the moon while awaiting reincarnation, whereas the sun road or "path of the gods" *(devayana)* was taken by the initiated, or those set free from the illusions of ignorance. In Iranian tradition, the souls of the dead, having passed the Cinvat bridge, went towards the stars, and if they had been good they went to the moon and then into the sun, and the most virtuous of all entered the *garotman*, the infinite light of Ahura Mazda. The same belief was kept in Manicheeism and existed in the East as well. Pythagorism gave astral theology a further impulse by popularizing the idea of the empyrean: the Elysian Fields, where heroes and Caesars went after death, were in the moon. The "Isles of the Blessed," and all the mythical geography of death, were set in the sky utilizing the moon, the sun, the Milky Way. Here, of course, we have clearly got formulae and cults impregnated with astronomical speculation and eschatological gnosis. But even in such late developments as that it is not hard to identify the traditional key ideas: the moon as land of the dead, the moon as receiver and regenerator of souls.

The Moon and Initiation

Death, however, is not final—for the moon's death is not. "As the moon dieth and cometh to life again, so we also, having to die, will again rise," declare the Juan Capistrano Indians of California in ceremonies performed when the moon is new. . . .

In Australian initiations, the "dead man" (that is, the neo-phyte), rises from a tomb as the moon rises from darkness. Among the Koryaks of north-eastern Siberia, the Gilyaks, Tlingits, Tongas and Haidas, a bear—a "lunar animal" because it appears and disappears with the seasons—is present in the initiation ceremonies, just as it played an essential part in the ceremonies of Paleolithic times. . . . Even when no lunar animals appear in the rites and no direct reference is made to the disappearance and reappearance of the moon, we are driven to connect all the various initiation ceremonies with the lunar myth throughout the area of southern Asia and the Pacific. . . .

In certain of the shaman initiation ceremonies, the candidate is "broken to pieces" just as the moon is divided into parts. . . . We find the same archetypal model in the osirian initiations. According to the tradition recorded by Plutarch, Osiris ruled for twenty-eight years and was killed on the seventeenth of the month, when the moon was on the wane. The coffin in which Isis had hidden him was discovered by Set when he was hunting by moonlight; Set divided Osiris' body into fourteen and scattered the pieces throughout Egypt. The ritual emblem of the dead god is in the shape of the new moon. There is clearly an analogy between death and initiation....If mystical initiation is achieved through a ritual death, then death can be looked upon as an initiation. Plutarch calls the souls that attain to the upper part of the moon "victorious," and they wear the same crown on their heads as the initiate and the triumphant.

~

Cosmo-Biology and Mystical Physiology

...Clearly, man's integration into the cosmos can only take place if he can bring himself into harmony with the two astral rhythms, "unifying" the sun and Moon in his living body. The "unification" of the two centres of sacred and natural energy aims—in this technique of mystical physiology—at reintegrating them in the primal undifferentiated unity, as it was when not yet broken up by the act that created the universe; and this "unification" realizes a transcendence of the cosmos....

By its mode of being, the moon "binds" together a whole mass of realities and destinies. The rhythms of the moon weave together harmonies, symmetries, analogies and participations which make up an endless "fabric," a "net" of invisible threads, which "binds" together at once mankind, rain, vegetation, fertility, health, animals, death, regeneration, after-life, and more. That is why the moon is seen in so many traditions personified by a divinity, or acting through a lunar animal, "weaving" the cosmic veil, or the destinies of men. It was lunar goddesses who either invented the profession of weaving (like the Egyptian divinity Neith), or were famous for their ability to weave (Athene punished Arachne, for daring to rival her, by turning her into a spider), or wove a garment of cosmic proportions (like Proserpine and Harmonia), and so on. It was believed in medieval Europe that Holda was patroness of weavers, and we see beyond this figure to the chthonian and lunar nature of the divinities of fertility and death. We are obviously dealing here with extremely complex forms in which myths, ceremonials and symbols from different religious structures are crystallized....[W]e find in them the syntheses of the moon and Mother Earth with all that they imply (the ambivalence of good and evil, death, fertility, destiny).

The Moon and Fate

The moon, however, simply because she is mistress of all living things and sure guide of the dead, has "woven" all destinies. Not for nothing is she envisaged in myth as an immense spider—an image you will find used by a great many peoples. For to weave is not merely to predestine (anthropologically), and to join together differing realities (cosmologically) but also to *create,* to make something of one's own substance as the spider does in spinning its web. And the moon is the inexhaustible creator of all living forms. But, like everything woven, the lives thus created are fixed in a pattern: they have a destiny. The Moirai, who spin fates, are lunar divinities. Homer calls them "the spinners," and one of them is even called Clotho, which means "spinner." ...

Lunar Metaphysics

We must try to get a general picture of all these lunar hierophanies. What do they reveal? How far do they fit together and complement each other, how far do they make up a "theory"—that is, express a succession of "truths" which, taken together, could constitute a system? The hierophanies of the moon that we have noted may be grouped round the following themes: (*a*) fertility (waters, vegetation, women; mythological "ancestor"); (*b*) periodic regeneration (the symbolism of the serpent and all the lunar animals: "the new man" who has survived a watery catastrophe caused by the moon; the death and resurrection of initiations; etc.); (*c*) time and destiny (the moon "measures," or "weaves" destinies, "binds" together diverse cosmic levels and heterogeneous realities); (*d*) change, marked by the opposition of light and darkness (full moon—new moon; the "world above" and the "underworld"; brothers who are enemies, good and evil), or by the balance between being and non-being, the virtual and the actual (the symbolism of hidden things: dusky night, darkness, death, seeds and larvae). In all these themes the dominant idea is one of *rhythm* carried out by a succession of contraries, of "becoming" through the succession of opposing modalities (being and non-being; forms and hidden essences; life and death; etc.). It is a becoming, I need hardly add, that cannot take place without drama or *pathos;* the sub-lunar world is not only the world of change but also the world of suffering and of "history." Nothing that happens in this world under the moon can be "eternal," for its law is the law of becoming, and no change is final; every change is merely part of a cyclic pattern.

The phases of the moon give us, if not the historical origin, at least the mythological and symbolic illustration of all dualisms. ... At every cosmic level a "dark" period is followed by a "light," pure, regenerate period. The symbolism of emerging from the "darkness" can be found in initiation rituals as well as in the mythology of death, and the life of plants (buried seed, the "darkness" from which the "new plant" (*neophyte*) arises), and in the whole conception of "historical" cycles. ...

It might be said that the moon shows man his true human condition; that in a sense man looks at himself, and finds himself anew in the life of the moon. That is why the symbolism and mythology of the moon have an element of *pathos* and at the same time of consolation, for the moon governs both death and fertility, both drama and initiation. Though the modality of the moon is supremely one of change, of rhythm, it is equally one of periodic returning; and this pattern of existence is disturbing and consoling at the same time—for though the manifestations of life are so frail that they can suddenly disappear altogether, they are restored in the "eternal returning" regulated by the moon. Such is the law of the whole sublunary universe. But that law, which is at once harsh and merciful, can be abolished, and in some cases one may "transcend" this periodic becoming and achieve a mode of existence that is absolute.... This myth of reintegration is to be found almost everywhere in the history of religion in an infinity of variations.... It existed at the most primitive stages, which indicates that man, from the time when he first realized his position in the universe, desired passionately and tried to achieve concretely...a passing beyond his human status.

The Myth of the Eternal Return

Eliade here explicates the archaic view of the sacred as it bears on the understanding of time and eternity. Archaic peoples seek release from the limitations of time; this longing to escape the "terror of history" seems to have been universal until the time of the ancient Hebrew prophets, who saw their God, Yahweh, as acting within history, not outside of it, for his chosen people. Christianity shares with Judaism this view of history as the arena of divine action and purpose. So, too, but in a very different sense, do modern philosophers since the time of G. W. F. Hegel in Germany. These "historicist" thinkers reject any belief in God, and so strive to discover ultimate meaning in history through devotion to some exclusively secular cause, such as a nation, class, or race, as in modern Fascism, Marxism, and nationalism.

[I] t is not our intention to exhaust the themes we encounter in this essay; we only wish to situate them in accordance with a common perspective: the need of archaic societies to regenerate themselves periodically through the annulment of time. Collective or individual, periodic or spontaneous, regeneration rites always comprise, in their structure and meaning, an element of regeneration through repetition of an archetypal act, usually of the cosmogonic

FROM: Eliade, Mircea: *The Myth of the Eternal Return, Or Cosmos and History.* © 1954 Bollingen. Reprinted by permission of Princeton University Press.

act. What is of chief importance to us in these archaic systems is the abolition of concrete time, and hence their antihistorical intent....We refer to archaic man's refusal to accept himself as a historical being, his refusal to grant value to memory and hence to the unusual events (i.e., events without an archetypal model) that in fact constitute concrete duration. In the last analysis, what we discover in all these rites and all these attitudes is the will to devaluate time. Carried to their extreme, all the rites and all the behavior patterns that we have so far mentioned would be comprised in the following statement: "If we pay no attention to it, time does not exist; furthermore, where it becomes perceptible—because of man's 'sins,' i.e., when man departs from the archetype and falls into duration—time can be annulled." Basically...the life of archaic man, although it takes place in time, does not bear the burden of time, does not record time's irreversibility;...Like the mystic, like the religious man in general, the primitive lives in a continual present....

That, for a primitive, the recognition of time is continually effected...is proven by the antiquity and universality of certain beliefs in respect to the moon. The moon is the first of creatures to die, but also the first to live again. We have elsewhere shown the importance of lunar myths in the organization of the first coherent theories concerning death and resurrection, fertility and regeneration, initiation, and so on.

$\sim$

We may note that what predominates in all these cosmico-mythological lunar conceptions is the cyclical recurrence of what has been before, in a word, eternal return....In a certain sense, it is even possible to say that nothing new happens in the world, for everything is but the repetition of the same primordial archetypes; this repetition, by actualizing the mythical moment when the archetypal gesture was revealed, constantly maintains the world in the same auroral instant of the beginnings. Time but makes possible the appearance and existence of things. It has no final influence upon their existence, since it is itself constantly regenerated.

Hegel affirmed that in nature things repeat themselves for ever and that there is "nothing new under the sun." All that we have so far demonstrated confirms the existence of a similar conception in the man of archaic societies: for him things repeat themselves for ever and nothing new happens under the sun. But this repetition has a meaning...: it alone confers a reality upon events; events repeat themselves because they imitate an archetype—the exemplary event. Furthermore, through this repetition, time is suspended, or at least its virulence is diminished....

[I]t is...probable that the desire felt by the man of traditional societies to refuse history, and to confine himself to an indefinite repetition of archetypes, testifies to his thirst for the real and his terror of "losing" himself by letting himself be overwhelmed by the meaninglessness of profane existence.

It matters little if the formulas and images through which the primitive expresses "reality" seem childish and even absurd to us. It is the profound meaning of primitive behavior that is revelatory; this behavior is governed by belief in an absolute reality opposed to the profane world of "unrealities"; in the last analysis, the latter does not constitute a "world," properly speaking; it is the "unreal" *par excellence,* the uncreated, the nonexistent: the void.

Hence we are justified in speaking of an archaic ontology, and it is only by taking this ontology into consideration that we can succeed in understanding—and hence in not scornfully dismissing—even the most extravagant behavior on the part of the primitive world; in fact, this behavior corresponds to a desperate effort not to lose contact with *being.*

~

History Regarded as Theophany

Among the Hebrews, every new historical calamity was regarded as a punishment inflicted by Yahweh, angered by the orgy of sin to which the chosen people had abandoned themselves. No military disaster seemed absurd, no suffering was vain, for, beyond the "event," it was always possible to perceive the will of Yahweh. Even more: these catastrophes were...foreseen by God so that the Jewish people should not contravene its true destiny by alienating the religious heritage left by Moses... Only historical catastrophes brought them back to the right road by forcing them to look toward the true God....

Through their terrifying visions, the prophets but confirmed and amplified Yahweh's ineluctable chastisement upon His people who had not kept the faith. And it is only insofar as such prophecies were ratified by catastrophes...that historical events acquired religious significance, i.e., that they clearly appeared as punishments inflicted by the Lord in return for the impiousness of Israel. Because of the prophets, who interpreted contemporary events in the light of a strict faith, these events were transformed into... Yahweh's "wrath." Thus they not only acquired a meaning...but they also revealed their hidden coherence by proving to be the concrete expression of the same single divine will. Thus, for the first time, the prophets placed a value on history, succeeded in transcending the traditional vision of the cycle (the conception that ensures all things will be repeated forever), and discovered a one-way time. This discovery was not to be immediately and fully accepted by the consciousness of the entire Jewish people, and the ancient conceptions were still long to survive.

But, for the first time, we find affirmed, and increasingly accepted, the idea that historical events have a value in themselves, insofar as they are determined by the will of God. This God of the Jewish people is no longer an Oriental divinity, creator of archetypal gestures, but a personality who ceaselessly intervenes in history, who reveals his will through events (invasions, sieges, battles, and so on). Historical facts thus become "situations" of man in respect to God, and as such they acquire a religious value that nothing had previously been able to confer on them. It may, then, be said with truth that the Hebrews were the first to discover the meaning of history as the epiphany of God, and this conception, as we should expect, was taken up and amplified by Christianity.

We may even ask ourselves if monotheism, based upon the direct and personal revelation of the divinity, does not necessarily entail the "salvation" of time, its value within the frame of history. Doubtless the idea of revelation is found... in all religions, we could even say in all cultures.... But these revelations occurred in *mythical* time, at the extratemporal instant of the beginning; thus, as we saw..., everything in a certain sense coincided with the beginning of the world, with the cosmogony. Everything had taken place and had been revealed at that moment, *in illo tempore*: the creation of the world, and that of man, and man's establishment in the situation provided for him in the cosmos....

The situation is altogether different in the case of the monotheistic revelation. This takes place in time, in historical duration: Moses receives the Law at a certain place and at a certain date. Of course, here too archetypes are involved.... Nevertheless, the moment of the revelation made to Moses by God remains a limited moment, definitely situated in time. And, since it also represents a theophany, it thus acquires a new dimension: it becomes precious inasmuch as it is no longer reversible, as it is historical event....

Under the "pressure of history" and supported by the prophetic and Messianic experience, a new interpretation of historical events dawns among the children of Israel. Without finally renouncing the traditional concept of archetypes and repetitions, Israel attempts to "save" historical events by regarding them as active presences of Yahweh. Whereas, for example, among the Mesopotamian peoples individual or collective sufferings were tolerated insofar as they were caused by the conflict between divine and demonic forces, that is, formed a part of the cosmic drama..., in the Israel of the Messianic prophets, historical events could be tolerated because, on the one hand, they were willed by Yahweh, and, on the other hand, because they were necessary to the final salvation of the chosen people. Rehandling the old scenarios... of the "passion" of the god, Messianism gives them a new value, especially by abolishing their possibility of repetition *ad infinitum*. When the Messiah comes, the world will be saved once and for all and history will cease to exist.... History no longer appears as a cycle that repeats itself *ad infinitum,* as the primitive peoples represented it (creation, exhaustion, destruction, annual re-creation of the cosmos).... Directly ordered by the will of Yahweh, history appears as a series of theophanies, negative or positive, each of which has its intrinsic value. Certainly, all military defeats can be referred back to an archetype: Yahweh's wrath. But each of these defeats, though basically a repetition of the same archetype, nevertheless acquires a coefficient of irreversibility: Yahweh's personal intervention.

But it must not be forgotten that these Messianic conceptions are the exclusive creation of a religious elite. For many centuries, this elite undertook the religious education of the people of Israel, without always being successful in eradicating the traditional Paleo-Oriental granting of value to life and history. The Hebrews' periodic returns to the Baals and Astartes are also largely to be explained by their refusal to allow a value to history, that is, to regard it as a theophany. For the popular strata, and especially for the agrarian communities, the old religious concept (that of the Baals and Astartes) was preferable; it kept them closer to "life" and helped them to tolerate history if not to ignore it. The Messianic prophets' steadfast will to look history in the face and to accept it as a terrifying dialogue with Yahweh, their will to make military defeats bear moral and religious fruit... because they were regarded as *necessary* to Yahweh's reconciliation with the people of Israel and its final salvation... demanded too great a religious tension, and the majority of the Israelites refused to submit to it.... It was more consoling, and easier, in misfortunes and times of trial, to go on accusing an "accident" (e.g., a spell) or a "negligence" (e.g., a ritual fault) that could easily be made good by a sacrifice (even though it were the sacrifice of infants to Moloch).

In this respect, the classic example of Abraham's sacrifice admirably illustrates the difference between the traditional conception of the repetition of an archetypal gesture and the new dimension, *faith*, acquired through religious experience. Morphologically considered, Abraham's sacrifice is nothing but the sacrifice of the first born, a frequent practice in this Paleo-Oriental world in which the Hebrews evolved down to the period of the prophets. The first child was often regarded as the child of a god; indeed, throughout the archaic East, unmarried girls customarily spent a night in the temple and thus conceived by the god (by his representative, the priest, or by his envoy, the "stranger"). The sacrifice of this first child restored to the divinity what belonged to him. Thus the young blood increased the exhausted energy of the god.... And, in a certain sense, Isaac was a son of God, since he had been given to Abraham and Sarah when Sarah had long passed the age of fertility. But Isaac was given them through their faith. His sacrifice by Abraham, although in form it resembles all the sacrifices of newborn infants in the Paleo-Semitic world, differs from them fundamentally in content. Whereas, for the entire Paleo-Semitic world, such a sacrifice, despite its religious function, was only a custom, a rite whose meaning was perfectly intelligible, in Abraham's case it is an act of faith. He does not understand why the sacrifice is demanded of him; nevertheless, he performs it because it was the Lord who demanded it. By this act, which is apparently absurd, Abraham initiates a new religious experience, faith. All others (the whole Oriental world) continue to move in an economy of the sacred that will be transcended by Abraham.... [T]heir sacrifices belonged to the "general"; that is, they were based upon archaic theophanies that were concerned only with the circulation of sacred energy in the cosmos (from the divinity to man and nature, then from man—through sacrifice—back to the divinity, and so on). These were acts whose justification lay in themselves; they entered into a logical and coherent system: what had belonged to God must be returned to him. For Abraham, Isaac was a gift from the Lord and not the product of a direct and material conception. Between God and Abraham yawned an abyss; there was a fundamental break in continuity. Abraham's religious act inaugurates a new religious dimension: God reveals himself as personal, as a "totally distinct" existence that ordains, bestows, demands, without any rational (i.e. general and foreseeable) justification, and for which all is possible. This new religious dimension renders "faith" possible in the Judaeo-Christian sense.

We have cited this example in order to illuminate the novelty of the Jewish religion in comparison with the traditional structures.... The same conception, enriched through the elaboration of Christology, will serve as the basis for the philosophy of history that Christianity, from St. Augustine on, will labor to construct. But let us repeat: neither in Christianity nor in Judaism does the discovery of this new dimension in religious experience, faith, produce a basic modification of traditional conceptions. Faith is merely made possible for each individual Christian. The great majority of so-called Christian populations continue, down to our day, to preserve themselves from history by ignoring it and by tolerating it rather than by giving it the meaning of a negative or positive theophany.

~

The Difficulties of Historicism

[Today] we find...the validity of "historicistic" solutions, from Hegel to Marx...being implicitly called into question. From Hegel on, every effort is directed toward saving and conferring value on the historical event as such, the event in itself and for itself.... [I]n fact, all the cruelties, aberrations, and tragedies of history have been, and still are, justified by the necessities of the "historical moment." Probably Hegel did not intend to go so far. But since he had resolved to reconcile himself with his own historical moment, he was obliged to see in every event the will of the Universal Spirit. This is why he considered "reading the morning papers a sort of realistic benediction of the morning." For him, only daily contact with events could orient man's conduct in his relations with the world and with God.

How could Hegel know what was *necessary* in history, what, consequently, must occur exactly as it had occurred? Hegel believed that he knew what the Universal Spirit wanted. We shall not insist upon the audacity of this thesis.... But there is an aspect of Hegel's philosophy of history that interests us because it still preserves something of the Judaeo-Christian conception: for Hegel, the historical event was the manifestation of the Universal Spirit. Now, it is possible to discern a parallel between Hegel's philosophy of history and the theology of history of the Hebrew prophets: for the latter, as for Hegel, an event is irreversible and valid in itself inasmuch as it is a new manifestation of the will of God—a proposition really revolutionary, we should remind ourselves, from the viewpoint of traditional societies dominated by the eternal repetition of archetypes. Thus, in Hegel's view, the destiny of a people still preserved a transhistorical significance, because all history revealed a more and more perfect manifestation of the Universal Spirit. But with Marx, history cast off all transcendental significance; it was no longer anything more than the epiphany of the class struggle. To what extent could such a theory justify historical sufferings? For the answer, we have but to turn to the pathetic resistance of...a Dostoevski, for example, who asked...how, from the viewpoint of the Hegelian and Marxian dialectic, it was possible to redeem all the dramas of oppression, the collective sufferings, deportations, humiliations, and massacres that fill universal history.

Yet Marxism preserves a meaning to history. For Marxism, events are not a succession of arbitrary accidents; they exhibit a coherent structure and, above all, they lead to a definite end—final elimination of the terror of history, "salvation." Thus, at the end of the Marxist philosophy of history, lies the age of gold of the archaic eschatologies. In this sense it is correct to say...that Marx... reconfirmed, upon an exclusively human level, the value of the primitive myth of the age of gold, with the difference that he puts the age of gold only at the end of history.... Here, for the militant Marxist, lies the secret of the remedy for the terror of history: just as the contemporaries of a "dark age" consoled themselves for their increasing sufferings by the thought that the aggravation of evil hastens final deliverance, so the militant Marxist of our day reads, in the drama provoked by the pressure of history, a necessary evil, the premonitory symptom of the approaching victory that will put an end forever to all historical "evil."

The terror of history becomes more and more intolerable from the viewpoints afforded by the various historicistic philosophies. For in them, of course, every historical event finds its full and only meaning in its realization alone....

For our purpose, only one question concerns us: How can the "terror of history" be tolerated...? Justification of a historical event by the simple fact that it is a historical event, in other words, by the simple fact that it "happened that way," will not go far toward freeing humanity from the terror that the event inspires.... We should wish to know, for example, how it would be possible to tolerate, and to justify, the sufferings and annihilation of so many peoples who suffer and are annihilated for the simple reason that their geographical situation sets them in the pathway of history; that they are neighbors of empires in a state of permanent expansion. How justify, for example, the fact that southeastern Europe had to suffer for centuries—and hence to renounce any impulse toward a higher historical existence, toward spiritual creation on the universal plane—for the sole reason that it happened to be on the road of the Asiatic invaders and later the neighbor of the Ottoman Empire? And in our day, when historical pressure no longer allows any escape, how can man tolerate the catastrophes and horrors of history—from collective deportations and massacres to atomic bombings—if beyond them he can glimpse no sign, no transhistorical meaning; if they are only the blind play of economic, social, or political forces, or, even worse, only the result of the "liberties" that a minority takes and exercises directly on the stage of universal history?

We know how, in the past, humanity has been able to endure the sufferings we have enumerated: they were regarded as a punishment inflicted by God, the syndrome of the decline of the "age," and so on. And it was possible to accept them precisely because...for the greater part of mankind, still clinging to the traditional viewpoint, history did not have, and could not have, value in itself. Every hero repeated the archetypal gesture, every war rehearsed the struggle between good and evil, every fresh social injustice was identified with the sufferings of the Savior (or, for example, in the pre-Christian world, with the passion of a divine messenger or vegetation god).... [B]y virtue of this view, tens of millions of men were able, for century after century, to endure great historical pressures without despairing, without committing suicide or falling into that spiritual aridity that always brings with it a relativistic or nihilistic view of history.

[I]t is above all the "elites" that are confronted with the problem, since they alone are forced, and with increasing rigor, to take cognizance of their historical situation. It is true that Christianity and the eschatological philosophy of history have not ceased to satisfy a considerable proportion of these elites. Up to a certain point, and for certain individuals it may be said that Marxism—especially in its popular forms—represents a defense against the terror of history. Only the historicistic position, in all its varieties and shades—from Nietzsche's "destiny" to Heidegger's "temporality"—remains disarmed. It is by no means mere fortuitous coincidence that, in this philosophy, despair, the *amor fati* [embrace of fate: ed.], and pessimism are elevated to the rank of heroic virtues and instruments of cognition.

Yet this position, although the most modern and, in a certain sense, almost the inevitable position for all thinkers who define man as a "historical being," has not yet made a definitive conquest of contemporary thought.... [I]t is worth noting that the work of two of the most significant writers of our day— T. S. Eliot and James Joyce—is saturated with nostalgia for the myth of eternal repetition and, in the last analysis, for the abolition of time. There is also reason to foresee that, as the terror of history grows worse, as existence becomes more and more precarious because of history, the positions of historicism will increasingly lose in prestige. And, at a moment when history could do what neither the cosmos, nor man, nor chance have yet succeeded in doing—that is wipe out the human race in its entirety—it may be that we are witnessing a desperate attempt to prohibit the "events of history" through a reintegration of human societies within the horizon... of archetypes and their repetition. In other words, it is not inadmissible to think of an epoch, and an epoch not too far distant, when humanity, to ensure its survival, will find itself reduced to desisting from any further "making" of history in the sense in which it began to make it from the creation of the first empires, will confine itself to repeating prescribed archetypal gestures, and will strive to forget, as meaningless and dangerous, any spontaneous gesture which might entail "historical" consequences. It would even be interesting to compare the anhistorical solution of future societies with the paradisal or eschatological myths of the golden age of the beginning or the end of the world.....

Freedom and History

... In the last analysis, modern man, who accepts history or claims to accept it, can reproach archaic man, imprisoned within the mythical horizon of archetypes and repetition, with his creative impotence, or, what amounts to the same thing, his inability to accept the risks entailed by every creative act. For the modern man can be creative only insofar as he is historical; in other words, all creation is forbidden him except that which has its source in his own freedom; and, consequently, everything is denied him except the freedom to make history by making himself.

To these criticisms raised by modern man, the man of the traditional civilizations could reply by a countercriticism that would at the same time be a defense of the type of archaic existence. It is becoming more and more doubt-ful, he might say, if modern man can make history. On the contrary, the more modern he becomes—that is, without defenses against the terror of history—the less chance he has of himself making history.... It is perfectly natural, for example, that Marxism and Fascism must lead to the establishment of two types of historical existence: that of the leader (the only really "free" man) and that of the followers, who find, in the historical existence of the leader, not an archetype of their own existence but the lawgiver of the gestures that are provi-sionally permitted them.

Thus, for traditional man, modern man affords the type neither of a free being nor of a creator of history. On the contrary, the man of the archaic civili-zations can be proud of his mode of existence, which allows him to be free and to create. He is free to be no longer what he was, free to annul his own history through periodic abolition of time and collective regeneration. This freedom in respect to his own history—which, for the modern, is not only irreversible but constitutes human existence—cannot be claimed by the man who wills to be historical... whereas archaic man recovers the possibility of definitively transcending time and living in eternity. Insofar as he fails to do so, insofar as he "sins," that is, falls into historical existence, into time, he each year thwarts the possibility. At least he retains the freedom to annul his faults, to wipe out the memory of his "fall into history," and to make another attempt to escape definitively from time.

Furthermore, archaic man certainly has the right to consider himself more creative than modern man, who sees himself as creative only in respect to his-tory. Every year, that is, archaic man takes part in the repetition of the cosmog-ony, the creative act *par excellence*.... In this respect, it is justifiable to speak not only of freedom (in the positive sense) or deliverance (in the negative sense) but actually of creation; for what is involved is creating a new man and creating him on a suprahuman plane, a man-god, such as the imagination of historical man has never dreamed it possible to create.

Despair or Faith

However this may be, our dialogue between archaic man and modern man does not affect our problem. Whatever be the truth in respect to the freedom and the creative virtualities of historical man, it is certain that none of the his-toricistic philosophies is able to defend him from the terror history.... What consolation should we find in knowing that the sufferings of millions of men have made possible the revelation of a limitary situation of the human condi-tion if, beyond that limitary situation, there should be only nothingness? Again, there is no question here of judging the validity of a historicistic philosophy, but only of establishing to what extent such a philosophy can exorcise the terror of history. If, for historical tragedies to be excused, it suffices that they should be regarded as the means by which man has been enabled to know the limit of human resistance, such an excuse can in no way make man less haunted by the terror of history.

Basically, the horizon of archetypes and repetition cannot be transcended with impunity unless we accept a philosophy of freedom that does not exclude God. And indeed this proved to be true when the horizon of archetypes and repetition was transcended, for the first time, by Judaeo-Christianism, which introduced a new category into religious experience: the category of *faith*. It must not be forgotten that, if Abraham's faith can be defined as "for God everything is possible," the faith of Christianity implies that everything is also possible for man.... Faith, in this context, as in many others, means...the highest freedom that man can imagine: freedom to intervene even in the ontological constitution of the universe. It is, consequently, a pre-eminently creative freedom. In other words, it constitutes a new formula for man's collaboration with the creation—the first, but also the only such formula accorded to him since the traditional horizon of archetypes and repetition was transcended. Only such a freedom (aside from its soteriological, hence, in the strict sense, its religious value) is able to defend modern man from the terror of history—a freedom, that is, which has its source and finds its guaranty and support in God....

We may say, furthermore, that Christianity is the "religion" of modern man and historical man, of the man who simultaneously discovered personal freedom and continuous time (in place of cyclical time). It is even interesting to note that the existence of God forced itself far more urgently upon modern man, for whom history exists as such, as history and not as repetition, than upon the man of the archaic and traditional cultures, who, to defend himself from the terror of history, had at his disposition all the myths, rites, and customs mentioned in the course of this book.... In the horizon of archetypes and repetition, the terror of history, when it appeared, could be supported. Since the "invention" of faith, in the Judaeo-Christian sense of the word..., the man who has left the horizon of archetypes and repetition can no longer defend himself against that terror except through the idea of God. In fact, it is only by presupposing the existence of God that he conquers, on the one hand, freedom (which grants him autonomy in a universe governed by laws...) and, on the other hand, the certainty that historical tragedies have a transhistorical meaning, even if that meaning is not always visible for humanity in its present condition. Any other situation of modern man leads, in the end, to despair. It is a despair provoked...by his presence in a historical universe in which almost the whole of mankind lives prey to a continual terror (even if not always conscious of it).

In this respect, Christianity incontestably proves to be the religion of "fallen man": and this to the extent to which modern man is irremediably identified with history and progress, and to which history and progress are a fall, both implying the final abandonment of the paradise of archetypes and repetition.

10

E. E. Evans-Pritchard: Primitive Religion and Modern Theories

Edward Evan Evans-Pritchard (1902–1973) is perhaps the most celebrated figure in modern anthropology, an intrepid traveler and scholar
who devoted himself to cultural inquiry and field research for nearly half a
century, from the 1920s to 1970, when he retired, multiple honors in hand,
from his post at Oxford University. Evans-Pritchard's chief claim to this
recognition rests on a series of systematic "in country" studies he prepared
in Africa, where he was able to immerse himself thoroughly in the customs
and beliefs of living tribal cultures. His close accounts of life among the
Azande and Nuer peoples of the Southern Sudan secured his reputation
as field-working ethnographer virtually without equal in descriptive skill
and analytical rigor.

Evans-Pritchard was the son of an Anglican clergyman. He attended
Exeter College, Oxford, where he took a degree in modern history. During
graduate study at the London School of Economics, his interest turned to
anthropology, and he began reading extensively both French and British
writings in this newly emerging discipline. He also met C. G. Seligman and
Bronislaw Malinowski, two pioneering figures who insisted that all anthropology begins with field anthropology. This was a precept he embraced
enthusiastically, and following Seligman's advice, he soon set off on his first
journey to Africa.

On arriving there, Evans-Pritchard settled first among the Azande,
who made him welcome as he learned their language and carefully noted
their customs over an interval of five years from 1926 to 1931. The fruit of
these labors took some time to ripen—till 1937 in fact, when he published
Witchcraft, Oracles and Magic among the Azande. Among certain intellectuals, it would prove one of the most influential books of the century.

The discussion in *Witchcraft* centers not on religion but on three topics
closely related to it. For the Azande, magic rests on the belief that certain
aspects of life are controlled by mystical powers. Evans-Pritchard says they

do not hold such beliefs because they are childish or ignorant, as Tylor and Frazer alleged; in fact, he finds the Azande "unusually intelligent, sophisticated, and progressive." Mystical ideas and related rituals hold a routine and rational place in their lives. For example, they think witchcraft is the cause of illness, so the source of the problem (usually a person trading in witchcraft who has a grievance against the victim) must be found. To do so, they turn to the poison oracle, selecting a small bird, forcing it to take poison, and posing a question. The bird's death or survival provides the answer: either Yes or No. If that process leads to a charge of witchcraft, measures are taken so the accused and victim are reconciled—a socially useful outcome.

The analytical precision in the accounts of these practices and the logic behind them is what has made *Witchcraft* a work of such keen interest to many anthropologists, social theorists, and even philosophers. Evans-Pritchard shows that the apparent absurdities of witchcraft and magic actually form a coherent and socially workable set of ideas and practices. They complement the Azande understanding of other causes and promote good conduct. Because witches are by definition disagreeable, people behave well to avoid suspicion. The magical world-view of the Azande thus functions in ways similar to our own. Within their overall conceptual system, they reason as logically about everyday beliefs and actions as we do within ours. The passage from *Witchcraft* reprinted here offers an exhibit of the logical pattern of magical thinking, as well as Evans-Pritchard's analytical method in describing it.

While preparing the Azande study, Evans-Pritchard began further field work with a neighboring tribe, the Nuer. The result of these efforts was an extended three-volume study exploring economics, kinship patterns, and religion. In *Nuer Religion,* the third in the sequence, published in 1956, he again put into service his trademark habits of close description and careful analysis. He notes that on first look the Nuer seem to be a people without religion; they appear to have no formal doctrines, sacraments, or organized worship. But appearances deceive. In fact, they possess all of these things, though in informal ways easy to overlook. Central to their religious life is the concept of spirit (for which their word is *Kwoth*) and the presence of spirits around them. But they are not primitive polytheists. For foremost among the spirits is the one sovereign God, whom they call *Kwoth nhial,* the "spirit of (or in) the sky." This divinity is conceived in terms similar to those of Western monotheistic religions: he is the creator of all things and ruler of the entire natural order, who also has the qualities of human personality and unselfishly loves humanity. This elevated notion of God fits ill with Victorian notions of primitive savagery and superstition. The same is true for other Nuer ideas. Totems, for example, are mere earth-spirits, held in low esteem. That fact is sharply at odds with the great importance assigned to totems by theorists like Frazer, Freud, and Durkheim. Tylor, we may recall, thought primitive the ideas of the gods developed as an extension of the idea of the human soul. For the Nuer, however, the human soul is different from, and even opposed to, the spiritual nature of the gods. Tylor's theory, so plausible in the scholar's study, accords poorly with the actual belief and practice of the Nuer. The same is true for Nuer ideas of personal conduct and morality, which are nearly puritanical in nature. For Evans-Pritchard, as the second selection provided here will indicate, Nuer religion stands well apart from such things as the savagery Freud suggested, the totemism that Durkheim envisioned, or the superstition imagined by Frazer in *The Golden Bough*.

Late in his career Evans-Pritchard returned to the theme of religion in a series of lectures entitled *Theories of Primitive Religion* (1968). This short, crisp discussion offers a kind of summary assessment of the most influential explanations of religion proposed over the course of the previous century. Most theorists, he observes, have never really encountered primitive people, but that has not kept them from voicing their opinions, however unfounded. They tend mostly to fall into two groups: those who offer psychological theories of the kind framed by Tylor, Frazer, and Freud, and those who offer sociological accounts—the sort developed by Marx and Durkheim or one of their many disciples and associates. The former stress the intellectual, emotional, and even irrational motives of primitive belief; the latter emphasize the role of the social factors and forces. Both groups offer ingenious, original, and sometimes quite compelling observations on their subject. But on the whole they are all beset by one problem: they rely on educated guesswork, rather than real knowledge of their subject. The third selection provided here offers a sample of this discussion, where Evans-Pritchard can be seen methodically dismantling the grand constructs of earlier theorists and making his point that good explanation always puts evidence ahead of speculation.

Witchcraft, Oracles, and Magic among the Azande

In this selection Evans-Pritchard discusses the nature of witchcraft, the use of oracles to discover it, the occasions when the Azande appeal to it, and its value in accounting for things that would otherwise be left without explanation.

I have described some of the prominent characteristics of witchcraft in Zande thought. Others will be developed in this and following chapters. It is an

FROM: *Witchcraft, Oracles, and Magic among the Azande.* © 1937 by The Clarendon Press, Oxford, England.

inevitable conclusion from Zande descriptions of witchcraft that it is not an objective reality....

The concept of witchcraft nevertheless provides them with a natural philosophy by which the relations between men and unfortunate events are explained and a ready and stereotyped means of reacting to such events. Witchcraft beliefs also embrace a system of values which regulate human conduct.

Witchcraft is ubiquitous. It plays its part in every activity of Zande life; in agricultural, fishing, and hunting pursuits; in domestic life of homesteads as well as in communal life of district and court; it is an important theme of mental life in which it forms the background of a vast panorama of oracles and magic; its influence is plainly stamped on law and morals, etiquette and religion; it is prominent in technology and language; there is no niche or corner of Zande culture into which it does not twist itself. If blight seizes the ground-nut crop it is witchcraft; if the bush is vainly scoured for game it is witchcraft; ... if a magical rite fails to achieve its purpose it is witchcraft; if, in fact, any failure or misfortune falls upon any one at any time and in relation to any of the manifold activities if his life it may be due to witchcraft....

When a Zande speaks of witchcraft he does not speak of it as we speak of the weird witchcraft of our own history. Witchcraft is to him a commonplace happening and he seldom passes a day without mentioning it. Where we talk about the crops, hunting, and our neighbors' ailments the Zande introduces into these topics of conversation the subject of witchcraft.... Witchcraft participates in all misfortunes and is the idiom in which Azande speak about them and in which they explain them. Witchcraft is a classification of misfortunes which while differing from each other in other respects have this single common character, their harmfulness to man.

Unless the reader appreciates that witchcraft is quite a normal factor in the life of Azande, one to which almost any and every happening may be referred, he will entirely misunderstand their behavior towards it.... To [the Zande]...there is nothing miraculous about it. It is expected that a man's hunting will be injured by witches and he has at his disposal means of dealing with them. When misfortunes occur he does not become awestruck at the play of supernatural forces. He is not terrified at the presence of an occult enemy. He is, on the other hand, extremely annoyed. Some one, out of spite, has ruined his ground-nuts or spoiled his hunting or given his wife a chill, and surely this is cause for anger! He has done no one harm, so what right has any one to interfere in his affairs? It is an impertinence, an insult, a dirty, offensive trick!...

Witchcraft...is so intertwined with everyday happenings that it is part of a Zande's ordinary world. There is nothing remarkable about a witch—you may be one yourself, and certainly many of your closest neighbors are witches....

But is not Zande belief in witchcraft a belief in mystical causation of phenomena and events to the complete exclusion of all natural causes? The relations of mystical to commonsense thought are very complicated and raise problems that confront us on every page of this book. Here I wish to state the problem...in terms of actual situations.

I found it strange at first to live among Azande and listen to naïve explanations of misfortunes which, to our minds, have apparent causes, but after a while I learned the idiom of their thought and applied notions of witchcraft as spontaneously as themselves in situations where the concept was relevant. A boy knocked his foot against a small stump of wood in the center of a bush path, a frequent happening in Africa, and suffered pain and inconvenience in consequence. Owing to its position on his toe it was impossible to keep the cut free from dirt and it began to fester. He declared that witchcraft had made him knock his foot against the stump. I always argued with Azande and criticized their statements, and I did so on this occasion. I told the boy that he had knocked his foot against the stump of wood because he had been careless, and that witchcraft had not placed it in the path, for it had grown there naturally. He agreed that witchcraft had nothing to do with the stump of wood being in his path but added that he had kept his eyes open for stumps, as indeed every Zande does most carefully, and that if he had not been bewitched he would have seen the stump. As a conclusive argument for his view he remarked that all cuts do not take days to heal, but on the contrary, close quickly, for that is the nature of cuts. Why, then, had his sore festered and remained open if there were no witchcraft behind it? This, as I discovered before long, was to be regarded as the Zande explanation of sickness. ...

In speaking to Azande about witchcraft and in observing their reactions to situations of misfortune it was obvious that they did not attempt to account for the existence of phenomena, or even the action of phenomena, by mystical causation alone. What they explained by witchcraft were the particular conditions in a chain of causation which related an individual to natural happenings in such a way that he sustained injury. The boy who knocked his foot against a stump of wood did not account for the stump by reference to witchcraft, nor did he suggest that whenever anybody knocks his foot against a stump it is necessarily due to witchcraft, nor yet again did he account for the cut by saying that it was caused by witchcraft, for he knew quite well that it was caused by the stump of wood. What he attributed to witchcraft was that on this particular occasion, when exercising his usual care, he struck his foot against a stump of wood, whereas on a hundred other occasions he did not do so, and that on this particular occasion the cut, which he expected to result from the knock, festered whereas he had had dozens of cuts which had not festered. Surely these peculiar conditions demand an explanation.... I present the Zande's explicit line of reasoning—not my own....

We must understand, therefore, that we shall give a false account of Zande philosophy if we say that they believe witchcraft to be the sole cause of phenomena. This proposition is not contained in Zande patterns of thought, which only assert that witchcraft brings a man into relation with events in such a way that he sustained injury....

In Zandeland sometimes an old granary collapses. There is nothing remarkable in this. Every Zande knows that termites eat the supports in course of time and that even the hardest woods decay after years of service. Now a granary is the summerhouse of a Zande homestead and people sit beneath it in the heat of the day and chat or play the African hole-game or work at some craft. Consequently it may happen that there are people sitting beneath the granary when it collapses and they are injured, for it is a heavy structure made of beams and clay and may be stored with eleusine [grass grown for grain: ed.]. Now why should these particular people have been sitting under this particular granary at the particular moment when it collapsed?... We say that the granary collapsed because its supports were eaten away by termites. That is the cause that explains the collapse of the granary. We also say that people were sitting under it at the time because it was in the heat of the day and they thought that it would be a comfortable place to talk and work. This is the cause of the people being under the granary at the time it collapsed. To our minds the only relationship between these two independently caused facts is their coincidence in time and space. We have no explanation of why the two chains of causation intersected at a certain time and in a certain place, for there is no interdependence between them.

Zande philosophy can supply the missing link. The Zande knows... why these two events occurred at a precisely similar moment in time and space. It was due to the action of witchcraft. If there had been no witchcraft people would have been sitting under the granary and it would not have fallen on them, or it would have collapsed but the people would not have been sheltering under it at the time. Witchcraft explains the coincidence of these two happenings.

I hope I am not expected to point out that the Zande cannot analyse his doctrines as I have done for him. In fact I never obtained an explanatory text on witchcraft, though I was able to obtain in the form of texts clear statements on dozens of other subjects. It is no use saying to a Zande "Now tell me what you Azande think about witchcraft" because the subject is too general and indeterminate, both too vague and too immense to be described concisely. But it is possible to extract the principles of their thought from dozens of situations in which witchcraft is called upon to explain happenings and from dozens of other situations in which failure is attributed to some other cause. Their philosophy is explicit, but is not formally stated as a doctrine. A Zande would not say "I believe in natural causation but I do not think that that fully explains coincidences, and it seems to be that the theory of witchcraft offers a satisfactory explanation of them," but he expresses his thought in terms of actual and particular situations. He says "a buffalo charges," "a tree falls,".... Herein he is stating empirically ascertained facts. But he also says "a buffalo charged and wounded so-and-so," "a tree fell on so-and-so and killed him,".... He tells you that these things are due to witchcraft, saying in each instance, "So-and-so has been bewitched." The facts do not explain themselves or only partly explain themselves. They can only be explained fully if one takes witchcraft into consideration....

[I]f Azande cannot enunciate a theory of causation in terms acceptable to us they describe happenings in an idiom that is explanatory. They are aware that it is particular circumstances of events in their relation to man, their harmfulness to a particular person, that constitutes evidence of witchcraft. Witchcraft explains *why* events are harmful to man and not *how* they happen. A Zande perceives how they happen just as we do. He does not see a witch charge a man, but an elephant. He does not see a witch push over a granary, but termites gnawing away its supports.... His perception of how events occur is as clear as our own....

Zande belief in witchcraft in no way contradicts empirical knowledge of cause and effect. The world known to the senses is just as real to them as it is to us. We must not be deceived by their way of expressing causation and imagine that because they say a man was killed by witchcraft they entirely neglect the secondary causes that, as we judge them, were the true causes of his death.... If a buffalo kills a man you can do nothing about it as far as the buffalo is concerned. But, though surely enough the buffalo has killed him, it would not have killed him if it had not been for the operation of witchcraft at the same time, and witchcraft is a social fact, a person. In a number of co-operating causes this single one is selected and spoken of as the cause of death because it is the ideological pivot around which swings the lengthy social procedure from death to vengeance....

Since Azande recognize plurality of causes, and it is the social situation that indicates the relevant one, we can understand why the doctrine of witchcraft is not used to explain every failure and misfortune. It sometimes happens that the social situation demands a common-sense, and not a mystical, judgement of cause. Thus if you tell a lie, or commit adultery, or steal, or deceive your prince, and are found out, you cannot elude punishment by saying that you were bewitched. Zande doctrine declares emphatically "Witchcraft does not make a person tell lies"; ... "Witchcraft" is in yourself (you alone are responsible)....

If a man murders another tribesman with knife or spear he is put to death. It is not necessary in such a case to seek a witch, for an objective towards which vengeance may be directed is already present....

In the instances given in the preceding paragraphs it is the natural cause and not the mystical cause that is selected as the socially significant one. In these situations witchcraft is irrelevant and, if not totally excluded, is not indicated as the principal factor in causation. As in our own society a scientific theory of causation, if not excluded, is deemed irrelevant in questions of moral and legal responsibility, so in Zande society the doctrine of witchcraft, if not excluded, is deemed irrelevant in the same situations. We accept scientific explanations of the causes of disease, and even of the causes of insanity, but we deny them in crime and sin because here they militate against law and morals which are axiomatic. The Zande accepts a mystical explanation of the causes of misfortune, sickness, and death, but he does not allow this explanation if it conflicts with social exigencies expressed in law and morals.

~

[Prior to the discussion below, Evans-Pritchard explains that the Azande ritually seek answers to certain questions about witchcraft and other important matters by forcing a poison (called *benge)* into small birds. The questions are stated as the poison is applied; if the bird lives, that fact forms the answer—perhaps a "Yes"—to the question; if the bird dies, that forms the opposite, or "No," answer.: ed.]

Problems That Arise from Consultation of the Poison Oracle

Magic and oracles are more difficult for us to understand than most other primitive practices and are therefore more profitable a subject for study than customs which invite easy explanations. Any European can at once comprehend, and even respect, a cult of the dead....For our own culture comprises notions of the soul and life after death and Gods, so that we are at once able to translate Zande beliefs about these entities into terms of our own culture and to find them reasonable, if mistaken. Along this path lie many pitfalls, because the desire to assimilate primitive notions to kindred notions of our own tempts us, in the first place, to read into their beliefs concepts peculiar to our own, and, in the second place, to interpret their beliefs by introspection or in terms of our own sentiments. But if the path of investigation into oracles and magic is safer, it is more difficult to follow.

I have described to many people in England the facts related in the last section and they have been, in the main, incredulous or contemptuous. In their questions to me they have sought to explain away Zande behaviour by rationalizing it, that is to say, by interpreting it in terms of our culture. They assume that Azande must understand the qualities of poisons as we understand them; or that they attribute a personality to the oracle, a mind that judges as men judge, but with higher prescience; or that the oracle is manipulated by the operator whose cunning conserves the faith of laymen....

The same, and other, problems naturally occurred to me in Zandeland, and I made inquiries into, and observations on, those points which struck me as being important, and in the present section I record my conclusions. Before setting them down, I must warn the reader that we are trying to analyse behaviour rather than belief. Azande have little theory about their oracles and do not feel the need for doctrines.

∽

It will have been noted that Azande act experimentally within the cadre of their mystical notions. They act as we would have to act if we had no means of making chemical and physiological analyses and we wanted to obtain the same results as they want to obtain. As soon as the poison is brought back from its forest home it is tested to discover whether some fowls will live and others die under its influence. It would be unreasonable to use poison without first having ascertained that all fowls to which it is administered do not die or do not live. The oracle would then be a farce.

If their mystical notions allowed them to generalize their observations they would perceive, as we do, that their faith is without foundations....

And yet Azande do not see that their oracles tell them nothing! Their blindness is not due to stupidity, for they display great ingenuity in explaining away the failures and inequalities of the poison oracle and experimental keenness in testing it. It is due rather to the fact that their intellectual ingenuity and experimental keenness are conditioned by patterns of ritual behavior and mystical belief. Within the limits set by these patterns they show great intelligence, but it cannot operate beyond these limits. Or, to put it another way: they reason excellently in the idiom of their beliefs, but they cannot reason outside, or against, their beliefs because they have no other idiom in which to express their thoughts.

But when faith directs behavior it must not be in glaring contradiction to experience of the objective world, or must offer explanations that demonstrate to the satisfaction of the intellect that the contradiction is only apparent or is due to peculiar conditions. The reader will naturally wonder what Azande say when subsequent events prove the prophecies of the poison oracle to be wrong. The oracle says one thing will happen and another and quite different thing happens. Here again Azande are not surprised at such an outcome, but it does not prove to them that the oracle is futile. It rather proves how well founded are their beliefs in witchcraft and sorcery and taboos. On this particular occasion the oracle was bad because it was corrupted by some evil influence. Subsequent events prove the presence of witchcraft on the earlier occasion. The contradiction between what the oracle said would happen and what actually has happened is just as glaring to Zande eyes as it is to ours, but they never for a moment question the virtue of the oracle in general but seek only to account for the inaccuracy of this particular poison, for every packet of *benge* is an independent oracle and if it is corrupt its corruption does not affect other packets of the poison....

Azande see as well as we that the failure of their oracle to prophesy truly calls for explanation, but so entangled are they in mystical notions that they must make use of them to account for the failure. The contradiction between experience and one mystical notion is explained by reference to other mystical notions.

Normally there is little chance of the oracle being proved wrong, for it is usually asked questions to which its answers cannot well be challenged by subsequent experience, since the inquirer accepts the verdict and does not seek to check it by experiment. Thus were a man to ask the oracle, "If I build my homestead in such-and-such a place will I die there?"... and were the oracle to reply "Yes," he would not construct his homestead in the ill-omened place.... Consequently he would never know what would have happened if he had not taken the advice of the oracle....

Furthermore, only certain types of question are regularly put to the oracle: questions relating to witchcraft, sickness, death, lengthy journeys, mourning and vengeance, changing of homestead sites, lengthy agricultural and hunting enterprises, and so forth.... One does not ask the poison oracle about small matters or questions involving minute precision with regard to time....

Indeed, I have noticed that as a rule Azande do not ask questions to which answers are easily tested by experience and that they ask only questions which embrace contingencies. The answers either cannot be tested, or if proved by subsequent events to be erroneous permit an explanation of the error. In the last resort errors can always be explained by attributing them to mystical interference. But there is no need to suppose that the Zande is conscious of an evasion of clear issues. In restricting his questions to certain well-known types he is conforming to tradition. It does not occur to him to test the oracle experimentally unless he has grave suspicions about a particular packet of poison.

Moreover, we must bear in mind that the main purpose of the oracle and its principal value to the Azande lie in its ability to reveal the play of mystical forces. When they ask about health or marriage or hunting they are seeking information about the movement of psychic forces which might cause them misfortune....

By means of his oracles a Zande can discover the mystical forces which hang over a man and doom him in advance, and having discovered them he can counteract them or alter his plans to avoid the doom which awaits him in any particular venture. These forces can be observed in no other way. Hence it is evident that the answers he receives do not generally concern objective happenings and therefore cannot easily be contrary to experience....

⌒

There is a final problem to discuss. As I have recorded in earlier sections, each situation demands the particular pattern of thought appropriate to it. Hence an individual in one situation will employ a notion he excludes in a different situation. The many beliefs I have recorded are so many different tools of thought, and he selects the ones that are chiefly to his advantage. Thus A consults the oracles, and it declares that B has committed adultery with his wife and B knows that he is innocent or wishes to convince others he is. A declares that the poison oracles cannot err and that in its revelations he has absolute proof of B's guilt. B can... say, "Their poison is foolish," or "They accuse me out of spite." A Zande does not readily accept an oracular verdict which conflicts seriously with his interests. The authority of a prince's oracle is the only way out of the impasse because such aspersions cannot be cast at a prince's oracle or person without serious consequences. But when A is in B's situation he will talk just as B talks. No one believes that the oracle is nonsense, but every one thinks that for some particular reason in this particular case the particular poison used is in error in respect to himself. Azande are only skeptical of particular oracles and not of oracles in general, and their skepticism is always expressed in a mystical idiom that vouches for the validity of the poison oracle as an institution....

In all this Azande are not employing trickery. A man uses for his individual needs in certain situations those notions that most favour his desires. Azande cannot go beyond the limits set by their culture and invent notions, but within these limits human behavior is not rigidly determined by custom and a man has some freedom of action and thought.

Nuer Religion

At the conclusion of his detailed account of Nuer religious practices and beliefs, Evans-Pritchard discusses the results of his work and their implications for the wider issue of interpreting religion, particularly the religion of so-called "primitive" peoples.

[T] hough during the last thirty or so years many and intensive investigations of primitive peoples have been made, there have been few

FROM: *Nuer Religion.* © 1956 by The Clarendon Press, Oxford, England.

systematic studies of what we may call, in order to include a wider range of phenomena than are usually placed under the rubric of religion, primitive philosophies. The word "philosophy" is used here, for want of a better, in the general sense of the German "Weltanschauung." We have, therefore, in the study of primitive philosophies to begin anew to build up a body of theory and to formulate problems in the light of it. There is only one way in which this can be done. A number of systematic studies of primitive philosophies has to be made. When that has been done a classification can be made on the basis of which comparative studies can be undertaken which possibly may lead to some general conclusions. This book is intended as a contribution which it is hoped may be useful in the building up of a classification of African philosophies.

Such a classification of African philosophies must naturally be by reference to their chief and characteristic features. Among all African peoples we find in one form or another theistic beliefs, manistic cults, witchcraft notions, interdictions with supernatural sanctions, magical practices, &c., but the philosophy of each has its own special character in virtue of the way in which among that people these ideas are related to one another. It will be found that one or other belief, or set of beliefs, dominates the others and gives form, pattern, and color to the whole. Thus, among some peoples, notably a large proportion of the Bantu, the dominant motif is provided by the cult of ancestors; among others, some of the Sudanic peoples for example, it is found in the notion of witchcraft, with which are bound up magical and oracular techniques; among others, such as the Nuer, Spirit is in the centre of the picture and manistic and witchcraft ideas are peripheral; and among other peoples yet other notions predominate. The test of what is the dominant motif is usually, perhaps always, to what a people attribute dangers and sickness and other misfortunes and what steps they take to avoid or eliminate them.

Nuer philosophy is, as we have seen, essentially of a religious kind, and is dominated by the idea of *kwoth,* Spirit. As Spirit cannot be directly experienced by the senses, what we are considering is a conception. *Kwoth* would, indeed, be entirely indeterminate and could not be thought of by Nuer at all were it not that it is contrasted with the idea of *cak,* creation, in terms of which it can be defined by reference to effects and relations and by the use of symbols and metaphors. But these definitions are only schemata, as Otto puts it, and if we seek for elucidation beyond these terms, a statement of what Spirit is thought to be like in itself, we seek of course in vain. Nuer do not claim to know. They say that they are merely *doar,* simple people, and how can simple people know about such matters? What happens in the world is determined by Spirit and Spirit can be influenced by prayer and sacrifice. This much they know, but no more; and they say, very sensibly, that since the European is so clever perhaps he can tell them the answer to the question he asks.

Nevertheless, we can reach certain conclusions about the basic features of the conception. We have seen that Nuer religion is pneumatic and theistic. Whether it can rightly be described as monotheistic is largely a matter of definition. I would say, for the reasons I have given, that it can be so described in the sense already discussed, for at no level of thought and experience is Spirit thought of as something altogether different from God. It follows from the conception of God as Spirit that though he is figured in many diverse figures he can be thought of both as each and as all alike and one. But if we say that in spite of the many different spirits Spirit is one and that Nuer religion is in this sense monotheistic we have to add that it is also modalistic. Spirit, though one, is differently thought of with regard to different effects and relations.

We have, indeed, in this matter to be particularly careful not to be led into false conclusions. A theistic religion need not be either monotheistic or polytheistic. It may be both. It is a question of the level, or situation, of thought rather than of exclusive types of thought. On one level Nuer religion may be regarded as monotheistic, at another level as polytheistic; and it can also be regarded at other levels as totemistic or fetishistic. These conceptions of spiritual activity are not incompatible. They are rather different ways of thinking of the numinous at different levels of experience. We found these different ways of thinking reflected in the complex notions involved in sacrifice; and also in the variety of Nuer attitudes towards Spirit, ranging from love to fear, from trust to apprehension, from dependence to hostility.

Since the basic feature of Nuer religion is the idea of Spirit it is not surprising that certain features of other African religions are unimportant among them or even entirely lacking. The conception of ancestral ghosts is altogether subordinate. Animistic ideas are almost entirely absent. Witchcraft ideas play a very minor role, and magic a negligible one. Both are incompatible with a theocentric philosophy, for when both fortune and misfortune come from God they cannot also come from human powers, whether innate or learnt. Likewise, it is easily understandable that there is no idea of an impersonal force, a dynamism or vital force, which we are told is characteristic of some African religions. It is true that when Nuer speak of *kwoth* without specifying any particular representation of it the impression may be conveyed that it has an impersonal character; but it is always understood that what is being referred to is Spirit conceived of either as God or as some particular hypostasis or refraction of him, though it may not be known which of them is concerned in the situation they have in mind. Moreover, it is certain that, for the most part at any rate, the many representations of Spirit we find in Nuerland today are a fairly recent introduction and development, and Nuer are aware of this. Another negative feature of Nuer religion is the complete absence of ritual, in the sense of ceremonial, interdictions, so prominent among other African peoples. No interdictions on food, drink, or sexual intercourse condition the efficacy of religious rites (nor, for the matter of that the success of any undertaking), and, there being no ritual interdictions, there can be no ideas of ritual purity and impurity. Nuer interdictions are not of a ritual order at all, but of a moral one, so that breaches of them result in a state of moral impurity or sin, of which the resultant situation and manifestation may be sickness or other misfortune. And what counts in sacrifice is not the outward, physical, state of the sacrificer, but his moral state, the sincerity of his intention.

We can say that these characteristics, both negative and positive, of Nuer religion indicate a distinctive kind of piety which is dominated by a strong sense of dependence on God and confidence in him rather than in any human powers or endeavors. God is great and man foolish and feeble, a tiny ant. And this sense of dependence is remarkably individualistic. It is an intimate, personal, relationship between man and God. This is apparent in Nuer ideas of sin, in their expressions of guilt, in their confessions, and in the dominant piacular theme of their sacrifices. It is evident also in their habit of making short supplications at any time. This is a very noticeable trait of Nuer piety.... [I]n western Dinkaland...a Nuer youth whose habit of praying to God for aid on every occasion of difficulty greatly astonished the Dinka. In prayer and sacrifice alike, in what is said and in what is done, the emphasis is on complete surrender to God's will. Man plays a passive role. He cannot get to God but God can get to him. Given this sort of piety, we are not surprised to find that the prophet is more influential than the priest.

In this sense of the totality of Nuer religious beliefs and practices forming a pattern which excludes conflicting elements and subordinates each part to the harmony of the whole, we may speak of their religious system. This does not mean, however, that it is an entirely consistent set of ideas. On the contrary, like other religions, it contains unresolved ambiguities and paradoxes, as that God is remote from men, a *deus absconditus* [hidden god: ed.] in the sky, and also very near to them, a *deus revelatus* [god disclosed: ed.] in human enterprises and affairs; and that he is both friend and foe, whom one summons for aid and asks to turn away, seeking at the same time union with him and separation from him. It might, indeed, be argued that the breaking up of the conception of Spirit into a number of different representations, evoked in different situations, could be regarded as a means of resolving both ambiguities; but there would be certain difficulties in this view. Both must always have been there, whereas the spirits are a new phenomenon. Also, they are not regarded as something different and apart from God, so that the ambiguities are not really resolved. Moreover, although some of the spirits have a capricious side to them and Nuer may be said to have in a way an aversion to some of them, they are, nevertheless, a coming down of Spirit to earth into a homely relationship to men, so that while they may trouble them they also put themselves at their service. In them man and Spirit meet. A prophet, indeed, seeks so complete a union with a spirit that he is no longer himself but the spirit. . . .

It is in the nature of the subject that there should be ambiguity and paradox. I am aware that in consequence I have not been able to avoid what must appear to the reader to be obscurities, and even contradictions, in my account. When one looks at Nuer religion from one angle it seems to be like this and when one looks at it from another angle it seems to be like that, and this and that do not always correspond. The difficulties of investigation and presentation have been further added to by the great increase in the number and types of spiritual forms.

The taking over from neighboring peoples of new spiritual conceptions has, if not produced, greatly accentuated the paradox of the one and the many, one of the chief problems of Nuer religion today, and one to which I have had to devote particular attention. And it has made yet more apparent a further problem, to which I have also given special attention—that of the relation of symbol to what it symbolizes—for every new representation requires, if it is to acquire more than nominal distinctness, a visible, material symbol. Indeed, our difficulties are everywhere greatly increased by historical changes in Nuer religion. . . . But if one has to admit that religious conceptions have some autonomy and pass from one people to another without our being able to say why they do so, we can show that they are much altered in the process, being made to conform to the already existing set of ideas into which they are taken. The ideas of *deng* [daughter of the air-spirit: ed.], *colwic* [spirits that once were human: ed.] and *kor* [internal body pain: ed.] are very different among the Dinka and the Nuer, that of *ther* [danger associated with pregnant women: ed.] has a very different place in Nuer thought to that which it has in Anuak thought, and *nyikang* [one of the air spirits: ed.] is a very different figure in Nuer religion from what it is in Shilluk religion. . . .

I have throughout my account emphasized, especially in my discussion of sacrifice, the difference between the personal and collective aspects of Nuer religion and that the first is more important for an understanding of its fundamental character. We learn from the collective expression of religion more about the social order than about what is specifically religious thought and practice. Its personal expression tells us more of what religion is in itself. If we recognize that the collective expression is only one form of religious activity we shall not make the mistake of trying to explain Nuer religion in terms of their social structure alone.

Sociological writers . . . have often treated religious conceptions . . . as a projection of the social order. This is inadmissible. That Nuer religious thought and practices are influenced by their whole social life is evident from our study of them....But the Nuer conception of God cannot be reduced to, or explained by, the social order.

In my first book on the Nuer I gave an account of their ecology, their modes of livelihood, and their political structure. I tried to show that some features of their modes of livelihood can be understood only if we take their environment into account; and also that some features of their political structure can be understood only if we take their modes of livelihood into account. I did not, however, try to explain their modes of livelihood as a function of their environment or their political structure as a function of their economy. In my second book I tried to show how some features of their family and kinship systems were more intelligible when seen in relation to tribal and lineage systems; but it is not suggested that they could be explained in terms of them. In this final volume I have tried to show how some features of their religion can be presented more intelligibly in relation to the social order described in the earlier volumes but I have tried also to describe and interpret it as a system of ideas and practices in its own right.

When the purely social and cultural features of Nuer religion have been abstracted, what is left which may be said to be that which is expressed in the social and cultural forms we have been considering? It is difficult to give a more adequate answer to this question than to say that it is a relationship between man and God which transcends all forms. It is not surprising therefore that we cannot give any clear account of what for Nuer is the nature of this spiritual relationship. We feel like spectators at a shadow show watching insubstantial shadows on the screen. There is nothing Nuer can say of the nature of God other than that he is like wind or air. They can speak of their experience of Spirit but can tell us nothing of Spirit itself. The spirits of the air are little more than names to them....It is much the same with the totemic representations of Spirit. They are not in themselves of a spiritual nature but only material symbols....Spirit in itself is for Nuer a mystery which lies behind the names and the totemic and other appearances in which it is represented.

We can, therefore, say no more than that Spirit is an intuitive apprehension, something experienced in response to certain situations but known directly only to the imagination and not to the senses. Nuer religious conceptions are properly speaking not concepts but imaginative constructions. Hence the response to them is imaginative too, a kind of miming. Words and gestures transport us to a realm of experience where what the eye sees and the ear hears is not the same as what the mind perceives. Hands are raised to the sky in supplication, but it is not the sky which is supplicated but what it represents to the imagination. Formal respect is paid to an animal not on account of what the animal is in itself but on account of what for some people it stands for in thought as a symbol....A piacular ox is the sacrificer himself and in the ox he dies in symbol. But the sacrificer is not present. The hand of the officiant on the back of the ox represents his hand.... To the mind sickness caused by sin is the sin and in the mind it is wiped out by the sacrificial act. We seem indeed to be watching a play or to be listening to someone's account of what he has dreamt. Perhaps when we have this illusion we are beginning to understand, for the significance of the objects, actions, and events lies not in themselves but in what they mean to those who experience them as participants or assistants. If we regard only what happens in sacrifice before the eyes it may seem to be a succession of senseless, and even cruel and repulsive, acts, but when we reflect on their meaning we perceive that they are a dramatic representation of a spiritual experience. What this experience is the anthropologist cannot for certain say. Experiences of this kind are not easily communicated even when people are ready to communicate them and have a sophisticated vocabulary in which to do so. Though prayer and sacrifice are exterior actions, Nuer religion is ultimately an interior state. This state is externalized in rites which we can observe, but their meaning depends finally on an awareness of God and that men are dependent on him and must be resigned to his will. At this point the theologian takes over from the anthropologist.

Theories of Primitive Religion

From his perspective as a field working anthropologist, Evans-Pritchard here offers an analytical review of major theorists from Tylor and his associates in the Victorian era through the first half of the twentieth century and up to his own time.

Tylor wished to show that primitive religion was rational, that it arose from observations, however inadequate, and from logical deductions from them, however faulty; that it constituted a crude natural philosophy. In his treatment of magic, which he distinguished from religion rather for convenience of exposition than on grounds of...validity, he likewise stressed the rational element in what he called "this farrago of nonsense." It also is based on genuine observation, and rests further on classification of similarities, the first essential process in human knowledge. Where the magician goes wrong is in inferring that because things are alike they have a mystical link between them, thus mistaking an ideal connexion for a real one, a subjective one for an objective one. And if we ask how peoples who exploit nature and organize their social life so well make such mistakes, the answer is that they have very good reasons for

---

FROM: *Theories of Primitive Religion.* © 1965 by The Clarendon Press, Oxford, England.

not perceiving the futility of their magic. Nature, or trickery on the part of the magician, often brings about what the magic is supposed to achieve; and if it fails to achieve its purpose, that is rationally explained by neglect of some prescription, or by the fact that some prohibition has been ignored or some hostile force has impeded it. Also, there is plasticity about judgements of success and failure, and people everywhere find it hard to appreciate evidence, especially when the weight of authority induces acceptance of what confirms, and rejection of what contradicts, a belief. Here Tylor's observations are borne out by ethnological evidence.

I have touched briefly on Tylor's discussions of magic partly as a further illustration of intellectualist interpretation and partly because it leads me straight to an estimation of Sir James Frazer's contribution to our subject. Frazer is, I suppose, the best-known name in anthropology, and we owe much to him and to Spencer and Tylor. The whole of *The Golden Bough,* a work of immense industry and erudition, is devoted to primitive superstitions. But it cannot be said that he added much of value to Tylor's theory of religion; rather that he introduced some confusion into it in the form of two new suppositions, the one pseudo-historical and the other psychological. According to him, mankind everywhere, and sooner or later, passes through three stages of intellectual development, from magic to religion, and from religion to science.... Other writers of the period ... also believed that magic preceded religion. Eventually, says Frazer, the shrewder intelligences probably discovered that magic did not really achieve its ends, but, still being unable to overcome their difficulties by empirical means and to face their crises through a refined philosophy, they fell into another illusion, that there were spiritual beings who could aid them. In course of time the shrewder intelligences saw that spirits were equally bogus, an enlightenment which heralded the dawn of experimental science. The arguments in support of this thesis were, to say the least, trivial, and it was ethnologically most vulnerable. In particular, the conclusions based on Australian data were wide of the mark.... No one accepts Frazer's theory of stages today.

The psychological part of his thesis was to oppose magic and science to religion, the first two postulating a world subject to invariable natural laws ... and the last a world in which events depend on the caprice of spirits. Consequently, while the magician and the scientist, strange bedfellows, perform their operations with quiet confidence, the priest performs his in fear and trembling. So psychologically science and magic are alike, though one happens to be false and the other true. This analogy between science and magic holds only in so far as both are techniques, and few anthropologists have regarded it as other than superficial. Frazer here made the same mistake in method as [philosopher Lucien: ed.] Lévy-Bruhl was to make, in comparing modern science with primitive magic instead of comparing empirical and magical techniques in the same cultural conditions.

However, not all that Frazer wrote about magic and religion was chaff. There was some grain. For example, he was able in his painstaking way to demonstrate...how frequently among the simpler peoples of the world rulers are magicians and priests. Then...he provided some useful classificatory terms, showing that these associations are of two types, those of similarity and those of contact, homoeopathic or imitative magic and contagious magic. He did not, however, go further than to show that in magical beliefs and rites we can discern certain elementary sensations. Neither Tylor nor Frazer explained why people in their magic mistake, as they supposed, ideal connexions for real ones when they do not do so in their other activities. Moreover, it is not correct that they do so. The error here was in not recognizing that the associations are social and not psychological stereotypes, and that they occur therefore only when evoked in specific ritual situations, which are also of limited duration, as I have argued elsewhere.

About all these broadly speaking intellectualist theories we must say that, if they cannot be refuted, they also cannot be sustained, and for the simple reason that there is no evidence about how religious beliefs originated. The evolutionary stages their sponsors attempted to construct, as a means of supplying the missing evidence, may have had logical consistency, but they had no historical value. However, if we must discard the evolutionist (or rather progressionist) assumptions and judgements, or give them the status of rather vague hypotheses, we may still retain much of what was claimed about the essential rationality of primitive peoples. They may not have reached their beliefs in the manner these writers supposed, but even if they did not, the element of rationality is still always there, in spite of observations being inadequate, inferences faulty, and conclusions wrong. The beliefs are always coherent, and up to a point they can be critical and sceptical, and even experimental, within the system of their beliefs and in its idiom; and their thought is therefore intelligible to anyone who cares to learn their language and study their way of life.

The animistic theory in various forms remained for many years unchallenged, and it left its mark on all the anthropological literature of the day....But voices began to be raised in protest, both with regard to the origin of religion and to the order of its development.

Before we consider what they had to say, it should be remarked that the critics had two advantages their predecessors lacked. Associationist psychology, which was more or less a mechanistic theory of sensation, was giving way to experimental psychology, under the influence of which anthropologists were able...to make use of its terms, and we then hear less of the cognitive and more of the affective and conative functions...of the mind; of instincts, emotions, sentiments, and later, under the influence of psycho-analysis, of complexes, inhibitions, projection, &c.; and *Gestalt* psychology and the psychology of crowds were also to leave their mark. But what was more important was the great advance in ethnography in the last decades of the nineteenth century and early in the present century. This provided the later writers with an abundance of information and of better quality....

~

It is necessary to say something, albeit little, about Freud's contribution.... [T]he conviction that the hard wall of reality can be broken through in the mind, or indeed is not there at all, was what Freud claimed to have found in his neurotic patients, and called omnipotence of thought.... The magic rites and spells of primitive man correspond psychologically to the obsessional actions and protective formulas of neurotics; so the neurotic is like the savage in that he "believes he can change the outer world by a mere thought of his." Here again we have put before us a parallelism between ontogenic and phylogenic development: the individual passes through three libidinous phases, narcissism, object finding, which is characterized by dependence on the parents, and the state of maturity in which the individual accepts reality and adapts himself to it; and these phases correspond psychologically to the three stages in the intellectual development of man, the animistic (by which Freud seems to have meant what others would have called the magical), the religious, and the scientific. In the narcissistic phase, corresponding to magic, the child, unable to satisfy its desires through motor activity, compensates by overcoming its difficulties in imagination, substituting thought for action; he is then under analogous psychic conditions to the magician; and the neurotic is like the magician too, in that they both over-estimate the power of thought. In other words, it is tension, an acute sense of frustration, which generates magical ritual, the function of which is to relieve the tension. So magic is wish-fulfilment by which man experiences gratification through motor hallucination.

Religion is equally an illusion. It arose and is maintained by feelings of guilt. Freud tells us a just-so story which only a genius could have ventured to compose, for no evidence was, or could be, adduced in support of it, though, I suppose, it could be claimed to be psychologically, or virtually, true in the sense that a myth may be said to be true in spite of being literally and historically unacceptable. Once upon a time—the tale deserves a fairy-story opening—when men were more or less ape-like creatures, the dominant father-male of the horde kept all the females for himself. His sons rose against his tyranny and monopoly, desiring to pleasure the females themselves, and they killed and ate him in a cannibalistic feast, an idea Freud gleaned from Robertson Smith. Then the sons had feelings of remorse, and instituted taboos on eating their totem, identified with the father, though they did so ceremonially from time to time, thus commemorating and renewing the guilt; and they established the further interdiction on incest which is the origin of culture, for culture derives from this renunciation. Freud's theory of religion is contained in this allegorical story, for the devoured father is also God. It may be regarded as an aetiological myth, providing a background to the drama enacted in those Viennese families of whose troubles Freud made clinical analyses which he believed to hold good in essentials for all families everywhere, since they arose out of the very nature of family structure. I need not elaborate. We all know the main features of his thesis, that, to put it crudely, children both love and hate their parents, the son, deep in his unconscious, wanting to kill the father and possess the mother (the Oedipus complex), and the daughter, deep in hers, wanting to kill the mother and be possessed by the father (the Electra complex). On the surface affection and respect win, and the confidence felt in, and the dependence felt on, the father become projected and idealized and sublimated in the father-image of God. Religion is therefore an illusion, and Freud called his book on the subject *The Future of an Illusion*; but it is only an illusion objectively. Subjectively, it is not so, for it is not the product of hallucination—the father is real.

There is no limit to interpretations on these lines....Magic and religion are...both reduced to psychological states: tensions, frustrations, and emotions and sentiments and complexes and delusions of one sort or another.

I have given some examples of emotionalist interpretations of religion. What now are we to make of it all? In my opinion these theories are for the most part guesswork of the..."if I were a horse" type, with this difference, that instead of "if I were a horse I would do what horses do for one or other reason" it is now "I would do what horses do on account of one or other feeling that horses may be supposed to have." If we were to perform rites such as primitives do, we suppose that we would be in a state of emotional turmoil, for otherwise our reason would tell us that the rites are objectively useless. It seems to me that very little evidence is brought forward in support of these conclusions, not even by those who not only offer them but have also had the opportunity of testing them in field research.

And here we must ask some questions. What is this awe which some... writers...say is characteristic of the sacred? Some say it is the specific religious emotion; others that there is no specific religious emotion. Either way, how does one know whether a person experiences awe or thrill or whatever it may be? How does one recognize it, and how does one measure it?...If we were to classify and explain social behaviour by supposed psychological states, we would indeed get some strange results. If religion is characterized by the emotion of fear, then a man fleeing in terror from a charging buffalo might be said to be performing a religious act; and if magic is characterized by its cathartic function, then a medical practitioner who relieves a patient's anxiety, on entirely clinical grounds, might be said to be performing a magical one.

There are further considerations. A great many rites which surely almost anyone would accept as religious in character, such as sacrifices, are certainly not performed in situations in which there is any possible cause for emotional unrest or feelings of mystery and awe. They are routine, and also standardized and obligatory, rites.... In some societies professional mourners are employed. Then, again, if any emotional expression accompanies rites, it may well be that it is not the emotion which brings about the rites, but the rites which bring about the emotion. This is the old problem of whether we laugh because we are happy or are happy because we laugh. Surely we do not go to church because we are in a heightened emotional state, though our participation in the rites may bring about such a state.

Then, with regard to the alleged cathartic function of magic, what evidence is there that when a man performs agricultural, hunting, and fishing magic he feels frustrated, or that if he is in a state of tension the performance of the rites releases his distress? It seems to me that there is little or none. However he may be feeling, the magician has to perform the rites anyway, for they are a customary and obligatory part of the proceedings.... I might add that in [Bronislaw: ed.] Malinowski's case [his fieldwork in the Trobriand Islands: ed.] I think it is possible that much of his observation of rites was of those performed for his benefit, and in return for payment, quite outside their normal setting, in his tent; and if this is so, it could hardly be held that any display of emotion there may have been was caused by tension and frustration....

For the same reason we must reject the wish-fulfilment theories. In comparing the neurotic with the magician they ignore the fact that the actions and formulas of the neurotic derive from individual subjective states, whereas those of the magician are traditional and socially imposed on him by his culture and society.... In classing primitive peoples with children, neurotics, &c., the mistake is made of assuming that, because things may resemble each other in some particular feature, they are alike in other respects, the *pars pro toto* [part for the whole: ed.] fallacy.... And, we may ask, who ever met a savage who believed that by a thought of his he could change the world? He knows very well that he cannot. This is another variety of the "if I were a horse" kind: if I were to behave in the way a savage magician does, I would be suffering from the maladies of my neurotic patients.

We are not, of course, to dismiss these interpretations out of hand. They were a not unhealthy reaction against a too intellectualist position. Desires and impulses, conscious and unconscious, motivate man, direct his interests, and impel him to action; and they certainly play their part in religion. That is not to be denied. What has to be determined is their nature and the part they do play.

What I protest against is mere assertion, and what I challenge is an explanation of religion in terms of emotion or even, in the sway of it, of hallucination.

Sociological Theories

The position of Durkheim, perhaps the greatest figure in the history of modern sociology, can only be appraised if two points are kept in mind. The first is that for him religion is a social, that is an objective, fact. For theories which tried to explain it in terms of individual psychology he expressed contempt. How, he asked, if religion originated in a mere mistake, an illusion, a kind of hallucination, could it have been so universal and so enduring, and how could a vain fantasy have produced law, science, and morals? Animism is, in any case, in its developed and most typical forms, found not in primitive societies but in such relatively advanced societies as those of China, Egypt, and the classical Mediterranean. As for naturism (the nature-myth school) [i.e., the view of theorist Max Müller, who argued that religion arose when early peoples, in describing natural objects or processes like the sun or storm, were led by their language, whose nouns have gender, to personify them as gods: ed.], was religion to be explained any more satisfactorily as a disease of language, a muddle of metaphors, the action of language on thought, than as a false inference from dreams or trances? Apart from such an explanation being as trivial as the animistic one, it is a plain fact that primitive peoples show remarkably little interest in what we may regard as the most impressive phenomena of nature—sun, moon, sky, mountains, sea, and so forth—whose monotonous regularities they take for granted....

[R]eligion...is...a social and objective phenomenon which is independent of individual minds, and it is as such that the sociologist studies it. What gives it objectivity are three characteristics. Firstly, it is transmitted from one generation to another, so if in one sense it is in the individual, in another it is outside him, in that it was there before he was born and will be there after he is dead. He acquires it as he acquires his language, by being born into a particular society. Secondly, it is, at any rate in a closed society, general. Everyone has the same sort of religious beliefs and practices, and their generality, or collectivity, gives them an objectivity which places them over and above the psychological experience of the individual, or indeed of all individuals. Thirdly, it is obligatory. Apart from positive and negative sanctions, the mere fact that religion is general means, again in a closed society, that it is obligatory, for even if there is no coercion, a man has no option but to accept what everybody gives assent to, because he has no choice, any more than of what language he speaks. Even were he to be a sceptic, he could express his doubts only in terms of the beliefs held by all around him. And had he been born into a different society, he would have had a different set of beliefs, just as he would have had a different language....

The second point which has to be borne in mind concerns the autonomy of religious phenomena. I will only mention it here....Durkheim was not nearly so deterministic and materialistic as some have made him out to be. Indeed, I should be inclined to regard him as a voluntarist and idealist. The functions of the mind could not exist without the processes of the organism, but that, he maintains, does not mean that psychological facts can be reduced to organic facts and be explained by them, but merely that they have an organic basis. At each level the phenomena have autonomy. Likewise, there could be no socio-cultural life without the psychical functions of individual minds, but social processes transcend these functions through which they, as it were, operate and, if not independent of mind, have an existence of their own outside individual minds....Religion is a social fact. It arises out of the nature of social life itself, being in the simpler societies bound up with other social facts, law, economics, art, &c., which later separate out from it and lead their own independent existences. Above all it is the way in which a society sees itself as more than a collection of individuals, and by which it maintains its solidarity and ensures its continuity. This does not mean, however, that it is merely an epiphenomenon of society, as the Marxists would have it. Once brought into existence by collective action, religion gains a degree of autonomy, and proliferates in all sorts of ways which cannot be explained by reference to the social structure which gave birth to it but only in terms of other religious and other social phenomena in a system all its own.

These two points having been made, we need delay no longer in presenting Durkheim's thesis. He started with four cardinal ideas..., that primitive religion is a clan cult and that the cult is totemic..., that the god of the clan is the clan itself divinized, and that totemism is the most elementary or primitive, and in that sense original, form of religion known to us. By that he meant that it is found in societies with the simplest material culture and social structure, and that it is possible to explain their religion without making use of any element borrowed from a previous religion. Durkheim thus agrees with those who see in totemism the origin of religion, or at least its earliest known form....

What then is the object revered in this totemic religion? It is not simply a product of delirious imagination; it has an objective basis. It is a cult of something which really does exist, though not the thing the worshippers suppose. It is society itself, or some segment of it, which men worship in these ideal representations. And what, says Durkheim, is more natural, for a society has everything necessary to arouse the sensation of the divine in minds. It has absolute power over them, and it also gives them the feeling of perpetual dependence; and it is the object of venerable respect. Religion is thus a system of ideas by which individuals represent to themselves the society to which they belong and their relations with it.

~

Such was Durkheim's theory. For Freud God is the father, for Durkheim God is society. Now, if his theory holds for the Australian aboriginals, it holds good for religion in general, for, he says, totemic religion contains all the elements of other religions, even those the most advanced. Durkheim was candid enough to admit this, that what is sauce for the goose is sauce for the gander. If the idea of sacredness, of the soul and of God, can be explained sociologically for the Australians, then in principle the same explanation is valid for all peoples among whom the same ideas are found with the same essential characteristics. Durkheim was most anxious not to be accused of a mere restatement of historical materialism [i.e., Marxism: ed.]. In showing that religion is something essentially social he does not mean that collective consciousness is a mere epiphenomenon of its morphological basis, just as individual consciousness is not merely an efflorescence of the nervous system. Religious ideas are produced by a synthesis of individual minds in collective action, but once produced they have a life of their own: the sentiments, ideas, and images "once born, obey laws all their own." None the less, if Durkheim's theory of religion is true, obviously no one is going to accept religious beliefs any more; and yet, on his own showing, they are generated by the action of social life itself, and are necessary for its persistence. This put him on the horns of a dilemma, and all he could say to get off them was that, while religion in the spiritual sense is doomed, a secular assembly may produce ideas and sentiments which will have the same function; and in support of this opinion, he cites the French revolution with its cult of Fatherland, Liberty, Equality and Fraternity, and Reason. Did it not in its first years make these ideas into sacred things, into gods, and the society it had brought into being a god? He hoped and expected, like Saint-Simon and Comte, that as spiritual religion declined, a secularistic religion of a humanist kind would take its place.

Durkheim's thesis is more than just neat; it is brilliant and imaginative, almost poetical; and he had an insight into a psychological fundamental of religion: the elimination of the self, the denial of individuality, its having no meaning, or even existence, save as part of something greater, and other, than the self. But I am afraid that we must once more say that it is also a just-so story. Totemism could have arisen through gregariousness, but there is no evidence that it did; and other forms of religion could have developed, as it is implicit in Durkheim's theory that they did, from totemism, or what he calls the totemic principle, but again there is no evidence that they did. It can be allowed that religious conceptions must bear some relation to the social order, and be in some degree in accord with economic, political, moral, and other social facts, and even that they are a product of social life, in the sense that there could be no religion without society, any more than there could be thought or culture of any kind; but Durkheim is asserting much more than that. He is claiming that spirit, soul, and other religious ideas and images are projections of society, or of its segments, and originate in conditions bringing about a state of effervescence.

My comments must be few and brief. While various logical and philosophical objections could be raised, I would rather base the case for the prosecution on ethnographical evidence. Does this support the rigid dichotomy he makes between the sacred and the profane? I doubt it. Surely what he calls "sacred" and "profane" are on the same level of experience, and, far from being cut off from one another, they are so closely intermingled as to be inseparable. They cannot, therefore, either for the individual or for social activities, be put in closed departments which negate each other, one of which is left on entering the other.... My test of this sort of formulation is a simple one: whether it can be broken down into problems which permit testing by observation in field research, or can at least aid in a classification of observed facts. I have never found that the dichotomy of sacred and profane was of much use for either purpose....

With regard to the Australian evidence cited: one of the weaknesses of Durkheim's position is the plain fact that among the Australian aboriginals it is the horde, and then the tribe, which are the corporate groups, and not the widely dispersed clans; so if the function of religion is to maintain the solidarity of the groups, which most require a sense of unity, then it should be the hordes and tribes, and not the clans, that should perform the rites generating effervescence.... What is the point of maintaining through ceremonies the solidarity of social groupings which are not corporate and which do not have any joint action outside the ceremonies?

Durkheim chose to argue his thesis on the evidence of totemism, and almost entirely on that of Australian totemism. Now, Australian totemism is a very untypical and highly specialized type of totemism, and conclusions drawn from it, even if accurate, cannot be taken as valid for totemism in general. Furthermore, totemic phenomena are by no means the same throughout Australia.... The assertion that Australian totemism is the original form of totemism is quite arbitrary, and rests on the assumption that the simplest form of religion is necessarily held by people with the simplest culture and social organization. But even if we accept this criterion, we would then have to account for the fact that some hunting and collecting peoples, as technologically undeveloped as the Australians and with a much simpler social organization, have no totems (or clans), or their totems are of no great importance for them, and yet they have religious beliefs and rites.... One must say also that there appears to be precious little evidence that the gods of Australia are syntheses of totems; though this is a clever attempt to get rid of their awkward presence. One sometimes sighs—if only Tylor, Marrett, Durkheim, and all the rest of them could have spent a few weeks among the peoples about whom they so freely wrote!

I have mentioned a few points which seem to me to be sufficient to raise doubts about Durkheim's theory, if not to invalidate it altogether....I must, however,...make a final comment on his theory of the genesis of totemism and therefore of religion in general. It contravenes his own rules of sociological method, for fundamentally it offers a psychological explanation of social facts, and he himself has laid it down that such explanations are invariably wrong. It was all very well for him to pour contempt on others for deriving religion from motor hallucination, but I contend that this is precisely what he does himself. No amount of juggling with words like "intensity" and "effervescence" can hide the fact that he derives the totemic religion of the Blackfellows [Australian Aborigine peoples: ed.] from the emotional excitement of individuals brought together in a small crowd, from what is a sort of crowd hysteria....The argument, like so many sociological arguments, is a circular one—the chicken and the egg. The rites create the effervescence, which creates the beliefs, which cause the rites to be performed; or does the mere coming together generate them? Fundamentally Durkheim elicits a social fact from crowd psychology.

~

There are grave objections to...the sort of sociological (or should we say sociologistic?) explanations we have been considering, not the least being the inadequacy of the data, which, as I have earlier said, are often confused and confusing. Then, we have here to urge again, negative instances cannot just be ignored. They must be accounted for in terms of the theory put forward, or the theory must be abandoned. What about primitive peoples who have clans and no totems;...who do not associate the right orientation with superior moral qualities; who have lineages but no ancestor cult; &c.? By the time all the exceptions have been registered and somehow accounted for, the remains of the theories are little more than plausible guesses of so general and vague a character that they are of little scientific value, all the more so in that nobody knows what to do with them, since they can neither be proved nor disproved in final analysis. If one were to test the theory of Durkheim...about the origin and meaning of religion, how could it be either substantiated or shown to be wrong?...How does one know whether religion maintains or does not maintain the solidarity of a society? All these theories may be true, but equally they may be false. Neat and consistent they may appear to be, but they tend to stultify further inquiry, because in so far as they go beyond description of the facts and offer explanations of them, they do not easily permit experimental verification. The supposition that a certain kind of religion goes with, or is the product of, a certain type of social structure would only have a high degree of probability if it could be shown historically not only that changes in social structure have caused corresponding changes in religious thought, but also that it is a regular correspondence; or if it could be shown that all societies of a certain type have similar religious systems.....

In concluding..., passing attention might be called to the similarity some of the theories we have touched on bear to those of Marxist writers, or some of them, who in many ways present the most straightforward and lucid exposition of a sociological point of view. Religion is a form of social "superstructure," it is a "mirror" or a "reflection" of social relations, which themselves rest upon the basic economic structure of society.... [R]eligion is "a reflection of production relations (particularly those of master and servant) and the political order of society conditioned by them" [quoting from Marxist Nikolai Bukharin: ed.]. So, religion tends always to take the form of the economico-political structure of society, though there may be a time-lag in the adjustment of the one to the other. In a society consisting of loosely connected clans religion assumes the form of polytheism; where there is a centralized monarchy, there is a single god; where there is a slave-holding commercial republic (as at Athens in the sixth century B.C.), the gods are organized as a republic. And so forth. It is, of course, true that religious conceptions can only be derived from experience, and the experience of social relations must furnish a model for such conceptions. Such a theory may, at least sometimes, account for the conceptual forms taken by religion, but not for its origin, its function, or its meaning. In any case, neither ethnography nor history (e.g. it is quite untrue that, as Bukharin asserts, in the Reformation the ruling princes all sided with the Pope) sustains the thesis.

Though I cannot discuss the matter further here, I would suggest that in their general approach to the study of social phenomena there is much in common, though they are dressed differently, between the French sociological school and the Marxist theorists. Though the latter regarded Durkheim as a bourgeois idealist, he might well have written Marx's famous aphorism, that it is not the consciousness of men that determines their being but their social being which determines their consciousness.

~

Modern Theories and the Primitive Mind

The great advances that social anthropology has made in and by field research have turned our eyes away from the vain pursuit of origins, and the many once disputing schools about them have withered away....

In these theories it was assumed, taken for granted, that we were at one end of the scale of human progress and the so-called savages were at the other end, and that, because primitive men were on a rather low technological level, their thought and custom must in all respects be the antithesis of ours. We are rational, primitive peoples, prelogical, living in a world of dreams and make-believe, of mystery and awe; we are capitalists, they communists; we are monogamous, they promiscuous; we are monotheists, they fetishists, animists, pre-animists or what have you, and so on.

Primitive man was thus represented as childish, crude, prodigal, and comparable to animals and imbeciles....

All this fitted in very well with colonialist and other interests, and some were prepared to admit that some of the discredit must go to the American ethnologists who wanted an excuse for slavery, and some also to those who desired to find a missing link between men and monkeys.

Needless to say, it was held that primitive peoples must have the crudest religious conceptions, and we have had occasion to observe the various ways in which they are supposed to have reached them. This may further be illustrated in the condescending argument, once it was ascertained beyond doubt that primitive peoples, even the hunters and collectors, have gods with high moral attributes, that they must have borrowed the idea...from a higher culture, from missionaries, traders, and others. Tylor asserted this, almost certainly wrongly, as Andrew Lang showed, about the Australian aboriginals....Modern research has shown that little value can be attributed to statements of this sort; but it was more or less an axiom of the time that, the simpler the technology and social structure, the more degraded the religious, and indeed any other, conceptions....

My task is expository, but I have also to put before you what seems to me to be the fundamental weakness of the interpretations of primitive religion which at one time appeared to carry conviction. The first error was the basing of them on evolutionary assumptions for which no evidence was, or could be, adduced. The second was that, besides being theories of chronological origins, they were also theories of psychological origins; and even those we have labeled sociological could be said to rest ultimately on psychological suppositions of the "if I were a horse" sort. They could scarcely have been otherwise so far as the armchair anthropologists were concerned, those whose experience was restricted to their own culture and society, within that society to a small class, and within that class to a yet smaller group of intellectuals....

$\sim$

Here and now I have a different task to perform: to suggest what should be the procedure in investigations of primitive religions. I do not deny that peoples have reasons for their beliefs—that they are rational; I do not deny that religious rites may be accompanied by emotional experiences, that feeling may even be an important element in their performance; and I certainly do not deny that religious ideas and practices are directly associated with social groups—that religion, whatever else it may be, is a social phenomenon. What I do deny is that it is explained by any of these facts, or all of them together, and I hold that it is not sound scientific method to seek for origins, especially when they cannot be found. Science deals with relations, not with origins and essences. In so far as it can be said that the facts of primitive religions can be sociologically explained at all, it must be in relation to other facts, both those with which it forms a system of ideas and practices and other social phenomena associated with it....

All this amounts to saying that we have to account for religious facts in terms of the totality of the culture and society in which they are found.... They must be seen as a relation of parts to one another within a coherent system, each part making sense only in relation to the others, and the system itself making sense only in relation to other institutional systems, as part of a wider set of relations....

I regret to say that very little progress has been made along these lines.... [W]hile in other departments of anthropology some, even considerable, advance has been made by intensive research, in the study of kinship and of political institutions for example, I do not think that comparable advance has been made in the study of primitive religion.... I am glad to say, however, since primitive religion in a broad sense has been one of my own chief interests, that lately there have been signs of a renewed interest in it, and from what we have called a relational point of view....

Now, sooner or later, if we are to have a general sociological theory of religion, we shall have to take into consideration all religions and not just primitive religions; and only by so doing can we understand some of its essential features. For as the advances of science and technology have rendered magic redundant, religion has persisted, and its social role has become ever more embracing, involving persons more and more remote and no longer, as in primitive societies, bound by ties of family and kin and participating in corporate activities.

If we do not have some general statements to make about religion, we do not go beyond innumerable particular studies of the religions of particular peoples. During last century such general statements were indeed attempted, as we have seen, in the form of evolutionary and psychological and sociological hypotheses, but since these attempts at general formulations seem to have been abandoned by anthropologists, our subject has suffered from loss of common aim and method....

~

I would propose instead that we do some research into the matter. Comparative religion is a subject hardly represented in our universities, and the data of what claims to be such are derived almost entirely from books—sacred texts, theological writings, exegetics, mystical writings, and all the rest of it. But for the anthropologist or sociologist, I would suggest, this is perhaps the least significant part of religion, especially as it is very evident that the scholars who write books on the historical religions are sometimes uncertain what even key words meant to the authors of the original texts. The philological reconstructions and interpretations of these key words are only too often uncertain, contradictory, and unconvincing, e.g. in the case of the word "god." The student of an ancient religion or of a religion in its early phases has no other means of examining it than in texts, for the people contemporaneous with the texts are no more and cannot therefore be consulted. Serious distortions may result, as when it is said that Buddhism and Jainism are atheistic religions. No doubt they may have been regarded as systems of philosophy and psychology by the authors of the systems but we may well ask whether they were by ordinary people; and it is ordinary people the anthropologist is chiefly interested in. To him what is most important is how religious beliefs and practices affect in any society the minds, the feelings, the lives, and the inter-relations of its members. There are few books which describe and analyse in any adequate manner the role of religion in any Hindu, Buddhist, Moslem, or Christian community. For the social anthropologist, religion is what religion does. I must add that such studies among primitive peoples have been few and far between. In both civilized and primitive societies herein lies an enormous and almost untilled field of research.

Furthermore, comparative religion must be comparative in a relational manner if much that is worth while is to come out of the exercise. If comparison is to stop at mere description..., we are not taken very far towards an understanding of either similarities or differences. The Indian monists, the Buddhists, and the Manichees may all be alike in desiring release from the body and detachment from the world of sense, but the question we would ask is whether this common element is related to any other social facts. An attempt was made in this direction by Weber and Tawney in relating certain Protestant teachings to certain economic changes. Indeed, far be it from me to belittle students of comparative religion on this score, for, as I hope I have shown in earlier lectures, we anthropologists have not made much progress in the sort of relational studies which I believe to be those required and the only ones which are likely to lead us to a vigorous sociology of religion.

Indeed, I have to conclude that I do not feel that on the whole the different theories we have reviewed, either singly or taken together, give us much more than common-sense guesses, which for the most part miss the mark. If we ask ourselves, as we naturally do, whether they have any bearing on our own religious experience…, I suppose the answer must be that they have little…, and this may make us sceptical about their value as explanations of the religions of primitives, who cannot apply the same test. The reason for this is, I believe, partly one I have already given, that the writers were seeking for explanations in terms of origins and essences instead of relations; and I would further suggest that this followed from their assumptions that the souls and spirits and gods of religion have no reality. For if they are regarded as complete illusions, then some biological, psychological, or sociological theory of how everywhere and at all times men have been stupid enough to believe in them seems to be called for. He who accepts the reality of spiritual being does not feel the same need for such explanations, for… they are not just an illusion for him. As far as a study of religion as a factor in social life is concerned, it may make little difference whether the anthropologist is a theist or an atheist, since in either case he can only take into account what he can observe. But if either attempts to go further than this, each must pursue a different path. The non-believer seeks for some theory—biological, psychological, or sociological—which will explain the illusion; the believer seeks rather to understand the manner in which a people conceives of reality and their relations to it. For both, religion is a part of social life, but for the believer it has another dimension. On this point I find myself in agreement with [Father Wilhelm: ed.] Schmidt in his confutation of [French scholar Ernest: ed] Renan: "If religion is essentially of the inner life, it follows that it can be truly grasped only from within. But beyond a doubt, this can be better done by one in whose inward consciousness an experience of religion plays a part. There is but too much danger that the other [the non-believer] will talk of religion as a blind man might of colours, or one totally devoid of ear, of a beautiful musical composition."

In these last lectures I have given you an account of some of the main past attempts at explaining primitive religions, and I have asked you to accept that none of them is wholly satisfactory. We seem always to have come out by the same door as we went in. But I would not wish to have you believe that so much labour has been to no purpose. If we are now able to see the errors in these theories purporting to account for primitive religions, it is partly because they were set forth, thereby inviting logical analysis of their contents and the testing of them against recorded ethnological fact and in field research. The advance in this department of social anthropology in the last forty or so years may be measured by the fact that, in the light of the knowledge we now have, we can point to the inadequacies of theories which at one time carried conviction, but we might never have obtained this knowledge had it not been for the pioneers whose writings we have reviewed.

11

Clifford Geertz: Religion as World-View and Ethic

Over the last quarter of the twentieth century, anthropologist Clifford Geertz (1926–2006) held a place of eminence in American intellectual circles comparable to that of Evans-Pritchard in Britain. Like Evans-Pritchard, he took it as an axiom that serious cultural inquiry must begin "in the field," and that theorists who wish to claim the warrant of scientific anthropology for their opinions must in some measure apprentice themselves through direct encounter with a culture or community other than their own. Like Evans-Pritchard also, Geertz took a keen interest in religion, though that was but one among multiple aspects of cultural analysis he pursued.

Geertz was born in San Francisco, California, in 1926. He served in the U.S. Navy in World War II, returned from duty to study at Antioch College, and entered Harvard University for graduate study, taking a doctorate in social anthropology in 1956. Before and again after taking his degree, he traveled to Indonesia, where he undertook fieldwork, initially in a town on the island of Java and later on the exotic island of Bali. At both sites his first mission was ethnography—the preparation of a close, integrated description of social behaviors and beliefs. Though he was personally nonreligious, this work led him quickly to discern the central place of religion in Indonesian life. In 1960 these labors led to his first monograph, *The Religion of Java*, a careful study of Javan symbolism, ritual, and custom that explored the complex religious blend of Islam, Hinduism, and native animist belief that governed all aspects of community life. A brief selection from this work devoted to death and mourning is provided in the first selection here.

In 1960 Geertz was appointed to the faculty at the University of Chicago, where he remained for the next decade. At the same time, he initiated a new field project in Morocco, where he was able to observe another (more exclusively) Muslim culture with a history and a geographical location very different from that of Indonesia. After multiple visits for field study at the Moroccan locales, he published *Islam Observed* (1968), an exploration of what he called two "styles" of Islamic society. He also examined the clash between traditional Islam, centered in Morocco on the figure known as the *marabout,* or warrior-saint, and alternative forms, including a rising protest movement he called the "scripturalist revolt," discernible in both countries. In retrospect we can see that the scripturalism Geertz identified bears a marked affinity to the Islamic fundamentalism which has now come to the center of world attention. A portion of Geertz's concluding chapter from this study serves as the third selection provided below.

While at Harvard Geertz had been exposed to a strong, independently American tradition of anthropology that reached back to the previous century, when an immigrant German-educated scholar, Franz Boas, established a school of anthropologists who capitalized on access to native American tribal cultures. This American school placed somewhat more emphasis on the human attitudes and dispositions that shape a culture than did Europeans, influenced by Durkheim and Marx, who stressed the reverse: society's role in shaping human attitudes. In addition, Geertz studied with Harvard social theorist Talcott Parsons, who was an admirer of Max Weber. Like Weber, Parsons stressed that a society consists of individual persons, a social system, and—not least—a "cultural system": a complex pattern of verbal and visual symbols that frame behavior, define relationships, mediate between the individual and the group, and address overarching questions of meaning and purpose.

In his theoretical work, Geertz embraced this American perspective in the form of "symbolic anthropology" and advocated its merits over purely functionalist social theory. This approach has also been called "interpretive anthropology"—inquiry animated not just by the scientific aim to explain human social structure, but by a more humanistic effort to interpret human culture, giving full weight to the role of ideas, beliefs, and emotions that confer meaning on life's activities. Geertz's favorite vehicle for advocating his "interpretive anthropology" was not the book, but the article, or essay. In the prime years of his career he produced a steady stream of intriguing, innovative journal articles reflecting this approach. The most important of these were collected into *Interpretation of Cultures* (1973), an award-winning volume which extended Geertz's reputation beyond the circles of professional anthropology. The lead essay of this volume, penned under the title "Thick Description," offered a kind of definitive statement on the issue. There he argues that the mission of anthropology is not just to describe, say, kinship groups or patterns of economic exchange, but to do so by grasping above all the network of cultural ideas and values that gives them significance and governs their use. The collection also featured "Religion as Cultural System," an essay that offered Geertz's signature statement on understanding, or (as he would prefer to say it) "interpreting," religion. Most of that essay appears in the second of these selections. In it Geertz lays out a multipart "thick" definition of religion, then explicates in detail each of its component parts. Along the way he elucidates the role of religion as, for most cultures, the first and final source of those general concepts of the world and life which furnish the framework of ideas and goals that govern communal life. He takes a position that in the end might best be described as a carefully qualified, nonreligious appreciation of religion's role as, in every culture, the creator of its "reality" and keeper of its ideals.

In 1970 Geertz became the first social scientist ever appointed to the faculty of the famous Institute of Advanced Studies at Princeton University, once the host of Albert Einstein and still today a magnet for the world's finest mathematicians and physicists. The entry of a literate, but "nonnumerate," social scientist to a circle of thinkers so committed to purely theoretical science of the highest order was not without controversy. Nonetheless, the honor stands as a testament to both the originality and influence of a theorist who, though little inclined personally to religion, found himself drawn to emphasize its crucial role in both the formation and function of culture.

The Religion of Java

This short selection depicts the religious mood that accompanies personal mourning in the Indonesian town of Modjokuto, on the island of Java, the site of Geertz' first anthropological field study.

The mode of a Javanese funeral . . . is not one of hysterical bereavement, unrestrained sobbing, or even of formalized shrieks of grief for the deceased's departure. Rather it is a calm, undemonstrative, almost languid letting go, a brief ritualized relinquishment of a relationship no longer possible. Tears are not approved of and certainly not encouraged; and one sees remarkably few of them. The effort is to get the job done, not to linger over the pleasures of grief. The detailed busy-work of the funeral, the politely formal social intercourse with the neighbors pressing in from all sides, the series of *slametans* [communal meals: ed.] stretched out at intervals for almost three years—the whole momentum of the Javanese ritual system—are supposed to carry one through the grief process evenly and without severe emotional disturbance.

Iklas, that state of willed affectlessness, is the watchword, and although it is often difficult to achieve, it is always striven for.

> I went to buy a sarong from Mudjito, whose wife died suddenly about two weeks ago. Mudjito was still rather upset about it evidently, smiling a nervous smile from ear to ear and talking about it without a pause for breath from the moment I came in....He said first, as Javanese inevitably do when they "have trouble," "I beg your pardon a thousand times because my wife is not here" (that is, please lighten my burden of grief by giving me your pardon); and I mumbled in return that I was sorry I had not come to see him sooner. He then went on at great length about how he was *iklas,* that it was God that took his wife away, and that he had no right to complain. He said that he was just *iklas* and bent to the will of God (Mudjito was a *santri* [Muslim: ed.] and thus more likely to ascribe things to the will of God than an *abangan* [traditional animist: ed.] would be). There was nothing he could do anyway. When first she died, he could see no reason to go on working (I noticed him already in the store the day after the death, people going in and out paying their respects). What was the point of it? He said that he felt his wife was not evil and had done no wrong, and he felt that she didn't deserve to die so young. But after a while he began to see that...he should be *iklas,* and now that he was truly *iklas* he didn't feel anything at all any more. He said that's the way one should feel. One's feeling should be flat, even, always on the same level....He said that happiness and unhappiness are irrevocably connected with one another; so, if one is happy now, he will surely be unhappy later on, and one should not indulge himself in either feeling....He said one shouldn't keep strong emotions locked up in his heart, but *iklas.* "Just like when I sell you this sarong, I should feel I got the right price, and you should too, so that neither of us is upset inside his heart. We must be *iklas* toward it, and that is the way I feel about my wife's death."...He said he felt at first as if he would like to die too, but then he talked himself out of it and said he had to carry on to see the children raised.

Sometimes this self-discipline proves too difficult and more direct measures need to be applied.

> I asked him if he was upset when his mother died a few years ago, and he said no, she was already old....He said one doesn't get upset when people are old and sick and then die. How about for babies, I asked. He replied, "Yes, for them you often get very upset. If they are only a month or two old, you don't get very upset, but if they are already a year or a year and a half and you

have been watching them play around and they are very cute and all and then they die, you can get quite upset." He said that when his youngest child died (evidently not so long ago) at the age of one and a half, his oldest son, who is about 17 or 18, cried solidly for a week, couldn't eat, couldn't sleep or anything. Finally, he went and got a *dukun* [magician: ed.] for him, and the *dukun* came and gave the boy some magic tea to drink and uttered a spell over the boy enjoining him to forget about the death, which he then did. He stopped crying and ate and slept normally.

Despite deviations such as this, most people do what can only be called a remarkable job of at least not showing their grief......

Whatever the deeper psychological reasons for this relative equanimity about personal extinction may be, assuming it is real, there are beliefs on the intellectual level to which one might point in partial explanation. One informant insisted that curers can never have any effect on the length of one's life. If one is going to die at thirty, he will die at thirty; if at sixty, sixty. All the *dukun* can do is make life easier for one.... There are variations on this belief in fate, however; for some hold that a man's life will be lengthened if he behaves ethically, and other people (or sometimes the same ones—the logical compatibility of separate beliefs is not usually a serious issue for *abangans*) think that premature death may be the result of sheer accident, sorcery, consorting with evil spirits, taking a false oath, an especially fast pace of living, persistent and prolonged emotional upset, or a sudden trauma of some sort.

But perhaps the major intellectual reason Javanese seem not to fear death so much as some other peoples is that it seems to them to bear the characteristics of that emptiness of emotional and intellectual content, that inner restraint of the will, that they value so highly.

He talked a little about this attitude toward death. It was all determined absolutely by God, so there was no use worrying about it and no use feeling sorry when someone else died. I asked him why some sinners flourished as the green bay tree, and so forth, and he said that he thought God was giving them a chance to understand. He laughed and said, "Yes, you often see old bent-over men who are real sinners." And he said he thought that God keeps them living in hopes they'll finally see the light, whereas the young good ones are all right anyway and so they die early, as a kind of reward, for it is a good thing to be dead. He spoke happily, not in any *weltschmerz* mood. I asked why he thought this, and he said, "Well, when you are dead, you don't want anything.... Like God—God doesn't need any money, or wife, or auto, does He? Well, that's wonderful, not to want anything...." I said, "Well, if it is so good being dead, why don't people kill themselves?" He was properly offended at this idea and said, "That would be wrong because it would be from your own will. It is up to God to decide when you should die, not yourself...." But he said he was ready to die anytime (he was about seventy); he thought it a good state not to want anything, not to need anything, like God....

Three separate notions of life after death, again often held concurrently by the same individual, are present in Modjokuto. The first is the Islamic version of the concept of eternal retribution, of punishment and reward in the afterworld for the sins and good deeds in this one. This is, naturally enough, strongest among the *santris,* often—especially among the more modern groups—complete with ideas of hell-fire, the constant moral inspection of the individual by God, and the awfulness of absolute Judgment.... One finds it throughout the society, although usually rather vaguely conceived and only half believed in outside of strictly Moslem circles.

Much more popular with *abangans* is the concept of *sampurna,* which means literally "perfect" or "complete" but which indicates in this context that the individual personality completely disappears after death and nothing is left of the person but dust. (Like many peoples around the world, the Javanese, although they often conceive of the dead as spirits annoying the living or demanding worship from them, never consider seriously what it must be like to be a spirit and never reflect that they will become one themselves. One sometimes hears the idea that spirits of the dead who attack people are those of individuals who have been evil in their lifetime, and sometimes also *setans* [spirits that possess: ed.] and the like are held to originate partly from this source, although this is as often explicitly denied.)

The third view, which is extremely widely held by all but *santris,* who condemn it as heretical, is the notion of reincarnation—that when a person dies his soul enters shortly thereafter into an embryo on its way to being born. The usual way in which this occurs is that a pregnant woman feels a sudden intense craving for some special food—an orange out of season or a duck egg—and the soul is inside this food and so enters the woman's womb and is reborn as her child. Often but not always reincarnation occurs within the same family, although the relationship may be rather distant and the individual in whom the soul is reincarnated need not necessarily be of the same sex as the deceased. It may be heralded by a dream on the part of the mother or established by a similarity of features in the child and the recently deceased or by a similar birthmark. It is not wise to tell a child when it is still young of whom it is the reincarnation, for this might make the soul within the child ashamed, and he would fall sick. After he is over six or so, it does not matter any more. When I asked people of whom they were the reincarnation, they never seemed to know, although they could almost always tell me of whom their children were reincarnations. Sometimes people hold to the Hindu notion of advancement and regression in the stages of being according to one's deportment while alive;

but most *abangans* leave this sort of thing to *prijajis* [Hindus] to reflect upon and use the idea of reincarnation primarily to explain personal peculiarities in their children and strange behavior on the part of an odd animal now and then, such as dogs who fast, as humans often do, on Mondays and Thursdays.

The Javanese have sometimes been said to worship their ancestors, but except for the vague apostrophes to "the ancestors" taken generally or to one's own ancestors as "grandfathers and grandmothers" in spells and at *slametans,* the burning of incense to "ancestors" on Thursday nights by a few people, and the decoration of family graves now and again, evidence of any kind of ancestor cult is absent in Modjokuto. Javanese claim they reckon kinship ascent eight generations back and have terms for each level (father, grandfather, great-grandfather...); but I never knew anyone who knew his ancestors by name back farther than his grandfather, and I have never heard of an ancestor, other than parents, being petitioned by name. Javanese "ancestor worship," in present-day Modjokuto at least, amounts to little more than a pious expression of respect for the dead plus a lively awareness of the necessity of being on good terms with one's own deceased father and mother and of being sure to feed them some rice or flowers when they appear in one's dreams.

Religion as Cultural System

This essay has been recognized as the definitive statement of Geertz' "symbolic" or "interpretive," anthropology as applied to religion.

Two characteristics of anthropological work on religion accomplished since the second world war strike me as curious when such work is placed against that carried out just before and just after the first. One is that it has made no theoretical advances of major importance. It is living off the conceptual capital of its ancestors, adding very little, save a certain empirical enrichment, to it. The second is that it draws what concepts it does use from a very narrowly defined intellectual tradition. There is Durkheim, Weber, Freud, or Malinowski, and in any particular work the approach of one or two of these transcendent figures is followed, with but a few marginal corrections necessitated by the

---

natural tendency to excess of seminal minds or by the expanded body of reliable descriptive data. But virtually no one even thinks of looking elsewhere—to philosophy, history, law, literature, or the "harder" sciences—as these men themselves looked, for analytical ideas. And it occurs to me, also, that these two curious characteristics are not unrelated.

If the anthropological study of religion is in fact in a state of general stagnation, I doubt that it will be set going again by producing more minor variations on classical theoretical themes. Yet one more meticulous case in point for such well-established propositions as that ancestor worship supports the jural authority of elders, that initiation rites are means for the establishment of sexual identity and adult status, that ritual groupings reflect political oppositions, or that myths provide charters for social institutions and rationalizations of social privilege, may well finally convince a great many people, both inside the profession and out, that anthropologists are, like theologians, firmly dedicated to proving the indubitable. In art, this solemn reduplication of the achievements of accepted masters is called academicism; and I think this is the proper name for our malady also. Only if we abandon, in a phrase of Leo Steinberg's, that sweet sense of accomplishment which comes from parading habitual skills and address ourselves to problems sufficiently unclarified as to make discovery possible, can we hope to achieve work which will not just reincarnate that of the great men of the first quarter of this century, but match it.

The way to do this is not to abandon the establishment of traditions of social anthropology in this field, but to widen them. At least four of the contributions of the men who, as I say, dominate our thought to the point of parochializing it—Durkheim's discussion of the nature of the sacred, Weber's *Verstehenden* methodology, Freud's parallel between personal rituals and collective ones, and Malinowski's exploration of the distinction between religion and common sense—seem to me inevitable starting-points for any useful anthropological theory of religion. But they are starting-points only. To move beyond them we must place them in a much broader context of contemporary thought than they, in and of themselves, encompass....

In working toward such an expansion of the conceptual envelope in which our studies take place, one can, of course, move in a great number of directions; and perhaps the most important initial problem is to avoid setting out, like Stephen Leacock's mounted policeman, in all of them at once. For my part, I shall confine my effort to developing...the cultural dimension of religious analysis. The term "culture" has by now acquired a certain aura of ill-repute in social anthropological circles because of the multiplicity of its referents and the studied vagueness with which it has all too often been invoked....[T]he culture concept to which I adhere has neither multiple referents nor, so far as I can see, any unusual ambiguity: it denotes an historically transmitted pattern of meanings embodied in symbols, a system of inherited conceptions expressed in symbolic forms by means of which men communicate, perpetuate, and develop their knowledge about and attitudes toward life. Of course, terms such as "meaning," "symbol," and "conception" cry out for explication. But that is precisely where the widening, the broadening, and the expanding come in. If [philosopher Suzanne: ed.] Langer is right that "the concept of meaning, in all its varieties, is the dominant philosophical concept of our time,"...it is perhaps time that social anthropology, and particularly that part of it concerned with the study of religion, became aware of the fact.

As we are to deal with meaning, let us begin with a paradigm: viz., that sacred symbols function to synthesize a people's ethos—the tone, character, and quality of their life, its moral and aesthetic style and mood—and their world view—the picture they have of the way things in sheer actuality are, their most comprehensive ideas of order....

The notion that religion tunes human actions to an envisaged cosmic order and projects images of cosmic order onto the plane of human experience is hardly novel. But it is hardly investigated either.... [T]he theoretical framework which would enable us to provide an analytic account of it...does not exist.

Let us, therefore, reduce our paradigm to a definition, for, although it is notorious that definitions establish nothing,... [t]hey...have the useful virtue of explicitness.... Without further ado, then, a *religion* is: *(1) a system of symbols which acts to (2) establish powerful, persuasive, and long-lasting moods and motivations in men by (3) formulating conceptions of a general order of existence and (4) clothing these conceptions with such an aura of factuality that (5) the moods and motivations seem uniquely realistic.*

A system of symbols which acts to...

Such a tremendous weight is being put on the term "symbol" here that our first move must be to decide with some precision what we are going to mean by it. This is no easy task, for, rather like "culture," "symbol" has been used to refer to a great variety of things, often a number of them at the same time.

In some hands it is used for anything which signifies something else to someone: dark clouds are the symbolic precursors of an on-coming rain....In...others, however, it is used for any object, act, event, quality, or relation which serves as a vehicle for a conception—the conception is the symbol's "meaning"—and that is the approach I shall follow here. The number 6...is a symbol. But so also is the Cross, talked about, visualized, shaped worriedly in air or fondly fingered at the neck....They are...symbols, or at least symbolic elements, because they are tangible formulations of notions, abstractions from experience fixed in perceptible forms, concrete embodiments of ideas, attitudes, judgments, longings, or beliefs. To undertake the study of cultural activity—activity in which symbolism forms the positive content—is thus not to abandon social analysis.... Cultural acts, the construction, apprehension, and utilization of symbolic forms, are social events like any other; they are as public as marriage and as observable as agriculture.

They are not, however, exactly the same thing; or, more precisely, the symbolic dimension of social events is, like the psychological, itself theoretically abstractable from those events as empirical totalities. There is still...a difference between building a house and drawing up a plan for building a house....

So far as culture patterns, that is, systems or complexes of symbols, are concerned, the generic trait which is of first importance for us here is that they are extrinsic sources of information. By "extrinsic," I mean only that—unlike genes, for example—they lie outside the boundaries of the individual organism as such in that intersubjective world of common understandings into which all human individuals are born.... By "sources of information," I mean only that—like genes—they provide a blueprint or template in terms of which processes external to themselves can be given a definite form. As the order of bases in a strand of DNA forms a coded program,... so culture patterns provide such programs for the institution of the social and psychological processes which shape public behavior. Though the sort of information and the mode of its transmission are vastly different in the two cases, this comparison of gene and symbol is more than a strained analogy.... It is actually a substantial relationship, for it is precisely because of the fact that genetically programmed processes are so highly generalized in men, as compared with lower animals, that culturally programmed ones are so important; only because human behavior is so loosely determined by intrinsic sources of information that extrinsic sources are so vital....

This point is sometimes put in the form of an argument that cultural patterns are "models".... The term "model" has, however, two senses—an "of" sense and a "for" sense.... In the first, what is stressed is the manipulation of symbol structures so as to bring them, more or less closely, into parallel with the pre-established nonsymbolic system, as when we grasp how dams work by developing a theory of hydraulics or constructing a flow chart. The theory or chart models physical relationships in such a way...as to render them apprehensible; it is a model *of* "reality." In the second, what is stressed is the manipulation of the nonsymbolic systems in terms of the relationships expressed in the symbolic, as when we construct a dam according to the specifications implied in an hydraulic theory or the conclusions drawn from a flow chart. Here, the theory is a model under whose guidance physical relationships are organized: it is a model *for* "reality." For psychological and social systems,... the case is in no way different. Unlike genes, and other nonsymbolic information sources, which are only models *for*, not models *of*, culture patterns have an intrinsic double aspect: they give meaning, that is, objective conceptual form, to social and psychological reality both by shaping themselves to it and by shaping it to themselves.

It is, in fact, this double aspect which sets true symbols off from other sorts of significative forms. Models *for* are found, as the gene example suggests, through the whole order of nature; for wherever there is a communication of pattern, such programs are, in simple logic, required. Among animals, imprint learning is perhaps the most striking example.... But models *of*—linguistic, graphic, mechanical, natural, etc., processes which function not to provide sources of information in terms of which other processes can be patterned, but to represent those patterned processes as such, to express their structure in an alternative medium—are much rarer and may perhaps be confined, among living animals, to man. The perception of the structural congruence between one set of processes, activities, relations, entities, and so on, and another set for which it acts as a program, so that the program can be taken as a representation, or conception—a symbol—of the programmed, is the essence of human thought. The intertransposability of models *for* and models *of* which symbolic formulation makes possible is the distinctive characteristic of our mentality.

...to establish powerful, pervasive, and long-lasting moods and motivations in men by...

So far as religious symbols and symbol systems are concerned this intertransposability is clear.... [T]he same self-discipline which rewards a Javanese mystic staring fixedly into the flame of a lamp with what he takes to be an intimation of divinity drills him in that rigorous control of emotional expression which is necessary to a man who would follow a quietistic style of life. Whether one sees the conception of a personal guardian spirit, a family tutelary, or an immanent God as synoptic formulations of the character of reality or as templates for producing reality with such a character seems largely arbitrary, a matter of which aspect, the model *of* or model *for*, one wants for the moment to bring into focus. The concrete symbols involved...point in either direction. They both express the world's climate and shape it.

They shape it by inducing in the worshipper a certain distinctive set of dispositions...which lend a chronic character to the flow of his activity and the quality of his experience. A disposition describes not an activity or an occurrence but a probability of an activity being performed....

So far as religious activities are concerned..., two somewhat different sorts of disposition are induced by them: moods and motivations.

A motivation is a persisting tendency, a chronic inclination to perform certain sorts of acts and experience certain sorts of feeling in certain sorts of situation....

As a motive, "flamboyant courage" consists in such enduring propensities as to fast in the wilderness.... "Moral circumspection" consists in such ingrained tendencies as to honor onerous promises, to confess secret sins in the face of severe public disapproval, and to feel guilty when vague and generalized accusations are made at séances.... Motives are thus neither acts (that is, intentional behaviors) nor feelings, but liabilities to perform particular classes of act or have particular classes of feeling. And when we say that a man is religious, that is, motivated by religion, this is at least part—though only part—of what we mean.

Another part of what we mean is that he has, when properly stimulated, a susceptibility to fall into certain moods, moods we sometimes lump together under such covering terms as "reverential," "solemn," or "worshipful." Such generalized rubrics actually conceal, however, the enormous empirical variousness of the dispositions involved, and, in fact, tend to assimilate them to the unusually grave tone of most of our own religious life. The moods that sacred symbols induce, at different times and in different places, range from exultation to melancholy, from self-confidence to self-pity, from an incorrigible playfulness to a bland listlessness—to say nothing of the erogenous power of so many of the world's myths and rituals. No more than there is a single sort of motivation one can call piety is there a single sort of mood one can call worshipful.

The major difference between moods and motivations is that where the latter are, so to speak, vectorial qualities, the former are merely scalar. Motives have a directional cast, they describe a certain overall course, gravitate toward certain, unusually temporary, consummations. But moods vary only as to intensity: they go nowhere. They spring from certain circumstances but they are responsive to no ends. Like fogs, they just settle and lift; like scents, suffuse and evaporate.... But perhaps the most important difference, so far as we are concerned, between moods and motivations is that motivations are "made meaningful" with reference to the ends toward which they are conceived to conduce, whereas moods are "made meaningful" with reference to the conditions from which they are conceived to spring. We interpret motives in terms of their consummations, but we interpret moods in terms of their sources. We say that a person is industrious because he wishes to succeed; we say that a person is worried because he is conscious of the hanging thread of nuclear holocaust. And this is no less the case when the interpretations are ultimate. Charity becomes Christian charity when it is enclosed in a conception of God's purposes; optimism is Christian optimism when it is grounded in a particular conception of God's nature. The assiduity of the Navaho finds its rationale in a belief that, since "reality" operates mechanically, it is coercible; their chronic fearfulness finds its rationale in a conviction that, however "reality" operates, it is both enormously powerful and terribly dangerous.

... by formulating conceptions of a general order of existence and...

That the symbols or symbol systems which induce and define dispositions we set off as religious and those which place those dispositions in a cosmic framework are the same symbols ought to occasion no surprise. For what else do we mean by saying that a particular mood of awe is religious and not secular, except that it springs from entertaining a conception of all-pervading vitality.... What any particular religion affirms about the fundamental nature of reality may be obscure, shallow, or, all too often, perverse; but it must...affirm something. If one were to essay a minimal definition of religion today, it would perhaps not be Tylor's famous "belief in spiritual beings."...

Usually, of course, religions affirm very much more than this: we believe, as James remarked, all that we can and would believe everything if we only could. The thing we seem least able to tolerate is a threat to our powers of conception, a suggestion that our ability to create, grasp, and use symbols may fail us, for were this to happen, we would be...helpless.... The extreme generality, diffuseness, and variability of man's innate (that is, genetically programmed) response capacities means that without the assistance of cultural patterns he would be functionally incomplete.... Man depends upon symbols and symbol systems with a dependence so great as to be decisive for his creatural viability and, as a result, his sensitivity to even the remotest indication that they may prove unable to cope with one or another aspect of experience raises within him the gravest sort of anxiety....

There are at least three points where chaos—a tumult of events which lack not just interpretations but *interpretability*—threatens to break in upon man: at the limits of his analytic capabilities, at the limits of his powers of endurance, and at the limits of his moral insight. Bafflement, suffering, and a sense of intractable ethical paradox are all, if they become intense enough or are sustained long enough, radical challenges to the proposition that life is comprehensible and that we can, by taking thought, orient ourselves effectively within it....

Of the three issues, it is the first which has been least investigated by modern social anthropologists (though Evans-Pritchard's classic discussion of why granaries fall on some Azande and not on others is a notable exception). Even to consider people's religious beliefs as attempts to bring anomalous events or experiences—death, dreams, mental fugues, volcanic eruptions, or marital infidelity—within the circle of the at least potentially explicable seems to smack of Tyloreanism or worse. But it does appear to be a fact that at least some men—in all probability, most men—are unable to leave unclarified problems of analysis merely unclarified, just to look at the stranger features of the world's landscape in dumb astonishment... without trying to develop... some notions as to how such features might be reconciled with the more ordinary deliverances of experience. Any chronic failure of one's explanatory apparatus, the complex of received culture patterns... one has for mapping the empirical world... tends to lead to a deep disquiet.... After all, even that high priest of heroic atheism, Lord Russell, once remarked that although the problem of the existence of God had never bothered him, the ambiguity of certain mathematical axioms had threatened to unhinge his mind. And Einstein's profound dissatisfaction with quantum mechanics was based on a—surely religious—inability to believe that, as he put it, God plays dice with the universe.

But the quest for lucidity and the rush of metaphysical anxiety that occurs when empirical phenomena threaten to remain intransigently opaque is found on much humbler intellectual levels. Certainly, I was struck in my own work, much more than I had at all expected to be, by the degree to which my more animistically inclined informants behaved like true Tyloreans. They seemed to be constantly using their beliefs to "explain" phenomena.... What they were *not* ready to do was... to leave events to themselves....

Nor is this to argue that it is only, or even mainly, sudden eruptions of extraordinary events which engender in man the disquieting sense that his cognitive resources may prove unavailing....More commonly it is a persistent, constantly re-experienced difficulty in grasping certain aspects of nature, self, and society... which renders man chronically uneasy and toward which a more equable flow of diagnostic symbols is consequently directed. It is what lies beyond a relatively fixed frontier of accredited knowledge that... sets ordinary human experience in a permanent context of metaphysical concern and raises the dim, back-of-the-mind suspicions that one may be adrift in an absurd world....

The second experiential challenge... the problem of suffering... has been rather more investigated, or at least described, mainly because of the great amount of attention given in works on tribal religion to... illness and mourning....

As a religious problem, the problem of suffering is... how to suffer, how to make of physical pain, personal loss, worldly defeat, or the helpless contemplation of others' agony something bearable, supportable—something, as we say, sufferable.... Where the more intellective aspects of what Weber called the Problem of Meaning are a matter of affirming the ultimate explicability of experience, the more affective aspects are a matter of affirming its ultimate sufferableness. As religion on one side anchors the power of our symbolic resources for formulating analytic ideas in an authoritative conception of the overall shape of reality, so on an other side it anchors the power of our, also symbolic, resources of expressing emotions—moods, sentiments, passions, affections, feelings....

For those able to embrace them, and for so long as they are able to embrace them, religious symbols provide a cosmic guarantee not only for their ability to comprehend the world, but also, comprehending it, to give precision to their feeling, a definition of their emotions which enables them, morosely or joyfully, grimly or cavalierly, to endure it.

Consider in this light the well-known Navaho curing rites usually referred to as "sings." A sing is a kind of religious psychodrama.... There are three main acts: a purification of the patient and audience; a statement, by means of repetitive chants and ritual manipulations, of the wish to restore well-being ("harmony") in the patient; an identification of the patient with the Holy People and his consequent "cure."... The sustaining effect of the sing... rests ultimately on its ability to give the stricken person a vocabulary in terms of which to grasp the nature of his distress and relate it to the wider world.... A sing is mainly concerned with the presentation of a specific and concrete image of truly human, and so endurable, suffering powerful enough to resist the challenge of emotional meaninglessness raised by the existence of intense and unremovable brute pain.

The problem of suffering passes easily into the problem of evil, for if suffering is severe enough it usually, though not always, seems morally undeserved as well, at least to the sufferer. But they are not, however, exactly the same thing.... For where the problem of suffering is concerned with threats to our ability to put our "undisciplined squads of emotion" into some sort of soldierly order, the problem of evil is concerned with threats to our ability to make sound moral judgments. What is involved in the problem of evil is not the adequacy of our symbolic resources to govern our affective life, but the adequacy of those resources to provide a workable set of ethical criteria, normative guides to govern our action. The vexation here is the gap between things as they are and as they ought to be if our conceptions of right and wrong make sense....

[T]he disquieting sense that one's moral insight is inadequate to one's moral experience, is as alive on the level of so-called primitive religion as it is on that of the so-called civilized....

Thus the problem of evil, or perhaps one should say the problem *about* evil, is in essence the same sort of problem of or about bafflement and the problem of or about suffering. The strange opacity of certain empirical events, the dumb senselessness of intense or inexorable pain... raise the uncomfortable suspicion that perhaps the world, and hence man's life in the world, has no genuine order at all.... And the religious response to this suspicion is in each case the same:

the formulation, by means of symbols, of an image of such a genuine order of the world which will account for, and even celebrate, the perceived ambiguities, puzzles, and paradoxes in human experience. The effort is not to deny the undeniable—that there are unexplained events, that life hurts, or that rain falls upon the just—but to deny that there are inexplicable events, that life is unendurable, and that justice is a mirage.... What is important, to a religious man at least, is that the elusiveness be accounted for, that it be not the result of the fact...that life is absurd and the attempt to make moral, intellectual, or emotional sense out of experience is bootless....

The Problem of Meaning...is a matter of affirming, or at least recognizing, the inescapability of ignorance, pain, and injustice on the human plane while simultaneously denying that these irrationalities are characteristic of the world as a whole. And it is in terms of religious symbolism, a symbolism relating man's sphere of existence to a wider sphere within which it is conceived to rest, that both the affirmation and denial are made.

... and clothing those conceptions with such an aura of factuality that...

There arises here, however, a more profound question: how is it that this denial comes to be believed? How is it that the religious man moves from a troubled perception of experienced disorder to a more or less settled conviction of fundamental order? just what does "belief" mean in a religious context? Of all the problems surrounding attempts to conduct anthropological analysis of religion this is the one that has perhaps been most troublesome and therefore the most often avoided, usually by relegating it to psychology....

It seems to me that it is best to begin any approach to this issue with frank recognition that religious belief involves not a Baconian induction from everyday experience—for then we should all be agnostic—but rather a prior acceptance of authority which transforms that experience. The existence of bafflement, pain, and moral paradox—of The Problem of Meaning—is one of the things that drives men toward belief....

In tribal religions authority lies in the persuasive power of traditional imagery; in mystical ones in the apodictic force of supersensible experience; in charismatic ones in the hypnotic attraction of an extraordinary personality. But the priority of the acceptance of an authoritative criterion in religious matters over the revelation which is conceived to flow from that acceptance is not less complete than in scriptural or hieratic ones. The basic axiom underlying what we may perhaps call "the religious perspective" is everywhere the same: he who would know must first believe....

If we place the religious perspective against the background of three of the other major perspectives in terms of which men construe the world—the common-sensical, the scientific, and the aesthetic—its special character emerges more sharply. What distinguishes common sense as a mode of "seeing" is...a simple acceptance of the world, its objects, and its processes as being just what they seem to be—what is sometimes called naïve realism....In the scientific perspective it is precisely this givenness which disappears. Deliberate doubt and systematic inquiry, the suspension of the pragmatic motive in favor of dis-interested observation...are the hallmarks of the attempt to grasp the world scientifically. And as for the aesthetic perspective, it involves a...suspension of naïve realism...in that...one merely ignores that experience in favor of an eager dwelling upon appearances....

The religious perspective differs from the common-sensical in that, as already pointed out, it moves beyond the realities of everyday life to wider ones which correct and complete them....It differs from the scientific perspective in that it questions the realities of everyday life not out of institutionalized skep-ticism..., but in terms of what it takes to be wider, nonhypothetical truths. Rather than detachment, its watchword is commitment; rather than analysis, encounter. And it differs from art in that instead of effecting a disengagement from the whole question of factuality,...it deepens the concern with fact and seeks to create an aura of utter actuality. It is the sense of the "really real" upon which the religious perspective rests and which the symbolic activities of reli-gion as a cultural system are devoted to producing, intensifying, and, so far as possible, rendering inviolable....It is, again, the imbuing of a certain specific complex of symbols—of the metaphysic they formulate and the style of life they recommend—with a persuasive authority which, from an analytical point of view, is the essence of religious action.

Which brings us, at length, to ritual. For it is in ritual—that is, consecrated behavior—that this conviction that religious conceptions are veridical and that religious directives are sound is somehow generated. It is in some sort of cer-emonial form...that the moods and motivations which sacred symbols induce in men and the general conceptions of the order of existence which they formu-late for men meet and reinforce one another. In a ritual, the world as lived and the world as imagined, fused under the agency of a single set of symbolic forms, turn out to be the same world....

However, though any religious ritual...involves this symbolic fusion of ethos and world view, it is mainly certain more elaborate and usually more public ones...which shape the spiritual consciousness of a people.... [W]e may call these full-blown ceremonies "cultural performances" and note that they represent...the point at which the dispositional and conceptual aspects of reli-gious life converge for the believer....

Where for the "visitors" religious performances can, in the nature of the case, only be presentations of particular religious perspective,...for participants they are in addition enactments, materializations, realizations of it—not only models *of* what they believe, but also models *for* the believing of it. In these plastic dramas men attain their faith as they portray it.

As a case in point, let me take a spectacularly theatrical cultural performance from Bali—that in which a terrible witch called Rangda engages in a ritual combat with an endearing monster called Barong.... [T]he drama consists of a masked dance in which the witch—depicted as a wasted old widow, prostitute, and eater of infants—comes to spread plague and death upon the land and is opposed by the monster—depicted as a kind of cross between a clumsy bear, a silly puppy, and a strutting Chinese dragon. Rangda, danced by a single male, is a hideous figure.... Her long red tongue is a stream of fire. And as she dances she splays her dead-white hands, from which protrude ten-inch claw-like fingernails, out in front of her and utters unnerving shrieks of metallic laughter. Barong, danced by two men fore-and-aft in vaudeville horse fashion, is another matter.... He is adorned with flowers, sashes, feathers, mirrors, and a comical beard made from human hair. And though a demon too,... the cluster of tinkling bells which hang from his absurdly arching tail somehow contrives to take most of the edge off his fearfulness. If Rangda is a satanic image, Barong is a farcical one, and their clash is a clash (an inconclusive one) between the malignant and the ludicrous.

This odd counterpoint of implacable malice and low comedy pervades the whole performance. Rangda... seems insane with fear and hatred as she screams deprecations at Barong amid the wild clanging of the gamelan. She may in fact go amok.... Barong, though he is charged with the same mana-like sacred power as Rangda, and his impersonators are also entranced, seems to have very great difficulty in being serious. He frolics with his retinue of demons... and generally prances about in paroxysms of narcissistic vanity.... The twin themes of horror and hilarity find their purest expression in the two protagonists and their endless, indecisive struggle for dominance, but they are woven with deliberate intricacy through the whole texture of the drama. They or rather the relations between them are what it is about.

It is unnecessary to attempt a thoroughgoing description of a Rangda-Barong performance here.... For our purposes, the main point to be stressed is that the drama is, for the Balinese, not merely a spectacle to be watched but a ritual to be enacted.... [B]y the time a full-scale Rangda-Barong encounter has been concluded a majority, often nearly all, of the members of the group sponsoring it will have become caught up in it not just imaginatively but bodily.... A Rangda-Barong struggle is inevitably marked by anywhere from three or four to several dozen spectators becoming possessed by one or another demon, falling into violent trances "like firecrackers going off one after the other," and, snatching up krisses, rushing to join the fray. Mass trance, spreading like a panic, projects the individual Balinese out of the commonplace world in which he usually lives into that most uncommonplace one in which Rangda and Barong live. To become entranced is, for the Balinese, to cross a threshold into another order of existence....

At length, when it seems as though Rangda will finally prevail, a number of entranced men rise, krisses in hand, and rush to support Barong. But as they approach Randga..., she wheels up on them and...leaves them comatose on the ground.... Then Barong moves among the kris dancers and wakens them by snapping his jaws at them or nuzzling them with his beard. As they return, still entranced, to "consciousness," they are enraged by the disappearance of Rangda, and unable to attack her they turn their krisses (harmlessly because they are entranced) against their own chests in frustration. Usually sheer pandemonium breaks out at this point with members of the crowd, of both sexes, falling into trance all around the courtyard....

It is in the direct encounter with the two figures in the context of the actual performance that the villager comes to know them as, so far as he is concerned, genuine realities.... The acceptance of authority that underlies the religious perspective that the ritual embodies thus flows from the enactment of the ritual itself. By inducing a set of moods and motivations—an ethos—and defining an image of cosmic order—a world view—by means of a single set of symbols, the performance makes the model *for* and model *of* aspects of religious belief mere transpositions of one another. Rangda evokes fear as well as hatred, disgust, cruelty, horror.... And on his side Barong not only induces laughter, he incarnates the Balinese version of the comic spirit—a distinctive combination of playfulness, exhibitionism, and extravagant love of elegance, which, along with fear, is perhaps the dominant motive in their life. The constantly recurring struggle of Rangda and Barong to an inevitable draw is thus for the believing Balinese both the formulation of a general religious conception and the authoritative experience which justifies, even compels, its acceptance.

...that the moods and motivations seem uniquely realistic

But no one, not even a saint, lives in the world religious symbols formulate all of the time, and the majority of men live in it only at the moments. The everyday world of common-sense objects and the practical acts is...the paramount reality in human experience.... The interweaving of the malignant and the comic, which the Rangda-Barong combat depicts, animates a very wide range of everyday Balinese behavior, much of which, like the ritual itself, has an air of candid fear narrowly contained by obsessive playfulness. Religion is sociologically interesting not because, as vulgar positivism would have it, it describes the social order (which, in so far as it does, it does not only very obliquely but very incompletely), but because, like environment, political power, wealth, jural obligation, personal affection, and a sense of beauty, it shapes it.

[R]eligious belief in the midst of ritual, where it engulfs the total person, transporting him, so far as he is concerned, into another mode of existence, and religious belief as the pale, remembered reflection of that experience in the midst of everyday life are not precisely the same thing, and the failure to realize this has led to some confusion, most especially in connection with the so-called primitive mentality problem. Much of the difficulty between Levy-Bruhl and Malinowski on the nature of "native thought," for example, arises from a lack of full recognition of this distinction; for where the French philosopher was concerned with the view of reality savages adopted when taking a specifically religious perspective, the Polish-English ethnographer was concerned with that which they adopted when taking a strictly common-sense one. Both perhaps vaguely sensed that they were not talking about exactly the same thing, but where they went astray was in failing to give a specific accounting of the way in which these two forms of "thought"—or, as I would rather say, these two modes of symbolic formulations—interacted, so that where Levy-Bruhl's savages tended to live, despite his postludial disclaimers, in a world composed entirely of mystical encounters, Malinowski's tended to live, despite his stress on the functional importance of religion, in a world composed entirely of practical actions....

It is this placing of proximate acts in ultimate contexts that makes religion, frequently at least, socially so powerful. It alters, often radically, the whole landscape presented to common sense, alters it in such a way that the moods and motivations induced by religious practice seem themselves supremely practical, the only sensible ones to adopt given the way things "really" are....

The nature of the bias religion gives to ordinary life varies with the religion involved, with the particular dispositions induced in the believer by the specific conceptions of cosmic order he has come to accept. On the level of the "great" religions, organic distinctiveness is usually recognized, at times insisted upon to the point of zealotry. But even at its simplest folk and tribal levels—where the individuality of religious traditions has so often been dissolved into such desiccated types as "animism," "animatism," "totemism," "shamanism," "ancestor worship," and all the other insipid categories by means of which ethnographers of religion devitalize their data—the idiosyncratic character of how various groups of men behave because of what they believe they have experienced is clear....

It is this particularity of the impact of religious systems upon social systems (and upon personality systems) which renders general assessments of the value of religion in either moral or functional terms impossible....One of the main methodological problems in writing about religion scientifically is to put aside at once the tone of the village atheist and that of the village preacher, as well as their more sophisticated equivalents, so that the social and psychological implications of particular religious beliefs can emerge in a clear and neutral light. And when that is done, overall questions about whether religion is "good" or "bad," "functional" or "dysfunctional"...disappear..., and one is left with particular evaluations, assessments, and diagnoses in particular cases. There remains, of course, the hardly unimportant question of whether this or that religious assertion is true, this or that religious experience genuine, or whether true religious assertions and genuine religious experiences are possible at all. But such questions cannot even be asked, much less answered, within the self-imposed limitations of the scientific perspective.

For an anthropologist, the importance of religion lies in its capacity to serve, for an individual or for a group, as a source of general, yet distinctive, conceptions of the world, the self, and the relations between them, on the one hand—its model *of* aspect—and of rooted, no less distinctive "mental" dispositions—its model *for* aspect—on the other. From these cultural functions flow, in turn, its social and psychological ones.

Religious concepts spread...to provide a framework of general ideas in terms of which a wide range of experience—intellectual, emotional, moral—can be given meaningful form. The Christian sees the Nazi movement against the background of the Fall which...places it in a moral, a cognitive, even an affective sense. An Azande sees the collapse of a granary upon a friend or relative against the background of a concrete and rather special notion of witchcraft and thus avoids the philosophical dilemmas as well as the psychological stress of indeterminism....A Javanese finds in the...concept of *rasa* ("sense-taste-feeling-meaning") a means by which to "see" choreographic, gustatory, emotional, and political phenomena in a new light. A synopsis of cosmic order, a set of religious beliefs, is also a gloss upon the mundane world of social relationships and psychological events. It renders them graspable.

But more than gloss, such beliefs are also a template. They do not merely interpret social and psychological processes in cosmic terms...but they shape them. In the doctrine of original sin is embedded also a recommended attitude toward life, a recurring mood, and a persisting set of motivations. The Azande learns from witchcraft conceptions not just to understand apparent "accidents" as not accidents at all, but to react to these spurious accidents with hatred for the agent who caused them and to proceed against him with appropriate resolution. *Rasa,* in addition to being a concept of truth, beauty, and goodness, is also a preferred mode of experiencing, a kind of affectless detachment, a variety of bland aloofness, an unshakeable calm....

The tracing of the social and psychological role of religion is thus not so much a matter of finding correlations between specific ritual acts and specific social ties....More, it is a matter of understanding how it is that men's notions...of the "really real" and the dispositions these notions induce in them, color their sense of the reasonable, the practical, the humane, and the moral. How far they do so..., how deeply they do so..., and how effectively they do so...are crucial issues in the comparative sociology and psychology of religion. Even the degree to which religious systems themselves are developed seems to vary extremely widely, and not merely on a simple evolutionary basis. In one society, the level of elaboration of symbolic formulations of ultimate actuality may reach extraordinary degrees of complexity and systematic articulation; in another, no less developed socially, such formulations may remain primitive in the true sense, hardly more than congeries of fragmentary by-beliefs and isolated images, of sacred reflexes and spiritual pictographs....

The anthropological study of religion is therefore a two-stage operation: first, an analysis of the system of meanings embodied in the symbols which make up the religion proper, and, second, the relating of these systems to social-structural and psychological processes. My dissatisfaction with so much of contemporary social anthropological work in religion is not that it concerns itself with the second stage, but that it neglects the first, and in so doing takes for granted what most needs to be elucidated. To discuss the role of ancestor worship in regulating political succession, of sacrificial feasts in defining kinship obligations,...or of initiation rites in...personality maturation...are in no sense unimportant endeavors, and I am not recommending they be abandoned....But to attempt them with but the most general, common-sense view of what ancestor worship, animal sacrifice...or initiation rites are as religious patterns seems to me not particularly promising. Only when we have a theoretical analysis of symbolic action comparable...to what we now have for social and psychological action, will we be able to cope effectively with those aspects of social and psychological life in which religion (or art, or science, or ideology) plays a determinant role.

Islam Observed

Geertz here discusses Indonesian and Moroccan Islam in the light of his views on the function of religion and the challenge that contemporary developments bring to these traditional religious cultures.

Some three or four decades ago...there raged in anthropology something of a great debate concerning what went on in the heads of savages. As in most such debates, the main participants were too busy talking to listen carefully....Yet it was, we can now see, the beginning, within anthropology at least, of something important: the conception of human culture as consisting not so much in customs and institutions as in the sorts of interpretations the members of a society apply to their experiences, the constructions they put upon the events through which they live; not just how people behave, but how they look at things.

Almost all anthropologists of any note contributed to this discussion of what unfortunately came to be known as the primitive thought problem; but perhaps the two most significant...were the Polish-English ethnographer Bronislaw Malinowski and the French philosopher Lucien Levy-Bruhl. Whether they intended to or not, these two men came to stand for the extreme positions in the debate: in Malinowski's case, primitive pragmatism; in Levy-Bruhl's, primitive mysticism. The dispute came down to...the question of whether savages as we then were free to call them viewed the world in an essentially common-sensical way, as a field of practical problems demanding practical solutions, or in an essentially affective way, as a series of emotional encounters demanding emotional responses.

To state the issue in so undressed a form is to expose its unreality; the conclusion that the dichotomy is a false one and that any man, civilized or not, is prudent and passionate by turns arises virtually of itself. And at length this was indeed the conclusion that was generally drawn, even by the protagonists themselves, who adjusted their polemics accordingly. But compromises, even reasonable compromises, are not always so advantageous in science as they are in politics, and in this case the "there is something to be said for both sides" position merely conduced to a wholesale missing of the point.

For the important question the primitive thought debate raised was not whether savages are rational or not, or even whether their mental processes differ from ours or not. They are and they aren't; they do and they don't. The important question the debate raised...was... "What are the differences between a commonsense orientation to the world and a religious one, and what are the relations between them?" What was taken to be an investigation of the "savage mind" was in fact an investigation of the varieties of human understanding, of the diverse ways in which men, all men, attempt to render their lives intelligible by ordering the separate events in which they find themselves caught up into connected patterns of experience.

～

The Religious Perspective

There is a dialectic between religion and common sense—as there is between art, science, and so on and common sense—which necessitates their being seen in terms of one another. Religion must be viewed against the background of the insufficiency, or anyway the felt insufficiency, of common sense as a total orientation toward life; and it must also be viewed in terms of its formative impact upon common sense, the way in which, by questioning the unquestionable, it shapes our apprehension of the quotidian world of "what there is" in which, whatever different drummers we may or may not hear, we are all obliged to live.

There has been, in short, a general shift in modern anthopological discussion of culture, and within it of religion as a part of culture, a shift from a concern with thought as an inner mental state...to a concern with thought as the utilization by individuals in society of public, historically created vehicles of reasoning, perception, feeling, and understanding—symbols, in the broadest sense of the term. In the study of religion, this shift is in the process of altering our entire view of religious experience and its social and psychological impact. The focus is now neither on subjective life as such nor on outward behavior as such, but on the socially available "systems of significance"—beliefs, rites, meaningful objects—in terms of which subjective life is ordered and outward behavior guided.

Such an approach is neither introspectionist nor behaviorist; it is semantic. It is concerned with the collectively created patterns of meaning the individual uses to give form to experience and point to action, with conceptions embodied in symbols and clusters of symbols, and with the directive force of such conceptions in public and private life. So far as religion is concerned, the problem becomes one of a particular sort of perspective, a particular manner of interpreting experience, a certain way of going at the world as opposed to other ways, and the implications such a perspective has for conduct. The aim of the comparative study of religion is (or anyway, ought to be) the scientific characterization of this perspective: the description of the wide variety of forms in which it appears; the uncovering of the forces which bring these forms into existence, alter them, or destroy them; and the assessment of their influences, also various, upon the behavior of men in everyday life.

But how are we to isolate the religious perspective at all? Are we not thrown back once more upon the necessity of defining religion, adding one more catch phrase—the "belief in spiritual beings," "morality touched with emotion," "ultimate concern"—to what is surely an endless catalog?...

Well, no. One can begin in a fog and try to clear it. One can begin, as I have in this book, with an assortment of phenomena almost everyone but the professionally contrary will regard as having something vaguely to do with religion and seek for what it is that leads us to think so.... We are attempting to articulate a way of looking at the world, not to describe an unusual object.

The heart of this way of looking at the world, that is, of the religious perspective,... is the conviction that the values one holds are grounded in the inherent structure of reality, that between the way one ought to live and the way things really are there is an unbreakable inner connection.... The world view is believable because the ethos, which grows out of it, is felt to be authoritative; the ethos is justifiable because the world view, upon which it rests, is held to be true....

Religious patterns such as those I have been discussing thus have a double aspect: they are frames of perception, symbolic screens through which experience is interpreted; and they are guides for action, blueprints for conduct....

The major characteristic of religious belief as opposed to other sorts of beliefs, ideological, philosophical, scientific, or commonsensical, is that they are regarded as being not conclusions from experience... but as being prior to it. For those who hold them, religious beliefs are not inductive, they are paradigmatic; the world... provides not evidences for their truth but illustrations of it. They are a light cast upon human life from somewhere outside it.

Social scientists, including anthropologists, have generally not been comfortable with this way of formulating things, not only because most of them are nonbelievers as indeed, I myself am, but because it seems to involve a departure from the path of strict empiricism. But there is nothing unempirical... about describing the way in which religious belief appears to the believer.... It is also, and this is more important, to neglect to ask or even to recognize some of the most critical scientific questions in this whole field of study, not the least of which is, "How is it that believers are able to believe?" Or, to risk even more being taken for an apologist for something otherworldly, "Whence comes Faith?"

Theological answers aside, it is clear that it comes from the social and psychological workings of religious symbols....

The main context... in which religious symbols work to create and sustain belief is, of course, ritual.... Individuals can, and in Indonesia and Morocco a few do, attain a concept of cosmic order outside of these institutions specifically dedicated to inculcating such a concept.... For the overwhelming majority of the religious in any population, however, engagement in some form of ritualized traffic with sacred symbols is the major mechanism by means of which they come not only to encounter a world view but actually to adopt it, to internalize it as part of personality.

The reasons why particular individuals are susceptible to the workings of sacred symbols at all, why they engage in rituals and why the rituals have... an effect, is of course another problem. Part of the answer is surely psychological, having to do with individual needs for nurturance, for external authority, or whatever, as well as capacities for trust, affection, and so on. Part, too, is surely social. In nonindustrial societies particularly, the social pressures toward religious conformity are very great.... In Morocco and Indonesia such pressures remain very strong....

In any case, besides the psychological and sociological factors impelling men toward belief, there are also cultural ones, arising, as I suggested, from the felt inadequacies of commonsense ideas in the face of the complexities of experience. It was this recognition that life continually overflows the categories of practical reason that Max Weber called "the problem of meaning," and it is most familiar to us... in the form of the problem of evil: "Why do the just suffer and the unjust prosper?"...Whatever else "Islam"...does for those who are able to adopt it, it surely renders life less outrageous to plain reason and less contrary to common sense. It renders the strange familiar, the paradoxical logical, the anomalous, given the recognized, if eccentric, ways of Allah, natural.

In societies like those of classical Morocco and Indonesia, then, psychological, social, and cultural factors converge to move men toward participation in the established religious rituals and toward the acceptance of the metaphysical beliefs implicit in such rituals. In such societies, believing is, so to speak, easy, almost as easy as speaking....

Secularization, Science, and Scripturalism

[But] [i]t is this religious ease that the changes of the last century and a half, not only in Morocco and Indonesia, but in the world generally, have progressively undermined. Inner need, community pressure, and the problems of meaning no longer converge so powerfully to impel the individual toward ritualized contact with sacred symbols. The symbols are still there, of course; so, for the most part, are the rituals, and they are still generally regarded as housing imperishable spiritual truths. But now people find it harder and harder, so to speak, to make them work....

As I have said several times, this process is only slightly advanced in Morocco and Indonesia, though it is rapidly gaining momentum. In the United States, where church attendance reaches new highs while the ability to internalize the Christian world view continues, apparently, to decline, it has gone much further. Whether the process, here, or elsewhere, is reversible...is, for the moment, beside the point. The fact is that the loss of power of classical religious symbols to sustain a properly religious faith, which the recent history of both Morocco and Indonesia displays, is general. So too, I think, is the major reason for this loss—the secularization of thought; so too, the major response to it—the ideologization of religion.

The secularization of thought in the modern world has had many causes and taken many forms; but on the cultural level it is in great part a result of the explosive growth of…positive science. In its pure form, the diffusion of the scientific way of looking at things to Third World countries like Morocco and Indonesia has been relatively slight. But the awareness that everyday experiences can be set in a broader and more meaningful context by resort to symbols which picture reality in terms of general laws inductively established…has spread to virtually every corner of either society. Even a century ago religious beliefs were about the only means available for plugging leaks in the hand-crafted dike of common sense. Today even the humblest peasant or shepherd knows that that is no longer so.

The long, rather unedifying history of the warfare between science and religion in the West has tended to lead in this century to the comfortable conclusion that "at base" they are not really in conflict. In the sense that one cannot subject expressions of faith to scientific tests nor disprove natural laws by quoting scripture, this is no doubt true. It is also no doubt true that there is no inherent reason why the view of reality generated by traffic with scientific symbols, in laboratories or wherever, need contradict the view of it generated by traffic with religious symbols, in mosques or wherever. And clearly, science and religion are not responses to exactly the same sort of inadequacies of common sense. Their fields of concern, though they overlap, are far from coincident, and they are not, therefore, simple alternatives.

But for all this, the brute empirical fact is that the growth of science has made almost all religious beliefs harder to maintain….Even if they are not direct antitheses, there is a natural tension between the scientific and religious ways of attempting to render the world comprehensible….Unless the importance of this "struggle for the real" is recognized and not passed off with easy pieties on either side, the history of religion, Islam or any other, in our times is, scientifically anyway, unintelligible. The warfare between science and religion…is not only not over; it is quite likely never going to end.

The scripturalists were at once the group in either society who felt this tension between the progressive secularization of thought in the modern world and the essentials of the religious perspective most keenly and who made the most vigorous response to it. The turn toward an exclusivist emphasis on the written sources of Islamic faith at the expense of those of the sort represented by Moroccan saint worship or Indonesian self-communion…made that tension, if not greater, surely less evadable. Again, the confrontation with scientific way of looking at things was made directly only by the most advanced leaders of the movement.…But the simple fact that for the scripturalists Islam became a set of explicit dogmas to defend projected them into the middle of the struggle for the real long before the more traditionalist groups in either society were even aware that it was going on.

Scripturalism was, in fact, the main agency in both societies, of what I have called... the ideologization of religion, and it is on these grounds rather than its theological contributions... that its adherents deserve to be called innovators. What the scripturalist movement accomplished... was to provide a general policy for Islam vis-à-vis the modern world, a public stance for it to take in a cultural setting in which secular modes of understanding... play the axial role that in classical societies was played by religious ones. Scripturalism began, in our countries anyway,... the intellectual revolution of which the more explicitly political concepts which accompanied and followed independence were the culmination. The scripturalists taught not just their followers but even more importantly their opponents how to formulate the ideals of an established civilization in such a way that they could survive, for a while anyway, in a modern world more than a little inhospitable to them.

There were essentially two strategies, not merely in our countries but in the movement generally, which the scripturalists devised for pursuing the struggle for the real: the absolute separation of religious matters from scientific ones, and the attempt to show that the scriptures, especially the Koran, anticipate and are fully consonant with the spirit and findings of modern science. The first approach consists of a denial of any metaphysical significance whatsoever to science...; its competence is strictly confined to the understanding of nature considered as some kind of mundane, self-contained system. Faith and reason are simply quarantined from one another.... The second approach consists of interpreting science as but an explicit spelling out of what is already implicitly present in religion, an extension and specification of the religious perspective rather than an autonomous mode of thought.

Taken together, these two notices make up a kind of Islamic deism: doctrinal essentials are protected from any sort of challenge by being locked away from human experience, while secular reason is left free to operate with full sovereignty in the ordinary world with the certain confidence that its findings can raise no problems for religious belief because such belief already implies them....

As by now might be expected, these two sides of the scripturalist response to a challenge posed by the secularization of thought have been differentially represented in our two societies. Both are present in both. But Indonesia, with her ingrained inclination to try to absorb all styles of thought into one broad, syncretic stream, has been naturally more receptive to the argument that Islamic doctrine and scientific discovery are really not conflicting but complementary forms of belief; while Morocco, with her as deeply ingrained inclination toward religious perfectionism and moral rigor, has been more receptive to the attempt to isolate a purified Islamic faith from contamination with everyday life. Scripturalism in both countries was and is a counter-tradition.... But its adherents are still Indonesians and Moroccans.... The Indonesian scripturalists have sought... to portray science, and indeed secular thought in general, as but an expression of Islam, merely another, for practical purposes perhaps more useful, way of putting what with greater depth if not equal explicitness the Koran has already said. Moroccan scripturalists have sought, contrariwise, to purge religious life of... superstition in order... to restore an idealized, hermetic Islam.... In the one case science poses no threat to faith because it is seen as religious; in the other, it poses no threat because it is seen as not....

[T]he achievements of scripturalism in providing an ideological stance for Islam in the modern world were applied with even more effectiveness in the service of the classical religious styles.... As nationalism grew out of scripturalism, it... carried the process of the ideologization of religion, the movement from religiousness toward religious-mindedness, to its final stages.... Whether these revamped traditions, having been constructed, can now persist depends upon whether the pattern of life they imply is viable in a semi-modern nation-state in the latter part of the twentieth century.

But this brings us to the guides-for-action side of religious symbols—to their influence upon how men actually behave....

The religious perspective, like the scientific, the aesthetic, the historical, and so on, is after all adopted by men only sporadically, intermittently. Most of the time men, even priests and anchorites, live in the everyday world and see experience in practical, down-to-earth terms—they must, if they are to survive. Further, the main setting in which the religious perspective, in the proper sense of the term, is adopted is, as I have said, in ritual, or at least in some special sort of socio-psychological context different from the ordinary run of life.... Even the pious see life in transtemporal terms only at moments.

There are a number of implications of this fact.... Because religious perception, the actual employment of sacred symbols to activate faith, takes place in special settings and in particular rituals, it is clear that it is extremely difficult to get phenomenologically accurate descriptions of religious experience. When anthropologists... talk to people about their religion... it is almost invariably in a setting about as far removed from the properly religious as it is possible to get. We talk to them in their homes, or the morning after some ceremony.... Rarely, if ever, can we get at them when they are really involved in worship....

Worship and analysis are simply impossible to carry out together, for the one involves being thoroughly... absorbed in one's experience,... while the other involves standing back and, with a certain detachment, looking at it.

I suppose that once this point is stated it seems so obvious as to be trivial. But it has gone virtually unrecognized, or at least undiscussed, in the comparative study of religion.... [E]ven with the best will in the world an informant will have some difficulty in recapturing... what religion amounts to for him....

Sometimes, as with Indonesian trance experiences, the subject simply often remembers nothing at all afterwards unless the vague sense... that he has had one hell of an experience can be counted as a memory. Other times, say after worshiping..., the subject may remember something but so cover it over with secondary revision that most of its vitality and real meaning, meaning for him, is lost.... So far as we are concerned with religion as a perspective, with the meaningful interpretation it gives to experience, we necessarily see through a pretty dark glass....

A clear distinction between religion experienced and religion remembered is thus an important analytical tool for understanding some otherwise difficult to understand phenomena. And not the least of these is the problem of the relation between belief and action.

When men turn to everyday living they see things in everyday terms. If they are religious men, those everyday terms will in some way be influenced by their religious convictions, for it is in the nature of faith, even the most unworldly and least ethical, to claim effective sovereignty over human behavior....

Or, to put aside images (which is very difficult to do when speaking of such matters), religious belief has its effect on common sense not by displacing it but by becoming part of it....

And here it is necessary to make a distinction between what I would call the *force* of a... religion... and what I would call its *scope*.

By "force" I mean the thoroughness with which... a pattern is internalized in the personalities of the individuals who adopt it, its centrality... in their lives. We all know that such force differs between individuals. For one man, his religious commitments are the axis of his whole existence, his faith is what he lives for and would quite willingly die for; he is god-intoxicated, and the demands flowing into everyday life from religious belief take clear precedence over those flowing into it from any other source—scientific knowledge, aesthetic experience, moral concern, or even practical considerations. For another man,... his faith is worn more lightly, engages his personality less totalistically; more worldly, he subordinates other forms of understanding to religious ones less automatically and less completely.... It is difficult to prove, but no one who has spent much time with Indonesians and Moroccans is likely to doubt that, on the whole, the latter take their religion a good deal more determinedly (which again is not to say necessarily more genuinely) than the former....

By "scope" on the other hand, I mean the range of social contexts within which religious considerations are regarded as having... relevance. Obviously, force and scope are related in that a man for whom religion is personally important will naturally be inclined to extend its dominion over wide ranges of life—to discern the hand of God in everything from stomach aches to election returns. Yet they are not the same thing. The force of religion is, generally speaking, greater in Morocco than in Indonesia, but, as I have suggested several times, its scope is narrower. In Indonesia, almost everything is tinged, if lightly, with metaphysical meaning, the whole of ordinary life has a faintly transcendental quality about it, and it is rather difficult to isolate one part of it in which religious beliefs and the attitudes derived from them play a more prominent role than any other. In Morocco, the bulk of ordinary life is secular enough to suit the most dedicated rationalist, and religious considerations, for all their intensity, are operative over only a few, fairly well demarcated regions of behavior, so that one gets a ruthlessness in, for example, commercial and political affairs which... reminds one of... some American racketeers.

In any case, it is necessary, in discussing the way in which religious beliefs and the sentiments they engender are absorbed into the stream of daily life, to distinguish between a vertical dimension, so to speak, of the process and a horizontal one, between the psychological grip of a culture pattern and the social range of its application....

The empirical point is not critical here. What is critical is that the complexities hidden in what seems to be a simple and straightforward question, how important is religious belief in the direction of human behavior, be recognized....

In these terms we can, then, state somewhat more exactly what has happened and is happening, to "Islam" in our two countries....

Over the centuries, and particularly in what I have called the classical period, roughly 1500 to 1800 in both countries, traffic with sacred symbols produced not only distinctive forms of faith but... also distinctive styles of life. World view and ethos reinforced one another because the way people thought they ought to live their lives... and the truths they thought they apprehended at saintly tombs or shadow plays were in tune with one another.... [T]he conceptions, values, and sentiments which guided everyday behavior were... influenced by what were taken to be... revelations of the basic order of existence.... What is different now is that even the spiritually responsive find revelations hard to come by....

The reflections, reverberations, projections... of religious experience in daily life remain very important in both Morocco and Indonesia. But they are, increasingly, the reflections, reverberations, and projections of experiences had by others than those who now depend upon them for filling out the crude framework of common sense.... [F]or more and more of them... the sort of ritually heightened consciousness of the really real... is inaccessible.... I do not want...to overstress the degree to which this disjunction...has proceeded in our two countries. It has really just begun: in Morocco, barely; in Indonesia, a shadow more than barely. But it has begun and it is the way things are moving, have been moving for at least a century, and are, in my opinion, likely to keep on moving for some time. In other Third World states, say Tunisia or Egypt, to stick to Muslim examples, it has perhaps gone further. And in the West, it has gone very far indeed....

So amid great changes, great dilemmas persist, as do established responses to them. In fact the responses seem to grow more pronounced as they work less well. The Moroccan disjunction between the forms of religious life and the substance of everyday life advances almost to the point of spiritual schizophrenia. The Indonesian absorption of all aspects of life—religious, philosophical, political, scientific, commonsensical, even economic—into a cloud of allusive symbols and vacuous abstractions is rather less prominent than it was...; but its progress has hardly been halted, much less reversed.

Original Source Page References
～

The readings in this book have been drawn from the following pages in the editions and translations of the original works as cited and acknowledged in the preceding chapters.

E. B. Tylor, *Primitive Culture,* Volume 1, pp. 27, 30-34, 70-71, 97-99, 102-4, 115-20, 424-34, 436, 438-46, 450-54, 457-60, 471-72, 474-78, 499-502; Volume 2, pp. 184-87, 247-50, 276-77, 331-36, 355-61

James Frazer, *The Golden Bough,* pp. 10-15, 17, 19-23, 25-26, 37-41, 45-52, 54-59, 61, 161-63, 265-70, 320-22, 324, 327, 337-38, 576-77, 711-14

Sigmund Freud, *Totem and Taboo,* pp. 140-52, 156-60; *The Future of an Illusion,* pp. 29-33, 42-44, 49-50; *Moses and Monotheism,* pp. 59-63, 66-70, 72-73, 77, 80-81, 83-86, 99-102, 110-11, 124

Emile Durkheim, *The Elementary Forms of the Religious Life;* pp. 36-44, 47, 87-88, 93-96, 101-4, 113-16, 119-20, 141, 144-45, 147-48, 150, 205-14, 218-23, 240, 242-46, 248-49, 258-59, 268-69, 280-81, 290-91, 293, 295-96, 299-300, 302-3, 305-12, 315-17, 326, 341, 346-49, 389-90, 396-97, 399-402, 415-19, 427-28, 430-34, 436-37, 444-47

Karl Marx, *Contribution to the Critique of Hegel's Philosophy of Law: Introduction,* pp. 175-76, 182-83, 186-87; "The Communism of the *Rheinischer Beobachter,*" p. 231

Karl Marx and Frederick Engels, *The Communist Manifesto,* pp. 494-96, 500-506, 519

Frederick Engels, *The Peasant War in Germany,* pp. 97-104, 107-18; *On Historical Materialism,* pp. 395, 398-99, 402-11, 413-16

Vladimir Ilych Lenin, "Socialism and Religion," pp. 83-87

William James, *The Varieties of Religious Experience,* pp. 26, 28-32, 38, 48, 87-92, 133-34, 162-67, 170, 171, 189, 196, 209-10, 247-49, 331, 332-33, 271-74, 326-35, 337-38, 377-82, 422, 424-26, 428, 430, 437, 442, 445-47, 455-56, 458, 483-85, 491, 494-504, 507-19, 523-27

Rudolf Otto, *The Idea of the Holy,* pp. 1-40, 136-42

Max Weber, *The Protestant Ethic and the Spirit of Capitalism,* pp. 47, 53-56, 71-75, 80, 81, 85-87, 89-92, 98-108, 110-19, 121-22, 124-25, 153-54, 162-63, 170-74, 176-83; *The Sociology of Religion,* pp. 424-27, 439-41, 447-48, 450-51; "The Social Psychology of the World Religions," pp. 284-92, 295-97, 299; "Religious Rejections of the World and Their Directions," pp. 325-28, 331-33

Mircea Eliade, *The Sacred and the Profane,* pp. 8-40, 43-47; *Patterns in Comparative Religion,* pp. 154-72, 174-76, 179-85; *The Myth of the Eternal Return,* pp. 85-86, 88-92, 102-11, 147-62

E. E. Evans-Pritchard, *Witchcraft, Oracles, and Magic among the Azande,* pp. 63-75, 312-13, 336-41, 349-51; *Nuer Religion,* pp. 314-22; *Theories of Primitive Religion,* pp. 26-30, 40-47, 53-57, 63-68, 75-77, 104-8, 111-14, 119-22

Clifford Geertz, *The Religion of Java,* pp. 72-76; "Religion as Cultural System," pp. 1-17, 19-36, 38-42; *Islam Observed,* pp. 90-91, 95-116

Printed in the USA/Agawam, MA
August 9, 2021

779264.025